Advance Praise ~~~

Mordecai Chertoff's extraordinary letters are history at its most compelling – vivid, detailed, immediate. His account of the reaction of Jerusalem's Jews to the UN partition vote is the best I've read anywhere. The narrative moves effortlessly between the historical and the personal, revealing a young man full of contradictions, self-absorbed and sometimes childish yet keenly observing the momentous events happening around him. At the same time, this book tells the touching story of a son's search for his elusive father, reminding us that, in the end, history is always personal. Together, father and son have written a unique narrative that gives us the vicarious experience of participating in Israel's founding. This book is a gift to the Jewish people.

– Yossi Klein Halevi
Senior Fellow, Shalom Hartman Institute
Jerusalem

Not that long ago, there was an era of dreams and hopes, bravery and idealism, recovery and rebirth. That was the era of Israel's birth, a world too often forgotten but to which Mordecai and Daniel Chertoff return us. Much more than a collection of letters or the story of a man, this is the story of a country and a nation. To read *Palestine Posts* is to learn Israel all over again, and to walk away enchanted and inspired.

– Dr. Daniel Gordis
Senior Vice President
Koret Distinguished Fellow and Chair of the Core Curriculum
Shalem College

Palestine Posts
An Eyewitness Account of the Birth of Israel

Toby

PALESTINE POSTS

AN EYEWITNESS ACCOUNT
OF THE BIRTH OF ISRAEL

Based on the Letters of Mordecai S. Chertoff
By Daniel S. Chertoff

The Toby Press

Palestine Posts
An Eyewitness Account of the Birth of Israel

The Toby Press
LLCPOB 8531, New Milford, CT 06776–8531, USA
& POB 2455, London W1A 5WY, England
POB 4044, Jerusalem 91040
www.tobypress.com

ISBN 978-1-59264-512-1, paperback

Printed and bound in Israel

To my children, Rachel, Ari and David, who followed in their grandfather's footsteps as Israeli soldiers and lovers of Zion; my wonderful children-in-law, Lior, Talya and Sara; my delicious grandchildren, Yehonatan Yaakov, Ofri Bareket, Eitan Moshe, Lia Ariel, Noam Zion, Eliana Miriam, Ilan Shmuel and most recently, Harel.

But most of all, to my wife, Arlene, who makes everything in my life possible.

Contents

PART IV: REFLECTIONS

Preface

> The instability of human knowledge is one of our few certainties. Almost everything we know we know incompletely at best. And almost nothing we are told remains the same when retold.
>
> Janet Malcom, "Strangers in Paradise,"
> *The New Yorker*, Nov. 13, 2006

I discovered the letters only after he died. Three weeks before the end, he was still taking buses downtown by himself to Café Hillel to flirt with the waitresses and watch the girls go by. But suddenly his blood sugar spiked and within a few days we learned he had advanced metastatic pancreatic cancer. Although I could not quite believe that he would soon die, I nevertheless rushed to simplify estate issues, learn where all his documents were, and have him identify people in the old photographs he had stored in wooden boxes. During his last three weeks, time seemed to slow down and nothing existed outside of his room. Jerusalem had just had one of the heaviest snowfalls in its history; travel was challenging, electricity was spotty, and worst of all, we had no telephone or internet. It was difficult to deal with all the medical and administrative issues. My father, Mordecai Samuel Chertoff, slipped away just two days before the end of 2013 in a gentle and, according to him, painless and peaceful process. He complained of being tired, increasingly slept and, finally, did not wake up. He was ninety-one.

Six years earlier, my father had left a large, spacious apartment in Greenwich Village, Manhattan and moved into two rooms in an assisted living facility in the Arnona neighborhood of southern Jerusalem near where my wife and I lived. We had moved to Jerusalem a few years earlier after living for more than twenty years in Efrat, a town in the Judean hills just south of Bethlehem.

When he left America he had consolidated his most precious belongings to bring with him to Israel. Now I stood alone in his apartment, surrounded by the distilled essence of what was important to him, of who he was. I wondered where to begin.

Slowly, I started going through everything. He was incredibly orderly and neat. Some of his drawers had dividers to enforce separation between pens, paperclips, penknives, and coins. Others held clothing, neatly folded and piled. I found some shirts, folded around cardboard and secured with paper tape, not worn since they were last laundered in New York, years earlier. Bills and papers were in neat, labeled folders. And in the bottom of a file drawer I had never opened before were folders filled with letters.

Leafing through them, I discovered the correspondence between my grandparents during the academic year of 1935–1936, when my grandmother took her three children to spend the year in Palestine, leaving my grandfather in New York; and the more extensive correspondence between my father and his parents and siblings when he lived in Palestine from 1947 to 1950, working as a journalist for the *Palestine Post* and serving in the Haganah.

I was stunned by the find.

Several years earlier, when my father was in his early eighties, he had started writing a memoir of his experiences living in Palestine/Israel during the birth of the State. I had encouraged him to develop it into a book for the family. The narrative was chiefly anecdotal and associative – he recorded his recollections, supported by a few old articles and some research, drifting from one topic to another with little logic. I had grown up hearing many of these stories, time and again, and was basically tired of them. Nevertheless, I wanted to be supportive and help him get it done, so I edited and produced it. But I had no idea that he had kept this trove of letters from the period.

My ambivalence toward the memoir reflected my ambivalence toward my father. I loved him, or at least wanted to love him, but he was hard to like. He was remote and self-involved; interested in ideas, not in people. He saw everyone, even his children, through the prism of his own needs and thoughts, and was a poor judge of character. He did not know how to engage and was the least empathetic person I have ever known. He could be charming when first meeting someone, but did not know how to behave in many situations. After he moved to Israel, I was compelled to adopt my mother's former role of telling him how to act and what to say. I doubt our relationship was unique among fathers and sons. Some of my friends' fathers were truly engaged, but I had only the sketchiest understanding of the kinds of relationships they might share. I brought my father to Israel for the last six years of his life and took care of him, but always felt guilty about my inability to give him the kind of affection and admiration he craved, despite his inability to bestow it himself.

The cache of letters I found had not featured at all in my father's memoir, and he had never mentioned their existence to me. There were about 400 in all – 65 that the family exchanged during the 1935–1936 trip to Palestine, roughly 120 that my father wrote to his parents and siblings between 1947 and 1950, and approximately 230 that he received from them in return. There were also a few letters from friends and lovers, and half a dozen or so notes from Gershon Agronsky, founder and editor of the *Palestine Post*. Among his papers were also photographs, and dozens of articles that he wrote for the *Post*, *Hadoar* (a Hebrew language periodical published in the US), and other publications.

* * *

My father was born into an intellectual, religious, Zionist family in the US, the youngest of three children. Both his parents were immigrants: his father, Shraga Feivel (Paul), from Belarus; his mother, Esther, from Romania. Paul had rabbinic ordination and taught Talmud at the Jewish Theological Seminary (JTS) in New York. My father was twenty-five years old and had almost completed his own rabbinical degree at JTS when he moved to Palestine in 1947. That year, his brother, Gershon, was thirty-two, single, and a pulpit rabbi in Elizabeth, New Jersey. His sister, Naomi, was a trained psychiatric social worker; she was thirty years old, married, and living in Cleveland, Ohio. All five members of the family were ardent correspondents, often using carbon paper to preserve copies of what they wrote and, perhaps with an eye toward posterity, saved almost everything.

Mordecai's letters were personal, but not private. Many of them are addressed "Dear Family," with the expectation that they would be passed around and shared. Nevertheless, he clearly had a different relationship and therefore a different kind of correspondence with each member of his family. He and his father wrote to each other in Hebrew; loving, tender, lyrical, and inspired letters. His mother seemed often at a loss as to what to write, focusing on her own activities, family matters, and projects and assignments for her son to carry out for her in Palestine. Mordecai and his brother discussed ideas, books, and current events, while the longest, most detailed and most intimate letters were between Mordecai and his sister. Early in their correspondence, Naomi offered to be his "therapist," a position for which she was professionally qualified. He gladly accepted the offer and took full advantage. While it is clear that most of the letters to individual members of the family were passed around, some of *their* correspondence was confidential – not to be shared. Overall, the correspondence reflects a very close, deeply loving family who seem to care more for each other than for anyone outside of their nuclear unit, including spouses and lovers.

Mordecai's siblings both wrote that their father was keeping an extensive "double entry bookkeeping system" for the correspondence, tracking what letters were sent and received and when, and the subjects they covered. According to Gershon, Paul then supposedly outlined key points which warranted responses and assigned them to his two other children accordingly. Although I've never found my grandfather's ledger, I suspect this description is no exaggeration.

Beyond the affecting experience of reading what my family wrote sixty-five and eighty years ago, I was moved by the logistics of such a correspondence as well as by the tactile aspects of hard-copy letters. In our digital age, when communication is instantaneous, when we can hold real-time video chats and expect responses to text messages within minutes and to emails within a day, it is hard to process the reality of what we now call "snail mail." People devoted hours to writing long, carefully composed letters, understanding that the letters would be read, reread, analyzed, consulted, and, ultimately, tied with ribbon and saved; that a letter could arouse strong emotions in those who read them and a response would be considered and composed with contemplation and deliberation. This exchange would have taken about six weeks during the 1930s and three to four weeks during the late 1940s. Imagine that this is all you have of a loved one; imagine not even hearing the voice of a parent or sibling for two years!

Even more important were the mechanics of composition. Word processing on a computer does not require forethought or planning. An author jots down ideas, rearranges them, edits, corrects spelling, and is, eventually, left with a finished text. But before word processing, writers had to plan and carefully organize what they wanted to say. They had to think and write in sentences, paragraphs, and whole sections. It was a very different, and more demanding, mental process.

Finally, handling the letters was a powerful tactile experience for me. The correspondence during the middle 1930s had traveled primarily by sea. Many of the letters were written with fountain pens, on thick, creamy paper. The letters between my father and his parents and siblings in the late 1940s were written on aerograms or thin onionskin, sometimes on both sides in an effort to save money. Most of my father's letters were typed so that he could use carbon paper and save a copy for himself, but several were handwritten. Most of the letters he received were handwritten. I recalled the comment by the Israeli novelist Aharon Appelfeld, who wrote in longhand, claiming that writing is a sensual art, "You have to touch [the paper] and feel it."[1] As I read the letters, holding paper my loved ones had handled, their pen strokes clearly visible, I had to agree.

As I read the letters, I began to realize how significant they were. Most were written during two of the most momentous years in Jewish history. They offer an eyewitness, real-time view of the struggle for Israel's rebirth, from the perspective of a young, articulate, religious,

---

1.   *The Paris Review* (Fall 2014), interview with Aharon Appelfeld.

idealistic Zionist New Yorker. Along with vivid descriptions of Jerusalem, the Yishuv (the Jewish community in Palestine), and the fight for self-determination for the Jewish people, they offer a fascinating glimpse into the American Jewish community of the 1940s. I realized that the letters might have a wider appeal, beyond family, especially if placed in context.

I also came to see a more personal significance in them. These letters are the private, intimate thoughts and observations of my father as a young man. Besides descriptions of events, historical figures, and Jerusalem of yesteryear, my father wrote of relationships with women, professional successes and failures, triumphs and disappointments, and his thoughts and feelings on a wide range of issues. What an incredible opportunity to get to know my father in his formative years, one participating in one of the most miraculous events of the twentieth century! As a character in William Boyd's novel, *Sweet Caress*, says, "Who wouldn't want to travel back in time and encounter their parents before they became their parents?"[2] Indeed! Here was just such an opportunity. But what would I find? What was he like then? How did he think? What kind of person was he at that stage in his life? Did he change? How would it influence what I thought and felt about him so many years later? This treasure trove was my opportunity to confront and better understand both the emergence of the State of Israel ... and my father.

In his first letters, written in early 1947, Mordecai focused on settling into his new home in Jerusalem and finding work. They are somewhat self-centered but include some interesting historical and cultural information. With the UN vote to partition Palestine in November 1947, the story accelerates and the letters become much more interesting. Mordecai's description of the twenty-four hours following the vote is a masterpiece. The letters deal increasingly with events, circumstances, and people of national importance. Although Mordecai continued to tell his personal story, he was also a fine observer of contemporary events, as both analyst and participant. Sitting in the offices of the *Palestine Post* while simultaneously serving in the Haganah gave him unparalleled access to news and events. He was a good writer; he knew how to tell a

2.   Bloomsbury USA, 2015.

story that was gripping, informative, and (perhaps due to his interest in photography) visual. He was sometimes a bit aloof, seemingly removed and unaffected, rarely totally involved or committed – except during the bombing of the *Post* and his daring excursions between Jerusalem and Tel Aviv when the highway was very dangerous.

Considering the letters, alongside the memoir that my father wrote more than half a century later, added an important dimension. The memoir fills in, supports, enriches, and distorts the information contained in the letters. In the preface to his *Lyrical Ballads*, William Wordsworth writes that "poetry is the spontaneous overflow of powerful feelings: it takes its origin from emotion recollected in tranquility." I would claim that, similarly, memoirs are descriptions of events and feelings recollected in tranquility, tempered by time, a lifetime of experience, imperfect memory, and a desire to justify or amend history. Mordecai's memoir provides a different, mature perspective on the events of those years. It also fills in some important details missing from the letters – information that my father was unable to disclose to his family at the time due to security considerations. I have therefore included selections from the memoir that fill important gaps.

* * *

I have always preferred fiction to non-fiction. But these letters are not fiction and the story they tell is no invention. Reading the correspondence was a more profound and gripping experience than being immersed in any novel. A world was opened up to me, containing characters living during a critical historic juncture, all of them more interesting than any fictional character could possibly be. This world was real, vibrant, current, and perhaps most importantly, at least for me, it was mine. It was also a world and a perspective worth sharing with others. But in order to do so I realized I would have to place the letters in their historical context – political and historical developments, events, people, and places. I was doing this for myself, for my family, for a potentially wider audience and also for my father, in an effort to make the letters come alive. Perhaps it would allow me to give him, at least posthumously, the love and respect he always sought.

In order to understand the letters more fully, I needed to immerse myself in the history of Israel's creation. For a basic source on the period I depended upon Benny Morris's *1948*, but soon found myself scouring many other sources for further information on everything my father mentions in his letters: events, people, speeches, places, etc. Many aspects of events remain controversial, especially the attack on Deir Yassin on April 9, 1948 and the Arab refugee issue, to identify just two. Since my purpose is not to advocate any particular narrative, but rather, to highlight my father's experience – in context – I made a concerted effort to present events as objectively as possible. To that end, I consulted a wide variety of sources, especially the accounts of key participants, including, for example, John Bagot Glubb, the British general who trained and led the Jordanian Arab Legion against Israel; UN mediator Count Folke Bernadotte; and Dov Joseph, Military Governor during the siege of Jerusalem, among others. Many of my sources are listed in the bibliography. The discovery of my father's letters and my subsequent research provided me with the opportunity to come to grips with the story of Israel's birth at a time when, seventy years later, its legitimacy is still questioned. It has significantly influenced my understanding of the current stalemate between the Israelis and the Palestinian Arabs.

In addition to books and articles, I skimmed every available issue of the *Palestine Post* printed during the period my father was in Palestine/Israel.[3] I thought it important because in his letters my father makes frequent references to events and articles discussed in "today's paper." Moreover, as his place of employment, the *Post* was the center of my father's daily existence, its rhythms a kind of "heartbeat" for him. He had an important role in putting out the paper every day and was intimately familiar with the contents of each issue. Reading them made me feel as if I were standing right next to him. It helped me better understand what he was experiencing and confronting each day. He wrote many unattributed articles, but each time I encountered his byline was, for me, poignant and filled me with pride.

---

3. Unfortunately, the *Post* archive is not complete. Some issues are unavailable and some are incomplete.

It proved to be a fascinating exercise in historical research. A daily newspaper published during a tumultuous time period is a valuable primary source, a contemporaneous view of what will later be reinterpreted and massaged into history. I read about events the way my father experienced them – on an accretive, day-by-day basis, rather than as processed history. Reading articles written about events as they are happening is vastly different from reading about them after the fact, knowing how they will end. One unforeseen aspect of reading these daily accounts of events was the experiential.

A powerful example was the *Post*'s ongoing coverage of the long odyssey of the *SS Exodus 1947*, a ship carrying 4,500 Jewish refugees from Europe attempting to reach Palestine in violation of the British limitations on Jewish immigration. The *Exodus* was part of the "Aliya Bet," the illegal Jewish immigration (discussed in detail below) organized by several Jewish groups at the time. The ship was tracked from the moment it left France on July 11, 1947, and, when close to Palestine, was attacked by the British with the immediate deaths of two refugees and a Jewish volunteer crewman. The refugees were subject to appalling abuses. They were pulled off the *Exodus*, loaded onto three smaller boats, and sent back to Port-de-Bouc in the south of France, where they refused to disembark. The French declared that they would not accept any refugees who did not disembark of their own free will. In frustration, the British threatened to send the refugees to Germany. At the end of August, the boats approached Gibraltar for refueling. An article in the *Post* includes a detail I have not found in historical summaries; despite a heatwave that made conditions intolerable, the refugee men, women, and children were locked in barbed wire cages in the hold in order to prevent their escape. The ships were refueled and again put out to sea.

Eventually, after almost two months at sea, the refugees were forced to disembark in Germany and were taken to camps horribly reminiscent of the concentration camps from which many of them had been liberated. Some of the refugees made subsequent attempts to reach Palestine but were caught and placed in British internment camps in Cyprus. Many of the *Exodus* refugees managed to reach Palestine by the time the State was declared on May 14, 1948 – almost a year after their original departure from France. But those who were interned in camps in Cyprus, where fifty thousand other Jews were held, had a longer wait. The British released the detainees at the rate of 1,500 per month; the last were finally released in January, 1949, when Britain formally recognized the State of Israel.

To read of the seasickness, the appalling sanitary conditions, of adults and babies dying, of the desperate refugees' determined refusal to disembark anywhere but Palestine, to feel the deepening sense of "Pharaoh hardening his heart"[4] as the British resolutely refused any mercy, despite worldwide condemnation and horror, is devastating. Even the United Nations Special Committee on Palestine (UNSCOP), present in Palestine at the time on a fact-finding mission, was appalled by the callousness of the British. The heartbreaking accounts of the agony of the victims unfolded in real time and it is impossible to remain dry-eyed. I found this a more "ethical" way to learn what happened, rather than reading massaged, historical summaries.

Reading the daily *Post* also gave me the opportunity to learn about contemporaneous events beyond Palestine, including the West's struggle with Russia over Germany and Berlin, Indian independence, the creation of Pakistan and "Hindustan," the communist takeover of Hungary, the "Texas City Disaster" (an industrial accident that killed over five hundred people), the assassination of Mahatma Gandhi, and Europe's ongoing struggle to recover from World War II. I was also fascinated by the advertisements for cigarettes, face cream, real estate, vacuum cleaners, and tourist attractions. Equally absorbing were the announcements of arrivals in Palestine, social events, concerts, reviews of cultural events, letters to the editor, etc. It is extraordinary to see that, in spite of the constant attacks – the bombs and sniper fire – and the uncertainty of what the future would bring, life went on as usual: Palestinian Jews flocked to concerts, sporting events, and the cinema. There were eight active movie theaters each in Haifa and Jerusalem and seven in Tel Aviv!

Shifting between these three main sources – a daily newspaper, history books, and my father's letters and memoirs – provided a rich perspective on the period. But it is the letters that are the most powerful. Historian Anita Shapira articulates perfectly what I discovered:

4. Exodus 8:32, for example.

"Autobiographical writing is an attempt to give expression to that fleeting moment, to freeze time, to perpetuate what happened in real time, before the historians and writers and agents of memory expropriate the past and control its shaping."[5]

* * *

Finding the letters was like stumbling upon a beautiful, ancient mosaic where some sections of the picture are full – dazzling, detailed, and vibrant – while others are sparse, faded, or missing. For some months there are many letters, but for others, like the invasion period immediately following the declaration of the State, when there was no mail service, there are almost none. There are also time periods during which much of moment happened, but, frustratingly, Mordecai writes only about personal matters. I have filled some of the gaps in his narrative with articles that he wrote, with other contemporary eyewitness reports (mostly by people he knew), and with the fruits of my reading and research. The resulting "restored" mosaic is a combination of all these sources.

Mordecai's parents and siblings were not only highly educated, but well informed about world affairs and the situation in the Middle East. They were also voracious consumers of news, especially with respect to Palestine. His letters home assumed this strong background in history, current affairs, culture, and literature. Therefore, in addition to filling in the gaps in the mosaic, I have tried to provide the background that Mordecai assumed in his readers. I am not a historian and do not presume to offer any novel interpretations of history or revelations. Nevertheless, I have included coverage of some aspects of the history of the period that seem rarely discussed, such as the tireless efforts by the UN to find a peaceful solution to the conflict, like the UNSCOP report and the proposals by UN mediator Count Folke Bernadotte. I have drawn on both primary and secondary sources in order to showcase the letters, but to a certain extent I have tried to restrict myself to what Mordecai knew or had read.

---

5.   Anita Shapira, "Jerusalem in 1948: A Contemporary Perspective," *Jewish Social Studies* 17, no. 3 (Spring/Summer 2011): p. 119.

This book is the result: a highly personal, subjective, and idiosyncratic work. It interweaves the letters – heavily annotated – with some of Mordecai's published articles, "editorials" he supplied to his brother, sections of his memoirs, and pictures and documents, in order to create a coherent narrative – his narrative – placed in its historical context. The result is both an eyewitness account of the birth of the State of Israel by an acute, well-positioned observer and participant, and the story of the inner life of a sensitive, educated young man, strongly attached to his family and far from home.

From a practical point of view, I observed all the normal conventions associated with editing a collection of letters. I made only basic corrections, fixing typos, normalizing spelling, format, etc. The names of publications and sailing vessels are in italics, even though my father obviously could not type in italics on his typewriter. In some cases I left charming misspellings and explained my father's word-play. I also deleted letters, or parts of letters, which I felt would not be interesting to the general reader.

All translations from the Hebrew are by Shira Koppel, except where indicated. People and places are identified only the first time they appear. Hebrew, and foreign language phrases are translated the first time they appear.

Finally, I suppose I should include what is known today as a "trigger warning." Mordecai was politically very incorrect, freely expressing racist views and evoking ethnic, gender, and racial stereotypes. He and his family were also very concerned with meeting "the right people" and could be snobbish and manipulative. These are not admirable qualities, but Mordecai and his family were "real" people who lived at a particular time. Some of their sentiments and expressions may be considered cultural artifacts.

One of the great pleasures of immersing myself in this long-gone world has been the opportunity to meet the descendants of some of the people mentioned in the letters and, indeed, in at least one case, to communicate directly with someone who played an important role in my father's life almost seventy years ago. Those encounters are described in context and in the acknowledgments. Perhaps this project will elicit responses from other participants in this drama. I hope so.

Chapter 1

Planting the Seeds: Palestine, 1935–1936

Mordecai's sojourn in Palestine/Israel during the late forties really began eleven years earlier, in 1935, when his mother took him and his siblings to Palestine for the academic year, leaving her husband in New York. (Paul would join them nine months later, for the summer months.) The trip was transformative for Mordecai. It established the Jewish homeland as the absolute center of his life, created the infrastructure that would sustain him during his later stay, and taught him how to manage on extremely limited resources. The letters he wrote to his father during that period, as a thirteen-year-old, foreshadow the issues, concerns, and habits that would be reflected in the letters he would write as an adult during the period leading up to and including Israel's War of Independence.

What was the complex political reality the family would encounter during their extraordinary trip?

Less than twenty years before, four centuries of Turkish rule in Palestine (from 1516 until 1917) had ended. Their Ottoman Empire had allied itself with Germany in World War I and had been defeated – specifically in Palestine – by the British. In recognition of the Jews' millennia-long attachment to their ancient homeland, on November 2, 1917, Britain's foreign secretary, Arthur James Balfour, "declared" in a letter to Lord Walter Rothschild, a British peer and leader of the British Jewish community, for transmission to the Zionist Federation of Great Britain and Ireland, that

> His Majesty's government view with favour the establishment in Palestine of a national home for the Jewish people, and will use their best endeavours to facilitate the achievement of this object, it being clearly understood that nothing shall be done which may prejudice the civil and religious rights of existing non-Jewish communities in Palestine, or the rights and political status enjoyed by Jews in any other country.

In 1922, the League of Nations awarded a mandate to the British to administer Palestine, a region whose original definition included what now constitutes Jordan,[1] the West Bank, Gaza, and modern-day Israel. The British government was tasked with implementing the Balfour Declaration,[2] and envisioned establishing a Jewish state in a large portion of Palestine. However, the Arabs of Palestine and the surrounding

---

1. At the same time, France was awarded a mandate to administer other Ottoman lands, including parts of Ottoman Syria, Lebanon, and Alexandretta, and parts of southeastern Turkey.

2. The Mandate was confirmed at the San Remo Conference, on April 25, 1920, and came into effect in 1923. Among the Conference's resolutions: "The Mandatory [i.e., Britain] will be responsible for putting into effect the declaration originally made on November 8, 1917, by the British Government, and adopted by the other Allied Powers, in favour of the establishment in Palestine of a national home for the Jewish people, it being clearly understood that nothing shall be done which may prejudice the civil and religious rights of existing non-Jewish communities in Palestine, or the rights and political status enjoyed by Jews in any other country."

   The question of what the Balfour Declaration meant by a "national homeland for the Jewish people" remains controversial. Minimalists claim the intent was an autonomous enclave for the Jews within an Arab state. Maximalists claim the intent was a sovereign Jewish state in all of mandatory Palestine, including what is now Jordan. There has been a recent resurgence of interest and scholarship on the subject in honor of the hundredth anniversary of the declaration.

countries were violently opposed to the possibility of a Jewish state of any size in Palestine.

Alarmed by the acceleration of Jewish immigration and land purchases, Palestinian Arabs responded to the Balfour Declaration with waves of riots and violence. In 1922, in an attempt to quell riots and appease the Arabs, the British issued a white paper[3] which, among other things, significantly reduced the immigration quota of Jews to Palestine and the amount of land to be allocated to them. But even these draconian measures were not enough to appease the Arabs. The riots worsened, and the disturbances of 1929[4] were rewarded by the 1930 Passfield White Paper, which further restricted Jewish immigration.

Nevertheless, in 1933 the rise of Nazism led to a significant increase in Jewish immigration to Palestine – 30,000 refugees in 1933, 42,000 in 1934, and 62,000 in 1935. This almost doubled the Jewish population, which grew to about 350,000 within only three years.[5] At the same time there were approximately 950,000 Arabs. Almost all Jewish immigration to Palestine during the 1930s was from Europe; about half from Poland, just over a quarter from Germany, and most of the rest from other Eastern European countries. Only one percent came from the United States.[6] Social scientists estimate that roughly nine thousand American Jews immigrated to Palestine between 1920 and 1939 – Orthodox Jews, pioneers, farmers and urban professionals. This rise in immigration would reach its peak in April 1936, barely two weeks after Paul arrived to meet up with Esther and the family.

The period between 1929 and 1936 was relatively productive in Palestine, despite the ongoing unrest and occasional riots. The British Mandatory government invested in infrastructure, transportation, and communications, and built beautiful public buildings. Palestine had long been a popular tourist destination, but these improvements increased

---

3.　White papers are authoritative statements of government policy preferences on an issue before it introduces legislation. Publishing a white paper tests public opinion on controversial policy issues and helps the government gauge its probable impact.

4.　In which roughly 250 Jews and Arabs were killed and at least 450 wounded.

5.　Bruce Hoffman, *Anonymous Soldiers* (Knopf, 2015), pp. 41–42.

6.　*A Survey of Palestine*, prepared in December 1945 and January 1946 by the British government in Palestine, p. 186.

its appeal and lead to the creation of new, comfortable, European-style hotels. Besides the obvious religious attraction for adherents of the three monotheistic faiths, the area, at the intersection of three continents – Africa, Asia, and Europe – boasted unique physical features and microclimates; deserts, mountains, the lowest spot on earth (the Dead Sea), coastal plains, the Jordan Rift Valley, and more. It also boasted a wide range of historical as well as religious sites of many different eras. There was an increasing number of knowledgeable guides, and many companies offered tourist packages with trips ranging in length from one to four weeks. In 1935, despite the sporadic violence, 107,000 tourists visited Palestine.[7]

This was the situation when Esther and her three children arrived in 1935. She was among the 3,804 "authorized American Jewish travelers registered by the government of Palestine Immigration Offices"[8] in Palestine that year.

But what kind of trip was this to be? A trip of a year's duration during those times was unusual. Perhaps it was a pre-immigration, pilot trip. Immigration to Palestine *was* a long-term dream of the family, although the Chertoffs had no intention of settling in Palestine permanently at that point, or even in the near future. They were unusual in this sense; while many American Jews supported the Jewish enterprise in Palestine, few actually wanted to move there themselves. Attitudes toward aliya among American Jews ranged from a rare sense of obligation to immigrate to strenuous *objections* to immigration – and everything in between. This reflected the diversity of answers to the questions of dual loyalty, assimilation, and the acceptance of Jews in wider American society. A central issue was the question of whether Jews were merely adherents of a religion, or a distinct nation in need of a state. This issue is discussed in some of the later correspondence between Mordecai and his family.

---

7. *Jewish Telegraphic Agency*, February 3, 1936. In fact, 1935 turned out to be the peak year for tourism, which began to decline in 1936 as a result of the Arab rebellion.
8. See Table 1 in Joseph B. Glass, *From New Zion to Old Zion: American Jewish Immigration and Settlement in Palestine 1917–1939* (Wayne State University Press, 2002), p. 19.

It is clear from the correspondence that the Chertoffs' dream of living in Palestine was an expression of their fervent religious Zionism. Although they were comfortable in the United States and grateful to their adopted country for providing them with a refuge from Europe, the center of their emotional lives was Palestine. Paul and Esther belonged to an intellectually elite milieu of American Orthodox Zionists; many of their friends were simultaneously religiously Orthodox and intellectually liberal and well-read scholars of Judaism. Nonetheless, that Paul and Esther were *so* Zionist as to commit to such an expensive, prolonged trip at such a dangerous time, and were willing to be apart for so long, was remarkable.

Who were these bold adventurers? I have little of my own perspective to offer. They were my grandparents, but I hardly knew them. When I was a child, they lived in New York while we moved around from one distant city to another. Although we visited them occasionally and spent some holidays together, I did not have an ongoing connection to them. On the rare occasions when we did see them they seemed ancient to me. My grandmother was sharp, acerbic, and cold, neither inviting nor loving, at least in my estimation. My grandfather was quiet and fragile – people were always hovering, fussing over him and asking, "Would Father like some tea?" His family always addressed him in the third person, "Father," with a capital "F."

When I was twelve years old we moved into my grandparents' apartment building on the Upper West Side of Manhattan. By that time, my grandfather had died but my grandmother still lived in the building, six floors above us. I remember her apartment, with the smell of decay and the dust that children associate with old people. The couches, too deep and too soft, difficult for a child to escape from, were upholstered in a rough red floral design. There were dishes of licorice which our grandmother would urge on us and which my sister, Jocelyn, and I loathed. My grandfather's study remained exactly as it had been when he was alive – beautiful glass-doored bookcases, a heavy desk with a green-shaded library lamp onto which my grandmother had glued, off-center, two birds kissing, and green and white plastic lawn furniture. My grandmother liked the folding lawn furniture because it was lightweight, comfortable, and inexpensive. There was a certain pragmatic logic, if not aesthetic sensitivity, to her choices, an interesting contrast to her love of high culture – she had an insatiable appetite for opera and jewelry. The study also boasted a large, framed picture of the Coliseum, the symbol of Roman culture, a reflection of my grandfather's appreciation of secular knowledge, not especially common among the religious Jewish intellectual elite.

Several years later my grandmother moved into an old age home where she lived until her death in 1973, during my first year of university. I hadn't gotten to know her while she lived above us and am embarrassed to write that I don't remember visiting her more than a few times in the home.

My understanding of who my grandparents were would deepen and change significantly after reading their letters. It was hard to recognize the cold and ancient couple I barely knew in the vivacious and loving letters I read. Gradually, my newly formed appreciation of their respective characters would be overshadowed by a sense of loss. As a child, I never glimpsed the fire and resolve my grandmother possessed, nor the deep love that my grandfather felt for and clearly expressed to his children. Perhaps time had stolen it from them; perhaps I was simply too young or too insensitive to recognize it. In light of the loving correspondence between my grandparents and my father, our infrequent visits and distant relationship to them later seem strange to me and I have no explanation. Moreover, given their intense involvement in their children's lives, it is hard for me to understand how they seemed to have been relatively uninterested in my sister and me.

* * *

6

My grandfather, Paul Chertoff, was born in 1881 as Shraga Feivel Chertoff, in the Haradok (or "Gorodok") district of what is today Belarus, then located in the Pale of Settlement, the only part of the Russian Empire in which Jews were allowed to live at the time. Conditions in the Pale were harsh; the area was overcrowded, there was religious oppression and very limited work opportunities. Conditions worsened further in 1894 with the ascension of Nicholas II, who encouraged attacks on Jews. In 1897, there were over five million Jews living in the Pale, of whom 724,548 lived in Belarus, making up almost 14 percent of the population. My grandfather's shtetl was small; less than fifteen hundred Jews by the time he left, but his family were not grindingly poor, like so many in those days; they even owned a share of the Wissotzky Tea company.[9]

Shraga Feivel was considered an *ilui*, a prodigy. He studied at the renowned Volozhin yeshiva, and in Smorgon, where Israel's first chief rabbi, Abraham Isaac Kook, lived for a time. He received rabbinic ordination in Russia in 1897, at the age of seventeen. Shortly after, he joined the tidal wave of emigration from Russia,[10] leaving the country together with his siblings – five brothers and two sisters – and settling in Rochester, New York. There, Shraga Feivel became Paul.[11]

There are no records of what Paul did during his first years in America, but a few years after the turn of the century found him studying simultaneously at Columbia University and the Jewish Theological Seminary, earning his MA in philosophy from Columbia in 1910 and receiving rabbinic ordination from JTS in 1911. The title of the twice-ordained rabbi's MA thesis reflects the breadth of his intellectual interests: "Happiness and the Object of Life as Viewed in the Works of

---

9. While known today as an Israeli company, Wissotzky Tea was founded in Moscow in 1849. According to a letter my father wrote to a genealogical researcher in the 1990s, his father sold their share in the company for a pittance once he arrived in the US.

10. Between 1880 and 1928, 2.3 million Jews left Russia – the vast majority for the US and a small number for Palestine. Ninety percent of the Jews who remained in Belarus were murdered during the Holocaust.

11. I have no knowledge of whether my grandfather's parents left Russia with their children. All of my grandfather's siblings eventually settled in Cleveland, Ohio.

Thomas Carlyle." I don't know why he pursued Conservative rabbinic ordination after receiving Orthodox ordination in Russia. Perhaps the earlier ordination was not recognized in the US, or it was easier to get a job as a pulpit rabbi in the Conservative movement.

Rabbi Paul and Esther Chertoff, 1914

After his ordination, Paul Chertoff became a pulpit rabbi, first in Rochester, NY, and then at Congregation Shaarei Zedek, which at that time was in Harlem, in New York City. In 1914, he married my grandmother, Esther Barish, who had immigrated to the United States from Romania. She was twenty-two years old on their wedding day, twelve years younger than he. I know almost nothing about the circumstances of her immigration or her family situation, only that she had a large, relatively wealthy family. Her letters to my father in 1947–48 make frequent references to family members and family events.

Gershon Baruch was born to the couple in 1915, Naomi in 1918, and Mordecai Samuel, my father, in 1922. The family lived in Brooklyn so that the children could attend the Chofetz Chaim Yeshiva, considered one of the best at the time.

Paul quickly discovered that the life of a pulpit rabbi was not for him. He joined a friend in the pants business, but this career move was not a success because, according to my father, "he was always in the back room with a Gemara[12] rather than out front with a customer."[13] In 1924, Paul found his intellectual home when he joined the faculty of the Teacher's Institute of the Jewish Theological Seminary. He ended up teaching there for forty years as Associate Professor of Rabbinics, commuting three hours a day to the Seminary until the family eventually moved to Manhattan. He was a gifted teacher; as a teen I met several of his students, all of whom told me how much they had loved him and learned from him. While teaching others, he continued his own studies, eventually earning a doctorate in Hebrew literature. To this day, JTS awards an annual prize in his name to an outstanding student in Talmud.

Meanwhile, Esther was at least as hungry for learning as her husband. Her education in Romania had been cut short due to her father's disapproval of studies for women. She was determined to continue her education in the United States and studied part-time while raising her children; although it took her ten years to do it, she succeeded in earning her high school diploma. Family legend has it that she would drop off baby Mordecai with the local newsagent for the day so that she could go

---

12.   A volume of the Talmud.
13.   From the memoirs.

to school,[14] though perhaps this is an exaggeration. When Mordecai was nine or ten years old, Esther began her undergraduate studies, receiving her BA from Hunter College at the age of forty-three.[15]

And then, in 1935, she embarked upon the journey of a lifetime, taking her three children, by then aged twenty, seventeen and thirteen, to live in Palestine for almost a year. While visas for immigration to Palestine were tightly restricted by the British authorities, tourist visas were more easily obtained. With all the paperwork in hand, Esther and the children boarded the *USS Rex* on July 9, 1935 and sailed to Palestine via Naples. Paul remained in New York, working. He would join them for a few months towards the end of their trip, in the spring of 1936.

Esther Chertoff was clearly extraordinary. It is hard to imagine this middle-aged woman leaving her husband for almost nine months to take her children six thousand miles away, to a primitive land seething with tension and occasional violence, where she did not speak the language (although her children did) and where – as the letters reflect – she did not have the financial means to live comfortably. But the odyssey is an indication of the extent of her will and the ardency of the family's Zionism. The trip was also a significant hardship for Paul, who was completely dependent on his wife and deeply involved in his children's intellectual development. Shortly after their departure, Paul moved temporarily into the Seminary dormitory.

The family's commitment to Zionism is reflected in my father's bar mitzva speech, delivered at Congregation Shomrei Emunah in Borough Park, Brooklyn, on June 22, 1935,[16] about three weeks before the family set sail for Palestine:

---

14. Naomi told this to her son, Adam, my cousin, who related it to me.
15. She would go on to earn a Master of Science in education from City College at the age of sixty-five. Her thesis was titled: "The Origin and Development of the Modern School in Israel."
16. There is a problem with the date of the bar mitzva which I cannot resolve. My father was born on September 7, the 14th of the Hebrew month of Elul, 1922. In 1935, the year he turned thirteen, his Hebrew birthday fell on September 12. Yet he celebrated his bar mitzva three months earlier. It is possible that he gave this speech in a gathering before he left and that he was only called to the Torah for

Rabbotai:[17] I have been granted a great privilege: in a few weeks I shall be going up to the Land of Israel. Perhaps it is just a coincidence that these two landmarks in my life – my bar mitzva and the trip to Eretz Yisrael – come together; and perhaps it is not a coincidence but, rather, a sign from Above; the finger of God pointing out the path I am to travel when I come of age.

It is, perhaps, a hint from Above, that in order to be a Jew faithful to our people and to our God, I must be faithful to our land too. I must learn of its brilliant past, know its prophets and seers, its scholars and great men, from whose waters we drank and from whose mouths we were nourished. I must also tie up my lot with her [Palestine's] future, which we hope will be even more brilliant, because Palestine, for us, is not only the land of our fathers, the land of the past, but also the land of the future, of the building sons.

We are already seeing the beginning of the redemption; sons are returning to their heritage from far and near...they gather in Zion to build her ruins, to make of her deserts an Eden and her desolate stretches a fruitful garden.

True, at my age I cannot be among the builders, but the new life in Eretz Yisrael, a life of stirring and re-awakening, a life of Jewish values and national conceptions, will take root in my heart and fill my soul, and their impress will not be erased all the days of my life. The spirit of new life, manifest in all that is happening there, will enter into me, too, and will arouse me, when I mature, to take my place among the builders of the House of Israel.

I thank God that I have been granted such good fortune. As Yehuda Halevi said: "Fortunate is the man who chooses to live in your streets; to see the good of your chosen ones, and to rejoice in your happiness as you return to the days of your youth."

---

the religious ceremony three months later, in Israel, but it is hard to imagine that either Mordecai or his father would have agreed to an arrangement that would have precluded Paul's attendance at such a momentous occasion.

17.   Hebrew, meaning "gentlemen."

> *"Bedam va'esh Yehuda nafla; bedam va'esh Yehuda takum!"*
> In blood and fire Judea fell; in blood and fire Judea will rise!

As will become clear, Mordecai was, indeed, setting out to become one of the builders of the Jewish state.

When the family arrived in Jerusalem, Esther rented a small apartment in the Bukharan Quarter – 70 Zefania Street – for seventy dollars a month (about $1,250 in 2018 dollars). Gershon and Mordecai shared a room while Naomi slept on a cot in the living room. In spite of the cramped quarters, they had frequent overnight guests. At first Mordecai attended the Tachkemoni School[18] but he quickly switched to the Hebrew Teacher's Seminary of Mizrachi; Naomi went to Yellin College,[19] and Gershon studied at the Hebrew University.

It was at this point, in the fall of 1935, that the Chertoff family's extensive correspondence begins. Between the summer of 1935 and the spring of 1936 my grandparents exchanged forty letters (others may be lost), all written in English. I have one or two by each siblings and another half dozen or so written by my father. Even as an American thirteen-year-old, Mordecai wrote to his father in Hebrew, a habit that would continue during his later extended stay, between 1947 and 1950.

Paul and Esther wrote to each other frequently. An exchange routinely took six weeks – three weeks each way – incomprehensible by today's standards. And until they got used to the vagaries of the mail service, both complained bitterly about the other not writing.

Paul's letters to Esther were loving and full of longing. Having caught a glimpse of her standing on deck as he watched the *USS Rex* pull away from the pier in New York, he wrote:

> The picture of you standing at the background of the white ship, which arose as a magnificent palace, was more than beautiful. It

---

18. The Tachkemoni School was founded in Jerusalem in 1909 by religious intellectuals who believed children should study Torah, modern science and other secular studies, and Zionism. According to Mordecai, the school even had a gymnasium. The school was a bastion of religious Zionism in the city.

19. Now called The David Yellin Academic College of Education.

didn't seem real, it seemed a dream, at least a moving picture!
(July 15, 1935)

A few months later, he wrote:

> My feelings toward you, dear, [are] measureless, limitless, [they]
> defy description ... an everlasting fire is burning – consuming my
> heart, my soul, my entire self is love for you ... these emotions are
> so sacred to me, that I wouldn't dare even to write them on paper.

Although Esther did not express her love for her husband quite so lyri-
cally, she credited him with the social success she found in Palestine,
and her appreciation for the difference he had made on her life is deep.
She wrote to him in November:

> If people take to me, dear, it is because of you, because I am the
> wife of Rabbi Chertoff. And if you contradict me and say no,
> because of myself, it is also because of you. For because of you
> I came out of my "shell." You know how depressed I was in my
> parent's home. Aside from the fact that I was kept in ignorance,
> I was always being put in my place. If there was company in the
> house I was careful not to open my mouth, for I knew that I
> stood a good chance of being "bawled out" because I said thus
> and so. So you see, dear, you really brought out the best there
> was in me. I always feel perfectly at ease in the greatest company
> and all due to you, sweetheart. When I think what my life might
> have been had I continued in the atmosphere in which I was
> brought up, I shudder.

While immersed in life in Palestine, Esther remained involved with
family life in America. She was bitterly disappointed when Paul was
not promoted from the Teacher's Institute to the Seminary and urged
him to do whatever it took, to speak with anyone who might be able to
help, to plead his case, make demands, etc. She was not one to give up.

She was practical, but had some peculiar views of social inter-
course. At one point she wrote to Paul that Gershon wanted some

money in order to take out a girl. She could not understand why he, a single man of twenty, would waste money on a stranger when he could simply take out his sister, Naomi, instead!

Esther had three main priorities in Palestine: see the country, meet people, and visit institutions – especially schools for girls. She vividly describes her day at the Evelina de Rothschild School in Jerusalem, her visits to Hadassah health clinics, the Girl's School for Farming in Jerusalem's Talpiot neighborhood, a home for babies, and other institutions.

Esther was a truly intrepid traveler, constantly on trips around the country, leaving the children alone for a week at a time. "One must see the country," she declared in a letter sent on February 4, 1936. She took buses, walked long distances, and stayed on kibbutzim, working for her board picking oranges. "I am willing to undergo all hardships to learn and experience Palestine," she wrote, telling her husband that she looked forward to retracing her steps with him when he arrived. At Christmas time she went to Bethlehem and to the Church of the Nativity and attended midnight mass. She was determined to see and experience everything.

Most of all, Esther was a relentless and strategic networker, successful in her determination to meet the "right" people, and socializing regularly with many of the pioneers of early Zionism. She wrote of spending an evening with Henrietta Szold, the founder of Hadassah (the Women's Zionist Organization of America), and helping to raise money for Szold's seventy-fifth birthday. She met Dr. Judah Magnes, a prominent Reform rabbi and one of the founders and first chancellor of the Hebrew University. She became a frequent guest at the home of Rabbi Meir Berlin (later Hebraized to Meir Bar-Ilan), with whom her husband had probably studied in Volozhin.[20] She socialized often with Dr. Alexander M. Dushkin and his wife. Dushkin had directed the bureau of Jewish education in Chicago and ultimately became professor emeritus of the education department of Hebrew University. She was also close to Eliyahu Ostoshinsky, head of the regional council of the town (now city) of Kfar Saba.

---

20. Berlin, an American rabbi of illustrious lineage, was one of the pre-eminent leaders of religious Zionism. Before moving to Palestine he had served as president of the Mizrachi movement, the official organ of religious Zionism.

Naomi, Gershon, Esther and Mordecai; caption
reads: "Dec 1935 Kerem Avraham"

Perhaps, Esther's most intriguing friend was Rose Viteles, whom
she may have already known in Ohio, where both women had family.
Viteles had moved to Palestine from America during the 1920s, not from
Zionist ideology but because her husband had been appointed general
manager of the Central Bank of Cooperative Institutions.[21] Once there,

---

21.   The bank provided loans for the development of cooperative institutions – kib-
      butzim and moshavim. It ultimately became a subsidiary of the Palestine Economic
      Corporation, an American company financed mainly by the Joint Distribution
      Committee.

however, she became integral to the life of the Yishuv: Invited to join the Union of Hebrew Women, she threw herself into its work, helping needy families, doing most of the fundraising, and ultimately becoming treasurer of the organization. She was also a member of the Palestine Council of Hadassah. More surprisingly for a woman of upper middle-class society, she became involved with the then highly illegal Haganah. When she joined the Haganah it was experiencing a financial crisis and Rose was instrumental in turning that crisis around. She ultimately became its unofficial treasurer. When the Yishuv had a complicated and/ or dangerous job involving money and international issues, they often turned to Rose Viteles.[22] Esther, of course, would have known nothing of these covert activities.

Paul's letters demonstrated a deep understanding of his wife. Through them he continued to encourage her personal development and fulfillment. On January 8, 1936, he wrote that he was glad that she was in the social swing in Palestine, "and meeting people of different types and standing":

> It turned out just as we planned. I knew that you needed, at least for some time, just this kind of life. In the ten, twelve, years of your college and teaching, you accumulated many ideas and views and you need to test those views and ideas in actual life, and exchange them with others who are interested in such subjects. Besides, during the years of your study and teaching you secluded yourself from society, and this phase of life, the social phase, was strange to you. As a result your interest[s] became somewhat circumscribed, limited. By nature you are very sociable, this phase of life in you is highly developed and being unable to exercise it you feel at times a certain dissatisfaction with yourself. Now you have a chance to be your true self, have all your faculties functioning harmoniously.

---

22. For more on the life and achievements of this fascinating woman, whose accomplishments should be more widely known, see https://jwa.org/encyclopedia/article/viteles-rose.

It would be hard to imagine a more perceptive and supportive husband.

All three children wrote to their father regularly. Unfortunately, there are no revealing details in the few letters I have from Gershon and Naomi, but Mordecai's letters offer a trove of information. In a letter to Esther, Paul commented that Naomi's letters were "sweet," Gershon's show "a real analytical mind, sharp, clear, and the style, a beautiful Hebrew," while Mordecai's letters were "always to the point, always clever, [with] a light veiled humor."

In one of Mordecai's letters, written shortly after they arrived and the day before his thirteenth birthday, he told his father about the various youth groups open to him, and asked, "Is it worth buying the two books of Avraham Mapu – *Ahavat Tzion* and *Ashmat Shomron*? I haven't read them, but one chapter they read to us at school and they're very interesting. They're written in the style of the biblical Prophets and Writings, and I want to read them." He also asked his father to send him the *New York Times* "Week in Review," demonstrating his precocious interest in journalism and current events.

In his response, Paul expressed his pleasure that his youngest son had joined the scouts and another youth group, and advised him that "*derekh eretz*"[23] for a boy his age certainly meant being engaged in sports and activities, but that he shouldn't forget "*Torah im Derekh Eretz*."[24] He also told him that "you may buy any Hebrew book you want, on condition you read it start to finish, that is the birthday gift from me."[25]

He asked Mordecai to write him all about his school, his studies, and his friends; told him he thought of him often; and "from the depths of my heart send you warm wishes, a father's blessings that you succeed in everything you do and in your studies, and rise always to

---

23. The Hebrew term "*derekh eretz*" literally means "the way of the land," but is used in this context to refer to a Jewish principle of living according to conduct that contributes to decency, respect, and social awareness.
24. "Torah with *Derekh Eretz*" is a philosophy of Orthodox Judaism articulated by Rabbi Samson Raphael Hirsch (1808–88), which formalizes a positive relationship between traditionally observant Judaism and the modern world. It uses the term *derekh eretz* in a subtly different sense, referring to secular studies.
25. This is a "deal" that my father gave me and my sister at about the same age.

greater heights in life and in society." He signed his letter "*avikha ohave-kha ahavat nefesh*" – your father who loves you with his soul.

Mordecai flourished in Palestine. He manifested his intense love of and facility with language by working on the Hebrew-language school magazine, *HaOketz*. As I read his letters to his father, I found myself fascinated and charmed by the young teenager who would later become my father.

In a letter written on January 1, 1936, Mordecai displays both his facility with language and his youth:

> I received your last letter just yesterday, and I want to let you know about a mistake I found in it. You wrote the word addressa for address when you should have written ketovet.
>
> You wrote to me kukhim (what I call small caves). I know the word kukhim. But it escaped my memory when I was writing the letter, and I was forced to settle for a sort of "description." Another thing, in my letter, I used the Aramaic word for please, b'mtuta. But thanks to Gershon's assistance I mixed up two letters and spelled it wrong. I don't want you to think that I really don't know how to spell the word correctly.
>
> Right now, I don't have the patience to write a whole saga because I am excited about the parade tomorrow, the tree planting,[26] the vacation day, etc. Therefore, I am ending.
>
> Lehitraot. Your son, who loves you deeply, Mordecai

In another letter (November 6) he wrote:

> My sister taught me a Hebrew slang expression that she heard from someone, "an innocent dove with a comma." When you attach a comma to the first letter of the word "dove," you get the Hebrew word for prostitute.[27]

---

26. For "Tu BiShvat," the Jewish New Year for Trees.

27. Indeed. The word for dove is *yona* and the word for prostitute is *zona*. It is true that if you add a comma to the letter yod (*y*), it will become the letter zayin (*z*).

In a letter sent on October 30, 1935, Mordecai sought his father's opinion on the delicate subject of the (illegal) Haganah:

> Are you happy about the "Jewish Haganah"? It's a large group of one thousand or fifteen hundred young Jewish men who gather and learn how to shoot rifles and pistols and how to use machine guns. The heads of the Haganah have secret ways to get information about the covert actions of the Arabs. A month before a riot, they know about it and prepare to fight the Arabs. A short while ago, the Arabs staged a strike because 153 cement tanks were found filled with arms, bullets, rifles, and pistols. The sender of the weapons was not found, but the Arabs claim that they were meant for the Jews, to fight against them. During the strike, members of the Haganah were on our roof to insure that if there would be a riot, they could defend us. The Arabs did not riot, but they demanded that the Jews surrender ten thousand rifles, fifty thousand hand guns, and one million bullets, and if not, they would arm themselves to defend against the "Jewish Danger."
>
> But it seems there is no danger from the Arabs (may their names be blotted out). They are too cowardly to fight, they just need to see the end of the gun and they will run away.[28]

Mordecai valued his father's opinion and expressed pleasure that his father equates knowledge of Hebrew with wealth, and that he believes that Mordecai is clearly growing wealthy.

He apologized for not sending photographs, due to "clouds and lack of sun." He also asked his father to save his letters; he will want them when he returns to the United States. And just before Chanukah, Mordecai described a hike he went on with a friend:

> I can tell you something very interesting. As you know, there is an Arab tribe called Bedouins, who wander from place to place. Once I went hiking with a friend in the hills near our house, we saw deep caves with smaller burial caves on the sides. Apparently,

---

28.   Unfortunately I have not been able to find Paul's response to this letter.

some time ago, they dug there and removed everything. Some time ago, Arabs lived there, but the foxes chased them away (foxes enter the caves at night, during the day there is no danger from them). We hiked about a mile and a half when suddenly we saw something you see and read about in books about the desert: a Bedouin camp. We went in and spoke to them a bit and they showed us woven rugs that they make themselves by hand that were beautiful. On the way back, I found the skull of a goat that was probably killed by a fox. The Bedouin have a donkey that is missing one ear that a fox took (for a memento perhaps?).

Mordecai wanted to share all kinds of details of his life with his father: that he was active in the scouts, was learning lots of songs and how to dance the Hora, and that he participated in a big holiday celebration:

> In honor of Chanukah, we traveled to Tel Aviv to see the parade of the candles. It was very nice. Thousands of students with menorahs and torches walked through the streets of Tel Aviv. A large stage, in the shape of a crown, with a menorah on it, was the starting point of the parade.

I read my father's letters from this period with amazement. He seems a charming thirteen-year-old, precocious, perceptive, and funny in an incisive, almost mature way. At the same time his writing displays a child's stream of consciousness, which, together with the total lack of self-consciousness and mistakes in spelling[29] and language, point to his youth. The letters display his budding love of language, literature, and the Bible, his interest in journalism and photography, his admiration for the Haganah, and his profound love for his father. And already, as a young teenager, he wanted his letters to be saved. I think I would have liked this young man!

Back in America, vicariously experiencing his family's adventures, Paul expressed how happy he was that his wife and children loved Palestine. On October 17, 1935, after they had been gone for three months, he wrote:

---

29. In later years Mordecai fondly remembered how his brother, Gershon, characterized his spelling as "bold and original."

I am very happy that you all like Eretz Yisrael... I am happy because if you like it you enjoy it, which is my ardent desire. Then loving the Land of Israel enriches the soul of the lover. It arouses in him feelings that were dormant in him, the feeling of a motherland! I am still lacking it, the feel of stepping on your own land, and am already eager to experience this feeling.

As Paul prepared to join the family in the spring of 1936, the correspondence turned to logistics. Since he planned to travel via Italy, both he and Esther worried about the impact of Italy's invasion of Ethiopia in October, 1935, and the hostilities with England. Paul was alarmed by President Roosevelt's warning that Americans should not travel aboard Italian ships. Heeding the President's advice, he eventually sailed from New York on the *RMS Berengaria* on March 18, and arrived in Haifa on April 1, 1936.

Paul landed in Palestine on the eve of an explosive period. Within days the Arabs would rise up in revolt against the British administration, a rebellion lasting until 1939.[30] Although the first stage of the unrest consisted primarily of a general commercial strike, it was accompanied by significant violence. Two weeks after my grandfather arrived in Palestine, an armed gang blocked part of the road between Nablus and Tulkarm, robbed travelers, and shot three Jews. In retaliation, members of the Haganah killed two Arabs. Two days later Jaffa exploded in violence: nine Jews were shot dead and ten wounded. On April 20, five more Jews were killed. Attacks continued throughout the country, including Jerusalem, where Jews were shot at while leaving a cinema and going to classes at Hebrew University.[31] By October 1936, eighty Jews, two hundred Arabs, and twenty-eight Britons were dead.[32]

I cannot imagine what my grandfather must have thought. For nine months he had been receiving glowing reports of his family's activities in Palestine – his wife's travels, lyrical descriptions of life in

---

30. The Arab revolt continued from 1936 to 1939.
31. Details from Bruce Hoffman's *Anonymous Soldiers: The Struggle for Israel, 1917–1947* (Knopf, 2015), p. 51.
32. Benny Morris, *1948: The First Arab-Israeli War* (Yale University Press, 2008), p. 16.

the Yishuv, his children's triumphs, Gershon's studies at Hebrew University. And suddenly, almost simultaneous with his arrival, the Yishuv was plunged into violence and uncertainty.

I have no information about the months during which the whole family was in Palestine, but there is one hint to Esther's expectations of her husband: among the items she told him to pack were his tuxedo and his cutaway suit! I wonder what events she thought they would attend.

* * *

The odyssey to Palestine reflects a side of Esther that was simply not visible to me as the young grandson of an old and seemingly cold and aloof woman. Her letters reveal her to be an adventuresome, curious, charismatic, highly intelligent, fearless, and driven woman. In fact, she was an early feminist. Although there are flashes of lyricism in her letters, she was far less sentimental than her husband; she wrote mostly about money, travel, housekeeping, and the people she was meeting and "cultivating" – a word later used by all the members of the family. Curiously, she wrote little about how it felt to be in Palestine, or how the children were doing. We don't hear much of their studies, friends, social activities, or growth.

Furthermore, as a child I do not remember having a single conversation with my grandfather, so his letters were also a revelation to me. These were not written by a fussy and frail old man; Paul's letters of 1935–36, and especially those of 1947–1950, reflect a sensitive, perceptive, and considerate man who adored his wife and children, and was passionately dedicated to their intellectual and social development. The letters show the depth of his engagement – he listened carefully to what he was told and responded accordingly and constructively. Perhaps this extreme sensitivity contributed to his eventual insecurity and dependence on his wife. Although his Hebrew is formal and archaic, Paul's writings also reflect deep knowledge of both secular as well as religious sources and abound with biblical, rabbinic, and classical allusions. In this he typified his circle, who were as familiar with

Carlyle and Homer as they were with Bialik, Ahad Ha'am, Rambam, and the Talmud.

The year in Palestine had a powerful impact on my father. Some of his memories are vividly captured in his memoirs. He writes:

> I never forgot the city itself, both the Old and the New, and the innocent pleasures of that year: pushing my bicycle up the hill of the unpaved, muddy Rehov Zephania to Rehov Malachi, scraping the mud off the wheels and mounting for the ride to school along Rehov Chancellor,[33] across Rehov Hanevi'im and then haring down the steep hill to Rehov Yaffo – once actually dodging under the neck of a camel, part of a caravan on its way out of the city; the pita-and-falafel lunches with harif (spicy pepper relish) washed down by fresh orange juice in the schoolyard; reading the adventures of Tidhar the Yemenite Detective in pamphlets hidden under the desk when we were supposed to be preparing to explain a passage in Sukkah in the Talmud class; donkey-riding in the Judean hills; walking around in the Old City.
>
> I remember the stone-throwing. The school was (and still is) across the street from the Mamilla Cemetery, where an abandoned stone-quarry retained enough rainwater to constitute a pool, and where we traded stones with the Arab children who swam there.
>
> I also remember my annoyance when my mother insisted I go with her to the Eden Hotel on Hillel Street, to be with her when she visited the famous Henrietta Szold of Hadassah. Years later I was delighted that I had met her.
>
> What was exciting for a thirteen-year-old was the trip to Kfar Giladi in Upper Galilee, where I met the widows of Yisrael Giladi and Yigal Portugali, founders of the kibbutz. I went to neighboring Tel Hai, where the one-armed hero of the Russian army, Joseph Trumpeldor,[34] was killed in an Arab attack on Tel

---

33. He may have meant Sderot Chancellor, now Rehov Strauss.
34. Joseph Trumpeldor (1880–1920), was an early Zionist activist and war hero. Born in Russia, he served as an officer in the Russian army and received four medals for bravery. He immigrated to Palestine in 1911, and during World War I he devised

Hai in 1920 – before I was born – but I knew all about him from the songs and stories with which I grew up.

The year in Palestine provided the model for Mordecai's later, longer sojourn; he watched how his mother managed, made do with inadequate funds, determinedly met the important people and actors of the time, traveled the country and "lusted after the land."[35]

With the correspondence ending in April, I can only assume that the family returned to New York during the summer of 1936. My father returned to New York transformed. Not only had he perfected his Hebrew and become completely comfortable in Palestine, he now felt a huge personal and communal stake in its development. The year established the infrastructure and contacts that would support him when he returned eleven years later. When he did so, he would be an adult, able to re-live his experiences on a much broader scale, against the backdrop of Israel's War of Independence.

The limited correspondence of 1935–1936 served as a gateway for me into the much longer and intense correspondence of 1947–1948.[36] It shook loose the images and assumptions I had about my father and his family, and about their relationships with one another. I read the later correspondence with an openness that I might not have otherwise had.

* * *

Back in the US, Paul continued teaching at JTS while Esther attempted to augment the family income by selling insurance – mostly unsuccessfully. Mordecai attended the Talmudical Academy High School in

---

and organized the Zion Mule Corps, a military transport unit in the British army, formed from volunteer Palestinian Jews. He died defending the settlement of Tel Hai in 1920.

35. As heard from Rabbi Shlomo Riskin. In the book of Numbers (13:2), God instructs Moses to send spies to spy out the land of Israel. Rabbi Riskin interprets the order to not merely spy, but to "lust" after the land.

36. The bulk of the correspondence is from 1947 and 1948. There are also some letters from 1949 and 1950, but they are not relevant to the story of the War of Independence.

Washington Heights, NY, where his studies in Palestine proved to have had been so successful that he was able to skip a grade. He continued his involvement with writing and journalism, becoming the managing editor of the *Academy News*. In his memoirs he writes that the yeshiva was "too easy," so he transferred to Stuyvesant High School, a renowned public high school in Lower Manhattan requiring a competitive entrance examination. After his graduation, he studied English literature at The City College of New York (ccny),[37] where he became a serious competitive fencer and president of the Hillel foundation.

Mordecai maintained his involvement in writing, becoming editor-in-chief of a glossy humor magazine, the *Mercury*, and editor-in-chief of the *Hillel News*. He wrote poetry and short stories, and translated Hebrew literature into English. He also published book reviews for *Commentary* magazine. He was learning the foundations of journalism and publishing. After receiving his BA, Mordecai went on to study for ordination at the Jewish Theological Seminary, following in the footsteps of both his father and his brother.

Mordecai Chertoff, CCNY graduation, 1943

---

37.   Now part of the City University of New York.

Mordecai's brother Gershon served as a military chaplain in Europe during World War II. Mordecai did not serve; he had a divinity student deferment and extremely poor eyesight. This seems to have troubled his conscience. Years later his sister would reassure him that any guilt he might have felt for not serving in World War II was more than expunged by his service in Israel.

The Chertoffs may have returned to America but their hearts were still in the Holy Land; they were more determined than ever to return there someday for good. But it was the youngest Chertoff who was most deeply affected by the year in Palestine. Despite their continued commitment to Zionism, his siblings were making lives for themselves in America. After receiving his ordination from JTS and serving as a chaplain in the US army, Gershon became the rabbi of Congregation B'nai Israel in Elizabeth, New Jersey, where he remained for his entire professional life. Naomi earned her masters of social work degree at Columbia, became a psychiatric social worker, married Monroe Seligman, and moved to Cleveland. Mordecai, meanwhile, was so driven by his desire to return to Palestine, that in January 1947, just one paper shy of completing his rabbinical degree, he left JTS. He could wait no longer; he had to return to Palestine.

It was difficult to get a visa to enter British-ruled Palestine. Although Mordecai had letters of introduction to the *Palestine Post*, where he hoped to work, he couldn't admit that to the British. For them, he assumed the role of perpetual student, claiming that he intended to study at Hebrew University, and was thus able to obtain a student visa. And so, at the end of January 1947, Mordecai Chertoff boarded the USS *Marine Carp* and set sail for Palestine, this time as an adult. He couldn't know what would befall him – the future of the country was uncertain and sure to be perilous – but he was determined to play his part. Being separated from his family for the first time, he would share as much of his experiences with them as he could, via the written word.

Part I

The Period Leading Up to the War (February–November, 1947)

Chapter 2

Introduction:
Context and Setting

The Chertoff family left Palestine during the spring or summer of 1936, a pivotal point in Middle Eastern history. A few months before they boarded a ship to the USA, the Arab revolt broke out, shortly followed by the arrival of the Palestine Royal Commission, headed by Lord Peel, to investigate the causes of Arab unrest. In an exhaustive 400-page analysis, the Commission concluded that the mandate was unworkable and recommended partition into independent Jewish and Arab states.[1] However, after three years of strikes, rioting, terrorist sabotage and murders, the British attempted to appease the Arabs by issuing the infamous White Paper of 1939 which rejected the Peel Commision's recommendation of partition in favor of an independent, bi-national state (with a large Arab

---

1.   In its review of the historical background, the Commission described the extensive and long-lived ancient Israelite kingdom and the arrival, hundreds of years later, of Arabs "from the Arabian desert." In what to contemporary ears would sound extraordinary, the Commission noted that some Jews remained in the area and "had clung throughout the centuries of *Moslem occupation* to what had once been *their national soil*" (emphasis mine). *Palestine Royal Commission Report*, July 1937 (chap. 1, sec. 3, point 14). Full text: https://unispal.un.org/pdfs/Cmd5479.pdf.

majority) to be established within ten years. It limited Jewish immigration to Palestine to seventy-five thousand people over five years – subject to the country's "economic absorptive capacity" – and stated that any further Jewish immigration would be contingent on Arab consent. The white paper also established stringent restrictions on land acquisition by Jews. In sum, it fundamentally repudiated the Balfour Declaration.

This brought on a particularly harsh response from the Jewish Agency for Palestine, essentially a quasi-governmental organization which administered the Jewish community in Palestine, headed by David Ben-Gurion. In an official rejection of the white paper, it declared. "It is in the darkest hour of Jewish history that the British government proposes to deprive Jews of their last hope…. The Jews will never accept the closing to them of the gates of Palestine nor let their national home be converted into a ghetto."[2]

Unofficially, the Jewish Agency did more than denounce the white paper. In response to the severe restrictions on Jewish immigration, and in light of the desperate situation of the Jews of Europe, a massive clandestine operation, code named "Aliya Bet,"[3] was undertaken to rescue Jews and bring them illegally to Palestine. The Aliya Bet had actually been started in 1934, upon the rise of the Nazi regime, but with the issuance of the white paper, efforts were stepped up considerably, and an official Jewish Agency department was established to coordinate them. Most attempts to enter Palestine were by sea. More than half of the 142 voyages on 120 ships were intercepted by British patrols and sent back to Europe. Over 1,600 refugees drowned in the process.

Efforts to bring in Jews continued after World War II ended. European Jewry had been decimated and the pitiful remnant that had survived the Nazis had nowhere to go. Their communities had been destroyed, their homes stolen from them. Hundreds of thousands were languishing in displaced persons camps,[4] unwelcome anywhere except by the

---

2. Quoted in Dina Porat, *The Blue and the Yellow Stars of David: The Zionist Leadership in Palestine and the Holocaust, 1939–1945* (Cambridge, MA: Harvard University Press, 1990), p. 14.
3. In contrast to legal immigration, "Aliya Aleph."
4. Benny Morris (*1948*, p. 40) places the number at approximately 400,000 Jewish displaced persons (DPs) in Europe after World War II.

Jews of Palestine – yet Palestine was barred to them by the British. Most refugees who were intercepted by the British attempting to enter the country were sent to internment camps in Cyprus and other camps in Europe. Between 1934 and 1948, clandestine immigration encompassed almost 123,000 men, women, and children (approximately 21,630 during the period leading up to WWII [1934–1939]; 16,456 during the war; and almost 85, 000 from 1945 to 1948).[5] In his letters, Mordecai discusses and provides details about several of the illegal ships that sailed for Palestine.

If Jews were to reach Palestine, who would protect them there? The British authorities could not be relied upon because they themselves posed a threat to the Jews. The leading self defense organization was the "Haganah," a paramilitary organization that had been protecting Jewish communities, farms, and kibbutzim from Arab violence since the 1920s. As its name ("defense") implied, the Yishuv's armed wing was dedicated to a defensive approach. There were those who objected to this responsive posture and advocated a more pro-active, muscular stance against Arab violence and British intransigence. In 1931, a second militia was formed, the National Military Organization, or Irgun Tzvai Leumi. Often known by its acronym, "Etzel," or simply as "the Irgun," it followed the revisionist Zionist ideology of Ze'ev Jabotinsky. Its stated principles were that every Jew had the right to enter Palestine; active retaliation would deter the Arabs; and Jewish force of arms would ensure the creation and survival of the Jewish state.

When World War II erupted, the Jews of Palestine were faced with a choice between two enemies – the British and the Nazis. The Jewish Agency, which commanded the Haganah, decided it was imperative to aid Britain against the Nazis and cooperated with the British. Thousands of Palestinian Jews volunteered for British fighting units. However, the Jewish Agency and the Haganah continued to defy the British by organizing illegal immigration into Palestine. David Ben-Gurion famously declared that: "We shall fight the War as if there was no White Paper, and the White Paper as if there was no War."[6] The Irgun, too, decided

---

5. *Haapala: Clandestine Immigration 1931–1948*, by Mordechai Naor, 1987. Ministry of Defense Publishing House and IDF Museum.
6. *Pioneer*, by Deborah Dayan, 1968, Massada, p. 68.

to cease their operations against the British. But one Irgun member, Avraham (Yair) Stern, had no intention of stopping his fight against the British. In 1940 he left the Irgun and founded yet another militia, "Lohamei Herut Israel," ("Fighters for the Freedom of Israel") known by its acronym, "Lehi," or pejoratively as "the Stern Gang."

In 1943, with the war slowly turning in Britain's favor, the Irgun decided it was time to once again fight the British. The continued attacks of the Lehi and the resumption of attacks by the Irgun on British policemen and soldiers enraged the British who demanded that the Jewish Agency reign in the two groups. The Jewish Agency was afraid that the continuing attacks on the British would undermine the political struggle for Palestine which would inevitably follow the end of the war. They initiated what became known as the *saison*, or "hunting season." A special Haganah force was formed in November 1944 to follow, arrest, interrogate and generally "neutralize" members of the Irgun and the Lehi. Some sources claim that the Jewish Agency used the *saison* to strengthen itself politically, but did manage to reduce attacks against the British while avoiding civil war within the Yishuv. The controversial *saison* was brought to an end in February 1945, and in October of that year, in an effort to work cooperatively, the three organizations formed an alliance, the *Tnu'at HaMeri HaIvri*, literally, the Hebrew Rebellion Movement. It was dissolved in August 1946 shortly after the explosion in the King David Hotel in Jerusalem.

The bombing of the King David Hotel, which housed the British Mandatory headquarters, is considered a turning point in the period leading up to Israel's war of independence. The operation, conceived and carried out by the Irgun with some Haganah cooperation, resulted in ninety-one dead, including Britons, Arabs and Jews, and almost fifty injured. The Irgun later claimed that they had given adequate prior warning so that the building could be evacuated, but the British claim they received no timely warning. The world was outraged.

Following the bombing, in an attempt to maintain safety for their personnel in Jerusalem, the British established four security zones, each surrounded by barbed wire. One encompassed the railroad, St. Andrews Hospice, and the neighborhoods of Katamon, the German Colony and Baka, within which most British personnel lived. A second included the Terra Sancta chapel, King George Street, the YMCA and the King David Hotel, as well as the Jewish Agency and parts of the neighborhoods of Rehavia and Talbieh. A third, known as the Jerusalem Fortress, was established downtown, and the fourth surrounded the Schneller compound which had once been an orphanage but had been turned into a British military camp. This had the effect of partitioning the city into east and west: "Jerusalem was an armed camp...barbed wire in great coils was everywhere, tanks could be seen at various locations, special pill boxes had been put above the entrance of the [King David] hotel, and on the roofs, and on the lawn of the imposing YMCA building across the street, soldiers manning machine guns surveyed all avenues and approaches."[7] The third zone, the Jerusalem "fortress," included the Russian Compound, the Anglo-Palestine Bank, the Central Post Office and part of Jaffa road. The Jews jeeringly referred to this area as "Bevingrad" – a neologism comprised of the name of the reviled British foreign secretary, Ernest Bevin, and of the Russian city, Stalingrad, which had been besieged by the Germans during World War II. Mordecai will make frequent references to "Bevingrad" in his letters; he considered it a reflection of British cowardice.

Jerusalem was a patchwork of neighborhoods of different ethnicities. Jewish neighborhoods often abutted Arab ones leading to friction between the two populations. The Arabs controlled the roads, both within Jerusalem and leading to the city. Arabs had four routes into Jerusalem – via Ramallah, Hebron, Jericho and Latrun – while the Jews had only one – Latrun. Arab snipers made walking through the city a dangerous proposition. The security zones, and the paperwork needed to pass through them, increased the difficulties for Jewish residents of the city. British troops struggled to both protect themselves and keep the two sides apart. The heterogeneous nature of Jerusalem, together with the presence of British troops and administrators, made for a volatile situation. By comparison, Tel Aviv, barely fifty miles away, was a virtual oasis of tranquility.

---

7. Bartley Crum, US delegate to the Anglo-American Inquiry on Palestine, quoted in *Anonymous Soldiers: The Struggle for Israel, 1917–1947*, by Bruce Hoffman, pp. 252–53.

While the three Jewish military organizations remained at odds with each other over tactics and targets, they all agreed on the importance of facilitating Jewish immigration to Palestine and preparing for the seemingly inevitable war with the Arabs that seemed bound to erupt as soon as the Mandate would end. For their part, despite the Haganah's cooperation, the British considered all three military groups terrorist and illegal with members of any subject to immediate arrest. In many of his letters, Mordecai expresses his antipathy for the Irgun and the Lehi, claiming, among other things, that they undermined the legitimate efforts of the Haganah.

By 1946, the Haganah had fifty thousand members, of whom the Palmach[8] brigade, an elite commando force, numbered five thousand; the Irgun had some 3,500–5,000 members, of whom 1,200–2,000 were combatants, and Lehi numbered somewhere between 250 and 500 fighters.[9]

Despite the best efforts of the British to limit Jewish Imigration, the Yishuv continued to expand. By the end of 1946, the population of Palestine had grown to approximately 1.9 million, of whom 1.14 million were Muslims, 600,000 were Jews and 145,000 were Christians. Most of the major cities were predominantly Jewish. The population of Tel Aviv totaled 183,000, all Jews except for 230 Christians, 130 Muslims and 330 "others." Jerusalem's population was 164,000, of which Jews made up 60 percent, with Muslims and Christians at 20 percent each. The population of Haifa numbered around 145,430, 52 percent of whom were Jewish, 28 percent Muslim and 20 percent Christian. Only Jaffa, with a population of 101,580, had a majority Arab population – 53 percent, while Jews represented about 32 percent and Christians, 16 percent.[10]

By February 1947, the British had become frustrated with the lack of progress in developing a permanent political arrangement for Palestine. Various arrangements were under discussion, including partition,

---

8. *Plugot machatz*, lit. "strike forces." The Palmach is discussed further below.
9. Bruce Hoffman, *Anonymous Soldiers: The Struggle for Israel, 1917–1947* (New York: Knopf, 2015), p. 244.
10. *The Palestine Post* report of June 1, 1947, based on estimates published in the *Bulletin of Current Statistics* for May 1947.

some kind of federation, and/or cantons of independent Jewish and Arab areas within a single state, but discussions with representatives from both sides were going nowhere. The Arabs categorically refused to accept a Jewish State in any borders and the Jews vowed to accept nothing less than the unrestricted return to their national homeland and statehood. On February 14, Ernest Bevin, the British foreign secretary, announced that Britain was referring the entire problem of Palestine to the United Nations.

* * *

This was the situation in Palestine when my father set sail from New York in January 1947. It was almost exactly two years after the liberation of Auschwitz, when the *USS Marine Carp* (which, in one letter, he refers to as the *"Crap"*) set out to Haifa. Since it was impossible for Jews to settle in Palestine without an immigration certificate from the British, Mordecai entered on a student visa, presumably to study at the Hebrew University. From his letters it is clear that he never really intended to study but, rather, to work as a journalist, ideally for the *Palestine Post*, the only English language daily in Palestine.

Chapter 3

Arrival in Palestine and Joining the *Palestine Post*

E ven before he receives his son's first letter, Mordecai's father, Paul, sends his thoughts and feelings about his son's journey:

Motzei Shabbat, February 8, 1947

My Dear Son Mordecai Shmuel,

It's been about ten days since your ship sailed, and during that time, not one hour has passed in which we have not thought about you and your journey. We constantly count the number of miles you have traveled from our shores, the number of days until you will reach the shores of Eretz Yisrael, and we wonder who will greet you there...

In truth, I must bless God and thank him for granting me the privilege to send one of my children to return and build the ruins of our land, to take part in building the land. When I stood on the pier, and saw the dancing and heard the singing of the young men and women who had come to see off their friends, the *"olim"*[1] – songs and dances full of sacred fervor and love of the homeland – my heart filled with awe at this wonderful sight, and I said to myself, "Here are these young men and women who have not yet even tasted the *galut*,[2] but they sense the taste of the homeland." Then I also filled with pride and said, "I too have a part in this joy, my son is among the 'nation returning to its homeland.'"

Indeed, on introspection, I am happy about your *aliyah*,[3] but the heart does not always obey the intellect. At home, I feel your absence, especially on Shabbat when Gershon is also gone. I look around me and the house is empty ...I go in and out of all the rooms, as though I am looking for something, searching for something precious I have lost. Indeed, it is a "lost object that returns,"[4] as I hope that in a year or fifteen months, we will see each other in Israel. But for now, I am, in the words of the prophet, like one "whose children have left him,"[5] and who have scattered to the winds, and we, your mother and I, remain alone.... Perhaps this is what our sages meant when they spoke about the time of the redemption as a period of "[birth] pangs of the Messiah." The pangs we are already experiencing. Let us hope that the Messiah too will arrive shortly.

...Naturally, we await your letter like those who await the rains in Eretz Yisrael. If this letter should arrive before you get to Eretz Yisrael, please write and tell us every detail about what has happened with you since you left New York.

With much love and eternal love,

Father

1. Hebrew, meaning, literally, "those who go up," i.e., those who ascend to the Land of Israel.
2. Hebrew, meaning "exile."
3. Hebrew, the noun form of "ascending" to the Land of Israel.
4. This is a reference to the laws regarding the return of lost objects, which appears in the Talmud in Tractate *Bava Metzia*.
5. A reference to Jeremiah 10:20: "My tent is spoiled, and all my cords are broken; my children are gone forth from me, and they are not; there is none to stretch forth my tent any more, and to set up my curtains."

Mordecai's older brother, Gershon, echoes many of his father's sentiments. His comment about religious observance being primarily national is particularly interesting:

> When I left you standing on the ship, I felt for the first [time] the taste of *galut* – that even America is exile. First, because at that very moment I understood that all the work I do with my community here will succeed only if the idea of Eretz Yisrael is uppermost in our thoughts. Religious observance is primarily national, as Abba showed, and, through this observance, the sages made Eretz Yisrael portable, as Zangwill[6] said. And besides observance, what purpose do our Jewish lives have here? ...And we can succeed with the young ones in school only in so far as we connect them to life in Eretz Yisrael, for example, if on Tu B'Shevat,[7] we tell them about the holiday in our land, etc.
>
> Second, and this is the main thing, with your journey, our family unit unraveled, if only temporarily. And in this we are no different from the exile in Russia, where some family member or other would leave home, this one to here and that one to there, until the members of a single family were scattered all over the world. Separation, and the pain it entails, [is] a clear sign of *galut*. You, however, have reached the end of your wanderings. And we too, through you, are in Israel. All our thoughts, yearnings, and hopes are directed to our land, which belongs to us by virtue of the "promise of God," and by virtue of your establishing yourself on our soil.
>
> ...Pave the way for us, and we won't tarry.
>
> Gershon Baruch

---

6. Israel Zangwill (1864–1926), a British Jewish author who was a strong proponent of cultural Zionism.
7. The fifteenth day of the Jewish month of Shevat is the "New Year for Trees."

Mordecai's first letter home:

On Board – S.S. Marine Carp

[undated – probably February 3rd or 4th, 1947]

Dear Folks,

Even the ship's officers admit that the weather has been rough. After all, when deck chairs chase you across the deck and loose trunks charge at you, when the walls and floors forget their respective special functions and substitute for each other – it ain't exactly calm. Still, in spite of it all, I was sick only for about ten minutes. The secret: stay out on deck, in the fresh air, and keep moving. The ten minutes came when a lurch of the ship threw Efros' daughter across the deck and knocked her out momentarily; Nat Cohen[8] and I brought her down to the sick bay. It was the heat and closeness there that convinced me to pay my tribute to father Neptune. Having paid my tax, I was free to come and go as I please, which I have been doing.

The ship is half empty: instead of a full load of 859 passengers, we have some three hundred. The food is by far the foulest slop I have ever seen – not tasted. For the first couple of days we consumed a prodigious amount of salami and bread, cookies, and halvah, which we had brought on board (we are eight Jews in one dorm section, with another half dozen someplace else). We finally got together and tackled the mess office with the result that we eat a few minutes earlier, and get salmon, tuna, sardines, lettuce and tomato, eggs – things unheard of in the cafeteria here where we were expected to eat. We are now eating fairly comfortably, although a meal on a stationary table will be quite welcome.

...I've gabbed with Tuviah Berlin[9] now and then, and of course been invited to his house already. I accepted. We

---

8.   He later sailed on the *Exodus 1947*.

9.   Toby Berlin, son of Rabbi Meir Berlin (later, Bar Ilan), leader of the religious Zionist movement, about whom more later.

had a real Chassidische minyan Shabbat morning, down in the so-called recreation hall. There are a couple of Jews on board who eat only from paper plates, using their own utensils. One has eaten only bread since we left New York – he has scruples against goyim[10] even seeing what he eats.

A last item for the present – we've been hearing the news casts via short wave, from both the US and England, and Palestine. It's the old British game again, war of nerves, excuses to sink, etc.[11] None of us on board are particularly worried though.

The weather has been rather foul, but ten dollars rents a deck chair, blanket and cushion for the trip, and so wrapped like the *Magic Mountain*[12] patients, we brave the cold and wet and sit on deck, gabbing and singing. All very friendly, very informal, very restful.

(We are now 1900 miles from NY, heading due East at full speed. We should hit the Azores sometime this evening). That is all for now.

Friday, February 7, 1947

230 miles from Gibraltar

The new American vice-consul to Palestine is on board, as are some members of the American consular staff in Baghdad. The Baghdadian (a Haaavard man) is married, and his wife is a tall, dark, very impressive, very polished hostess type. Nat Cohen (Masada guy, and a good man) and I turned on the charm on Wednesday, and exchanged a few pleasantries with them. Yesterday, with the sea smooth and the sun shining, everybody was on deck, and they were on our end of it. Nat and I went to work, and before long the five of us were in a semi-circle swapping autobiographical lies and discussing

---

10. Hebrew, literally meaning "nations," used to refer to anyone non-Jewish.
11. He is referring to the British naval patrols which were stopping ships with illegal immigrants from docking in Palestine.
12. A novel by Thomas Mann.

music, books, etc. Your own darling son really carried the afternoon. The magic circle broke for dinner, and then we met again downstairs in the "game room" (which has a loud-speaker, records, a few Coca-Cola bottles) while a horse-racing thing was run off, with Mrs. Harris (Baghdad) presiding very wittily. After the racing, her husband invited us to tea in the snob dining room, where the waiter groveled and cringed, and didn't dare ask us whether we belonged there, since we were with the "State Department." We sat there for about three hours, over tea and salmon-sardine-tuna sandwiches, discussing the Middle East. Nat and I are very carefully culti-vating the trio: the Harrises, for their own merit, their charm and affability, her hostess perfection – and because consular personnel keeps changing, and they may very well end up in Palestine some fine day too. We are making "friends" of them, and we very carefully shove in a little Zionist dig. So far, so good...

Give Tooltolleh[13] my regards.

Eight hours of sleep is more than we ever get. Watch-men of our health deplore our long hours, but to no avail. Landing is what worries us most. Without doubt, that Cus-toms House will be more than just a time-consuming head-ache. Credentials as students will make no difference when it comes to opening trunks, and I can just picture the scene: Belongings all over the floor, packages spilled, and chaos confounded. With the prospect of Bernie Popkin meeting us with a truck, to take us to Jerusalem, we have what is supposed to be a silver lining. Our other Haifa friends will no doubt be at the boat to meet us as well. Things don't look too bad, really.

---

13.   "Tooltolleh" was the nickname of Samuel Bavli, son of Hillel Bavli, professor of Hebrew literature at JTS. The Bavlis were close family friends of the Chertoffs, and Tooltolleh is mentioned frequently in the correspondence, although his nickname is spelled many different ways. At the time of these letters, Tooltolleh was three years old. He is currently a medical doctor specializing in endocrinology, diabetes and metabolism and internal medicine, with numerous publications to his credit.

Flash – Portugal visible off the port bow (that means to the left, landlubbers). We reach Gibraltar at one tonight. Incident: We were standing on the Bridge, with the Chief Officer (we cultivated him too), and Rachel Weiner was looking through the field glasses, at the Azores. "Oh, look," she chortled excitedly as the glasses brought everything right up to her nose, "there's a rock there." The Chief turned pale, and went down on his knees, just about ready to sound the Abandon Ship. "No, no," she says, I mean in front of the island." Mr. Healy got to his feet again, still a bit pale, and came out with: "Your phrasing is horrible, lady!" And I had asked "when do we hit the Azores" just a few hours before that...

Sunday, February 9, 1947

Back to my friends, the Harrises. They have succeeded in teaching me an asinine card game, one which we would call "Oh S**t," but which their breeding leads them to call "Oh Hell." Either appellation is appropriate. But *hert sich a myseh* (Yiddish, that was).[14] In the course of one of our by-now traditional midnight (really ten-thirty) coffee klatches ("Teas"). I was asked "Coffee or tea?" by Rud (that's Mrs. H) and answered, with a broad Russian (or what I fondly believe to be a Russian) accent – *"tea, ov coarse,"* and made some remarks about me on the *benks ov de Vulgar*. After a few more neo-Russianisms, Spook (that's Mr. H) turned to me and said: "How long did you live in the States?" Giving him a chance to compose himself, I assumed a conspiratorial air and whispered: "Since birth." He masked his amazement with true diplomatic aplomb. I might mention, incidentally, for Naomi's benefit, that Rud's mother seems to be a bit of all right, from her daughter's account: first woman legislator in Florida, first woman ambassador to Denmark (by the name of Owen, incidentally), proud possessor of six honorary

---

14. Meaning, "Listen to a story."

degrees.[15] Meanwhile, I've swapped dirty jokes with the new American vice-Consul to Jerusalem, who is now sitting a deck chair away, reading I.F. Stone's[16] *Underground [to Palestine]*. We had a boat drill yesterday – *ah sollchem vey!*[17] If we ever hit one of those famous mines (for which the Mediterranean is still famous, and which earns extra pay for the sailors as long as they sail upon it) I shall dive overboard, typewriter in one hand, tallis and tefillin in the other, and swim. By the time they get the boats launched I shall have landed in Haifa...But we have radar on this ship, and a de-magnetizing outfit...so we don't worry too much (please notice the postmark, and don't be uneasy – we will have made it by the time I mail this). Nu – enough, for now. More later.

Bet Hakerem, Jerusalem, Sunday, Feb. 16, 1947

Dear Family,

To bring things up to date in my peregrinations: We arrived in Haifa bay Friday morning, at six. I stood on the bridge in the rain, shmoozing with the captain, as the ship moved in past the breakwater, staring at the Carmel and feeling very queer. We went through the passport control office on board ship, and after a long delay finally disembarked

---

15. Mrs. Harris (Rud) was the daughter of Ruth Bryan Owen. Owen, a Democrat, became Florida's (and the South's) first woman representative in the United States Congress in 1929, coming from Florida's 4th district. Representative Owen was also the first woman to earn a seat on the House Foreign Affairs Committee. In 1933 she became the first woman appointed as a US ambassador to another country when President Roosevelt selected her to be ambassador to Denmark and Iceland. Harris's grandfather was William Jennings Bryan (1860–1925), 41st UN Secretary of State and orator who delivered the famous "Cross of Gold" speech.

16. I. F. (Isidor Feinstein) Stone (1907–1989) was an American journalist and author. He went to Palestine after WWII to report on the migration of European Jews. During Israel's War of Independence he was the correspondent for US-based *PM* (possibly short for Picture Magazine). He went on to write for other periodicals and was best known for his *I. F. Stone's Weekly* which ran from 1953 to 1971.

17. It is possible that this is supposed to be *Ah Zochen Vey*, a Yiddish phrase that essentially means, "it's pretty bad if it's come to that."

in small boats (for "security reasons" ships do not dock to discharge passengers) and plunged headlong into the chaos that is Customs. We had been met on board ship by [Jewish] Agency people, and it felt damn good to hear real Hebrew. In the Customs there was a guy from the HU[18] and an "expediter" who nearly clawed the inspector's eyes out every time he tried to open a bundle. All went well for the small things, but when the big trunks came along the s.o.b. chief inspector decided to have a look, and the guy really put me through the wringer. He leafed through books, read a few *Frontier* articles, looked at pictures, and squeezed tubes of toothpaste and made himself thoroughly obnoxious. I was a limp rag by the time it was over, and it was, of course, too late to go to Jerusalem. We spent Shabbat in a Haifa hotel, and the Milgrims[19] came to see me – a wonderful reunion.

Shabbat afternoon I walked down to the port, and spoke to some of the kids from Cyprus[20] as 765 of them got off the *Ocean Vigor* and were taken to be distributed around the country. In my slick suit I felt like a criminal as I saw their rags, and listened to the stories of two years on the road from Romania. I damn near cried to see them smile so happily at having finally arrived. They were in fair health, and wonderful spirits. ... I'm booked for dinner at Berlin's on Friday night, and will take care of Gomel[21] in the Yeshurun,[22] as I originally planned....

We left Haifa 6:30 this morning, arrived here [in Jerusalem] a bit before ten, and went up to the HU [Hebrew University] for lunch, where I met the Seminary

---

18. Hebrew University.
19. This may be Jacob Milgrom (1923–2010), who became a prominent American Jewish Bible scholar and Conservative rabbi, best known for his comprehensive Torah commentaries and work on the Dead Sea Scrolls. The name is mentioned in several other letters, usually spelled "Milgrim."
20. Jewish refugees who had been detained in DP camps in Cyprus.
21. The prayer of thanksgiving for delivery from danger.
22. Synagogue in Jerusalem where Mordecai and his family had gone for High Holiday services twelve years earlier, before the synagogue was finished.

contingent, ... Mrs. Van Vriesland[23] was much more than cordial (Hadassah[24] is with the Joint,[25] in Italy) and she and Yehudit are fighting over having me. We dropped in to Viteles[26] too, (next door) and they all asked for you all.

Jerusalem is a tired looking city, but beautiful in spite of the barbed wire and the damn soldiers all over the streets. They all looked scared stiff, and travel with machine guns over their shoulders, in groups of three! I've been walking the streets like a madman – staring at people, eavesdropping on conversations, and generally beaming all over the place. (Friday night we were eating in the Hotel Zion, in Haifa, when the orchestra played *"hevenu shalom aleichem"*[27] and then broke into a hora.[28] Your little son joined in, and was soon in the middle, showing off with a sabra and then a few more. When someone at another table said "hora *niflah*"[29] after it was over, I answered that it had to be – it was the first since we arrived – that afternoon. There were gasps and astonished eyebrows all over the place at that, and a chorus of *"broochim habaim"*[30] and *"ad me'ah ve'esrim shanah."*[31] It was really wonderful.) But it is Jerusalem which really feels like home, and I think today will go down in my personal

23. Mrs. Jeanette Van Vreisland, née Hoofien, will be mentioned frequently in the correspondence. She was born in Utrecht, The Netherlands in 1886. Her first marriage was to Leonard Salomon Ornstein, a prominent theoretical physicist at the University of Leiden. He committed suicide in 1941, six months after being barred from the university by the authorities. She later married Siegfried Adolph van Friesland, a lawyer and later an executive and official in various Palestinian commercial and public service enterprises.

24. Her daughter, Hadassah Van Vriesland, not to be confused with Hadassah Frisch, is mentioned frequently in Mordecai's later correspondence.

25. The Joint Distribution Committee, the world's leading Jewish humanitarian organization.

26. Rose Viteles, discussed above.

27. A popular song, the title means "we brought peace upon you."

28. A traditional Jewish folk dance.

29. Hebrew, meaning "a wonderful hora."

30. Hebrew, meaning "welcome," literally, "blessed are those who have come."

31. Hebrew, literally "until one hundred and twenty," referring to the age – a traditional Jewish blessing for long life.

history as my happiest. I feel a little delirious, drunk *"v'lo me-yayin."*[32] If you could only be here!

...

Item: A three-year-old in a kibbutz was sitting on the pot, when his mother tried to hurry him with *Nu Histader,*[33] to which the little *tachshit*[34] [sic] answered:*"Hahistadrut eina yozeit."*[35] Such a child, *oy veh!*

Plan: dinner with Yehudit tomorrow, Magnes Tuesday, Viteles Saturday, and lunch with Van Vriesland on Tuesday. A good beginning... I'll see Abe Herman[36] and Agronsky[37] tomorrow, and investigate jobs and such immediately. Next week I shall go on a *tiyul* (hike, that is) and see something of the country. I'll break off now, the boys want to feed me, and then there is a *mesibah*[38] to which I have been invited, to meet the rest of the HU kids, as well as some other friends. By the time you get this you will have received a wire from me, so I can mail this a day or two later...

Monday evening [February 17, 1947]

I am now comfortably ensconced in Rehavia,[39] with the Friedens, where I shall remain for a while, how long I can't say yet. They were very excited to have me, and more than eager to hear all the news about the family. I wired you

---

32. Hebrew, meaning "and not from wine."
33. Hebrew, meaning "get on with it!"
34. Hebrew, meaning "gem."
35. Hebrew, meaning, "The Histadrut (the Israel labor organization) is not coming out" (a play on the words *histader* and *histadrut*).
36. Abraham Herman (1878–1947) was the president of HIAS, the Hebrew Immigrant Aid Society.
37. Gershon Agronsky (Agron) founded the *Palestine Post* in 1932 and was its editor-in-chief until 1955. He was mayor of Jerusalem from 1955–1959. Mordecai often refers to him as "GA" or "*Hamelech*" (the king) in his letters.
38. Hebrew, meaning "party."
39. Upscale neighborhood in West Jerusalem, near the city center.

this afternoon – not that I had anything urgent to say, but because I know you'll rest better from the time you receive it. (I know my tenses are wrong there – *nu*.)

Received a letter from *Commentary*,[40] with a blast at me from the editors of the "Barabbas" obscenity, asking me to write a rebuttal, which I shall do within the next few days.[41] Incidentally, it means more money, you know.

I'm beginning to catch up on lost sleep: slept twelve hours last night (missed the hour [work] stoppage over the deportation of the 800,[42] about which you probably read) and now feel fit as a fiddle. The food is good, and not too expensive: a steak dinner, a la Rosenbloom['s], or rather Gluckstern's,[43] cost half a pound, which at the current practical rate is less than two dollars, (all money changing outside of the banks, and all over Jaffa Road are such changers, pays between 29 and 33 *grush*[44] on the dollar, depending on the international and local scene. As for jobs – I haven't seen those people yet, I want to soak in a little more of the local scene and rest up completely before I embark on anything big.

---

40. A monthly Jewish American magazine founded by the American Jewish Committee in 1945.

41. Mordecai published a scathing review of Emery Berkessy's book, *Barabbas: A Novel of the Time of Jesus* in *Commentary* on January 1, 1947. Their archive shows at least six reviews by Mordecai beginning January 1, 1946, when Mordecai was twenty-four years old.

42. Palestine Jewry staged a one-hour strike on February 17 in protest of the deportation of eight hundred illegal immigrants to Cyprus. Reported in *The Cornell Daily Sun*, vol. 64, no. 73, February 18, 1947.

43. Rosenbloom's and Gluckstern's were two kosher restaurants in New York.

44. Between 1918 and 1927, the legal tender in Palestine was the Egyptian lira, which was divided into one hundred "*qurush*" in Arabic, or *grush* in Hebrew. Even after the Palestine pound, which was divided into one thousand "mils", replaced the lira, the word *grush* continued to be used as slang, with one *grush* being worth ten mils.

And that is all for the present, I am going to mail this letter now, and hope that it finds you all well, and happy that the first fifth of our private dream[45] has finally come true.

Goodnight now, and love to you all.

Be'ahava Raba,[46]

Mordecai Shmuel

[Undated, but postmarked Feb 26, 1947]

Dear Family – Father, Mother, Gershon, Naomi, Monroe:[47]

As you can imagine, the brat is getting along quite well. I met Zifroni[48] the other day, and spent a long time shmoozing with him. He, in turn, introduced me to some of the other newspaper guys (Feller – *Hatzofe*,[49] Mike Eskolski, *Palestine Post*, etc). I am a regular feature at all Agency press conferences, and will go with an Agency group to the Negev in a day or two,[50] after which I'm off on my *tiyul*, which I intend to stretch over a few weeks. It all depends on [our] friend Agronsky. I saw him the other day, and gabbed over coffee and cake at his house. He asked me to come over the office tonight, with some of my stuff, to talk business. Needless to say, I shall be there. I shall leave this letter unfinished, so that I can let you know how I make out with him.

...

---

45. I.e., that the entire family, all five members, will one day live in Israel.
46. Hebrew, meaning "with much love."
47. Naomi's husband, Monroe Seligman. They were married the previous October.
48. Gabriel Zifroni was a journalist at *Do'ar Hayom*, a Hebrew-language daily newspaper, and *Hazit Ha'am*, the weekly publication of the revisionist movement. In later life, he became head of Israel's national theater, Habimah. He died in 2011 at the age of ninety-five.
49. *Hatzofe* was a daily newspaper for the religious Zionist sector. It was published between 1937 and 2008, when it merged with *Makor Rishon*.
50. It is unclear what status Mordecai had that enabled him to be part of the group. He was not yet an accredited journalist.

Things have been rather quiet around here – just a little blasting of the oil lines,[51] and an attack on a military installation up north – almost nothing to get excited about. Today's papers all carried stories of another boat having been captured,[52] but officially, (Agency and British) it is still only a rumor. I never realized before how personally and how seriously these deportations are taken – as Goldie Meyerson[53] said to a small meeting of the new American kids here – it is worse than an execution. It is worse, even, than the barbed wire in Jerusalem and the frightened British soldiers walking around in groups to keep themselves "safe." What is most amazing is that life goes on normally, in spite of the political situation. The only real evidence is in the barbed wire, and in the cafes, which are pretty empty most of the time – in Jerusalem, that is: I haven't seen anything else, outside of Haifa, (which is a beautiful city).

I shall be seeing Miller[54] later this week, as well as all our other friends and relations throughout the country, and will say to them whatever has to be said. The University says I can keep away until I get that paper done for the Seminary,[55] which means that I register in the fall as a research student, at a saving of 36 Lira (either $146 or about $110, depending on where you change your money).

Mrs. Van Vriesland and Viteles have both "entertained" me – but I don't care for their American cliques. I

---

51. On February 20, the Irgun bombed the Iraq Petroleum Company pipeline in the north.
52. The *Palestine Post* of February 23 carried a small item about a ship carrying six hundred refugees from central Europe being captured by the Royal Navy. It is unclear which ship it was.
53. Later Golda Meir, Prime Minister of Israel from 1969 to 1974. In 1947, she was head of the political department of the Jewish Agency, and the principal negotiator between the Jews of Palestine and the British mandate authorities.
54. Paul Chertoff's friend from Belarus, who then lived in Palestine.
55. Mordecai had one last paper to finish in order to complete his rabbinical degree at the Jewish Theological Seminary in New York (JTS).

prefer the Malkoff's Palestinians.[56] And by the way – my next letters are going to be in Hebrew: I shall be on the road, without my typewriter, and want to spare you the agony of having to read my writing: my Hebrew is far more legible. Besides – it's time I wrote a bit of Hebrew... Had dinner Friday night with Berlin, who asked for you all and was very impressed with my description of Monroe (blush, guy, I'm press-agenting for you!) and my reports that the family will all be here one of these days. (What else – I must fill the sheet, postage is high in these parts....)

(I break now to finish after I've seen Agronsky)

You know, of course, that this is an Eastern country, with some eastern customs. I sat and gabbed with Agronsky, with Lurie,[57] with half the staff, and finally left some stuff for them to read. I see Agronsky tonight again, for a decision. Something tells me I shall not have the patience to sit down and write after I've seen him, so I'll send this off, and you'll hear again very soon whether I got the job or not. For the present, then,

Shalom uvracha,[58] and all my love,

Mordecai

P.S. I'm now on the *Palestine Post*. Details later in the week.

The attacks that Mordecai describes as "almost nothing to get excited about" were not seen that way by the British and were followed by others. On February 28, the Lehi bombed a building in Haifa and on March 1, the Irgun attacked the British Officers' Club in Jerusalem, killing eighteen and wounding about a dozen more. In response to these

---

56. In those days, Jews living in Palestine were called Palestinians; the Arab inhabitants didn't use the term.
57. Ted Lurie joined the staff of the *Post* in 1932. He was its editor from 1955 until his death in 1974, at the age of sixty-four.
58. A traditional goodbye in Hebrew, it means literally, "peace and blessing."

ongoing terror "outrages,"[59] on March 2, the British declared martial law and instituted a draconian curfew on Jewish areas of Jerusalem, Tel Aviv, Petach Tivkah and Ramat Gan. From five in the afternoon until ten in the morning, seventeen hours out of twenty-four, nobody was allowed out on the streets. Immediately after martial law was declared, two Jews were killed by Arab snipers, one a four-year-old girl standing on the balcony of her home.

The British operations against the Jewish resistance were called Operation Hippo in Jerusalem and Operation Elephant in Tel Aviv. They were met with stiff resistance. Among other attacks, on March 9, a British army camp was attacked in Hadera, and there were pitched battles between British forces and Jews in the Tel Aviv security zone[60] and in Sarona, an area then outside Tel Aviv originally founded by German Templers. On March 12, the Irgun attacked the Schneller military base in Jerusalem. The press used the names Hippo and Elephant interchangeably and printed reports on the consequences of the operation on civilians. One headline read "700 Taxi Men are Elephant Victims." The article protested that, "the tread of the Elephant having deprived them of all means of earning their livelihood, 700 local taxi drivers, with about 3,600 dependents, have been out of work for over ten days now...."[61] Seventy-eight Jews suspected of being members of the resistance were arrested. Although martial law was lifted on March 17, the curfew remained in force in Jerusalem until early April.

The March newspapers also carried stories on the trials of Jews accused of terrorism, including Moshe Barazani,[62] Dov Gruner,[63] and

---

59.   *Palestine Post*, March 2, 1947.
60.   A security zone, similar to the ones in Jerusalem, was established around Citrus House in Tel Aviv, where a branch of British security headquarters was located (http://trove.nla.gov.au/newspaper/article/56774543).
61.   The *Palestine Post*, March 12, 1947.
62.   Moshe Barazani, (1926–1947) was a member of the Lehi. He was captured carrying a grenade, en route to an assassination operation against a British Brigadier.
63.   Dov Bela Gruner (1912–1947) was a Hungarian-born member of the Irgun. He was a member of the Jewish Brigade of the British army during WWII. He was wounded and captured on his second Irgun operation, an arms raid against a police station in Ramat Gan.

the two Irgun members accused of blowing up the Jerusalem Railway station on October 30, 1946.

By the end of March, the Americans had come to support the British decision to refer the matter of Palestine to the United Nations. The UN responded by setting up a special commission (United Nations Special Committee on Palestine, UNSCOP) that was to begin its deliberations in May, 1947.

Sunday, March 16, 1947

Dear Family,

You'll have to excuse a brief letter – I'm doing what is known hereabouts as a "*shvitz,*" a rush, hustle-bustle, hurly-burly, etc. Why? well, as Gershon said, one must start from the top. Also: a few days ago I undertook some translation for the [Jewish] Agency – nothing important, but a source for a few extra bucks, and a decent contact. I intended to do it this morning, not knowing that there was going to be an upheaval in the *Palpost*, which there was. Our foreign editor has just been invited to Paris, to give an exhibition of his paintings (surrealist stuff), and has taken a three-months leave which may well be permanent.[64] Last night, I was invited into Ted Lurie's office (after G.A.'s[65] talk with him) and invited to take over the job. This promotion has its drawbacks: by accepting it I have incurred the undying enmity of the foreign-news sub-editor... with a lot of experience, but not capable of handling the job, which includes not only bossing her (iron hand in the silken glove stuff) but – it includes what is known as makeup. In other words, little Mordecai will be deciding, as of Thursday

---

64. It was. The editor-turned-artist was Reggie Weston (1909?–1967). He was born in London and moved to Palestine in 1936, where he was a journalist and an editor of *The Jerusalem Post*. He had already begun to paint and taught at Bezalel Art School until he moved to Paris in 1947 to be an artist, full time. Weston was almost immediately successful, exhibiting in London, New York, Brussels and Tel Aviv. His works remain in demand and he is currently represented by the Annandale Galleries in Sydney, Australia.

65. Gershon Agronsky.

night (Wednesday night, rather, sorry it's a careless typewriter) just where each article goes, what is important and why, and whose stuff get thrown out altogether. It's a tremendous job, with a whale of a lot of responsibility and a mass of technical detail attached, all of which I have to learn in three days. Happily, I know something about it from my college days, but some of the stuff I know I'll have to forget because our style is different from the *NY Times*…. And please, Chertoffs, pray for me. By the time you get this I will have been on the job, on my own, for about a week, and will be getting very little help from Ted, – so – put in a plug for me upstairs, every little bit helps…. It's the kind of break that does not come very often, and I'm infinitely lucky that I've been working here for the last three weeks – I know the workings of the paper, and I have some halfway decent chance of not fouling up the job completely. When I think now of how I used to watch this Reggie (my predecessor) working on stone (seeing to the arrangement of type down in the printing room) so calmly, so sure of himself, I was terribly impressed. Who knows, maybe some day I'll be watched the same way by somebody! Here's hoping, anyway.

Frisch[66] called me at the office – with love from Mother. He took me to dinner at the Eden Hotel – town's snazziest, and was very pleasant indeed. He invited me to tour the country with him, but of course I couldn't….

I went to Shertok[67] for *Shalosh Se'udot*,[68] and he was charming. He got quite a kick out of Naomi's very recent

---

66. Probably Daniel Frisch, president of the Zionist Organization of America (ZOA) and father of Hadassah, about whom (much!) more later.

67. Moshe Shertok, later Sharett, (1894–1965), was one of the signatories of Israel's Declaration of Independence. At this time, he was secretary of the political department of the Jewish Agency. During the 1948 war of Independence, he was foreign minister for the Provisional Government of Israel. He was the second prime minister of Israel (1954–55), serving for a little less than two years between David Ben-Gurion's two terms. Despite the similarity in names, the Shertok and Chertoff families were probably not related but were close.

68. Literally, "three meals," referring to the third meal of Shabbat, usually eaten late on Saturday afternoon.

history, and was charmed by the letter. Seemed to like me too, asked me to come up again, and see him before he leaves for Washington again. I felt very comfortable there, inasmuch as I'm settled with a job and a room, and am not coming to ask for anything.

...

Father's letters continue to be a delight, and you're all writing the kind of stuff which, on reading, makes me feel almost there with you. Incidentally, Gershon my pet, I sincerely regret not having sent you any editorials,[69] but things have been so hectic here I haven't had the time to sit down and think about anything but the *Post* for the present. AND – now I'm beginning to ask for things:[70] I need a few towels (they cost L.P. 1–2[71] for a bath towel), and a 220 volt resistance unit for the E.A.Co. Percolator #3434. Send it with somebody. ...

And now to that translation, so that I can learn a bit more of my job tonight.

Shalom u'vracha, and all my love,

Mordecai Shmuel

---

69. Mordecai's brother, Gershon, had asked Mordecai to supply him with editorials and material for sermons. Some of the letters below have editorials embedded in them.
70. Mordecai's letters are peppered with requests that his family send him various things that were either hard to obtain in Palestine or very expensive. In letters below I have deleted such requests.
71. Between one and two Palestinian pounds.

Mordecai's *Palestine Post* press card

Palestine Post staff, April, 1948. Standing (from left): Gershon Agronsky, unknown, Lea Ben Dor, unknown. Sitting (from left): Mordecai Chertoff, Marlin Levin, Mike Eskolsky, Hugh Orgel

Chapter 4

Illegal Immigration and Joining the Haganah

I n the following letter Mordecai mentions three (of the twenty-two) ships that sailed for Palestine carrying illegal immigrants during 1947.[1] He also refers to "Bergsonians" – with considerable vitriol. These were not followers of the French philosopher, Henry Bergson, but rather the specific inner circle of Irgun members who worked with and for Hillel Kook, whose alias was Peter Bergson. Kook/Bergson was the son of the chief rabbi of Afula, and the nephew of the first Ashkenazi[2] chief rabbi of Mandatory Palestine, Abraham Isaac Kook. He took the name Peter Bergson to avoid embarrassing his prominent rabbinic family while conducting his Irgun-related activities. In 1931, Kook had helped found the Irgun and became a spokesman for it and for Revisionist Zionism, which espoused the Jewish right to sovereignty over

---

1.   See Mordechai Naor, *Haapala: Clandestine Immigration 1931–1948* (Ministry of Defence Publishing House, 1987).

2.   There are two chief rabbis in Israel, one for the Ashkenazi community and one for the Sephardi community. Basically, most Jews from Central and Eastern Europe are Ashkenazi while those from the Iberian Peninsula and Arab countries are mostly Sephardi. Their respective religious practices are slightly different.

the whole territory of historical Israel. He was involved in fundraising in Europe and America and his group focused much of their efforts on raising money for the transport of illegal immigrants to Palestine, sponsoring several shipments of refugees. American members of the group included the prominent author and screenwriter, Ben Hecht, and the illustrator and political artist, Arthur Szyk. Kook and his followers were widely opposed by more mainstream American Zionist organizations who took particular issue with his public campaign, during wartime, against the US' refusal to extend help to the Jews threatened by the Nazi campaign of murder. Mordecai expresses profound antipathy for the Bergsonists.[3]

The letter also addresses the issue of salaries and the cost of living in Palestine, subjects in which the Chertoffs were very interested and which persist as topics of conversation throughout the correspondence. The family was concerned with salaries both as a means of living comfortably, but perhaps more importantly, as a measure of recognition and personal value. In their letters, they press Mordecai for details about his compensation and tell him, in great detail, about his brother-in-law Monroe's starting salary and prospects.

March 23, 1947

[Sunday, 2 Nissan – Hebrew date]

[MSC typed the first part of this letter in Hebrew and then switched to an English typewriter.]

My dear family,

Two days ago, I received the "official press card," and now I scoff at the curfew. Besides that, the barbed wire fences are like nothing to me. ... I can enter the security zone, but besides soldiers, there's nothing to see there except for the Schocken Library (which I will visit tomorrow

---

3.   In referring to the Irgun, Mordecai used the terms Irgun, Revisionists, Bergsonsians, and Bergsonists somewhat interchangeably.

or the next day, to see Yitzchak Shenberg[4] and talk to him about translating his book) ...

A few days ago, I walked between the barbed wire fences, and I saw what "they" have done to our beautiful capital. Soldiers, every step of the way, and guns and armored cars on every corner. The security zone is a British fortress; from now on, I will stay away from their fortress and spend my time among our Jews.

I visited Shertok on Shabbat, and we sat and spoke Hebrew the entire time. A woman came to visit, and Shertok continued in Hebrew. After about half an hour, she turned to me and asked: "Do you also speak English?" I answered that I speak English during work hours only! Shertok laughed, and she sat there confused.

By the way, everyone is surprised by how quickly I settled in here, and especially by the fact that I started work nearly as soon as I arrived in the Land. Even my explanation that I am "almost a Sabra"[5] doesn't suffice – after all, there are plenty of Sabras here and none of them works at the *Palestine Post*. And my quick advancement is also considered "a bit unusual." ...

(11:45, and now I have to wait to proof the first page, correct it, and supervise the final layout. After that, I have to write a bit of new material for the second edition, see to the corrections–and go home to sleep.)

I saw Frisch a second and third time, and he wants me to write for him – I gave him a short article about eliminating military rule, and I was paid handsomely. Regarding

4.   Yitzchak Shenberg/Shenhar (1902–1957), was born in Voltshisk, on the border of Galicia, and moved to Palestine in 1921. He became a writer, a literary adviser to publishing firms, an editor and a translator.

5.   Sabra (*tzabar* in Hebrew) is a slang term for a Jew born in the Land of Israel. The *tzabar* fruit is known as prickly pear in English. It grows on cactus and is native to Israel. It is covered with sharp spines on the outside and is soft and sweet on the inside – a metaphor for the stereotypical Israeli character.

his request that I send him material from here I have to think some more ... it's possible .... In any case, Frish represented me to Silver,[6] and I spoke to him twice. We don't live by his word, but then neither do we live by the words of his opponents. In general, I try – and succeed – to stay away from politics here: it's not worth getting embroiled. ...

(No Hebrew typewriter here at home, so here goes in English....)

My aching reality principle! Every Jew in Palestine who has heard (and almost all have) is amazed that within three weeks I've become Foreign Editor of the *Post*. Excuse me for being sore – no, I'm not hiding anything. The salary is not mentioned simply because a new one must be set since the initial sum discussed. In other words, I'll be getting well over 40 pounds. How much more I don't know yet, and you people seem too damned impatient to wait to find out. The salary is secondary for the present, since the job itself calls for a good one, and my acceptance as permanent Foreign Editor, which can be after a few months, automatically means increase. So forget that. Besides, all of us journalists do outside writing as well, to supplement, and so I'll be making a good (for Palestine) living. I don't go to the office until seven [pm], when I read and correct what my subordinate has done, and take charge. I see the paper through two editions, and read the Hebrew papers. I sleep from 2:15 or 2:30 to 10, then breakfast, and read the Hebrew papers. I spend the day reading, sunbathing, taking tea with your lousy Americans (Mrs. Archibald Silverman, Viteles, Van Vriesland) and with my Palestinians (Frieden, Shertok, Zifroni) or with just plain people, like

---

6. Abba Hillel Silver (1893–1963), American Reform Rabbi and Zionist leader instrumental in orchestrating support in America for the establishment of the State of Israel. He was a forceful spokesman for Jewish Statehood, appearing in the United Nations several times during 1947. Mordecai devotes most of an article to him (below).

Biggert (*Tribune*) or Stone[7] (*PM*)[8] or Frisch or Silver, or Cantor. Frankly, I don't like the snobs, but I tolerate them for political and social reasons. I saw Shenberg the other day, and while he has nothing for me now, he was very friendly. I shall take days now and then to see the Tel Aviv clique – but one does not spend time in Palestine "getting to know people" by hanging around. I have far more status as an American on the *Post*, knowing Hebrew and from the Seminary, than if I were a lazy HU student. My job speaks in my favor, and impresses them all. It is a job I should keep for at least a year or two, simply for the experience (if not to keep permanently, as a basic-income earner). I can always get stuff in the Hebrew papers, I have the contacts, all I have to do is write. I'm not writing yet because I have nothing to say – yet. Give me time. I've been here just a month! Within the next few days I'll be getting to work for *Frontier* and *Commentary* (just received January and February, but not March yet, and no *Frontiers* at all!), and I've written to Pete about other work. The pigeon story[9] will be retyped and sent you in a few days.

In a pleasanter vein now: Gershon, my own gullible brother: the *Ben Hecht* never arrived in Palestine, because it

7.   I. F. Stone, an investigative journalist whose book, *Underground to Palestine*, Mordecai describes reading on the ship to Palestine.

8.   *PM*, a liberal-leaning daily newspaper published in New York City from June 1940 to June 1948. It was financed by Chicago millionaire, Marshall Field III. The paper printed large photos and, in order to remain free of pressure from business interests, did not accept advertising.

9.   A short, humorous sketch about pigeons that Mordecai wrote and sent to the author (and very close friend and mentor) Maurice Samuel for critique. Samuel responded with a detailed and blunt analysis, calling it "ponderous" and "overwritten." More interesting, perhaps is the fact that in his letter, Samuel sends regards to Kepi, the woman with whom Mordecai was supposed to NOT be having a relationship. (See below.) Later in the correspondence my father refers to Samuel as "Moish." Mordecai was apparently also working on a novel. Samuel (1895–1972) was a British-American novelist, translator and lecturer. He wrote widely on both Jewish and non-Jewish subjects, both fact and fiction.

never existed.[10] The *Abril*, a converted PBY[11] which had been a private yacht before the war, did arrive after a good deal of ballyhoo. NOBODY GOT AWAY in landing.[12] Those (excuse me, father and mother) f**king Bergsonsians lie in their teeth. Their 700 ton boat, the *Shoshanna* (*Shabtai Luzinsk*i) which landed near Gaza, did get quite a few ashore, and someday I'll tell you the story.[13] Right now it's still hot, and more people than I can tell you are involved. So – don't believe what you read in the papers, not even the *Palestine Post*. By the way, neither martial law nor curfew touched me. My little green book (issued by the PIO Palestine Information Office – gov't stuff) works like a charm.

...

Correct[ion?] – the *Abril* arrived. Advertised long before it appeared, and caught, inevitably. There is even a very strong doubt as to whether, after all the shouting, it was a Bergson ship! They lie, like rugs...: they printed a "picture" in their "Answer"[14], showing a British soldier on-guard with a "vicious looking knife" in his hand: they simply scraped away part of the negative, and re-touched – in a blank the shape of a knife – nor was it even a smooth job either! I'm checking that *Abril* thing anyway, and will write more about it. In the meanwhile, the *Herzl*, with 2,700 aboard, is approaching Haifa, but we are not allowed to print the story yet (censorship)...so – this

10. The *Ben Hecht* was the name the Irgun gave to the ship that had previously been the *Abril* when it was bought by them to transport refugees to Palestine.
11. A flying boat and later amphibious aircraft used extensively in WWII.
12. The *Abril*, or *Ben Hecht*, had sailed to Palestine on March 1, 1947 from Marseille, with over six hundred immigrants and crew. In his book, *Seventy-five years of Hebrew Shipping in Eretz Yisrael*, Hillel Yarkoni writes that the ship was purchased with money donated by the American-Jewish organization, League for the Free Land of Israel, with money donated to them by Ben Hecht from the proceeds of his play, *A Flag is Born*. The ship was intercepted by the British and the refugees aboard exiled to Cyprus. The American crew eventually returned to the US.
13. The *Shabtai Luzinsky* was originally registered as the *Susannah*. It set sail on March 4, 1947 from Italy and arrived undetected in Palestine on March 23, with 823 passengers.
14. Newsletter of the Bergson Group, published in the US.

is a scoop.[15] (Stone was scooped on the Haifa oil-well story, just because he was there on the spot: it takes an extra two hours for a cable to get to NY from Haifa than from here, and so he missed his deadline! Boy – was he sore!) On the change of terminology just announced by the govt, "controlled area" instead of "statutory martial law area", Stone cracked: "British government combats terrorism with euphemism." ...

Good-by for now, with much love

Mordecai

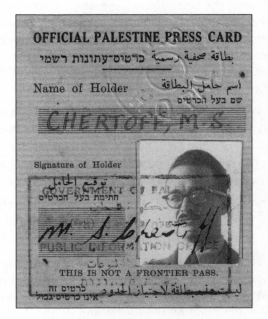

Mordecai's official press card

---

15.   The *Theodor Herzl* left France on April 2, 1947, with 2,641 passengers and arrived off the coast of Palestine on April 13. The ship was captured during a gale by the destroyer *Haydon* and the frigate *St. Bridges Bay*. There was heavy resistance which resulted in three refugee deaths and twenty-seven injuries. The ship was then towed to Haifa bay. As this occurs well after the date written at the top of the letter, I can only surmise that my father did not send the letter when he first began it but kept adding new information until he was able to send it.

[April 2–5?, 1947]

[The beginning of the letter is missing.]

I want to...go to work. (Which consists of: reading the stuff already sent down to be set-up in type, and correcting the galleys of it, reading of *Reuter* and *UP* material, selecting and preparing it for the printer, showing the guy where to put articles ("working on stone") and then supervising the corrections of the page-proof (seen by Lurie, Agronsky). After the first edition, I see whether anything new and usable has come in on *Reuters*, and send it down, supervise its insertion at the right place and cut what needs cutting to accommodate the new material, then have a sandwich while they put it into the presses, and we get a copy and go home. Okay, clear enough?

...Incidentally, Horowitz and Shertok both told me my work is important, so you should react accordingly. And it is so interesting, actually, what with me making the news, that the time speeds by with only a little drag after the final check has been made, waiting for the paper to come up. I love the work and feel that I belong in it. Can you ask for anything more?

I'm going to it now...

(And as our little Jew-operator on the *Reuter* ticker signs off every night – "Editors: we are now signing off. Good night everybody, good night to all. 'LAYLA TOV AND KOL TUV'." [Good night and All the Best]– and do the Arabs burn up! Thursday night the sign-off was "...and to the night shift (which does not work Friday night, and so begins its Shabbat after work Thursday night)... *Shabbat Shalom 'kol Tuv*." These damn Jews are everywhere...!

All my love,

Foreign Editor, the *Palestine Post*, Jerusalem, Palestine. OKAY?

My love to the Bavlis I'll write them very soon now...

G'night!

Sunday, April 6, 1947

Dear Toots [Naomi],

You deserve a separate, special letter all for yourself. Although I should preface it with a kick in the pants for your "hints" that things can't be as good as I paint them. You're right – they're better. The only b**ch I have at present – and it's a real one – is that apparently I'm indispensable, which means very little time off. I'm still working six nights a week, and it is really rough, believe me. I have the assurances of both Dallek (who will write you soon, he was too tied up, he told me) and Shertok, that what I'm doing is important, and that compensates me for not having taken that long *tiyul*, and for not having all the time I would like. Still, as Gershon invariably says, *c'est la vie* – and it certainly is.

Chag Sameach[16] – and was I at a Seder![17] Forty people, all Sabras, and of one family, representing four generations in Palestine (with the exception of one branch, which is here five). It was in Ramat Gan, in a palatial home built fifteen years ago in a modernistic style which is just beginning to be used in the more expensive homes in the States. They were terribly impressed by my Hebrew, particularly its grammatical, un-slangy quality, which I owe to father and NY. What I've read – and am reading – in Hebrew impressed them even more. But that is not too important. I too have been swimming – in Tel Aviv, the morning of the first Seder. It was beautiful, and not too warm.

---

16. Happy Holiday – it was Passover.
17. In his memoirs, Mordecai identifies his host as Nahum Slouschz (1871–1966), a Russian-born writer, translator and archeologist who was an important figure in the political and cultural activities of the Hovevei Zion movement in Odessa. He taught at the Sorbonne, then settled in Israel in 1919 and revived the Palestine Exploration Society. He died in 1966 at the age of ninety-four.

I've taken to eating home-cooked meals, right here in my own room. The restaurant food, while not too expensive, is too richly prepared for me. And as you should know by now – *Tag-essen*[18] does not last indefinitely, people tire too easily. Van Vriesland and Malkoff are the only ones I care to visit for food – the others are too formal, and make too much of an occasion of it. Besides, I don't like being presented as a celebrity, a newspaper man who knows it all. There are things I don't know (really) yet.

Somehow, I have little to say. Today is hot, but beautiful, and tonight will probably be another of those clear, cool, starlight work-loused nights. I know that one night a week (besides Friday night) would make all the difference, and we're all waiting for some new blood on the staff to make it easier for us all. Agronsky seems pleased with the speed with which I've learned the job, and the next couple of days should see an easement of our personnel problems.

Elias Epstein[19] called me the other day, and with "Agronsky is a friend of mine, I don't want to take you away from him, but" he offered me three-four jobs: propaganda for England, for the States, write for his magazine, a JNF propaganda office job. We finally left it at freelancing for him, because this is no time to change jobs. In the meanwhile, I'll be able to go on local trips, which he will arrange for me and which will cost nothing. Negev, etc.

Incidentally, your fears about both martial law and curfew were unfounded. My little green best-seller (official press card) did the trick, and made things quite easy.[20]

---

18. This is Yiddish, meaning "eating days," referring to the tradition in Eastern European yeshivas – which lacked dinning facilities – where yeshiva students would be hosted for meals in different homes on different days.
19. Elias M. Epstein (1895–1958) was overseas director of the Jewish National Fund (JNF).
20. While life under curfew and martial law may have been easy with a press card, the same cannot be said for the non-journalist citizens of the city. Thousands of

Leonard Bernstein is due here soon,[21] and the whole country is agog. I'll be able to get off for that concert – I may have to raise a little hell, but I'll be there.

...

Just had a talk with Ted Lurie about my job, and here is the story: 40 pounds per month, for the duration of the "trial period" (which will be three months altogether), and then a "grading" and a slight raise. We are now going over into five nights a week: this week, because of Pesach, and next – because we'll have the new guy we need. Agronsky and Lurie don't know it – but they too are on trial – I'll see how the five night week suits me, and then decide whether to stay or drop the job. The point is – it will be the only 5 day (okay – night) job obtainable around these parts, and 2 days off is a big thing.

I'm going to drop this letter now – so it catches the next plane. Meanwhile – be good, but not more than necessary.

...

That's all for now – be well, and my love to the whole family, even though they have fallen down a bit on the letter-writing angle. (And I felt quite at home with my four-generation, 40 sabras at the Seder).

Nu – happy birthday to Gershon.

Love,

Mersh

Jerusalemites were displaced because of designated security areas. Beyond the isolation and difficulties the curfew imposed, it was impossible for many to make a living.

21. The famous composer and conductor (1918–1990) was music director of the New York City Symphony at the time and just embarking on tours to other countries. Bernstein arrived on April 23 for a three week concert tour with the Palestine Philharmonic Orchestra. It was his first visit of what would become a lifelong association with Israel. In a later letter Mordecai describes his conversation with Bernstein backstage at the concert. I was surprised to find Bernstein's home address and phone number in my father's address book from the period.

April 14, 1947

Dear Family,

This letter had better be organized: there's been a lot of stuff in your last few, and I want to cover it all. So – I'm cueing from the very last and working my way backwards to the earliest which I've ignored. Here goes.

What's to get excited about just because I've been promoted? Gershon, I'm on trial until the end of May (because the guy I've replaced is due back then, and may want the job, depending on how his picture exhibit in Paris succeeds, and if they commit themselves to me – i.e., put me on a permanent basis, there'll be a conflict when he comes back) and may be back on the local desk at that time. Still, Brilliant[22] (of the Tel Aviv office, who just returned to Palestine) tells me that after two months I can't be fired altogether, and I've already done my two months, so I definitely have a job on the *Post* as long as I want it. Incidentally, GA (*"Hamelech"*)[23] read a cable story I wrote up the other day, and actually went so far as to say that it was very good. He, and Ted, have both expressed themselves as delighted with particular page-shapes on a number of occasions, not to me (horrors – that would be telling!) but to the stone-man (no relation to Neanderthal man, who is extinct, but simply referring to the guy who puts the articles – while in type – where I tell him), and he passed it on to me. So – it looks pretty good. At any rate, I had dinner at [Rav Meir] Berlin's the other night, and when he heard just what it is I am doing on the paper his eyebrows hit the ceiling. He was terribly impressed, particularly since he knows what a newspaper is. I have been assured by a number of people then when I'm

---

22. Moshe Brilliant (1915–1995), was born in New Jersey and moved to Palestine when he was eighteen. Starting as a messenger for the *Post*, he became a reporter and ultimately, Tel Aviv bureau chief. He was also a contributing correspondent for the *New York Times*.

23. "The king," i.e., Gershon Agronsky.

ready to switch over to a Hebrew paper it will be very easy for me to get a good job. Maybe, in a few years, when I'm a "veteran" newspaper man (below the age of 30!) At present I'm working from 7 to 2 in the morning, five nights a week. Which means I can go to performances too – *Mechashe-fah*[24] Thursday night – it's only 12 years old! As soon as we get out new press (a cylinder job, which welds all the lead together into a solid sheet and presses it around a drum, so that as the drum spins the paper is printed -15,000 copies an hour!) I'll be through much earlier, because second edi-tions will be very rare (the trouble to chisel out the mate-rial to be replaced and fit in the new, in solid lead, is rather great – too great except for emergencies). I love it though, there's never a dull moment.

Here is "*darki bakodesh*":[25] When I arrive at the office at seven, my subordinate has already sent down (to the lino-typers, to be set into lead on a machine much like a type-writer with a box of molten lead instead of a ribbon) about 15 stories (articles), which I read and check over when they come up in galley form. I go over the "clip" – *Reuter* news service – and see whether she's missed anything important, and begin to send down stuff myself. That means taking the long sheets from the ticker:[26] and editing them, writing headlines and indicating size and kind of type I want for them.

---

24. A famous Yiddish musical, *Di Kishufmacherin* (The Sorceress), by Abraham Gold-faden, known as the father of Yiddish theater. It was translated into Hebrew by Natan Alterman in 1935.

25. This means, "My way in holiness." It is Mordecai's teasing way of describing his schedule.

26. The teleprinter machine was an early form of high speed, remote printed commu-nication. It consisted of a device like an electric typewriter linked to a dedicated telephone line. News agencies such as Reuters would transmit a continuous stream of stories that would be printed onto long rolls of paper on the machines of subscribers. The copper wires connecting device to the telephone system lead to the news agencies that used them being known informally as "wire services." The term "ticker" was an anachronism by the 1940s, harking back to the original ticker tape machines that printed stock prices on narrow, "ticker tape."

Meanwhile, Daniel, a little sefardi, comes in and takes our *nash*[27] orders and goes out for the food. When I have stuff ready for the press room, I push a button and a copy boy comes scurrying (nu – comes) to bring it downstairs. By 9:30 all the main stuff is down, and I make a "Dummy" (slop-sheet of approximately where the articles will be on the first page) and go down with it, ready to sweat. The first few days Ted used to go over it with me, now he doesn't bother to do more than ask me – sometimes tell me – what the feature story is. I walk downstairs armed with chutzpah and the dummy, and immediately begin to tell the grown men there, who have been doing this stuff all their lives, just what to do. And they listen. They even do it. My *yekke*[28] subordinate keeps sending stuff down, which I read, check and plan for on the run as it comes. Meanwhile, I'm writing the heads for the big "top" stories, and seeing that they're placed correctly in the form. When the form is all full (after I've cut articles as I read them upside down and inside-out in lead, to make room) a page-proof is pulled, and I first check and correct all the mistakes they've made – inevitably – in the headlines, see what important stuff is still out (in the "overset" sheet I get) and with Ted or GA, decide what has to be squeezed in, after which I start to squeeze. Once the corrections are made, and another check pulled and scanned, it goes to press – and I have time to eat, pee, etc. Then, I read the latest *Reuter* stuff, see if any of it is worth using, edit it and send it down, decide, with Ted if he's around, otherwise without him, but with anxiety – as to what can be left out of the second edition, and see that the changes are all made. At that time, I

---

27. Snacks, in Yiddish.
28. Yiddish, meaning German Jew, but is used to refer to anyone who shows what are considered to be the typical characteristics of German Jews – formality, strictness, punctuality, etc. The word is an acronym of *Yehudim keshai oref*, "stiff-necked Jews." Or, possibly, from the German *jacke* ("jacket") which the German Jews who emigrated to Palestine/Israel continued to wear even for work on the kibbutz. (See "Hebrew as She Is Spoke: Ivrit, Sabrit, Sleng and Pinglish" by Ruth Gruber, in *Commentary*, November 1, 1950.)

whistle for Yaakov, who drives me home in either the big, old, decrepit Ford with the illuminated "Press" sign on its nose, or in the little baby Austin. And so to bed, with all the ink not quite washed off my elbows but not particularly concerned over such minor matters. Just the for hell of it, I'm enclosing the *Reuter* sign-off of Erev Pesach – I think you'll like it, tho' I know the Arab papers did not...Teleprint is, incidentally, a wonderful thing. The other day I went in to the *Haaretz*[29] office in Jerusalem, and teleprinted a message to our Tel Aviv office, to have [Moshe] Brilliant meet me when I arrived in Tel Aviv (this was the day before Seder, and I swam in Tel Aviv that morning). We had barely finished typing the message, and adding *bevakasha le'asher*[30](in Hebrew type, of course) when the *b'seder*[31] came right back. 'S wonnerful! Incidentally, I just received my *Mikraot Gedolot*[32] from the Schocken office-head here, a neighbor, who got it from friends, etc. – the Chumash in five volumes, Prophets in two – you may send me the new Schocken *Ketubim*[33] (published in Boston very recently) when you get the chance. And for Gershon's information – the Gemara is no Esau act[34] – I want my *Ketubot,*[35] with my notes from Lieberman's class. Until it comes I shall continue with the *Baba Kama*[36] which I bought in Mea Shearim[37] a few days ago. I've bought a few volumes of Kabak,[38] and am reading him now preparatory to writing

---

29. A left-wing Hebrew language newspaper in Israel founded by Gustav Schocken (1912-1990) who was its editor from 1939 to 1990. He was also a member of Knesset for the Progressive Party between 1955 and 1959.
30. Hebrew, meaning "Please approve."
31. Hebrew, meaning "Okay."
32. Bible printed with multiple commentaries on each page.
33. The "Writings" is the third section of the Bible (Torah, Prophets, and Writings).
34. Mordecai does not want to trade editions with his brother – a reference to Esau selling his birthright to Yaakov for a bowl of lentils.
35. A tractate of the Talmud that deals primarily with marriage contracts.
36. A tractate of the Talmud dealing with civil matters such as damages and torts.
37. Ultra-Orthodox neighborhood in Jerusalem.
38. Aharon Avraham Kabak (1883–1944), Hebrew novelist, critic, and translator, was born in Smorgon, a city in Belarus, and died in Jerusalem. He wrote for Hebrew and

that damn paper on him that the Seminary wants. (If I could only give them three months of the *Post*, with all the work I've done on it, instead!)

Yes, Gershon, I prefer *Haaretz* to *Davar*,[39] simply because the former is a better newspaper, though its line is as you say (like the *Times* and the *NY Post*, for example). Both evening papers are somewhat unreliable, I'll save their orientation for the list I'm getting for you of all papers and their affiliations.

[The last page of the letter is missing.]

As is only natural, during his first couple of months in Palestine, Mordecai (known to his family also as "Mersh" and sometimes, "the Brat" and sometimes "Butch") writes mainly about the many details of beginning a new life in a new country; the people he meets and "cultivates"; the rooms he finds to live in; the paperwork he has to complete to be able to move around; the new job at the *Palestine Post* that he acquires and masters. One crucial detail of his life at that time, however, is completely absent from the letters: he says nothing of the fact that, within a month or so of his arrival in Palestine, he was recruited into the Haganah. A clear description of that has to wait until his letter of July 8, 1948, below. It seems clear from his openness with his family that this is something he would have shared with them had he been able. He was not at liberty to tell them what he was involved in, and even if he had permission, he wouldn't have been able to write anything down for fear of discovery if his letters fell into the wrong hands. The Haganah was still an illegal organization as far as the British were concerned.

Yiddish newspapers and periodicals and then turned to composing short stories in Hebrew. Kabak is regarded as a pioneer of the Hebrew novel in the twentieth century.

39. *Davar* (lit. speech or word) was a Hebrew-language newspaper established in 1925 by leaders of the Labor movement in Palestine. They called it "The Newspaper for the Workers of the Land of Israel."

Almost immediately upon his arrival in Palestine, Mordecai was trans-lating Haganah radio broadcasts into English.[40] He also served in an intelli-gence-gathering capacity (about which, more below) and wrote summaries of news from Arab countries. After the state was formally declared and the Haganah became the Israel Defense Forces, Mordecai was formally drafted.

He describes his early recruitment in the memoir he wrote decades later, but even there the chronology is never completely clear; possibly he is being intentionally vague:

> Afternoons we used to hang out at the Atara Café,[41] on Ben Yehuda Street. One afternoon I met Yoel Malkoff there. His wife had been my sister's teacher in Bet Hakerem, back in 1935–36, and he was a big shot in the Haganah. British C.I.D. men hung out there, too, but you could always spot them by their haircuts. They never did find the "terrorists" they were presumably looking for.
>
> "Go to Kupat Holim,"[42] Yoel told me.
>
> "But I feel fine!"
>
> A kick under the table. "Go to Kupat Holim, and ask for Yehezkel."
>
> So I did. The interview was brief:
>
> "Do you want to be with the Americans, or the Palestinians?"[43]
>
> "The Palestinians."
>
> "Can you drive a truck or a car?"
>
> "Of course not; I'm a New Yorker."
>
> I was then sworn into the Haganah.

---

40. I have several such transcripts in my possession.
41. Café Atara was an institution in Jerusalem. Opened in 1938 by a German immigrant, Heinz Greenspan, the European-style café became a center for Zionist intellectuals, Haganah fighters and British officers alike. It stayed open through thick and thin, only closing its doors permanently in 1996 (it moved to Rehavia for a while and then closed a few years later). It was frequented not only by activists and politicians, but by many of the giants of Hebrew literature, including Shai Agnon and Aharon Appelfeld, and appears as a setting in books by Agnon and Amos Oz.
42. Health Care Provider.
43. In those days, the Jews were the "Palestinians" while the Arabs were still "Arabs," as noted above.

It was neither the Bible nor the pistol which were intimidating; they were staples of so many spy books and movies – it was the oath itself:

"I declare that I am joining the Haganah voluntarily, and of my own free will; I swear to be faithful to the Haganah, to its rules and regulations, as set forth by its Supreme Command; I swear to obey the Haganah for the rest of my life; to accept its authority without conditions or reservations, and to obey when it calls me to active duty at any time and place; to fulfill all commands and carry out all instructions; I swear to give all my strength, and even my life, to protect and fight for my nation and my homeland, for the freedom of Israel and for the redemption of Zion."

My code name would be Eeter (in the Tanach, Ehud ben Gera, one of Israel's Judges, is referred to as "*eeter yad yemino*," lit., his right hand was weak, i.e., he was a lefty). My boss would be "Shfifone" (Viper). I was certain when I left Kupat Holim to go to the office, that you only had to look at me to know that I was in the illegal, dangerous, anti-British underground.

One day I asked Agronsky for a week off.

"Want, or need?"

"Need."

"Okay – just be careful."

He understood.

The week was spent at a kibbutz, Ramat Rachel, south of Jerusalem. …We were also taught to handle a Sten gun,[44] and practice throwing grenades – or rocks – the closest thing we could get to grenades. We Americans, who had all played baseball as kids, got the rocks closest to the targets – garbage cans. When the call came: *Slik!*[45] – it meant the British were coming. By the time they got into the kibbutz, the guns were hidden, and we were listening to a lecture on Zionist history….

---

44. British submachine gun used extensively by British and Commonwealth forces throughout World War II. They had a simple design and very low production costs, making them effective weapons for resistance groups such as the Haganah.
45. *Slik* – Hebrew slang for "hide."

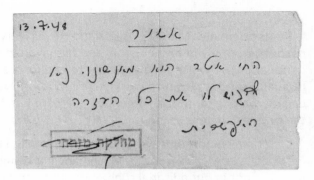

"This is 'Eeter.' He is one of our people.
Please give him every assistance." Mizrachi
Dept. (Haganah intelligence – Jerusalem)

April 27, 1947

Dear Family,

... Gershon, you are enjoying my reviews. I must say, that's quite a legacy I left those two magazines. I had completely lost track of how many I had written, and thought that the March *Commentary* (which I just received) was the last of the lot.[46] The more the merrier, of course. If they would only send me books here for review! Maybe if we tell them "who" I am they will! Thank you for the books, which I look forward to (tch tch, poor grammar) and for the stuff which came on the *Crap*.[47] I am now engaged in a search for second-hand Shmaryahu Levin[48] stuff, but it is going very slowly.

---

46. As noted above, Mordecai wrote at least six book reviews for *Commentary* during 1946–47.

47. Mordecai is referring to the *USS Marine Carp*.

48. Shmaryahu Levin (1867–1935) was a Jewish Zionist activist in the Russian Empire, then in Germany and in the United States, and member of the first elected Russian parliament for the Constitutional Democratic Party in 1906. He was a strong advocate for the creation of the Technion, the Israel Institute of Technology.

...

Incidentally, Mrs. Van Vriesland *kleibs* very noisy *naches*[49] from my published stuff, and has given me some material on art which I may be able to use for a story (a local art scandal, I'll get to work on it very soon). And I'm eagerly waiting for Moish[50] to appear – I want him to read the pigeons[51] before I send them.

(Time out for some work now) – Incidentally, Leonard Bernstein is now conducting in Tel Aviv, and it is being broadcast. But not in our editorial room – too distracting. S**t.

I shall be off on Wednesday, and may ... take in a performance in Habimah[52] or someplace else, I'll see. Meanwhile, they're all running after me. JNF wants me to edit a monthly news bulletin, I'll see how much they're offering (the work would take about one or two days to do, every month) and then consider the deal. I doubt it, of course. Incidentally, Naomi did a terrific press agenting job for me here. Everybody knows about me, everybody thinks I'm good – I just have to be careful not to show them any work, lest I spoil the impression. The promising young man must not spoil any promises...

This must of necessity be a short letter. I have a little time now, and I want to read some Kabak[53] before the page comes up, because I have a hunch Lake Success[54] cables will

---

49. I have not found a source for the Yiddish. It may be similar to "*shepping nachas*," i.e., taking pride in something or someone.
50. Maurice Samuel, the author.
51. A short story Mordecai wrote. Maurice Samuel wrote a detailed critique. It appears that Mordecai eventually abandoned the story.
52. One of the first Hebrew language theaters in Palestine, Habimah, in the center of Tel Aviv, was built in 1945 and became the national theater of Israel in 1958. It was the home of the eponymous Habimah theater company that had been founded in Czarist Russia in 1912. The company moved to Palestine in 1928.
53. Probably Aharon Kabak's trilogy, *Shlomo Molcho* (see chapter 5, footnote 29).
54. The village of Lake Success, NY, was the home of the United Nations headquarters between 1946 and 1951.

be coming in soon, and we'll be here rather late. So, good-night for now, and my love to all. Don't send anything just keep writing those wonderful letters. Love to Bavlis.

Mordecai

Chapter 5

The United Nations Special Committee on Palestine (UNSCOP)

The "Lake Success" cables to which Mordecai refers were dispatches from the Special UN Session on Palestine, prompted by Britain's decision in February to refer the matter of Palestine to the United Nations. The General Assembly met on April 28 and continued to deliberate for the next seventeen days. It finally resolved to appoint a fact-finding committee, the United Nations Special Committee on Palestine (UNSCOP) composed of representatives from eleven "neutral" countries: Australia, Canada, Czechoslovakia, Guatemala, India, Iran, Netherlands, Peru, Sweden, Uruguay, and Yugoslavia. It intentionally excluded the "Big Five" permanent members of the UN Security Council – USSR, USA, UK, France, and China. The committee toured Palestine from June 15 to July 3. It held twelve public hearings (July 4–17) during which thirty-one representatives from twelve Jewish organizations gave testimony and submitted written depositions. It generated thirty-two tons of material. Jewish Agency representatives such as David Ben-Gurion,

Moshe Shertok, and Abba Eban[1] testified, along with Chaim Weizmann. UNSCOP also heard testimony from anti-Zionist religious and non-religious Jewish representatives, as well as from the Palestine Communist Party and a few Arab organizations.[2] The Arab Higher committee boycotted the investigation.[3] Mordecai would participate in some of UNSCOP's travels in Palestine and report on some of the testimony.

There were three potential solutions to the problem of Palestine under consideration by the committee: partition into two separate states, a unitary state with a fixed Arab majority, and a federal state divided into cantons. The British were pushing for a five-year trusteeship under their auspices, essentially an extention of the Mandate.

On April 16, twelve days before the UN Special Session was convened, the British imposed a country-wide curfew in Palestine while they hanged four members of the Irgun: Dov Gruner, Yehiel Dresner (alias, Dov Rosenbaum), Eliezer Kashani, and Mordehai Alkahi. Gruner had been captured in March 1946 and the other three in December. The executions suffered from severe irregularities. The four had no prior notice that their sentences were going to be carried out, had not been allowed to say goodbye to their families (supposedly for security reasons), had no last meal, and no spiritual support from a rabbi. Even more egregious was the case of Dov Gruner, for whom the appeals process had not run its course. All four were hastily and secretly executed on April 16, in contravention of British law. All went to the gallows singing *Hatikvah*, the other prisoners joining their defiant song. They were four of the twelve "Olei Hagardom," (lit., "those who went up to the

---

1. Abba Eban (1915–2002) born Aubrey Solomon Meir Eban, was an Israeli diplomat and politician. In 1947 he was liason officer to the United Nations Special Committee on Palestine (UNSCOP) and, from 1950–1960, Israel's ambassador to the UN. He was Israel's foreign minister from 1966–1974. He was an extremely eloquent spokesman for Israel.

2. For a list of individuals and organizations that testified see *The Summary of AG-057 United Nations Special Committee on Palestine (UNSCOP) (1947)* https://archives.un.org/sites/archives.un.org/files/files/Finding%20Aids/2015_Finding_Aids/AG-057.pdf.

3. The Arab Higher Committee was the leading Palestinian Arab representative body at the time. It had been founded in 1936 by the Grand Mufti, Amin al-Husseini. Al-Husseini was in exile in Egypt in 1947, avoiding prosecution for war crimes arising from his collaboration with the Nazis.

gallows"), the Jewish pre-independence fighters who were executed by British mandate authorities.

The Americans were among those who considered the British acts cruel. The executions of Moshe Barazani and Meir Feinstein were scheduled to occur five days later. Barazani had been convicted of planting a bomb at the Jerusalem Railway station on October 30, 1946, which resulted in the death of a British constable. Feinstein was accused of possessing a hand grenade. Rather than allow themselves to be hanged, the two men planned to blow themselves up next to the gallows, together with the British hanging party. Visitors had smuggled them a grenade hidden inside an orange. When they learned that a rabbi would be present at the hanging, they changed their plans and killed themselves in their cell just before the planned execution.

In response to these harsh sentences, there were numerous attacks on British army personnel throughout the month, as well as a daring operation undertaken by the Irgun on May 4 to break prisoners out of Acre prison. Twenty-eight incarcerated Irgun and Lehi members were freed although some of the liberators were captured. Mordecai will make reference to some of these events below.

These events, along with the activities at the United Nations, led Mordecai's father to despair. On April 30, he writes:

> I must admit, Mordecai, that my heart is not now in the writing of letters. I don't have the peace of mind or serenity for it. Because these days – the days of the U.N. assembly – are fateful days – for us. Our fate – the fate of the land and the nation – have been cast into their hands, they will determine our fate. I read the report of the assembly daily, and my heart is horrified from humiliation and fury... humiliation at our lowly status among the nations. They all sent their delegates, and we have not a single delegate, as though we are not a nation, and as though it has nothing to do with us. And fury – at the audacity of the Arabs and the indifference of the delegates! We have not a single friend, and there is not so much as a spark of justice or compassion in their hearts.... They talk about Eretz Yisrael

as merchandise sold in the market, which goes to the highest bidder.... we can lean on none other than our Father in Heaven and on our strength. "Let the nations rage and the peoples mutter, He who sits in the heavens laughs, the Lord derides them."[4]

May 7, 1947

Dear Family,

...Just moved to a new room, with Katznelson,[5] head of the Kupat Holim. It is next door to Agronsky, in the heart of "the" section – Rehavia, and for the same price, includes both phone and Frigidaire and permission to cook all I want. ...

Heard Leonard Bernstein the other night – and spoke to him afterwards in the dressing room. There is nothing for me to say about him as a musician – you can read the local papers – but – he said he would like to build him[self] a house here, and poor thing he had *shilshul*[6] all through the program! The country has gone wild over him, and he's promised to be back next year. He says our orchestra is potentially the best in the world...[7]

We had a little fire at the *Post* the other day and it kept me busy so that I missed the kids who were going to

---

4.   Psalms 2:2, 4.
5.   Dr. Reuven Katznelson (1895–1961) was an early researcher in the interdisciplinary blending of social work with political science. He was a pioneer in public health and social work and established the first independent network of public health clinics (Kupat Holim) in the country. He served as assistant to Henrietta Szold in the formative years of the Hadassah movement. His daughter, Shulamith, founded Ulpan Akiva in 1951 (see chapter 5, footnote 131) and his son, Shmuel Moshe Tamir, was minister of justice when Menachem Begin was prime minister.
6.   Diarrhea.
7.   In the *Post* of May 2, Bernstein is quoted, "The Palestine Philharmonic has the highest potential of any orchestra I've ever conducted, and I have no doubt that it could easily be the greatest in the world." He goes on to explain that it needs a permanent conductor of its own and a good concert hall.

Shechem[8] for the *Shomroni korban pesach,*[9] so as compensation I treated myself to a trip to Tel Aviv, and saw the Habimah [Theater]do *Oedipus* – and did it superbly. There isn't a company in your country that would attempt it, that could do it if it wanted to, etc., etc. I sat in the first row, free (you have to know people in this country), and afterwards, following a snack, we dropped in on *"Li-La-Lo"* (supposed to be satire), doing a skit called *"Lo Yoter Midai"* (not too much) which stank. We caught their second act, and all they have is Shoshana Damari, a Yemenite singer who is terrific.[10] She's going to the States in a few months, for a few months, and I've given her your name and address, to look up. I think you'll get a kick out of her...

So – the family apparently thinks I do have something on the ball – well, well. For the last two issues I have been writing the lead-all story for the second edition (our lead-alls now are all on the UN meetings, and we have a guy who does the first edition story, using all the junk that comes in throughout the day. I pick up where he leaves, and the second edition story is mine, with a little of his remaining here and there if I think it worth keeping). Last night, as we were going home, GA (on the same *"mishkal"*[11] as "JJ," CB, etc., as

8.   Nablus.
9.   The Passover sacrifice as performed by the Samaritans or Shomronim. Named for Samaria, a region of ancient Israel, their religion is closely related to Judaism. Samaritans believe that theirs is the true religion of the ancient Israelites from before the Babylonian exile. In the fifth century, the Samaritan population is thought to have topped 1.5 million, but religious persecution, conversion and economic hardship had nearly erased the community by the early twentieth century. In 1931 there were only 182 Samaritans recorded in the Palestine census; at the beginning of 2015 there were exactly 777. Half lived near Nablus, on Mt. Gerizim, the group's holiest place and the site of its yearly Passover sacrifice. The other half live in a compound in the city of Holon, near Tel Aviv. The Samaritans are also characterized by a strong fidelity to the land – they did not go into the Diaspora. They are afforded a unique status in Jewish religious law.
10.   Shoshana Damari (1923–2006) was a Yemeni-born Israeli singer known as the "Queen of Hebrew Music." She had an extremely successful singing career and became a national Israeli icon.
11.   Hebrew, literally "weight," but here intending status or level.

used by all big executive people) invited me in to have an almost-morning snack. We shmoozed, he showed off his library, and it was all very cozy. Then I went next door and so to bed. Lead story is all well and good – it will be a while before I do a "leader" (editorial) though. I think he wants me to do some book reviews for the *Post* now too – he asked what kind I like to do (they pay extra, of course).

... And as far as suing the British gov't for governing according to the illegal White Paper – don't be naive my dear brother. What about not making laws retroactive (which the British did after the Gruner execution) and any one of a dozen other little items – they label it all "security" – and there you are. Curfew, dispossesses from homes, turning half of Jerusalem into a fortress – are all these legal? Still they're done, and all in the name of security....

How is mother, and when is she going to write?

I'll be sending you a week's *Posts* every week now, there will always be stuff there that Gershon can use for an edit*orial*. There is one in particular which I'm going to send as a clipping, for use the next time you hear of a boat being turned back the people deported (there's bound to be another soon...).

...

My Ramat Gan Sabra is Adi Cohen. The family is the Shluoh family,[12] of the Tel Aviv municipality – a big shot.

And what is that blackmail to which you so glibly refer, my dear sister? Are you just sending one of those tiresome "letters to the (foreign) editor" or have you something specific in mind? Incidentally – I finally received a nice little letter from Hadassah...

---

12. Probably "Shlush," or Chelouche. Aharon Shlush or Chelouche was a founder of the Tel Aviv Neighborhood of Neve Zedek. There is also an Aharon Shlush born in 1921, who joined the Haganah as a teenager.

Nothing to add – except that I haven't had anything from you now for over a week.

Love to all –

Mordecai

The "Hadassah" that Mordecai mentions is Hadassah Frisch, daughter of Daniel Frisch, president of the Zionist Organization of America. Mordecai originally met Hadassah through his sister, Naomi, who was her counselor at Camp Cejwin in New York. Mordecai dated Hadassah in America and proposed marriage. He will not receive a definitive response until November of 1947. During this entire period his letters are strangely silent about her.

(Courtesy of Vivien Bacaner)

Hadassah Frisch

Friday, May 16, 1947

Dear Family,

I saw Miller in Rehovot yesterday, and he … gave me a bit of interesting information: He has been asked (I forget by whom) to negotiate with Alexander M. Dushkin,[13] the Great, for the latter to serve as head of education in Palestine.

...

Some people are never satisfied. How can Father complain that I am not writing editorials yet? I have one of the most responsible jobs on the paper. Above me there are only two – Agronsky and Ted Lurie – and that in the course of two weeks. Ye gods and little fishes – I still have to learn the business. My greatest trouble to date, all along, has been that I have acquired responsibility too soon, with serving an apprenticeship. CCNY *Mercury*[14] is just one example, this might very well be another were it not for the fact that Ted – and GA – realized from the beginning that I would need help, and gave it. The job is still new and exciting to me, and there is still a lot I can learn doing just what I'm doing. Jakie – step down from duh vaggon, please![15] As for the paper itself – it gives what is considered to be literary stuff on Friday – you may have seen it already in the weekly bundles I've been sending – but it's pretty poor stuff. We did print Izzy Stone's Cyprus

---

13. Prof. Alexander M. Dushkin (1890–1976) was one of the movers and shakers of the Yishuv with whom Esther socialized when she lived in Palestine in 1936. Born in Poland, he was educated in the United States, receiving his PhD from Columbia University. He was also a graduate of the Teachers Institute of the Jewish Theological Seminary of America. Prior to leaving for Palestine he was director of the Board of Jewish Education in Chicago, as well as executive superintendent of the Jewish Education Committee in New York. He joined the Hebrew University faculty in 1949, and became the founder of its School of Education. He was awarded the Israel Prize for education in 1968.

14. Student humor magazine of City College of NY of which Mordecai was editor-in-chief.

15. A reference to one of Mordecai's favorite jokes. In brief, a family in the shtetl fantasizes about leaving for greener pastures. In the meager comfort of their home, they recount their fantasies, which become humorously specific and extend to what they will pack, etc. The son, Jakie, is very excited and keeps exclaiming that he will sit next to the wagon driver. The father finally gets exasperated and yells, "Jakie, get off the wagon!" Mordecai invoked it frequently, to warn, "don't get ahead of yourself."

visit, and a series by him on Turkey, but the section is sad. Part of the trouble is the obsession with pleasing the English reader[16] – hence crap like this Gubbins[17] and the sports, etc. However – I suggested to GA that I do a page in the supplement one of these days, devoted to Franz Kafka (Brod,[18] his biographer and literary executor is here) and said I should send home for the books...

The new Seminary Museum sounds interesting, Maw, let's hear more about it. And do you mean to tell me that that little group of yours actually meets?[19]

Mordecai here returns to the UN's deliberations on the issue of Palestine, beginning with one of its procedural quirks.

As Alistair Cooke (Manchester *Guardian* guy in NY)[20] put it – the Political Committee adjourned, Aranha[21] waved his Magic Wand – and it reformed again as the Assembly: 55 grown men moving into a new meeting hall to decide

---

16. British personnel in Palestine, rather than the Jewish readers.
17. Nathaniel Gubbins (1893–1976), a noted British journalist and humorist, had a regular column in the *Post*.
18. Max Brod (1884–1968), was a Czech author, composer, and journalist who moved to Palestine in 1939, fleeing the Nazis. A prolific writer in his own right, he was also the friend, literary executor and biographer of Franz Kafka.
19. Mordecai's mother, Esther, created an organization (which she refers to as "The Project") of Zionist young people who would meet regularly to socialize and discuss issues of interest. In keeping with Esther's elitism, it was exclusive: "we shall abide by that standard; people who did not have the advantage of a fine cultural background are not eligible." Each meeting was to consist of a discussion on a specific topic, refreshments and dancing. The inaugural meeting was held on March 2, 1947. The meetings continued for some time and Esther considered the project a great success. She updates Mordecai several times as to its progress. I have not found any third party reference to this group.
20. Alistair Cooke (1908–2004) later became known to American audiences through his role as host of PBS's "Masterpiece Theater." The rest of the world knew him as the celebrated presenter of "Letter from America," the longest-running speech radio programme hosted by one individual in history.
21. Osvaldo Aranha (1894–1960), Brazilian politician, diplomat and statesman, and at that time, president of the UN General Assembly.

whether they approve of what they did in the old meeting hall! (Shades of Pooh-Bah).[22] But it hasn't come out badly at all, so far. The Arabs are sore, US and USSR seem to be for partition – we may even get it. All I know is we must get something, soon, because things here are getting worse by the day. The streets are deserted at night, people are afraid to go out – and every once in a while their fears are born out when an Englishman gets knocked off. It's unpleasant. For me, of course, it makes no difference because during those dead hours I'm at work. It's bad though, bad for the city and for the people living in it. I seem to recall some curiosity over my schedule: well, after having gotten in at about 2–3 am the night before, I usually sleep until ten thirty or so, and then make myself breakfast, do some shopping, and take care of some of the fantastically numerous details of keeping legal here – today I went to Immigration for the third time, to get my visa renewed ....

My crowd at present is the newspaper crowd – Zifroni, Agronsky, Lurie, Clifton Daniel (*NY Times*) Homer Biggart, Eliav Simon (*UP*) and his assistant, who came over with me, Mrs. Van Vriesland, the Molkoffs, Moshe Brilliant in Tel Aviv, a couple of local kids. I'll send a full-day in my next letter.

...It's almost time for Shabbat Shalom. Love all –

As Irgun and Lehi attacks continued, the British added layer upon layer of security in an attempt to protect their soldiers and police. British forces were ordered to walk in groups of no fewer than four, and vehicles were required to have at least one armed guard, literally "riding shotgun."

---

22. In Gilbert and Sullivan's comic operetta, *The Mikado*, Pooh-Bah holds numerous offices, including First Lord of the Treasury, Lord Chief Justice, Commander-in-Chief, Lord High Admiral, Archbishop, Lord Mayor, and Lord High Everything Else. The name Pooh-Bah has come to be used as a mocking title for a pompous pretender to great influence. Mordecai loved Gilbert and Sullivan and knew large portions of many of the operettas by heart.

May 22, 1947

Dear Family,

Here are some details to fill in my time schedule: Now that the UN Assembly meetings are over – and that was quite a rave notice father gave Silver![23] – I've been finishing work on the old schedule again – 1:45, 2:00, sometimes 2:15, and it almost feels as though I'm not working (you know, the Jew and the goat and the rabbi).[24] As a result I've been getting up by 9:30. I putter around for breakfast, shop for same, and am ready to work by about 11:00. So far I've done a piece for Epstein, a piece for Frisch, two for Gershon, and have begun to collect my material for a piece on censorship.

...

I haven't been around to Rishon [Lezion] or Kfar Vitkin[25] yet – I'll have to wait for a real leave until GA gets back from the journalists conference in Prague (he's leaving the end of this month) but the other more local relatives I shall see soon. You can't imagine the reluctance I have ... to go out of the house at all during the day – the heat these days is really something – a nice little persistent khamsin.[26] The trouble is that it means I see few people, because I work at night.

....

---

23. Abba Hillel Silver, a key figure in the mobilization of American support for the founding of the State of Israel, presented Israel's case to the Political Committee of the UN Special Assembly on Palestine on May 8.
24. Mordecai compares his attitude to his lightened workload to the Jewish joke about the man who complains to his rabbi that his house is too small. The rabbi advises him to bring in a horse, then a goat, chickens, and more. When the rabbi finally tells the man to remove all the animals, the house suddenly feels spacious. Although Mordecai's workload is still heavy, it now seems mild to him in comparision to recent exertions.
25. A moshav near Netanya where Mordecai had (has) relatives.
26. Arabic, meaning "heatwave," literally a dry hot sandy wind blowing in from the east.

My really big problem now is to get that damned Kabak paper done.[27] I've been thinking of the possibility of giving Bavli a translation of either a volume of Kabak or of the by now famous *Maagalot*[28] instead – it would serve the double purpose of a piece of work for him, a job for me which would pay off in the long run – and a third advantage – would give me the extra time I need for the job. On a six-day week, particularly as I was living it before, looking for rooms and getting organized and finishing work very late at night, I hardly had a chance for much reading. I read *Shlomo Molcho*[29] but that's not enough to write a paper on. I'm writing to him this week, but I wish Father would talk to him and ask him if my substitution idea is acceptable – that is, not ask, but help "explain" to him the difficulty of getting it done on time for Commencement (when is it?). The books themselves are very hard to get – all but *Shlomo Molcho* are out of print, and I think the only guy who might lend the others to me is Davidson – and I haven't seen him yet and can't ask him for them just "*stam azoy.*"[30]

Moish[31] has arrived, and is in Rehovot at Weizmann's.[32] I hope to see him one of these days. Meanwhile Agronsky has suddenly realized that the book [Moish's book, *Web of Lucifer*] has not been reviewed in the *Post*, and has applied to me for a review. (Who else could do it – I'm the only one in the country who's read the book!) I read it quite a while ago, but I think I'll manage.

---

27. Probably the last paper Mordecai needs to submit to the Jewish Theological Seminary in NY in order to receive his rabbinical ordination.

28. *Maagalot*, (lit. circles) was a bestselling novel published in 1944 by Polish-born David Meletz, a pioneer of the early kibbutz movement who was nevertheless able to write critically about kibbutz life.

29. A trilogy written by Aharon Kabak, based on the life of Solomon Molcho (Diogo Pires), a Portuguese mystic (1500–1532) who declared the coming of the Messiah. Born to "New Christian" Marrano parents, Molcho was convicted of apostasy by the Inquisition and was burned at the stake.

30. Yiddish phrase meaning "just like that."

31. Maurice Samuel.

32. Possibly Chaim Weizmann (1874–1952), scientist and first president of Israel, or perhaps another Weizmann.

...

I assume that Naomi's characterization of the UN session as foul was pre-Gromyko[33] (have you heard about the kids running around [saying] "didn't I tell you Soviet Russia had Shomer Hatzair[34] leanings?") and his very surprising statement.[35] I should have liked to have seen NY Jews get excited about that. Father, I am sure, will call it just a Russian bluff, trusting them as he does. But then – what are they, after all said and done – *goyim*![36]

...

Love –

Mordecai

Wednesday, May 28, 1947

Dear Family,

... Erev Shavuot[37] dinner at Berlin's house was very nice, and was topped by a visit from Herzog's son, Yaakov[38] (the

---

33. Andrei Gromyko (1909–1989), a Soviet statesman. At this time, Gromyko was the Soviet Permanent Representative to the United Nations. Despite a longstanding and vehement ideological opposition to Zionism, miraculously, in the crucial period from 1944 to 1948 the USSR supported the creation of a Jewish state.

34. Hashomer Hatzair is a left-wing Zionist youth group. Here Mordecai is referring to a popular joke. It had been common to condemn Hashomer Hatzair as having Soviet leanings. The extraordinary reversal of Russia's policy on Zionism led wags to invert the popular criticism.

35. Mordecai here is referring to an extraordinary speech that Gromyko gave at the UN on May 14, 1947. In a dramatic volt-face from open hostility to Zionism, the Soviet representative voiced a moving recognition of Jewish suffering during WWII, and unequivocal support for the Partition Plan. Soviet support would not be limited to diplomacy; communist Czechoslovakia would supply arms to the infant Israel during the War of Independence.

36. Non-Jews.

37. Jewish festival which occurs seven weeks after Passover.

38. Yaakov Herzog (1921–1972) was born in Dublin, Ireland. His father was Yitzhak HaLevi Herzog, the second Ashkenazi chief rabbi of Israel. His brother, Chaim Herzog, became the sixth president of Israel. The family immigrated to Palestine in

guy who Zeitlin[39] roasted for his Mishnah translation and commentary). Instead of standing *tikkun*[40] ourselves, we went around town and saw how the other Jews do it: Kurds, Yemenites, Bukharim[41] and the Gerer Chassidim (you should have heard me ask, in flawless Yiddish, where the Gerer *shtibel*[42] was!) as well as other assorted Sephardic Jews. We stayed at each place for a few minutes, caught a two-hour nap, and then went down to the Kotel and watched the communities gathering: they came from every side, in massed ranks, singing and dancing and clapping their hands as they came down the long hundred-odd steps (or is it 500 – I was too tired to count on the way up, and didn't care particularly on the way down). We *chapped arein*[43] a davening[44] there, and then sat with some friends of his in the Old City where we had a *kibbud*,[45] and watched the retreat from the Kotel. By 7:30 (am) we left the [Old] City and went back home, to retire for most of the rest of the day. *Chag Sameach*!

1937. After he was ordained as a rabbi in the Harry Fischel Seminary in Jerusalem, Herzog studied law at the Hebrew University of Jerusalem and London University. He earned a doctorate in international law from McGill University in Montreal. Herzog served in the Shai unit (intelligence, "*sherut yidiot*") in the Haganah. He went on to become a close advisor to Israel's leaders and a noted diplomat.

39. Probably Aaron Zeitlin (1898–1973), author of several books on Yiddish literature and poetry and, for a time, Professor of Hebrew literature at the Jewish Theological Seminary.

40. Literally, *tikkun* means rectification. Mordecai is referring to the tradition of *Tikkun leil Shavuot*, "the rectification of the night of Shavuot" – which consists of staying up for the whole night of Shavuot to learn Torah. The tradition has its source in a midrash (Talmudic legend), which relates that the night before the Torah was given, the Israelites went to sleep early so as to be well-rested for the momentous day ahead. But they overslept, and Moses had to wake them up because God was already waiting on the mountaintop. To rectify this perceived flaw in the national character, the tradition was instituted of staying up all night to learn Torah.

41. Jews from Central Asia who historically spoke Bukhari, a dialect of the Tajik-Persian language.

42. Yiddish for "little house" or "little room," *shtibels* are used for communal Jewish prayer but are less formal than synagogues.

43. "Grabbed," in Yiddish.

44. "Prayer service," in Yiddish.

45. "Refreshments," in Hebrew.

I addressed a clever little note to the *"Beth Din shel Mattah,"*[46] G. Agronsky, *Yoshev Rosh,*[47]" and as a result I shall see something of the country next week: Toby Berlin just got a car (on my name) and since he's leaving for the States again soon he's anxious to get around in it, So – with me and Yaakov Herzog (nothing but the best families – three sons-of-rabbis!) we are taking a four-day *tiyul*[48] up to the Upper Galil. In planning the itinerary, I saw to it that Kfar Vitkin and Merhavia[49] (some of Bavli's *mishpacha*[50] there) were included. We leave Sunday morning, and will be back on Wednesday before the road curfew descends (7 at night).

Yesterday I went riding for a few hours in a beautiful new car with an American flag on the license plate: my vice-consul friend and I went for a spin, after which we retired to my villa (of which I rented all but one room, since all I need for myself is that one room – hah!) for a little cognac. And so to work.

I did a review of Samuel's *Web,*[51] and did it rather well, I think. It will be in the Friday supplement (day after tomorrow) and of course I'll mail a separate clip immediately.

...

I'm off to the Food Control[52] now – and my next week's letter may be a few days *tiyul*-delayed, so don't worry (though I'll try to write en route too). That's all for

---

46. Literally (in Hebrew), "the lower court," as opposed to the heavenly court over which God presides.
47. "Chairman," in Hebrew.
48. Hebrew word used for both "hike" and "trip" – in this case, a trip.
49. A kibbutz in the north, close to the town of Afula.
50. "Family" in Hebrew.
51. *Web of Lucifer*, by Maurice Samuel. The review, "A Renaissance Novel," appeared on page 7 of the *Palestine Post* of May 30.
52. An office originally set up by the British and then taken over by Jewish municipal authorities of Jerusalem to manage the allocation of food and water during the

now – regards from Maurice, whom I haven't seen yet. (He's at Weizmann's[53] for a few weeks, then to Agronsky).

Love,

Mordecai

Wednesday night, June 4, 1947

Dear Family,

...It's a beautiful country all right. ... We left Sunday morning in Roy's '46 Chrysler, and zipped over to Netanya, the most gorgeous beach I've ever swum (swam or swimmed) at, and then went up to Kfar Vitkin. The old man is not too well, he sits around the house and does next to nothing. Chayim is still built like the rock of Gibraltar, and looks every bit as permanent.[54] He has a shy little red-head for a daughter, really cute, and his wife protests very volubly that there is nothing like moshav[55] life. When I get a real vacation again I intend to spend a few days there. This time a couple of hours had to do, and from there we went up to Zichron Yaakov,[56] where we saw Friedland's house (now a recuperation place) with a beautiful view of the surrounding neighborhood. From there to Naharia,[57] where we spent the night, and where

---

siege of the Jewish sections of the city. Jewish residents of Jerusalem had food ration books, and local grocers kept lists of customers. Arab residents of Jerusalem did not suffer from food or water shortages.

53. It is unclear to which Weizmann he is referring.
54. The "old man" and Chayim were relatives of the Chertoffs in Kfar Vitkin.
55. A moshav is a particular type of cooperative agricultural community. It relies on cooperative purchasing of supplies and marketing of produce, but unlike a kibbutz, farms are individually owned.
56. A town located at the southern end of the Carmel mountain range, overlooking the Mediterranean Sea. Part of the Haifa district, it was founded in 1882 by Baron Edmond James de Rothschild and named after his father (the name means "Jacob's Memorial").
57. A northern coastal city in Israel. It was founded in 1935 as an agricultural village, but for a number of reasons agriculture failed in Naharia and it soon became a tourist destination.

they have one of the Hollywood-style seaside cafes with good music and very impressive outdoor colonnades and soldiers in mufti trying to forget that they're in enemy territory, and playing at being the kids they really are.

From there we went up to Har Meron[58] (the next morning) and saw the grave of Bar Yochai[59] (with the usual palm-crossing for the attendants) and almost all of Palestine from the top of the mountain there. Next year I plan to go there for the *hillulah*.[60] From Meron to Safed, and the old city there, as well as a good meal, and then to Yesod Hamaalah, a very old moshava,[61] and to Hulata, a ten-year-old fishing kibbutz, with very little to show for themselves but a record of hardship and suffering. They've moved on to their new spot now though, and things look brighter.

We were driving along from there, looking for Kfar Blum (the American Habonim[62] joint) when I spotted the Trumpeldor[63] monument to the left and so went in – to [Kibbutz] Kfar Giladi. We spent the night there in the Rest House (Keilah[64] was not around, and one feels like a heel

---

58. A mountain in the upper Galilee containing the grave of Rabbi Shimon bar Yochai and the site of the annual pilgrimage on the 33rd day of the counting of the Omer (the period between Passover and the Feast of Weeks commemorating the giving of the Torah).

59. Rabban Shimon bar Yochai was a sage who lived in the second century, active after the destruction of the Second Temple in 70 CE. He was one of Rabbi Akiva's disciples, and said to be the author of the *Zohar*, the chief work of Kabbalah.

60. Literally this means festivity. It refers to the *yahrzeit*, the anniversary of the death, of Shimon bar Yochai (it has also come to refer to the yahrzeit of any great teacher of kabbala or Chassidut). There is a widely observed custom to visit Shimon bar Yochai's grave on Lag Ba'Omer, and celebrate with torches, song, and feasting. This celebration specifically requested by Rabbi Shimon bar Yochai of his students.

61. Not to be confused with a moshav, a moshava is a small settlement where all land/housing is privately owned. The one Mordecai visited was one of the first settlements of the entire Yishuv, founded in 1883.

62. "The Builders," a Socialist-Zionist cultural youth group originally founded in Great Britain in 1929.

63. See chapter 1, footnote 34.

64. Keilah Hagar Barish, Mordecai's great-aunt.

sponging in a kibbutz that has a guest house) and we took a quick little side trip to Metullah[65] and the Tanur [waterfall].

Yesterday morning we left for Kfar Blum, and actually found the road: we were travelling along the dirt path, slowly, when we were jolted by a rock in the middle of the road which smashed our steering apparatus. Toby went for a cab and went back to Kfar Giladi (which now has a terrific garage) while I sat on the hood of the car exchanging *"marchaba"*[66] with every Arab and his brother – and there must have been at least a thousand who passed me on the way to and from the village and the market-grounds before it. They were very pleasant, and one little four-year-old waved to me and kept grinning at me until her parents took her around the bend, out of sight. And we went back to Giladi, ate, and took a bus to Tiberias. From there to Merhavia,[67] via the whole Emek[68] (Kinnereth,[69] Degania,[70] Bet Alpha,[71] etc.). Regards to Naomi from Caller in Kfar Giladi, and from "Aziz Efendi"[72] – in Merhavia. We split up after Tiberias, with Toby and his wife staying on overnight while I gave the Bar-Adonim a chance to exercise their hospitality. They did, very nicely. They live rather exotically (uncomfortably, that is, with the john way out in the back yard, and no flushing. It's very primitive, and they seem quite delighted with it. Their kid is cute, but nothing to compare with Tultelleh (they have a nice picture of the latter). And the home would be the envy of Greenwich Village

---

65. Town on the border with Lebanon.
66. Arabic greeting – hello, or welcome.
67. Either the kibbutz or moshav.
68. *Emek* means valley – he must be referring to Emek HaYarden, the Jordan Valley.
69. Mordecai could be referring to the lake, the archeological site, the kibbutz or the village, all of the same name.
70. The first kibbutz in Israel, which sits on the banks of the Kinneret.
71. Another kibbutz.
72. Pesach Bar-Adon was a Polish-born archeologist and writer who spent some years living among Bedouins, during which time he took the name Aziz Effendi ("Sir Aziz"). Mordecai is using this name to send greetings to Naomi; in the next sentence he mentions staying with the Bar-Adonim, using the writer's real name. Pesach's wife was Dorothy Kahan, an American-born author.

denizens could they see it. A tremendous room upstairs has only mats and work tables, and it is where they both work. Very comfortable, requires absolutely no housekeeping at all.

I'm still too tired and too excited by the trip to be able to do it justice – from time to time I'll be sending you bits of "adds" on things that happened on the way, and particular things we saw – such as the Arab funeral and the Arab wedding (very little difference between them, really).

...

Love,

Mordecai Shmuel

P.S. I sent Bavli 2 stories and the Bar-Adonim send their love.

When Mordecai left New York for Palestine, he had been at the Jewish Theological Seminary for three-and-a-half years and had completed all the requirements for ordination save one paper, to which he has referred several times in previous letters. Presumably, he had since completed and sent in the paper and was waiting to find out whether it was enough to allow him to graduate in absentia. It must have been, because on June 9, 1947 he received a telegram from his family that reads, simply: "Congratulations Rabbi Chertoff, Love, Family." He had been awarded his rabbinical degree from the Jewish Theological Seminary at their commencement ceremony the previous day, June 8.

Mordecai's father is overjoyed; the day after he sends the telegram, he writes to his newly ordained son:

"This is the day we awaited; we will rejoice and be glad in it."[73] I thought of this verse when Dr. Finkelstein called your name, the first among the graduates, and crowned you all with the crown of: Rabbi, Sermonizer, Teacher. And indeed we have what to be happy and rejoice about! First, we, your parents merited that both of our sons are rabbis of Israel,

---

73. A variation on Psalms 118:24.

the second generation of rabbis, the beginning of a dynasty of rabbis. And that is not something to take lightly! This is the finest pedigree in our nation, the pedigree of Torah. And the second – I don't know whether you will use your title and position of rabbi or not, but whatever will be, you have acquired an important vocation that you can rely on for your livelihood if the need arises. This feeling – that you will be able to draw your livelihood from another field, should you wish to do so – gives you greater security also in the field of literature. Moreover, whatever a person does, not out of need, but rather of his free will, that kind of work gives him pleasure; it is sport and not work. (June 10, 1947)

It is noteworthy that while Paul considers the rabbinate a vocation, he sees it as one to rely on only "if the need arises," viewing it as secondary to a more primary occupation. It is clear that he is not encouraging his son to be a full-time pulpit rabbi.

As the correspondence continues, it becomes clear that Mordecai is both moved and excited by his new status as a rabbi. The low wages received in journalism and the ability to work as a rabbi enter his calculations as he considers his future. His new professional option feeds his increasing doubts about a career in journalism. He seeks an "intellectual life" in which he can ponder ideas and write. He has a romantic image of the rabbinate and is unrealistic about its demands. Over the coming years in Jerusalem, Mordecai will complain, intermittently, of financial matters and of boredom and frustration with journalism. He will seek more rewarding work, consider graduate work in literature and philosophy, and will oscillate between leaving and remaining in Palestine. His frustration and rationalizations will be reflected in his letters, especially those to his sister.

Mordecai's father understands his son very well. In a letter written some months later, he shares his thoughts on the purpose of Mordecai's aliya.

...I must look first at the purpose of your travels to Eretz Yisrael... Certainly you recall that your main purpose was to acquire the Hebrew language so you would command it the way you do English. We had another hope—but an additional one, and not the original—that after you would acquire the language at a high level perhaps you would occupy for yourself a place in the Land and become rooted there... As soon as you made Aliyah, you were accepted as an assistant at the P. P., and after a few weeks, you were promoted to editor. Of course, we were all happy about this job... but we never thought, and certainly neither did you, that this would become your life's work! We believed this was a temporary job until you would become known to the family of authors in the Land and become familiar with the people and institutions who could give you a few hours of work per day so you could support yourself, and the bulk of your time you would devote to studying in university or under the mentorship of some Hebrew author. [October 26, 1947]

The correspondence will continue to reflect Mordecai's indecision about his professional direction as well as the question of leaving or remaining in Palestine.

June 10, 1947

Dear Family,

...I haven't received Cohen's article yet, but I did get a long six page outburst from Robert Graves[74] because of my review of his *King Jesus*.[75] I found the letter at Malkoff, whom I hadn't seen for a few weeks, and it had been there for some time, too long for me to answer it now. Besides, *ain cheshek*.[76] I don't see me getting upset over every angry

---

74. Robert Graves (1895–1985) was a celebrated and prolific British poet, historical novelist, critic, and classicist. His works include memoirs of his early life (including service in the British army in WWI), *Good-Bye to All That*, and the historical novels, *I, Claudius* and *Claudius the God*.

75. Mordecai reviewed Grave's historical novel *King Jesus*, in the April 1, 1947 issue of *Commentary*. It was a critical review (objecting to the author's "total irresponsibility in his handling of Jewish religious tradition") which is presumably why Mordecai subsequently received the six-page outburst from Graves.

76. Hebrew, meaning "can't be bothered."

writer's reaction to a review, and I haven't the tools here for a proper answer – so to hell with him. And I'm too busy now with my censorship article and the UN commission to take the time. Received a lovely note from Samuel, and will see him at Rehovot, with Chaim, on Sunday.

...

Let's finish the send me business right now: (Gershon): ... Also – a copy of Father's book. I want Herzog[77] to read it. (His son and I are hitting it off well – he's quite a guy, and responsible for that Mishna and Commentary in English, which Zeitlin reviewed in the *JQR*. ... and send me *Metamorphosis*[78] too, incidentally. In short: I must become a Kafka expert, see? Then I can do a good job on it, and maybe something for the Hebrew as well. ... Are you interested in Buber[79] on Moses? I'm reading it now, and it seems good. If you want me to, I'll send it on when I'm through. (Just received these books from Sarah Neiman: Ted White,[80] Toynbee,[81] Schauss,[82] *Shock of Recognition*.[83] ... I also sent Bavli two short stories in Hebrew – I wonder what he thinks of them. Shimmy Halkin[84] is due here on Friday – I feel like

77. Ashkenazi chief rabbi of Mandate Palestine, afterwards chief rabbi of Israel, Yitzchak HaLevi Herzog.
78. By Franz Kafka.
79. Martin Buber (1878–1965), Austrian-born Jewish philosopher. He lectured in Germany until Hitler came to power, settling in Jerusalem in 1938, where he became a professor at Hebrew University lecturing in anthropology and sociology.
80. *Thunder out of China*, by Theodore H. White, published in 1946.
81. Arnold J. Toynbee (1889–1975), was a British historian, philosopher of history, and author of many books. He was a widely read scholar and fierce opponent of the Jewish state.
82. He first asked for this book, *The Jewish Festivals, History and Observance* by Hayyim Schauss, in a letter dated March 16, so it took almost three months to arrive.
83. *The Shock of Recognition: The Development of Literature in the United States Recorded by the Men Who Made It*, edited by Edmund Wilson, published in 1943.
84. Simon Halkin (1899–1987), was a novelist, poet, teacher, and translator. Born in Russia, his family moved to America in 1914. He taught Hebrew literature in America, then immigrated to Israel in 1949, becoming head of the department of Modern Hebrew Literature at Hebrew University.

a s**t for not having written, but you know how it goes in the Middle East: we're so poor, financially speaking, and have to be so parsimonious with money we like to feel prodigal in another way, so we spend time like drunken sailors spend money. That's all.

...

Enough *narrishkeit*[85] – I have to get work on my censorship. ... That's all for now – and all my love to all – Rabbi-Foreign-News-Editor.

Mordecai

Below is an article which appeared in *The New Palestine*, a periodical published by the Zionist Organization of America, under Mordecai's pen name, "Shmuel Bar Abba."[86] The article describes the impact of several speeches delivered at the Special Session of the UN which established UNSCOP (the United Nations Special Committee on Palestine). It highlights the favorable stance of the Russians toward the Zionists presented by the Russian representative, Andrei Gromyko, and the speech made by American Zionist leader, Dr. Abba Hillel Silver, who presented Israel's case.

Contemporary readers may be surprised to read of Russia's strong support for the Zionist cause during this period; support that would become even more evident during the vote for partition on November 29, 1947. In the article, Mordecai points out that Russian support for the Jews undermined Britain's claim of the need to appease the Arabs. Dr. Silver was filling in for David Ben-Gurion, who had been delayed, and who spoke on May 12. Silver was a key figure in the mobilization of American support for the founding of the State of Israel.

---

85. Yiddish, meaning nonsense.
86. Shmuel bar Abba (Heb. "Samuel, the son of the father") was a Talmudic sage. Perhaps Mordecai chose him as his pen name as a reference to how close Mordecai felt toward his father.

Echoes of UN in Palestine

By Shmuel Bar Abba
SPECIAL TO THE NEWS REPORTER
June 13, 1947

JERUSALEM – Here in Palestine, we have become so accustomed to the spectacle of fact-finding commissions and royal commissions and Anglo-American commissions (there have already been eighteen such here to quiz and question us), that the idea of a nineteenth was received with hardly more than a disgusted shrug and a fitting sneer at British stalling – and by sporadic increases in underground activity. And were it not for something that happened at Lake Success, we would expect nothing more from a new commission than has appeared from the last – books "telling all" by some of its members, trying to work off the frustration of being ignored by those who commissioned them.

The something that happened was not the invitation by the Political Committee to appear before it, a considerable victory in itself for a small nation grown weary of protesting in vain, nor was it the final resolution of the terms of reference, which excluded the independence clause we battled against and are wide enough to permit investigation even in the DP camps of Europe.

It was Gromyko's speech, which climaxed the Jewish fight at the Session. The speech in itself was an analysis of Jewish plight and right in already familiar terms, and endorsed a Palestine-solution which the Agency itself suggested months ago – before the Congress. It was important not only as the first official Soviet pronouncement on policy, as a repudiation of the Arab claims of Russian support, and as the appearance as a new friend (motives aside) for Zionism, but even more so as evidence of a startling fact: not all the delegates came to the session with their minds made up. The debate meant something; we protested – and for the first time – not in vain.

The reports received here tell us that Mr. Gromyko listened very carefully to the Arab and Jewish spokesmen, and was impressed by both: by the Arab extravagance and by the Jewish sobriety, logic and justice.

British Myth Demolished

A "Sabra," who arrived in New York in time to hear the discussions, wrote that the Jews succeeded "in convincing the Russians that Zionism was not simply a wagon in an imperialist train ... The Arabs, by their own hands, demolished the romantic notions that had been built around their Eastern costumes and their reticence, which had been misinterpreted as diplomatic dignity and reserve. But the biggest myth to be exploded was that on which the cornerstone of British policy had rested, namely, that it was necessary to appease the Arabs in order to prevent them from moving toward Russia."

A former colleague of mine, also in New York at present, wrote me about the man responsible for the Gromyko conversion (and, incidentally, for the friendly Austin statement which it inspired); Dr. Abba Hillel Silver.

The Sabra, an old Shomer Hatzairnik, (and so almost "by definition" opposed to Dr. Silver and sympathetic to the vicious anti-Silver campaign run by his party newspaper)[87] with something of the poet in his makeup, permitted himself

---

87.   Hashomer Hatzair is a socialist-Zionist youth group that was founded in 1913 in Galicia, Austria-Hungary. It was initially Marxist-Zionist, and propounded the belief that Jewish youth should move to Palestine and live on kibbutzim. The group argued for a bi-national state in Palestine. After World War II, Hashomer was involved in the Aliya Bet and many members joined the Haganah and the Palmach. The movement remains active today worldwide. Mordecai may have assumed that the "Old Shomer" would be opposed to Dr. Silver because Silver was a Republican, albeit one who championed the rights of workers and other social causes.

some fancy imagery in his letter, and I include it only
because of its writer's background – it has been well said
that the convert makes the most ardent disciple:

"Yesterday was 'Israel's Day' at the UN. Dr. Silver
spoke before the delegates of the nations of the world, i.e.,
before the world itself. Like at the revelation at Mt. Sinai,
no bird sang and none flew, nor did any bull give voice,
but the whole World kept silent, listening to every word
pronounced by that strong, sweet voice, varying as the
message varied, rising and falling, soothing and arousing
as only he can.

"The impression made was so great as never to be
forgotten. So must William Jennings Bryan have sounded
when he delivered his famous 'Cross of Gold' oration at a
moment far less crucial in a nation's history.

"His worst enemies admit that it was a speech wonderful for content, style, delivery – and effect. It was not
histrionics, it was great public speaking. It was indeed a
great day for us Jews, a victory – may we have many more!"

And the man-in-the-street in Jerusalem, who gets his
news from the Hebrew press and the one English daily, feels
a renewed strength and confidence in the future in spite of
the barbed-wire all around him, in spite of the tanks and
armored cars, in spite of the "identity checks" and arrests
and prison sentences and deportations to Kenya[88] and yes,
in spite even of the shattering midnight executions.

For we have been heard by the world, we have been
listened to very carefully, and England will no longer be
able to ignore world opinion and us, and her obligations
to us in Palestine. And from Jerusalem, let one at least, say,
"Thank you, Dr. Silver."

---

88. Following a series of escapes from the internment camp at Latrun, a number of
internees were deported by the British authorities to various internment camps in
the UK's African colonies. They were kept in camps in what is today Eritrea, the Su-
dan, and Kenya, from 1944 to 1948, released finally only after Israeli independence.

The speech was, indeed, powerful.[89] In it, Abba Hillel Silver reminded those assembled that twenty-five years before World War II and the destruction of European Jewry, the Balfour Declaration had acknowledged the historical connection of the Jewish people to Palestine and "the grounds for reconstituting" the Jewish State. He asserted that the British Mandatory government was now interfering with the right of the Jews to reconstitute their home in Palestine and quoted the 1937 testimony of former British prime minister, David Lloyd George,[90] who admitted that restricting Jewish immigration had "never entered into the head of anyone engaged in framing the policy" of building a Jewish commonwealth. Silver stressed that the Jewish State would not be racial or theocratic, but would be "based upon full equality and rights for all inhabitants without distinction of religion or race and without domination or subjugation." He urged the UN delegates to the Special Session to visit the area and see what the Jews had already achieved:

"The task was enormous: untrained hands, inadequate means, overwhelming difficulties. The land was stripped and poor, neglected through the centuries, and the building took place between two disastrous world wars when European Jewry was shattered and impoverished. Nevertheless, the record of pioneering achievement of the Jewish people in Palestine has received the acclaim of the entire world. And what was built there with social vision and high human idealism has proved a blessing, we believe, not only to the Jews of Palestine, but to the Arabs and to other non-Jewish communities as well."

Silver made sure to remind those listening that there were Arab leaders who had fully supported the Zionist idea:

"That the return of the Jews to Palestine would prove a blessing not only to themselves but also to their Arab neighbors was envisaged by the Emir Feisal, who was a great leader of the Arab peoples, at the Peace Conference following the First World War. On 3 March 1919, he wrote the following, "We Arabs ... look with the deepest sympathy on

---

89.   The text of the speech may be found at goo.gl/HgtAea, and a video clip may be found at https://goo.gl/7v9imx. The video clip is well worth watching.

90.   David Lloyd George (1863–1945) was prime minister of Britain at the time of the Balfour Declaration and an ardent supporter of Zionism.

the Zionist movement. Our deputation here in Paris is fully acquainted with the proposals submitted yesterday by the Zionist Organization to the Peace Conference, and we regard them as moderate and proper. We will do our best, in so far as we are concerned, to help them through; we will wish the Jews a most hearty welcome home.... I look forward, and my people with me look forward, to a future in which we will help you and you will help us, so that the countries in which we are mutually interested may once again take their places in the community of the civilized peoples of the world."

Silver argued that the development of the Jewish homeland would improve the standard of living in the Middle East, and would foster the development of the concepts of social justice and modern scientific method in the Middle East. He made an impassioned entreaty on behalf of the thousands of Jewish refugees still languishing in DP camps in Europe, and concluded by pleading that surely the Jewish people were as entitled to self-determination as any other nation.

Mordecai's article was printed just before UNSCOP arrived in Palestine. The Special Committee had completed the first phase of their work and developed a four-point plan for how to proceed.[91] They would now tour the country and hear from various actors in the conflict and learn about the situation firsthand. They spent five weeks in Palestine and conducted both public and private meetings, even meeting twice with Menachem Begin,[92] head of the (very illegal) Irgun. They then

---

91. "...Upon its arrival in Palestine, the Committee should take the following measures: first, ask the Government of Palestine to furnish factual information on its constitution and functions, together with other relevant data; second, request the Arab and Jewish liaison officers to present observations on this statement; third, make a brief survey of the country; and fourth, conduct hearings." *United Nations Special Committee on Palestine Report to the General Assembly, Volume 1,* Chapter 1 (A) Item 27 (F).

92. Menachem Begin (1913–1992), born in Brest-Litovsk, trained as a lawyer and became head of Polish Betar. When Germany invaded Poland, he fled to Russia, but was arrested by the Soviet authorities for his Zionist activities. He eventually reached Palestine in 1942 with the Polish Free Army, and upon his discharge, he joined the Irgun. After the War of Independence, Begin became the leader of the political party, Herut, and then of its successor, Likud. He led the parliamentary opposition for many years before becoming prime minister of Israel from 1977–1983.

toured Lebanon, Syria, Jordan and displaced persons camps in Germany and Austria. The *Post* carried detailed accounts of their daily activities. Mordecai participated in some of their excursions within Palestine, and includes descriptions in several of his letters below.

June 17, 1947

Dear Family,

All I have heard from you in the last two and half weeks is that I am now a Rabbi. How did it happen, who was there, what was said aside from Macdonald's remark that Rabbis should spend a year in Palestine before getting their degrees, etc. etc. Silverman and Pesach Kraus, both a class below me in the Seminary, arrived together last Friday, and I met them on Jaffa Road looking well and bewildered...

Shertok was funny the other day. We were running a long story of his appearance before the UNSCOP,[93] and he came up to the office, sat himself down at a desk, and "subbed" the galleys of his stuff. ("subbed" means edited). Afterwards, I led him to Agronsky's office, where Zipporah was waiting for him, and went in with them. GA wanted to know how they knew me (he had met me at the Shertok house last Shabbat afternoon) and they brushed him off as though it were unthinkable that they should not know me. My *baal habayit*,[94] incidentally, is one of the hordes who made the pilgrimage to Mt. Scopus to pay their respects to Naomi when she was busy taking in two enemas a day: Dr. Katznelson, of the Kupat Holim.[95]

UNSCOP is a good opportunity for me: I am going to go with them to the Dead Sea and Jericho on Friday, unless they change their plans and don't go. Meanwhile, I'll be

93. The article ran on June 18.
94. Hebrew, meaning "landlord" (literally, master of the house).
95. On their earlier visit to Palestine, Mordecai's sister, Naomi, became ill and was treated by Dr. Katznelson.

attending some of the open sessions. I missed the first, since my press card was not ready. (We get special yellow cards in addition to our little green books).

At a party in Ted Lurie's house the other night – really a *chanukkat habayit*[96] but used as an excuse to invite the press and the powers and spread a little good will and bad likker – an Old Friend repulsed a Man of Distinction: Clifton Daniel (*New York Times*, who looks like a Calvert ad) got no-place with Kepi[97] (*Reuter Press Service* – a British firm – who looked as though she were on her way to the opera). She is living way out in Katamon, a swanky section past Rehavia....

I saw Maurice Sunday. By mistake, I went to the Chief's house instead of the Ziff institute. If you recall, there's a long straight road leading up to the house, and a small house squatting over the road. I came striding up, looking neither to the right nor the left, and was about a yard past the little squatter-house when I heard a rifle-bolt click behind me and a "*slach li*."[98] I turned around to find a rifle-barrel in my stomach, and behind it, a husky looking little Jew-boy. We didn't argue – I identified myself, he went to check on my kashrut, and everything was fine.

...

Love,

Mersh

...P.S. Just received your "commencement" letter. Are you sending <u>Hebrew</u> diploma? Did mother cry? Naomi?

---

96. Hebrew, meaning "house warming" or "dedication of a new house."
97. About whom, much more below.
98. Hebrew, meaning "excuse me" (literally, forgive me).

Frolicking in the Dead Sea with UNSCOP; Mordecai is second from the left
(Photo by Hugo H. Mendelson) [99]

June 30, 1947

Dear Family,

I guess I did forget to tell you how I feel now that I'm a member of the fraternity.[100] You see, I glowed so much around here I must have felt, subconsciously, that you could see it there. However – let me say now that I'm really thrilled, and all day Sunday of the Commencement I kept figuring out what time it was in NY and whether I still was a layman or already a Rabbi. Now I know. I was even a bit afraid to picture the ceremony, since I was not quite sure I was graduating, and until your wire came I was still unsure. Now that I know – and a bit has appeared in the *Palestine Post*, put there by

99. Despite extensive research, I am unable to identify the current copyright holder.
100. Of rabbis.

Agronsky[101] (I'll send it in another letter since no enclosures permitted in this [air letter]) a real cause for worry has disappeared. You see, all is not gravy here: one thing that has been bothering me is that despite the free time I have, I have been able to do very little, since I've been very tired. I've been told that it takes a few months to overcome the need for extra sleep – I'm about due on it now. If it does not pass, it will be time to reconsider my job: I can't see me doing this work only, with no energy for a real intellectual life at the same time.

It's coming slowly, it will have to come much more quickly if this is to be my life. More of this at some later date. Perhaps my extreme depression now is a result of Gershon's cable – I'll get back to that later, after I've told you that I went to the Dead Sea with the Commission, and then to the Negev with them too. Both trips are written up in the *Post*, and I'll send you copies in a day or two. There is a lot left out of them, of course for many reasons, but I haven't the *nachat ruach*[102] now to fill them in. Some other time, perhaps. Incidentally, I am still acting foreign editor, and will be until we hear something definite from my predecessor. And I need my diploma so that I can register at the Hebrew University as a research student,[103] and get back about $200 of my deposit with them. I'll write to the Student Body, mainly because I've been misquoted, and because I think they should know what is going on here. Indiscriminate killing is not justified, regardless of the provocation or the goal. We Jews are the last bastion of morality and ethics in the world, if we capitulate what can we expect from the goy? ...I just received a note from Frisch with *The New Palestine* and SBA's article.[104] Who is the guy? Not bad at all. There should be another soon, signed by MSC. And I hope to do some UN stuff, real stuff, very soon (as soon as I shake

---

101. Not found
102. Hebrew for "peace of mind."
103. Mordecai entered Palestine on a student visa and must maintain that appearance.
104. His own Shmuel Bar Abba article, reproduced above.

this depression) – I've met Gerold Frank[105] and Victor Bernstein[106] here – both very nice guys, and Bob Miller, a terrific *UP* man, one of the best journalists in the US.

... And my dear sister: I sold out, as you so vulgarly put it,[107] to father's impression of the UN meeting and Silver at it. You, with your high connections, never let me know what's going on anyway, how can I know when I've gotten hold of the wrong end of the stick? However, I now believe that the UNSCOP will produce, for us, pure s**t, and shall write a piece saying so, in spite of Silver and in spite of Gromyko. And I'll thank you to put the evidences of my early indiscretions – all of them – some place where I can find them someday and utilize them for legitimate fictional purposes. Don't be a stinker!

In the next page of this letter I shall comment on Naomi's and Monroe's plan for settling in Palestine, as well as upon the subject of Gershon's very foolish wire. I had the impression that as Rabbi and a responsible writer, foreign editor, etc., etc., I might be credited with some sense, and I resent the family alarm as an insult to me and to my *saichel*.[108]

The "very foolish wire" sent by Gershon, and the "frantic cables" from his parents to which Mordecai refers in his next letter, express the family's strenuous disapproval of the relationship that had developed between Mordecai and a woman whom we will call "Kepi."[109] Kepi and

---

105. Gerold Frank (1907–1998,) was a Jewish-American author and ghostwriter. He was a war correspondent in the Middle East during World War II. His best-known book was *The Boston Strangler*.
106. Victor H. Bernstein (1904–1992), journalist and foreign correspondent known for his coverage of the Nuremberg trials. Bernstein was foreign editor of *PM*. He wrote *The Final Judgment*, an account of the Nuremberg trials, in 1947.
107. Apparently, Mordecai's sister, Naomi, did not share her brother's enthusiasm for Dr. Silver. On June 20, 1947, she wrote, "You should be crucified. At least you sold out for Silver – I think your article reeked with Silver idolatry – My only hope is that you make it pay well."
108. Yiddish, meaning "intelligence."
109. To save her family any possible discomfort as a result of this disapproval, I have decided to omit identifying details.

Mordecai had a relationship that began in the US and either resumed or continued in Palestine. The family apparently received reports from people returning from Palestine about Mordecai and "his girlfriend."

"Kepi"

Kepi grew up in a small town in Massachusetts, in a traditionally religious, non-Zionist family. She eventually graduated from a prestigious university in 1949. The relationship with Mordecai presumably ended in the fall of 1947, when Kepi returned to America to continue her studies. It is unclear from the correspondence why the family thinks she is unsuitable, but that is clearly what they think. In addition to the cables, there are multiple, long letters from each member of the family urging Mordecai to break off the relationship. Gershon even writes a cautionary tale of a man whose career is ruined as a result of an improper match.

I have had the pleasure of getting to know various members of Kepi's family, especially her daughter. They have been very helpful in furthering my understanding of my father "as a young man," as well as the attitude of some American Jews toward the Zionist enterprise. They were open in explaining to me that Kepi's later life was troubled. Perhaps my father's family anticipated potential problems in the future and wanted to make sure that the relationship did not turn into something permanent. Alternatively, their disapproval may have derived from the intimate nature of the relationship; perhaps they thought it inappropriate for a future rabbi, or that it reflected negatively on Kepi. In addition, if I am reading the correspondence correctly, Mordecai was enjoying an intimate relationship with Kepi while his marriage proposal to Hadassah remained outstanding. This may also have contributed to the family's attitude. The fact that Mordecai is virtually silent about Kepi in his letters (until later) suggests that he is well aware of their disapproval.

Mordecai's father is distressed by his son's frustration with his work and its lack of intellectual fulfilment. In a letter dated July 17, Paul writes:

In your letters you touched on important issues of interest to you and to the nation of Israel. Take the question about your future employment, whether you should make literature your life's work. This is a weighty and complicated question. I'll tell you the truth, this question has troubled me, and continues to trouble my mind for some [time]. Our sages said that *sofrim*, authors, are poor. In truth, they meant *sofrei Stam*[110] but the truth is that it relates to modern authors as well. And it's difficult for me to make peace with the idea that you could remain poor your entire life. On the other hand, to return to America and work in the rabbinate and also in literature, you'd have to leave the Land and return to the Diaspora and my life's dream, as you know, was that our family would finally settle in the Land. This is the question—but I think that a big part of the solution depends on the solution of the question of Eretz Yisrael in general. If we are to have sovereignty[111] in Eretz Yisrael, or even in just a part of it, the look of things will

---

110. Men who copy Torah scrolls, *tefillin*, and *mezuzot*. The Hebrew word "*sofer*" means both author and scribe. Scribes of holy texts are called "*sofrei stam*," *stam* being an acronym of *sefer Torah*, *tefillin*, and *mezuzot*.

111. The Hebrew says "*melukha*," which literally means "kingship" but is also used to refer to government.

change and new and various opportunities will arise for a young man like you. Therefore, now is not the time at all to search for a solution to the question of your life's work...

At the same time he is proud of his son's condemnation of the Irgun (Etzel):

Mordecai my dear, the more pleasant impression that your letter made on me is the assumption in your letter regarding the Etzel, in other words, your statement that the nation of Israel is the single bastion of morality and good attributes left in the world, and we have no right to create breaches in it! How correct are these words of yours and how dear to me are these feelings and ideas of yours! Whenever I think about your words I am proud and say how lucky I am that I raised a son like this for the people of Israel!

July 1, 1947

Dear Family,

To continue, from yesterday: I imagine there must be a lot that Monroe can do here to live comfortably, as Naomi says, although why she and Monroe should be any different from the rest of us I don't know. The point is that the only thing that pays a decent sum here is business, wages are all low and when they supply the one income, very inadequate if one wants to live as in New York. For example: I get 45 LP per month, plus a 12% cost-of-living increase, which brings it up to 50, plus. Minus taxes and a few other little items which the Yishuv extracts, I receive about 37 LP per month. Of this 10 goes to rent, which leaves me 27 (or about $100) per month for food, clothes, books, entertainment, travel, etc. etc. etc. – not very much.

My rent is for one room, of course, but for an apartment it would be much more, out of proportion to the added number of rooms. And I may add that the *Palestine Post* pays "well," compared to other institutions, firms, etc. In business, of course, there is no limit. You can even build yourself a fabulous house like Zananiri's[112] in Jerusalem and have as your biggest worry whether to use the new Buick, the new Studebaker or the new motorcycle. But that does not happen to everybody.

All the men in my field hold at least two jobs, some three. Almost all the women work. When they don't – such as Ted Lurie's wife, who is burdened with two wonderful kids – the husband has still another job (if he can get it. Ted has the *Post*, CBS short-wave broadcasting and some South African paper). I have no idea what there is in the Maritime field – why not write Meerovitch[113] and ask him. I can see him the next time I go to Tel Aviv (for some swimming and to see Davidowitz) but what good it will do I have no idea. However – come out, by all means, and at least see the country before you make up your mind (to Monroe, this line is) and at the same time you can see what's here for you.

NOW – please let's not have any more of these frantic cables. Ridiculous as its cause, its content upset me so that I couldn't sleep worrying about Father, and consequently had a hell of a time trying to do my work properly. Nobody is destroying anything or anybody. Kepi came to Palestine on her own, got herself a job, an apartment, and [is] well-organized. I have made no commitments, and neither has she – she may even be leaving at the end of the year to finish [college]. We are both working very hard and have little time for mutual destruction anyway. On some nights off I go to Tel Aviv, on others I stay in Jerusalem and go out with

---

112. Owner of "Zaniri," a housewares store established in Jerusalem in 1936. It moved to Amman, Jordan in 1951.
113. Manashe Meerovitch (1860–1949), was a noted agronomist and activist in the BILU, a movement dedicated to the agricultural settlement of the Land of Israel. He wrote several books about Palestine. He was nicknamed, "The Last of the BILU," as he was reputed to be the only member of that early Zionist group to see the foundation of the State of Israel.

her – I haven't met anyone else, incidentally. And that's all I have to say on the matter.

(11:45 – there goes the bloody siren. Wait...12: a blast someplace in Rehavia, but you'll know long before you get this letter what your friends in the IZL or Stern Gang have pulled. I must get to work now.)

Shalom u'veracha – and don't be so foolish.

Love – Mordecai Shmuel

In the above letter, Mordecai explains his financial situation. He writes that his net salary per month is 37 LP (Palestine Pound, also called the "Lira") and his rent is 10 LP (for one room). The Palestine Pound (and, from 1947, the Israeli Lira) was pegged to the British pound Sterling at 1 LP = 1 BP (and remained so until 1954).[114] Converting his salary to dollars,[115] Mordecai took home $166.50 month and paid $45/month in rent ($1,780 and $500 respectively in 2017 dollars).[116] A rough comparison of his situation to that of a journalist in New York at the time would have shown expenses to have been about the same, but with income being significantly more in the US – a situation that persists to today in Israel. Later, serving as an IDF soldier after the declaration of the state, Mordecai's salary will be 2 LP/month, approximately a fifth the cost of his rent! It is no wonder that he will not be able to make ends meet.

The following letter traverses a wide range of Jewish attitudes toward the establishment of a Jewish state, some of which were reflected in testimony Mordecai hears from speakers at the UNSCOP hearings. Those speakers included, among many others, Ben-Gurion, Chaim Weizmann, Moshe Shertok (Sharett), and Judah Magnes. Ben-Gurion, Weizmann and Shertok we know were "typical" Jewish Zionists, pursuing the dream of a Jewish state, while Magnes favored the creation of a bi-national state, and the "*peyah* Jews" presumably Chassidim, opposed the creation of a Jewish state utterly, unless it was through an act of God following the arrival of the Messiah.

---

114. In 1980 Israel switched to the Israeli shekel (IS) and in 1985 to the "New" Israeli Shekel (NIS).
115. https://www.uwyo.edu/numimage/currency.htm.
116. https://www.measuringworth.com/uscompare.

July 15, 1947

Dear Family,

This may sound somewhat ungrateful, but I must ask mother to spare me the ordeal of having to read her hand-writing on the back of a typed letter: One side interfered with the other and makes reading very difficult.

UNSCOP: I've traveled with them, I've heard Benny, Chaim, Shertok, Magnes and the Communists testify, I've watched them at the hearings and listened to the questions. The least we shall get from them is *kadoches*[117] on toast, the most – a bi-national state. They were very much impressed by Magnes,[118] who, while supposedly giving testimony and presenting a brief, behaved in the usual rabbinical manner, drawing from the well of his wisdom and giving them to drink of the cooling draught. He did not testify, he preached, and each time he breathed the word "parity" – with all the passion he could muster, like some guys I know who invoke Freud (and the way Jung invokes God – and you can mentally see him spelling it G-d for greater sanctity) – I half expected a *bat kol*[119] to answer "amen," or at least a halo to settle around his head (I would prefer a halo around his neck, rather snug too). Speaking of halos – sitting up in the press gallery, Ben Gurion's white hair framing a red, bald expanse of top-of-the-head did look just like one. Only a few Jews stand to benefit from the inquiry – we journalists, who re-saw the country at their expense, riding in comfort-able '47 Hudson's and Studebakers. But that seems silly now, with martial law in Netanya.

---

117. Yiddish, meaning "fever."
118. Judah Leon Magnes (1877–1948), prominent Reform Rabbi in both the US and Mandatory Palestine. He was a leader in the pacifist movement during WWI, and an advocate of a bi-national Jewish-Arab state in Palestine. Needless to say, Mordecai was no fan.
119. Hebrew, meaning "heavenly voice."

...Gershon and Naomi: I see that even the ZOA has come out anti-terror...and you, son, are very naive to think that it makes any diff at all whether UNSCOP is here or not when British soldiers are shot. I may add that as a full member of the Chertoff *Bet Din*[120] I protest against one member's apparent complete disregard for questions of morality and ethics, and recall to him the Rabbis comments concerning *"mitzva ha ba'ah be'averah."*[121] The only conceivable defense for them would lie in a claim of selective shootings – that there was even an attempt to knock off the bastards, (like Conquest, the CID chief in Haifa who met a bloody end)[122] and not to pick on youngsters who have no idea of what it is all about. Incidentally, don't believe that s**t about the Bergsonists parachuting refugees into the country. As we say in Hebrew (translation for your convenience) – neither forest nor bears![123]

...

Official Communique from me to you, insisted upon by the object of your – and Father's – displeasure: "Tell him there is and will be nothing between us."[124] It was said seriously, deliberately, and not simply as a stop-gap or appeasement line.

---

120. Hebrew, meaning "court of law."
121. An obligation (related to Jewish ritual or otherwise) which is fulfilled only through committing a violation (for example, paying taxes or buying matza with stolen money) is not considered acceptable by the rabbis.
122. A. E. Conquest, head of the Criminal Investigation Department in the city of Haifa, was killed by two young Jews believed to be members of the Lehi in downtown Haifa on April 25, 1947.
123. In Hebrew, the expression is *"lo dubim v'lo ya'ar."* The intended meaning is that something didn't happen; there isn't a shred of truth to it. It derives from a Talmudic discussion of a verse in Kings II. The prophet Elisha was traveling between Jericho and Bet-El when a large gang of children appeared and mocked him. He cursed the children, upon which two bears came out of a wood and killed forty-two of them. The Talmudic discussion revolves around whether the appearance of the bears was a miracle or the appearance of both bears and forest was a miracle. The second opinion was that there had been no forest or bears in the area until Elisha cursed the children – hence the expression, "no bears and no forest."
124. That is, Kepi tells Mordecai to tell his father that there is nothing between them.

So relax. (I'm still waiting for an answer from Hadassah[125] to my last letter – has Frisch said anything himself?)

...

That's all for now – I want to retype my answer to Cohen. Send me a few Max Lerner[126] editorials on the Truman Plan and the Parts Talks, on Russia and the Marshall Plan – pretty please?

...Shalom u'vracha, and all my love,

mersh

(oops – I mean Rabbi M).

This letter once again reflects Mordecai's abhorrence for the Irgun and Lehi. His comment to his siblings suggests that they were critical of the timing of Jewish terrorist attacks (i.e., while UNSCOP is present) rather than the fact of such attacks. In spite of his antipathy to the British, Mordecai remained sympathetic toward the British "youngsters," i.e., young soldiers, "who have no idea what it is all about" and absolutely disapproved of terrorist activity against them.

As we will see, Mordecai's pessimism about UNSCOP's deliberations will prove to be misplaced. In their thorough final report, published on September 1, the main recommendation was to partition Palestine into separate Jewish and Arab states – exactly what the Zionists had hoped for. This is discussed at length below.

Wednesday, July 23, 1947

Dear Family,

There is an unfortunate time-lag between incidents here and your receipt of my description of them where you

---

125. Hadassah Frisch, who lived in the US but traveled abroad frequently with her father, Daniel Frisch, the president of the ZOA.
126. Max Lerner (1902–1992), was an American journalist and educator known for his syndicated column in the *New York Post*. He wrote several influential books.

are. Last night, for instance, there was a lot of shooting.[127] It
sounded like the end of the world; Purim[128] and 4th of July
to the nth power – and all the casualties were a girl grazed
in the leg by a bullet and a few people scratched by flying
glass. Why there were so few is very simple: "Can you see a
target?" "No, but we keep shooting, maybe we'll hit something." (Overheard near an armored car on Saturday night).
Added to that, they were just shooting into the air last night.
I was going to work, walking along at a comfortable pace,
when I heard a few shots, and the sirens. I judged distance
and direction, and saw that my way was not blocked. Realizing that there would be no going out to eat (and not too
happy with the stuff our canteen guy makes) I dropped in
and bought a kilo of grapes and wended my way along JNF
road,[129] then down King George, watching the army cars
rushing past me and the people rushing towards me, back to
Rehavia. On King George a girl came running up to me – can
I get her to Bet Hakerem right away, she has to pack so as to
able to leave for Haifa and sail for America tomorrow on the
Carp. We discussed it for a while, and then she dropped in,
on Ben Yehudah [street], to an aunt's house. I started down
the street and saw soldiers at the end of it, so I turned right
around and into that house where I sat tight, eating open
sandwiches and drinking tea, until the all-clear sounded,
when I went back to work. And so, through a couple of hundred rounds of pointless shooting, I met a very pretty little
sabra (this one's sister). My "hostess," incidentally, will drop
in on you or at least give you a ring, when she arrives. Her
name is Aviva Halaban[130] (her pop's in The Agency, where, I

127. He probably means Saturday night, July 20. There was rioting over the *Exodus*
refugees and the *Post* reported heavy gunfire. Several firebombs were thrown at
British vehicles. The refugee ship the *Exodus* was discussed in the preface and will
be discussed further, below.
128. A Jewish holiday which celebrates the deliverance of the Jews from the villain
Haman in ancient Persia, as recounted in the Book of Esther. It is characterized
by a festive atmosphere, costumes, feasting, and drunkenness.
129. Today known by the JNF's Hebrew name, Keren Kayemet LeYisrael Street.
130. She became a well-known Israeli operatic soprano, frequently performing in the US.

don't know). Of course by now last night's farce is old stuff, and there are a few more to talk about (they always shoot at the water tanks, so that they drip and people sit helplessly in their houses, hearing the precious water run out and unable to go up on the roof and plug the holes.

And that's all for this bulletin. Here's something that must be done immediately: Mother – write a letter to Shulamith Kaznelson,[131] 10 Rashbah, Jerusalem (Rehavia – where I'm living) inviting her to live at our house in NY. This will enable her to get an American visa – she wants to study psych in the States for a year. Her father is the Kupat Holim big-shot, but she still needs her maintenance "guaranteed." Mention that since I'm living here, you want her there, etc. You know how to do it so that the goyim at the Consulate here will say yes. And please do it immediately, since these things take time. They've been very nice to me here, and in spite of the smallness of the room, have made me very comfortable (I can even use their pots and dishes, let alone the Frigidaire, telephone, perpetual hot-water, etc.). And it's a little thing for an unfortunate family, with a son[132] moldering away in Kenya and his wife languishing here (married six months!). So please – do it immediately.

...

---

131. Shulamith Katznelson (1919–1999) did study in the United States, although I don't know whether my family played a part in getting her there. She pioneered the idea of learning language through immersion. In 1951 she founded the private language school Ulpan Akiva in Netanya, where Jews learn Arabic, and Arabs, Hebrew. Some eighty thousand people from 148 countries have attended its courses. The instructors include Jews, Christians, Muslims and Druze. Students have included President Chaim Herzog and Defense Minister Moshe Ahrens. Katznelson was awarded the Israel Prize in 1986, and was nominated for the Nobel Peace Prize in 1992, and again in 1993.

132. Shmuel Katzenelson (latter Tamir) (1923–1997) went on to become a leading politician in Israel, serving as Minister of Justice in the government of Menachem Begin.

      And that's all for now – I have some work I must do. Did you get the editorial I wrote? NU?

Love to all --

P.S. – a buzz from the office – the boys just blew-up the *Empire Rival* in Haifa Bay,[133] after the last refugee had disembarked...

---

133. Mordecai probably means the *Empire Lifeguard*, which was sunk on July 24 in Haifa. The British Troopship, *Empire Rival*, was blown up in Haifa Bay by "swimming saboteurs using limpet mines" on August 21, 1946 (reported in *Lewiston Evening Journal* and *Lawrence Journal-World*). The *Empire* ships were used to transport illegal immigrant refugees back to Europe or Cyprus.

Chapter 6
The Sergeants Affair

J uly 1947 was an extremely eventful month for Palestine and the Yishuv. As described above, Israeli officials, including David Ben-Gurion, Moshe Shertok, Eliezer Kaplan,[1] and Chaim Weizmann, along with a number of rabbis representing a range of organizations and religious orientations, addressed UNSCOP; the *Exodus 1947*,[2] as well as several other ships carrying refugees, were intercepted; there were numerous attacks on British soldiers, and curfews were instituted in Haifa, Netanya and Jerusalem. The country's most destabilizing incident, however, was the widely condemned "Sergeants Affair," which Mordecai discusses in the following letter.

---

1. Eliezer Kaplan (1891–1952), Zionist activist, Israeli politician, signatory of Israel's declaration of Independence, and the country's first minister of finance and deputy prime minister.
2. Discussed at length in the preface, the *SS Exodus 1947* carried 4,500 Jewish refugees from Europe but was intercepted by the British off the coast of Palestine. The ship was escorted back to Europe but the refugees refused to disembark anywhere but Palestine. After two months at sea, under strict British control, the refugees were forced to disembark in Germany where they were placed in camps. The last of the *Exodus* refugees finally reached Israel in January of 1949, eight months after the establishment of the state.

The affair began on July 12 when the Irgun kidnapped two British Army Intelligence Corps NCOs, Sergeant Clifford Martin and Sergeant Mervyn Paice. But its roots were planted earlier – with the capture of three Irgun members – Avshalom Haviv, Meir Nakar and Yaakov Weiss – during the Acre Prison Break of May 4. They had been tried and convicted of illegal possession of arms and for having intent to kill or harm a large number of people. For Palestinian Jews under the British mandate, these crimes carried the death penalty. Despite many appeals for clemency, including by the UNSCOP committee – the three had not actually harmed anyone – they were due to be executed at the end of the month.

The Irgun threatened to kill the two sergeants they had kidnapped if the death sentences were carried out. This tactic had worked once before; in 1946, captured Irgun fighters Michael Ashbel and Yosef Simchon had been sentenced to death, but when six British officers were kidnapped and the threat of reprisal killings was made, their sentences were commuted to life imprisonment – and the British officers were released.

The Irgun was acting alone; the Jewish Agency described the kidnapping of the sergeants as a provocation. The Haganah even cooperated with the British in trying to locate the kidnapped sergeants. The men had been kidnapped in Netanya and the British put a cordon around the city and the twenty settlements surrounding it, and began an extensive search effort. The area was placed under martial law and almost 1,500 people were interrogated, but to no avail.

On July 27, it was announced that the order had been given to carry out the executions of the Irgun members on the 29th. In contravention of official policy, the executions were to be carried out in secret, instead of publicly, and the families of the men were not permitted to visit beforehand. As a result, the superintendent of the prison refused to carry out the executions and was relieved of his duties. The men were executed in the early hours of the 29th of July and buried on the 30th.

Later that same day, the booby-trapped bodies of the two British sergeants were found hanging in a eucalyptus grove near Netanya. Mordecai heard this news during the writing of the following letter.

July 30, 1947

Dear Family,

Gershon is a good boy; he's written some nice long letters, and sent some nice books (which I now expect daily). That he's forgotten *the New Yorker* I can forgive him.[3] As for decisions – how can one decide anything in Palestine today? We are counting a new *sefira*[4] here – how many days will pass since the latest triple murder[5] before the boys blow up, and really make trouble. Since the hangings, there's been one hand grenade thrown, an incident hardly worth mention. The big question is – will IZL kill the two kidnapped sergeants (one of whom is really a friend). The deed would undoubtedly provoke martial law, or at least provide the excuse for it, their release would, at least, postpone the trouble everybody expects. That it would not change the British policy is almost an unnecessary observation to make. Martial law in all of (Jewish) Palestine would mean a breakdown of our economy, and would set us back many years.

OOPS – I better keep away from prophecy – the bodies of the two have just been found, with the government claiming that they were tortured (a damn lie, that's not IZL style, say what you will about them – although they should have snatched Farran,[6] and given him the works for the Rubowitz business, instead of two guys whose mother's milk was still on their chins). However, they did what they did, and the latest rumour is a 2-hour "spree" to be allowed

---

3. It seems Gershon gave his younger brother a pep talk. In response to a letter that is lost, in which Mordecai apparently called himself just a "good bullsh***er" with no real talent, his brother wrote to reassure him that he was truly talented and that Agronsky called him "undeniably brilliant." He listed others who thought highly of Mordecai. Insecurity and the need for reassurance are recurring themes in the correspondence. Gershon then adds a request for more editorials.
4. Hebrew, meaning "counting." "New" because the *omer*, the period of counting the days from Passover to Shavuot, had ended not long before.
5. Referring to the execution of the three Irgun fighters captured during the Acre Prison Break.
6. The Farran affair is discussed at length below.

the soldiers, in which to retaliate. Fortunately, by the time you get this letter, today will be a thing of the past, and you won't have a chance to worry over it. It may be just another one of those rumours, of course, in which Palestine, and particularly Jerusalem, abounds.

UNSCOP in Beirut was covered by our local man, who spent all his time phoning us to give us his stories, there wasn't much fun to the trip. Besides, we're all pretty sick of the whole farce anyway, and nobody here expects any good from them. They count for little that they couldn't even delay the latest triple-murder ("execution") or help the *Exodus* exiles in any way. And now Bevin... accuses *us* of not wanting to abide by the UN decision! Of all the unbounded gall!

Send me a copy of Danny's interview – let's see what's being said about censorship – my favorite subject. When I have time, I'll finish the article on it that I'm doing.

And, my dear brother, there is little discussion of anything on a high level in *Davar* either, the paper has slipped way, way down. I'm not paying *Post* postage, so I'll keep sending them, since I think you're interested in seeing how a local paper handles the news, and how much we have to leave out, etc. The chief is in NY now – let Naomi pull the strings for an autographed photo. ...

And now for a really wonderful, welcome letter from Naomi, which, although it covered what Gershon had previously written, was great to read anyway: *Mazal tov, v'chol tuv*![7] That sounds like a wonderful break for Monroe, and the beginning of a really good thing.[8] How he did it I can't imagine (not how he got the break; that part I should expect, but how he got in to see the right guy, in order to be able

7. Hebrew, meaning "congratulations and all the best."
8. The letter described the job that her husband, Monroe, had just been offered in Cleveland, in the textile industry. This launched his life-time occupation.

to turn on the charm, etc., and get himself in). *Bravo, bra-vissimo*! (As the kids here would put it – "*Eisen*!"[9])

The ship, the *Exodus '47* – ! We were stunned here, and when the Haganah blew up the radar stations, it served to let off steam for all of us. Not enough, of course, but then what can one do, really? Someday I'll give you a description of Jerusalem, with its military and police and tanks, etc. It's a very, very quiet city, really.

My frequent protestations, my dear sister, are directed, for the most part, not to Father, but to you: in spite of his system of bookkeeping,[10] I receive only the letters you write, and there have been precious few of those.

...As for rapes in the holy land – I could tell you a gory story about some foreign correspondents and a girl in the back of an Arab cab, and the fight the Arabs of that company started over the public exhibition the stalwart CBS correspondent gave, and how he was almost fired for it, but I don't want to shock you. If I wanted to, I could tell you about the UNSCOP in Beirut, where they went hunting after having been browned off by Ted Lurie here (they asked for a red light district, and he said: what do you want that here for, you're going to the most notorious country in the world for that, Beirut is all red) and what spectacles they made of themselves, drinking and running after women in the native quarters, but I don't want to shock you. So there. Besides, I know that scandal does not interest you, least of all Naomi.

My own plans: to stick to the *Post* for the present, and see: GA may come across with the weekly he's planning, or the air-mail edition, which would be wonderful: good hours, shorter, and more time for me. Or – I'm applying for a ZOA fellowship, if I get it I may stop working and really go back to study for a year, and then see. For the present, no change is at all advisable, even if only for security reasons: (that

---

9. Yiddish for the metal "iron."
10. For keeping track of the correspondence with Mordecai (described in preface).

little green book[11] is almost armor-plate). I'm comfortable where I am, the family is very nice to me, very friendly (I came in 4:30 the other morning, we did a *mishmar*[12] waiting for news of the hangings, and Dr. K[13] woke up when I came in. I gave him the news – he worries just like Father – and we sat down to coffee in the kitchen, after which – about 7:30, I went to sleep, and slept almost all day).

It's up to you Jews in America now, to get a decent political break. Nothing can be done from here, the government has proven itself a thousand times over as beyond all consideration for the peace and good of the country, if at the same time it means a break for the Jews. They're cutting off our noses to spite everybody's faces. The stupidity of their approach and the knowledge of it does not help us very much – sometimes it isn't so easy to laugh – and thinking about it, I find that I'm much more serious than I've been before now, like everybody else, I think I smile less, and know that I joke far less.

...

I'm quitting here, so that I can mail these together. So long for now, and all my love to everybody – I miss you all, I suppose it's to be expected...

Love,

Mersh

By the end of this mostly informative and chatty letter, it is apparent that Mordecai is being affected by the tension and violence in the country, as well as by the political machinations. The sense of helplessness he feels is palpable. Intensely empathic, Paul internalizes and seems to personally experience his son's periods of despair. He writes:

---

11. His press credentials.
12. Hebrew, meaning "vigil."
13. Dr. Reuven Katznelson.

...it was not pleasant for me to read in your letter that your special quality, the quality of a man with a smiling countenance, a shining face, has been transforming into a disposition of despair and worry ... besides the fact that worry breaks the body of a person (and I see this on my own flesh), you know that "the divine spirit does not dwell in a place of sadness," but only in a place of happiness.[14] You are the child of a family of Hasidim,[15] and you must awaken the Hasid in you, the happiness and confidence of the Hasid. Ultimately, the worries, and the decrees, and the troubles will pass, they are temporary because "the Glory of Israel will not lie"[16] and that which was promised to us will be fulfilled and we should not abandon eternal life for the worries of the moment.

The killing of the two sergeants was widely condemned in both Palestine and the UK. Yishuv officials denounced the murder of the two innocents. The head of the Netanya council, Oved Ben Ami, called it a despicable crime that defiled the war of liberation. And as Mordecai predicted, the reaction from the British was not long in coming. Whether the soldiers were truly allowed a two hour "spree" as Mordecai claims, or they simply erupted in rage, on the evening of July 31, the day after the sergeants' bodies were found, groups of British policemen and soldiers rampaged through Tel Aviv, breaking shop and bus windows, overturning cars and attacking Jewish pedestrians. The rioters were joined by British mobile police units in armored vehicles. They shot at two buses, killing four Jews and injuring others. They detonated a grenade in one café, and tried to abduct someone from another but were beaten back. The British military, supposedly meant to protect civilians, killed five Jews and wounded fifteen. Some policemen were punished, but no criminal charges were ever brought.

---

14. Babylonian Talmud, *Shabbat* 30b.
15. This was news to me!
16. I Samuel 15:29.

The reaction in Britain to the hangings was also severe. Despite an outpouring of condemnation and shame from Anglo-Jewry, anti-Jewish riots began in England on August 1. In numerous locations throughout the UK, synagogues and Jewish-owned shops were attacked and burned, and anti-Semitic signs and slogans were widespread. The rioting was most intense in Liverpool; it lasted five days and over three hundred Jewish properties were damaged.

Mordecai refers to these events in the next letter, a passionate expression of the profound contempt he clearly feels for the Irgun and for what he considers its unethical methods, as well as the growing disgust and rage he feels toward the British. He seems to feel squeezed between these two actors. While he sympathizes with the aims and motivations of the Jewish terrorist organizations, he nevertheless rejects their methods and worries about their future influence on the emerging Jewish, democratic state. Begin's decision to hang the seargents is sometimes represented as tragic rather than as unethical. But, it should be noted, the tactic worked – the British conducted no more hangings. Nevertheless, Mordecai is increasingly shocked and enraged by the behavior of the British who feigned evenhandedness but clearly favored the Arabs.

Aug. 4, 1947, 12:46 am!

Dear Gershon,

Youz is a good boy! Your little note from my friends on the corner of Broadway and 111th[17] was very welcome indeed – it seems I just can't make ends meet (a book or a pair of sandals is beyond my budget). I just received a batch of letters – from you, father, mother, Naomi – all such lovely people!

I guess I'll have to bow to your superior numbers – and judgment, as to my ability,[18] and indulge in a little self-love...

---

17. In 1947, there was a bank on that corner.
18. A reference to the pep talks he received from various members of his family in response to his self-criticism.

But my dear brother, you don't seem to absorb what I say about the Irgun and its pals: It's like dis: (this might even mean edit[orial])

As Jews, our attitude towards the Irgun and the Stern gang must be determined — or should be, anyway — by yea olde saying of the Rabbis — which I quoted some time ago.[19] As long as we adhere to a moral criterion, there is no question of condoning their acts. On the other hand, should we be purely pragmatic about it, and ignore the ethical issue, we will eventually come to the same decision, for a number of reasons. First, the question of the Yishuv itself. If we build our state on the Irgun, we'll have them always with us — a consummation devoutly to be avoided, since no *fascist* (and you can consult any dictionary on the meaning of that word) group can possibly be considered a beneficial element. Just today they killed a cashier while robbing Barclays Bank in Haifa; a few days ago it was the horrible affair of the two sergeants (horrible if only because of the booby-trapping of the bodies,[20] an old Nazi stunt, if my veteran brother[21] recalls aright), a very simple instance of wanton murder, with no semblance of justice behind it, no possible excuse for the deed. Encouraging such an element in our midst means their entrenchment and permanence — our own little underworld, to make the little Jewish State complete! As for its effect on the British — just think of Tel Aviv, last Thursday night, and let me tell you of the spate of letters we've received, swearing vengeance for the hanging. The effect on English public opinion may be seen very

---

19. Probably *"mitzva haba'a be'avera"* – "a good deed that comes from a violation" (derived from Isaiah 61:8), i.e., that positive results are not a justification for illigitmate methods.
20. When the Irgun strung the bodies of the sergeants up in a forest clearing near Netanya, they buried an anti-personnel mine in the ground below. It exploded when the bodies were being removed, blowing the body of Sergeant Martin to pieces and wounding the captain cutting it down.
21. Gershon served as a chaplain in Europe during WWII.

concretely – the riots in Liverpool, *lemashal*.[22] Must I go on? Oh yes, I may add that they are not the great patriots you imagine them to be. Many are drawn from the same kind of slum which produces the NY gangster, and while some are, of course, honestly motivated, they certainly can't be considered "good" citizens, not by any stretch of the imagination. Did I write you that there was a regular schedule of payments for different kinds of *pe'ulot*[23] which the "professional" arm carries out? The youngsters they get come in wide-eyed, and then must remain lest they be turned in to the authorities – a neat kind of blackmail. And they send them to their death with no compunction – witness the death of the kid sent to "attack" the RAF billet in Jerusalem last Friday[24] – with not a chance of getting out of it alive. They're a bunch of murderers, son, and see that you have no truck with them!

...

And I'm sick and tired of UNSCOP – as is everybody else here. We anticipate no good from them, and are expecting more fun in October, from the Arabs. (But we can handle them, it's the British we're having a little trouble with). Vic Bernstein's[25] gone and he didn't get *PM* here anyway. Aviva Halaban is rather nice – maybe? You'd better brush up on your Hebrew, son! I have Pearlman's *Mufti*,[26] forget it, and forget Crossman[27] (the turncoat louse – coming out

---

22.   Hebrew, meaning "for example."

23.   Hebrew, meaning "actions," "activities" or "operations."

24.   Aharon Musayoff (and others) attacked the RAF billets on the Ibn Gabirol Street perimeter of Zone B in Jerusalem on August 1. He was riddled with bullets and killed; eight accomplices were arrested. There were no British casualties.

25.   See chapter 5, footnote 106.

26.   Moshe Pearlman, *Mufti of Jerusalem: The Story of Haj Amin El Hussein* (Palestine: Gollancz, 1947).

27.   Richard Crossman, British member of the Anglo-American Committee on Palestine. He wrote an account of his experiences, *Palestine Mission: A Personal Record*, that Mordecai had previously asked his family to send him.

against illegal immigration!) and Crum[28] too – I've seen them already. Haven't heard from Bavli yet. What is "Telem Bayam?"[29]

Thanks oodles, again, for the check – it means a little elbow-room financially speaking.

Thrill – spoke to New York the other day! I went with [Mike] Eskolsky when he did a broadcast to the States: it was recorded by ABC for use last night in their week's roundup of the world news... before the recording, and I heard Mackay, the NY announcer, as though he were in the same room. For the ten minutes we had to wait for the recording room to get ready, we heard part of a chamber music concert from NY. It was a nice feeling! If I had a contact in the States to do a radio spot once a week or two, I'd really be in the chips – and just think of hearing me at such a distance! (If I were ever to get such a spot, I would arrange for you to be in the studio when I make the recording, so's you could say hello as we get the stuff ready – such a nice pipe dream!

...

Just was told of the arrests of Rokach and Sapir and Ben Ami,[30] and the *outlawing of the Revisionist party!* Where are we, in Rumania, where the opposition Peasant party was outlawed, and its leaders arrested, or in the US – where Communism is taboo now? Unsympathetic as I am to the party, its suppression is a crime, and completes the abrogation of civil liberties (so far we've had arrest without warrant, imprisonment with-

---

28. Bartley Crum, an American member of the Anglo-American Committee on Palestine, had also written an account of his experiences – *Behind the Silken Curtain*.
29. In an earlier letter MSC mentions that he is thinking of translating Bar-Adon's "Telem BaYam" so it seems strange that he is asking Gershon what it is. It is possible that Gershon is replying to Mordecai's earlier letter, and Mordecai has simply forgotten what Telem BaYam is.
30. Israel Rokach, mayor of Tel Aviv, Yosef Sapir, mayor of Petach Tivkah, and Oved Ben Ami, mayor of Netanya. All three were arrested by the British authorities on August 5, accused of aiding the Jewish underground groups.

out trial, suppression of papers and broadcasts with no sort of reason and mass punishment for individual acts (higher gasoline price, the two martial law periods, and now even the destruction by the army of houses near which arms are found. Great stuff – the mighty British Empire in its death throes is thrashing around pretty violently, and smashing all it can at the same time…. I'm taking a malicious inhuman pleasure in their economic crisis – let the bastards starve, let them suffer, for what they're doing to us. And while I'm in the mood – our British friends are going the way of all *tzorr'rey Yisrael*[31] – the way of Greece and Rome and Egypt – and as we outlived the earlier ones, we'll live on to put Bevin in his proper place in our history, in our list of downfallen tyrants and human beasts.

…

The raise is really very little – five pounds (I get £45 now) plus a cost-of-living bonus of £5.400, which is paid only twice. However, I have yet to be paid for my editorial, and book reviews (I'll be doing another soon) also pay extra. It still is not much of a living though, if one wants to live at all comfortably. For a bachelor, it's enough, but I hate to think of what it would be like now if I were married! (without a real working wife, who earned about as much as I do, that is). Still, the fascination of the work is ample compensation for the low pay, and these days there is no other work worth doing in Palestine from that point of view. I may mention, incidentally, that I feel little desire to write these days, but much to read, and to run around in the streets and watch how people take the shocks as they come. I want to go to Tel Aviv one of these days and sample the *matzav ruach*[32] there…

---

31.   Hebrew, meaning "foes of Israel."
32.   Hebrew, meaning "mood" or "atmosphere."

Nu – this is about all for now. I'm going downtown to see what the devil is going on now that some sixty Jewish leaders have been arrested. I wonder whether we're in for another July 29,[33] or whether August 5[34] will be something special all by itself. Well, goodbye now, I'm off.

Love to you all,

P.S. Special love and mazel tov, again, to Naomi and Monroe. I'm glad for her and very proud of him.

In the middle of writing the letter, Mordecai learned that the British had suddenly arrested the mayors of Tel Aviv, Netanya and Petach Tikvah and had interned them at a detention camp in Latrun. In what they described as "part of the security forces' campaign against terrorism," the British also arrested many other Jewish leaders. They claimed they had arrested thirty-five people; Jewish sources put the number closer to two hundred. The official government statement announcing the operation said that all the prisoners were being held under the Defense (Emergency) Regulations[35] and that "the military authorities are satisfied that in each case grounds exist for the detentions."[36] They took further measures: the Revisionist youth organization, Betar, closely associated with the Irgun, was outlawed, and its property declared liable to confiscation; all Jews were forbidden to leave the country until the operation was completed; heavily-reinforced guard units were placed at all ports and airports, and off-duty soldiers were restricted to barracks, the British fearing that they would be targets for reprisal attacks.

---

33. I'm not certain as to what Mordecai is referring. Several things happened on July 29: the *Exodus 1947* refugees refused to disembark and the three Irgun operatives were hanged in Acre prison, while frantic searches continued for the missing British sergeants and the British cabinet was debating what measures to take to return calm in Palestine.

34. Although dated August 4, Mordecai obviously wrote the letter over several days, something he often did.

35. A wide-ranging and draconian set of laws introduced by the Mandatory government in 1945.

36. Quoted in an article released by the Jewish Telegraphic Agency (JTA) on August 6, 1947. Many of the other details mentioned here are also found in the JTA article.

The fears proved to be well founded; reprisal from the Irgun was swift. Barely two hours after the arrests and new restrictions were announced, two Irgun members planted a bomb in the Jerusalem Department of Labor building. They then walked over to the chief clerk and quietly told him to evacuate the building. It was evacuated successfully, but when British police attempted to remove the bomb, it exploded, killing three constables and seriously injuring a fourth. A dusk-to-dawn curfew that had been in effect for sixteen days and lifted only that morning, was re-imposed. Mordecai refers to the attack in the following letter.

The British decision to execute young men who had no blood on their hands, and the Irgun decision to retaliate by hanging the two sergeants, led to an escalation in the hostilities between the Palestinian Jews and the British. This process was critical to ending the British mandate. In a letter written fourteen years later, Arthur Creech Jones, the British colonial secretary in 1947, included the Sergeants Affair (and its repercussions) as one of the main reasons the British made the final decision to relinquish the mandate of Palestine.[37]

Friday, Aug. 22, 1947

Dear Gersh,

...Re the pipes – which I really missed, and will greatly appreciate having back, and the pen, which I hope will be a fine point (not the finest, which I understand is too thin, but finer than the average) – they can be sent with either (Rabbi) Jack Milgrom, or with Carmi Charny[38] or Zipporah

---

37. In a letter written on October 23, 1961, to Elizabeth Monroe, one of the founders of the Middle East Centre of St. Antony's College, Oxford, Creech-Jones described the hanging of the two sergeants as a "deadly blow against British patience and pride," including it as the last of four elements that had led the British cabinet to conclude, in September 1947, that the mandate was no longer tenable. For more, see Bruce Hoffman's *Anonymous Soldiers, the Struggle for Israel, 1917–1947* (Vintage, 2016), p. 472.

38. Carmi Charny, later known as "T. Carmi" (1925–1994) was a prominent Hebrew poet and translator of, among other things, Shakespeare's plays. During this period, Carmi was Mordecai's roommate and close friend. His brother, Israel Charny, is an expert on the Armenian genocide. I had the pleasure of interviewing him on November 16, 2015.

Borowsky,[39] who are coming on the ZOA fellowship for this year. I suggest that mother call Borowsky, if Carmi does not call the house (right after Rosh Hashanah – which I shall spend at the Yeshurun,[40] where I spent my first full Yom Kippur fast, occupying Toby Berlin's seat).

All talk about *tachlis*[41] will have to wait, until we see how things go here. It seems UNSCOP will have more to do with my career than they imagine. I want a Photostat of my diploma for me, essentially, and it will be handy for the University too.

Sandstrom was not involved in the red-lighting,[42] but some of the other regulars were. Incidentally, read Don Burke's piece in the Aug. 18 issue of *Time*, on the blowing up of the Labor Department – he did a good job. (He's a nice guy, and used some of the stuff I fed him in that piece – about the kids.)

...

That's all for now – your edit will be out soon – I want to see what happens with the *Exodus* refugees first; and when I've done my Kafka I'll write a long letter.

My love to all, and best wishes to Gertrude.

Love,

Mordecai

---

39. Zipporah (Zippy) Borowsky arrived in Palestine in October, 1947. In later life, she published a collection of her letters from that time, in which Mordecai is mentioned several times: Zipporah Porath, *Letters from Jerusalem: The War of Independence and the Establishment of the State in the Eyes of an American Girl* (Scranton, PA: 1998). I had the pleasure of interviewing her on May 15, 2017 when she was ninety-three years old.
40. Synagogue in Jerusalem, see chapter 3, footnote 22.
41. Hebrew, meaning "practical matters" or something essential, purposeful.
42. The chairman of UNSCOP, Justice Emil Sandstrom. According to Mordecai, he did not participate in the quest for prostitutes during UNSCOP's tour of Lebanon. See letter of July 30.

Mordecai and Carmi Charny

Since Mordecai wrote an average of three or four letters a month during 1947 (and five or six per month in 1948) it is likely that some letters
from September are missing. It was another eventful month in Palestine, but in the only surviving letter, penned sometime between the 17th
and 23rd, Mordecai focused almost exclusively on personal matters.[43] I
assume that in the missing letters he discusses the arrival of the *Exodus
1947* refugees in Hamburg on September 9, and the continuing British
action against other desperate, would-be immigrants.

Given Mordecai's close involvement with UNSCOP (he traveled
with them in Palestine, followed their activities, reported on their hearings and wrote articles about them for the *Post*), I assume he must have
written letters about their final report to the United Nations General
Assembly, issued on September 3. Throughout this period, Mordecai
had peppered his letters home with numerous snide, derogatory, and
pessimistic comments about the likely results of their work. But his pre-
dictions proved wrong. Even if UNSCOP did not give the Jews everything
they had hoped for, it nevertheless recommended what the Jews sought
most – partition and independent statehood.

Specifically, the plan

> envisages the division of Palestine into three parts: an Arab State,
> a Jewish State and the City of Jerusalem. The proposed Arab State
> will include Western Galilee, the hill country of Samaria and

---

43.   The letter was clearly written after Rosh HaShana but before Yom Kippur.

Judea with the exclusion of the City of Jerusalem, and the coastal plain from Isdud to the Egyptian frontier. The proposed Jewish State will include Eastern Galilee, the Esdraelon plain, most of the coastal plain, and the whole of the Beersheba sub-district, which includes the Negeb. The three sections of the Arab State and the three sections of the Jewish State are linked together by two points of intersection, of which one is situated south-east of Afula in the sub-district of Nazareth and the other north-east of El Majdal in the sub-district of Gaza.[44]

The report recommended that these two states be joined in economic union. They should also be democratic, i.e., representative in character, with guarantees of essential human rights and fundamental freedoms and safeguards to protect the rights and interests of minorities.

It advised that statehood should occur as quickly as possible, after a transition period to be managed by the United Nations, rather than by Britain, and that during this transition period 150,000 Jews be allowed to immigrate to the Jewish area. Longer term, it insisted that the UN General Assembly address the larger problem of distressed European Jews, of whom approximately 250,000 were languishing in assembly centers, "as a matter of extreme urgency."

There was also a minority report, from three of the eleven UNSCOP member states, which recommended a federal arrangement; Palestine would consist of separate states or cantons under a federal government to be administered by the Arabs. The Jews would be permitted only limited immigration.

The report is fascinating and well worth reading. UNSCOP did a thorough job. Their intensive and efficient efforts resulted in their completion of their task in the mandated three months – a remarkable accomplishment. Their efforts required extensive preparation and included a 2,200 mile fifteen-day tour of Palestine, a five day trip to Lebanon and Syria, a visit to the king of Transjordan in Amman, a

---

44. Part II, *Boundaries*, Official Records of the Second Session of the General Assembly, Supplement No. 11, United Nations Special Committee on Palestine, Report to the General Assembly, Volume I.

2,700 mile seven-day tour of displaced persons camps in Germany and Austria, the holding of thirteen public hearings during which thirty-seven persons representing six Arab states and seventeen Jewish organizations gave evidence, and the holding of four private hearings. A total of thirty-nine private meetings were held by the Committee; its four sub-committees and its three working groups held additional formal and informal private meetings.[45]

The Committee produced a comprehensive, detailed, objective and honest picture of Palestine as of the fall of 1947. Its three-volumes include extensive descriptions of the geography, agriculture, industry, and demographics of Palestine. They analyzed the British Mandate and its political situation, summarized the views of the Jews and the Arabs, and offered detailed responses to arguments raised on both sides. They emphasized that the new states must be democratic and representative and stressed the need to protect minority rights.

Particularly striking, in a report that is the epitome of even-handedness, is the obvious admiration the Committee had for what the Jews had managed to accomplish in so little time and under such adverse circumstances. They cite the extensive administrative infrastructure (a "state within a state") that had been functioning for decades, the highly developed and advanced industrial and agricultural infrastructure, and describe how the Arabs had benefitted from the success of the Jews.

There is extensive discussion of the Balfour declaration, and of the exact meaning of a "national home" for the Jews. They quote Winston Churchill's comments about the declaration, and about coexistence, and stress that, "it is essential that [the Jewish people] should know that it is in Palestine as of right and not on sufferance. That is the reason why it is necessary that the existence of a Jewish National Home in Palestine should be internationally guaranteed, and that it should be formally recognized to rest upon ancient historic connexion."[46]

Although disappointed by the small geographical area awarded to it, the Jewish Agency accepted the report. In contrast, the Arab Higher

---

45. UNSCOP press release, August 31, 1947.
46. Item 77, "The mandate in practice."

Committee rejected the report entirely, claiming that the Jews had no moral or legal right to Palestine and that the only possible outcome must be an Arab state in the entirety of Palestine.

The General Assembly of the UN established a committee to consider the report and invited delegations of both the Arab Higher Committee and the Jewish Agency to make further representations. The British officially agreed with the conclusions of the report, but unofficially Bevin felt it was unjust to the Arabs and declared that Britain would not impose partition unless it was acceptable to both the Arabs and Jews.

Between the issuance of the report on September 3, and the actual UN vote on its recommendations, there was intense political jockeying and a dramatic increase in violence. The period was tense, stressful and full of suspense. A thorough description would read like a political thriller. Still, during this period Mordecai's surviving letters remained focused on personal matters.

September 1947

Dear Family,

This is the first respite I've had in a long time – we had added *AP* to our press services and I had had to go through that too, with the result that I was too knocked out to do any kind of writing. I did a piece on Kafka,[47] and found myself going through a real Sturm und Drang, of the kind I thought I had left behind me a long long time ago. Result? Just this: I think it time I did some real studying. Culture is very decidedly a function of leisure, and as the latter grows, the former waxes strong as well. I found myself sitting back in awe before things I myself wrote months ago, and wondering at my past erudition – a hell of a situation. I've applied to Columbia and Harvard, for admission to the graduate schools, to do work in literature and take some philosophy, in both of which I find myself feeling woefully inadequate, particularly after the

---

47. M. S. Chertoff, "New Interpretations: More about Kafka," *Palestine Post*, September 12, 1947, p. 7.

reading I did for the Kafka piece (enclosed, and which does not reflect it, either. However, for the *Post*, it was the only kind of article possible). I had long felt that there must come a time at which one must stop playing with books and study and go out to earn a living – to hell with that now. I feel that it is nobody's business how long I go to school and play with books, as long as it comes out of my own pocket. Sooo – if I'm accepted to either school, I'll accept, and consider myself fortunate. There is enough for me to do around most any big city now to earn a living on part-time work, and be able to study. I think I need another year or so before I can settle down here without feeling that I'm losing out somewhere along the intellectual line. Gershon envies my being here – I envy his reading and studying and the oodles of hours of leisure he has at his disposal.

I have also decided that as *tachlis*, this racket is not for me: to rise even to GA's job, the pinnacle of success here, would mean not having a moment for anything but the paper – and I don't think it's worthwhile devoting my life to. Further, it means not only my days, but nights as well. It is a rare treat for me to see Jerusalem at night. My job has changed slightly now, and I do all the makeup, so that I don't have to come before 8:30, which gives me more time during the day, but I never get to see anybody or be anywhere when anything is happening. I don't like the idea, as a permanent portion. *L'shem shport*[48] it's okay. But more of this later on.

...have you seen Graves'[49] letter attacking me....

GA will bring you two Etrogim, for Father and Gershon: I would have sent Bavli one too, but I dared not impose on the boss. He volunteered to bring them (he's

---

48. *L'shem* means "for the sake of" in Hebrew; I think Mordecai is being cute here, altering the word "sport" so it sounds more like Hebrew. So he means, "for the sake of sport."

49. A response to Mordecai's review of Robert Graves' *King Jesus* in the April 1947 edition of *Commentary*.

leaving *motzei* Yom Kippur)[50] when he heard that Kepi's flight has been postponed, and she may not get back in time for the first days of Sukkot. Some time after she does get back, you will enjoy the fruits of a son in Palestine: I've trudged the streets of Jerusalem, Tel Aviv and Bethlehem (with little luck) and managed to scare together a few things for you all. They're meant as birthday gifts, but since mailing is such a lousy business, have them all at once, call them what you like -- only enjoy them, with all my love and wishes for a really good year.

...I've written Finky,[51] Mandelbaum,[52] thanking them for notes to me about my graduating, and am sending a little gift for Tultuleh. For the Bavlis pa and ma, I had no idea what to get, and still less money with which to do so – give them my love anyway, and I wanted to wire Tultuleh on our birthday, but had to start work at four that day (my assistant was off), and since the post-office is closed from 1–4, and I was barely ready by one (after a grueling Saturday night, with everything late) I couldn't get to the post-office on time. I'll do better next year.

Something else, now, for this year. I don't like the undercurrent of anti-Kepi propaganda which has flowed along in some of the letters, particularly Naomi's and Gershon's. I feel rather strongly about this since I happen to care for her, a good deal. She's leaving now to finish her ... degree, and then plans to come back to Palestine. I hope nothing goes wrong with her plans. If it hadn't been for my having invited her to the house at the time Monroe was around, when all attention was concentrated upon him and distraction was resented, I'm sure the whole family attitude would have been different. However, I don't feel called upon

---

50. Jewish days begin at sunset and end at nightfall the next day. *Motzei* means "end of" in Hebrew. *Motzei* Yom Kippur is the night on which Yom Kippur ends.
51. Professor Louis Finkelstein, chancellor of the JTS.
52. Probably Bernard Mandlebaum, a rabbi, and from 1966 to 1971, president of the Jewish Theological Seminary.

to apologize or explain anything, I'm a big, balding boy now and if and when I make up what mind I have, it will be me making it up, not the family. I don't want to sound *"broyges,"*[53] and I hope the admonition is unnecessary, but I trust you will be your sweet selves when she comes to NY to see you and bring my gifts and love. You might stop for a moment and consider that she has been closest to me here, and by her sympathy and understanding made things a good deal easier for me than they might have been. Just stop and think and you'll realize that there have been no unhappy letters and gripes since she's been here. And I'm somewhat lonely already at the thought of her leaving. She knows everything of my comings and goings here, so what I've forgotten she can fill in.

Nu – Gmar Chatima Tova[54]

Love,

Mordecai

This letter may provide a preliminary clue as to one of the possible reasons Mordecai ultimately decided to leave the newly established State of Israel in 1950 and not return, despite his devotion to it and to the Zionist cause. He is frustrated by the long hours and relative unimportance of his work and misses the intellectual fulfillment he finds in more literary pursuits. He contrasts his life with his fantasy of his older brother's life as a pulpit rabbi, with its "oodles of leisure time" to read and study. (He has no idea of how hard his brother works.) At this point he is only considering the possibility of leaving for a short period of time and imagines that after a further period of study he will be able to find life more satisfying in Israel. Mordecai's dream of a leisurely life of letters

53. Yiddish, meaning "angry" or "upset."
54. Traditional Jewish greeting during the High Holiday season, meaning, "May you receive a good final seal." According to Jewish tradition, one's fate for the coming year is written down by God on Rosh Hashana, and sealed, or signed by Him, at the end of Yom Kippur.

is best described by his friend, (Rabbi) David Greenberg, in a letter to Mordecai dated Yom Kippur, 1947. Greenberg writes:

> Your letter seems to indicate that you are acquiring a valuable store of journalistic experience, albeit working very hard and living a Spartan existence. You are at long last doing what you want. Of course, it's a long way from the realization of the fond dream of the spacious home, graced by a charming hostess, its gates opened wide to Palestine's literary greats and aspirants. Chertoff – patron, publisher, publicist, literary lion, deft and delightful critic, proud citizen of the sovereign Jewish state.

It is also noteworthy that Mordecai (finally) defends Kepi, explaining to his family how important she has been to him and how she enriches his life.

Chapter 7

Enter the Third Woman

G iven his dissatisfaction with his working life, at least Mordecai is juggling an active social life. It is clear that his relationship with Kepi is far from over, yet his feelings must be ambivalent because in the following letter, written to his sister a month later, it is clear that he views his relationship with Kepi as temporary or expedient and that he still thinks of Hadassah.

In the meantime, Naomi has met the Strauss family of Cleveland and discovered that they have a daughter living in Palestine. She thought the girl sounded like a potentially good match for her baby brother and in a letter dated August 19, writes:

> I got another babe for you. Her family is terrific... The rich
> Strausses of Cleveland... She became a Zionist just recently.
> Her name is Ann Strauss and she is working for Yassky[1]

---

1. Dr. Chaim Yassky (1896–1948), was an ophthalmologist. In 1931, he became the director of the Hadassah Medical Organization in Palestine and was one of the driving forces behind the establishment of the Rothschild-Hadassah University Hospital on Mount Scopus, which opened in 1939. The Yasskys were family friends of the Chertoffs.

> as his secretary at the [Hadassah] hospital. She is 23 or
> 24, a college grad, attractive, smart, etc., etc. ... Date her,
> toots, and tell me about her. I really think you'll like her.

The Strausses were, indeed, wealthy. Ann Strauss's maternal grand-father was Salmon Halle, co-owner of the Halle department store in Cleveland. In a later letter Naomi describes her visit to the chateaux which the Halle brothers had dismantled in France and brought to Cleveland and reassembled, brick by brick. Ann's mother, Marion Halle Strauss, was president of Hadassah in Cleveland and her father, Abraham Strauss, was the head of a surgical department at Mount Sinai Hospital in Cleveland. Ann graduated from Bryn Mawr College in 1944. She studied English literature; and minored in geology, which included map-making from aerial photographs, a skill later put to use by the Haganah.

Wealth aside, Ann will become an important and close friend to Mordecai.

(Courtesy of Roy Shenkar)

Ann Strauss

Monday Oct. 13, 1947

Dear Toots,

Just received your letter. I plead guilty, claim extenuating circumstances and plead for special consideration. After the first furious round of visiting it began coming out of my ears, and I stopped suddenly and completely. I resented people's astonishment at my knowledge of Hebrew and objected to the sly innuendos that I was beating the anti-Semitism inspired exodus from America. Then Kepi showed up, and I had a feeling that it would not do to visit too many people with her because I knew she would not last and did not want to be too closely identified with her in people's minds (I was right, too, because it would have, for example, fouled up any possible running around with Ann Strauss, who is so close to Yassky). I did make a few attempts to see him after she left, but found him on the verge of leaving too, and usually not at home (I did not try to call, but went over to his house instead). However, I shall fill in the omission when he returns – I have been feeling a good deal more sociable lately. I've visited Nishry[2] a couple of times – he's a nice guy (she was out) and has a lot to say about the country, having been there so long. He says it too.

Ann Strauss is a good kid. She has personality, sense, looks but no complexion, completely unaffected and sweet. But – she's about where Hadassah was two or three years ago on things religious, has contempt for the Rabbinate (not in its deviations from its ideal, but in its ideal per se). She is the only one I date now on my infrequent days-off. She's nice, but – I wish Hadassah were here. I expect a letter from her any day now, and we'll see how things stand.

...Incidentally, in Pakidstan (a *pakid* is a bureaucrat, toots) or Mapaistan, both of which are being bruited about

2. Perhaps Israel Nishry (1898–1949). The name appears many times in Mordecai's letters but I cannot positively identify him or explain the relationship.

as possible names, the unit of coinage will in all probability be a shekel, with 7 shekalim making a baksheesh and 10 baksheeshim a *protektzia*, with the system probably on the *dunam* standard.[3]

... And – how does Dallek know what kind of job I'm doing? You can tell him that the Jewish State can have my invaluable services if they'll pay a living wage (not that I'd work for money: all I want is the traditional compensation for "*bitul melacha*").[4] I'll send you a couple of pieces I wrote recently – the great Max Brod found it necessary to attack me, stupidly, ineptly, childishly, ineffectively, for *my Kafka piece. I did not deign to reply. (Howzat for dignity?)*

There is no question of my leaving here now – desertion[5] is a serious thing. We ran a report on Weizmann's speech, I'm checking for the complete text now, to read as you suggest.

...

Wrote to the folks for my old passport so I can arrange for a permanent visa. When that's done, I'll trouble Gershon

---

3. This is word play – Mordecai is joking about what the new state might be called. This is his first reference after the UNSCOP report to the idea that there may actually be a state. Just as is true in Israel today, much depends on who you know, rather than what you know, so he is joking that the state may be named for the bureaucrats who run the Yishuv, or the Labor party (Mapai). Baksheesh can mean tip or gratuity in Arabic, but in Eastern Europe it is used exclusively to mean a payoff, or bribe. Having *protektzia* is essentially about knowing the "right" people and thus having clout or being the recipient of nepotism. But he is wrong about the shekel. Israel's first unit of currency as an independent modern country was the lira. It became the shekel in 1980. A dunam is a unit of area, defined in Mandatory Palestine and contemporary Israel as 1,000 square meters (10,764 sq ft).

4. More wordplay. "*Bitul melakha*" is used in Jewish Law to mean a time when work (*melakha*) is forbidden, e.g., when one is required to leave work to go to a funeral. Here he is purposely using it as an anology of the concept of "*Bitul Torah*," i.e., wasting time with any activity other than the study of Torah. The implication is that Mordecai should at least be well compensated if he is to work.

5. In addition to the figurative meaning, Mordecai is now secretly a soldier so it would literally be desertion.

to seeing to it that my books are crated and shipped out here. I could use them. Most of all, I could use a Jewish Encyclopedia here. Nu. I'll finish this letter either later tonight or tomorrow. Incidentally, I've sent you two the most beautiful Chanukah menorah in all Palestine, and the most beautiful I've ever seen. It cost less than you wanted it to, but never mind how much. I have nobody to spend my money on these days anyway. Use it in good health. (The extra little pitcher is the *shamas*,[6] but the thing looks much richer with the urn in the center (cruse, I mean) under the arch of the leaves. I'm sure Monroe will have no trouble putting it together again.

...

Later: Just got a letter from the folks. Now that Father knows I'm staying here he says there is renewed reason to come, and I get the impression that they will get busy on their visas. I see, too, that Mother is busy with Hadassah, as well as half a dozen other things in addition to her insurance.[7] That's good.

Just made a date for tomorrow night! (A date is a big thing in my wild, bachelor life here) I'm taking Ann to see the Hebrew version of *You Can't Take It With You*.[8] It is supposed to be very good, with local color added.

And for the record, my pet – when are you kids coming out here to at least visit? You won't recognize our gorgeous little country (now in its winter coat of mud and rain and fitful sunshine) if you don't hurry.

---

6.   Yiddish, meaning "helper" (*shamash* in Hebrew). A chanukiah has nine branches, for nine candles – eight for the eight nights of Chanukah, with an additional candle lit each night until on the final night, all eight are alight – and the ninth branch to hold the *shamas* or *shamash*, the candle used to light all the others.

7.   Mordecai's mother sold insurance in an effort to supplement the family income.

8.   Comedic play by George S. Kaufman and Moss Hart which premiered on Broadway in 1936, and won the 1937 Pulitzer for drama.

Incidentally – Dallek thinks I'm OK – someday I'll bother him for a real job in the Political Department. I don't think I'll want to do night work all my life. Nu – my love to all. And keep writing – your letters are swell. You might even goad your handsome husband into writing a few lines – it's time I heard something about and from him. How does his work go, how does he like it, etc. It is eminently unfitting a member of our family to be so quiet.

Got work to do. Incidentally – have you found out as yet what you're supposed to be doing in your job?

That's all for now.

Love

Mersh

Chapter 8

The Farran Affair

The next letter is in the form of an editorial for Gershon about the trial, in early October, of Major Roy Farran, for the kidnapping and murder of Alexander Rubowitz five months earlier.[1] Farran was the commander of a plainclothes British "special squad" tasked with fighting Jewish terrorism. On May 6, sixteen-year-old Alexander Rubowitz, was putting up notices for the Lehi when he was abducted. Witnesses saw a boy struggling furiously with men who were pushing him into a car. Rubowitz's body was never found, and all evidence – including a confession – pointed to Farran. The evidence connecting Major Farran to the disappearance was circumstantial but compelling.[2] Witnesses saw a boy being chased down Ussishkin Street by a large, blond man, then

---

1.   Mordecai made a passing reference to it in his letter of July 30, 1947.
2.   The details of the Farran case presented here are taken largely from the essay, "The War on Terror that Failed: British Counter-Insurgency in Palestine 1945–1947 and the Farran Affair" by David Cesarani, in *British Ways of Counter-Insurgency: A Historical Perspective,* edited by Matthew Hughes (Routledge, 2013). Cesarani's source was the original police report on the investigation – *Report on the Alleged Abduction and Murder of Alexander Rubowitz and Subsequent Police Investigation,* by K. P. Hadingham, Superintendent of Police, Jerusalem District, 19 June 1947, The National Archives CO 537/2302.

caught at the intersection of Ussishkin and Keren Kayemet L'Yisrael Streets where he was forced into a waiting car. The boy struggled so fiercely with his pursuer that a second man had to get out of the car to help subdue him. One of the witnesses, a fifteen-year-old named Meir Cohen, was brave enough to approach the car and ask what they were doing. The man who had gotten out of the car snarled that they were policemen, showed him a police ID, then threatened that he'd be shot if he didn't leave. The boy retreated, but not before he heard the prisoner cry out, in Hebrew, that he was from the Rubowitz family. As the car sped away, a grey hat was seen lying in the road. There was a name on the headband that looked like "Far-an," or "Farkand."

When Alexander Rubowitz did not return home, his parents went to the police, but the police claimed to know nothing and to not have him in custody. The Rubowitzes knew that their son was involved in the Jewish underground so they assumed that he would have given a false name if he *had* been picked up. After a few more days, when he still hadn't turned up, they went to the Jewish press. When *Haaretz* published a photograph of Alexander, together with his description, the witnesses who had seen the abduction went to the police with their information, and with the hat. The police still did nothing and claimed not to know anyone by the name of Farran. At this point public suspicion was mounting that this was no simple crime, nor merely the kidnapping of a minor Lehi activist by a rival group, as had been known to happen, but that in some way, British forces had been involved. And then an anonymous tip was sent to the family informing them of the existence of Major Roy Farran.

Roy Farran, who had served in the SAS during WWII, had been brought to Palestine to command a covert special forces unit tasked with hunting down Jewish insurgents. The unit was not subject to the same restrictions as the police in terms of what they were and were not allowed to do to suspects. Farran reported to Brigadier Bernard Fergusson, and it had been to Fergusson, the day after Alexander Rubowitz disappeared, that Farran had confessed. It had been his men who had picked up Rubowitz. He had joined them, and they had taken the boy to a forest outside of Jerusalem. After a brutal interrogation in which nothing was learned, Farran reportedly crushed the boy's head with a rock, killing him.[3] He and his men then stripped Alexander's body, burned his clothing, and then stabbed his corpse repeatedly. They left it there and returned to Jerusalem.

None of this was made public. Fergusson didn't arrest Farran for murder nor tell anyone else what he had heard. It was only after the newspapers picked up the story of the missing boy that he went to the inspector general, Lieutenant-Colonel William Nicol Gray, and told him about Farran's confession. Gray did nothing with the information until the end of May, just before he was due to leave Palestine. Only then did he tell his second-in-command, Arthur Giles, what he knew and instructed him to take the 'correct action.' Giles went to Sir Henry Gurney, chief secretary of the Palestine government and told him everything. Gurney instructed Giles to "proceed with the case as an ordinary criminal offence with the object of bringing Farran and any other accused to trial." Superintendent Hadingham was put on the case, interviewed Fergusson, and decided, together with the attorney general, that Farran should be arrested and charged with murder.

Although this took place in early June, the trial only began in October. Farran escaped from Palestine twice before he was brought to trial, fleeing first to Syria, and then a second time, to Jordan. He resigned from the colonial service, which meant that he would be tried by court-martial rather than in a civilian court, and assumed complete responsibility for the incident. As a result, none of the men in his squad who had assisted in kidnapping and beating the teenager were brought to trial.

October 1947

Dear Gershon,

Nobody expected anything else, we all knew that Roy Alexander Farran would not be executed for the murder-kidnapping of Alexander Rubowitz. Few of us expected as clean a bill of health, as Farran was guilty. All of us nursed a secret prayer in our hearts that he would pay as we felt he

---

3. Another account claims that an Arab was tasked with disposing of the body.

should. There was hardly anybody in Palestine who believed the trial would be as it was: little better than a farce.

Could it be anything else when Col. Fergusson, with whom Farran had had a long tête-à-tête the morning after the alleged kidnapping, refused to talk lest he incriminate himself; Farran's own scrap book of his exploits in the Holy Land was considered inadmissible as evidence on the grounds that it was privileged as his preparation of his defense for the trial;[4] the crucial hat, with the name FARRAN printed in it, was found, during the trial, to have no more than a smudge where the once-clear letters had been?[5]

Fergusson should have been forced to testify, or else tried as an accomplice-after-the-fact: that neither he nor his superiors consider his hands clean may be seen in Fergusson's going on leave the day after the trial.

Evidence in the possession of the police should certainly not have been mysteriously altered past all usefulness.

The last point of the defense, that there was no body, and so the very fact of murder had not been established, let alone the identity of the murderer, can stand a little examination.

The boy is missing.

Police reported him "dead" to his family.

How do they know?

It might even be useful to interrogate certain Bedouins in the Dead Sea area about a cremation they were paid – and handsomely – to carry out.

---

4. Notes made by Farran while in custody and found after he escaped reportedly contained a confession, but they were judged to be preparation for his defense and inadmissible under the rules of lawyer-client privilege.
5. Farran claimed not to have been present when the boy was snatched. He told Fergusson that he had loaned his hat to one of the men who had been there.

But then maybe Rubowitz himself staged the whole thing. Maybe he was tired of life in Jerusalem, and fled to Syria – where Farran spent some time AWOL before he gave himself up. Maybe Farran was looking for Rubowitz!

A day or two after the trial the *Palestine Post* ran a story of a Japanese admiral who was acquitted of charges of war crimes. He walked out of the prison gates towards his waiting friends and fell down dead of a heart attack.

Under it there appeared a story speculating on the whereabouts of Captain Roy Alexander Farran, recently acquitted of charges of murder.

That's all for now.

Love,

Mordecai

Roy Farran left Palestine under high security. Fergusson, too, was told to leave. A year later, Lehi sent a parcel bomb to Farran's family home in Staffordshire but Roy was not at home and his younger brother, Francis Rex, opened it and was killed.

Alexander Rubowitz's body has never been found.

* * *

In his next letter, Mordecai offers a surprisingly mild and weak response to a shrill and irate letter from his mother about his continuing involvement with Kepi. Perhaps he is too weary to offer a more vigorous response. His father's letter, which also mentions Kepi is, indeed, "moderate" in comparison, as Mordecai remarks. Here are the relevant sections of their respective letters:

Esther Chertoff writes:

And now the most important and unpleasant part of the letter. When we were in Montreal last summer, some neighbor of [Kepi's]... greeted us in such a way as to imply that we had accepted her, and we were of course very much surprised and disappointed. Mordecai, it seems that we have been deceived all along. I can hardly believe my eyes reading about the "anti-Kepi propaganda." When you left here, you had completely broken with her, you were determined that it was all at an end. But it seems that she changed your mind for you. When we heard rumors that she is there, we didn't believe that either.

We wrote you, Gershon cabled you, and we wrote you again and again. Each time you denied the whole story, you said that there is nothing in it, and you were hurt that we didn't trust you, and that you are no child, and that we must believe you.

There never was an "undercurrent of anti-Kepi propaganda," it was all entirely on the surface. There were no innuendos, it was all on the surface, you knew that we were and are completely and entirely against. The children shouted it from the house tops and father and I agreed, but we thought it good politics not to mention it. Now here you are with the bomb-shell. We are thoroughly shocked: when you were exasperated at the mere thought that we suspected you of going with her. I can't imagine what's happened to you.

Your having invited [Kepi] to the house when Monroe was here, has nothing to do with this thing. She had been here long before Monroe came upon the scene, and the impression which she created was not a favorable one. What people tell you, that she is pretty, charming, and all the rest is playing diplomacy. It stands to reason that if one person is interested in another, the third one is not going to say anything but the most flattering things about the person involved. "Your best friend won't tell you:" the only ones are those of your family: the ones who really love you disinterestedly, and who want to see you happy, really happy.

...I repeat, nobody loves you like your family; loves you whole heartedly, disinterestedly. All that your family wants of you is to see you happy and contented. If I repeat myself, it is because I feel so strongly about it, and my reason backs me up. ...

Now [Kepi] spent five hours here last Monday, and both father and I were wonderful to her: just as sweet and nice as can be. But we were doing it for your sake, dear. We love you so much, we did not want to hurt you through her, so we followed your instructions, but it was merely a good act.

You are young and handsome and charming and brilliant. You are an unusual guy, in every way, and you have an unusual family. I guess that there is nothing for me to say further, except that I wish you every happiness together with us.

His father writes:

In your letter, you touched on two important matters. The first – about your returning to America to study – is truly and worthy of particular consideration. This matter has occupied my thoughts for a while already. About the second matter – that is, Kepi – I couldn't understand the tone of your words, your tone of anger. Where is that coming from? You maintain that this matter is personal, individual, and that others have no right to interfere. But it seems to me that precisely because of this, that the matter is so personal, that your future happiness depends on it, that you must listen to the opinion of those who are interested in your happiness and in your future. You know that it's easier for others (obviously those sincerely interested in your happiness) to judge things like this and see all the sides to the matter, the strong side and the weak,[6] than it is for the

---

6. Written in Hebrew as "הצד החזק והרפה" (*hatzad heḥazak veharafeh*), which is similar to the wording Moses uses in his instructions to the spies in Num. 13:18.

person directly involved. You know the explicit halacha of "one who has a vested interest is an invalid witness."[7]

For now, I'm not determining anything, that is, I am not deciding anything not about the first matter nor the second, not yes and not no. You know that I am not a person who decides weighty matters in panic or haste. I need deep study, consideration, to turn the matter over and over in my head until it becomes clear from every perspective. My decision must come, not from emotion, but from clear thought. I also think we have enough time to think about these issues and we don't have to jump the gun. My advice to you is that you too not rush to decide; delve into it, turn it over in your mind,[8] and think about the other side of the coin, because every coin, that is, every question, has two sides. (October 6, 1947)

October 14, 1947

Dear Family,

I'm writing now simply because I haven't written in some time, in spite of me being in far from the mood for writing: I'm just too dammed lonely and out of sorts.

Mother's letter was quite upsetting, and therefore Father's moderate letter, following by a day or two, was so welcome. But what is this I hear about your planning not to come if I decide to return to the States this summer?

...

I do know that my job has settled down into dull routine, finally, and is far from satisfying. I'm very much afraid that my future will have to be elsewhere. But more of that some other day, when the sun is less strong and I am more

---

7.   As per a mishna in Tractate *Sanhedrin*.
8.   Written in Hebrew "הפוך בה והפוך בה" (*hafokh bah vehafokh bah*) as per Mishna *Avot* 5:22.

so. Finky[9] sent me a very nice thank you note – clever move there, Pop! One never knows, indeed.

...

Love – Mordecai

Mordecai's father continues to take his son's despair seriously and responds with his usual incisiveness and sensitivity:

> About the main question, which is whether to settle in the Land or come back here, you need to consider this: What are your chances of a livelihood here? It seems to me that working in literature is not a reliable source of income here. And then, you'd have to get a position as a rabbi, but also not give up the literature. And, in truth, that's not at all a bad idea for you. The hardest part about the rabbinate is the sermons, but for you that part is easiest. The salary of a rabbi and his income add up to a fair amount, also his standing in society is important and honorable. And your literary pursuits will add to your income, and also to your standing. Therefore, it doesn't appear as though there's any question here. It's obvious![10]
>
> Even so, the question is how can a Jew leave Eretz Yisrael now, as we stand on the threshold of the Redemption? Just yesterday, Herschel Johnson[11] announced, as you know, that our government is inclined to recognize the Jewish government in another eight months! And if the position of America is accepted—then we are poised on the eve of actual independence, and how can a person with a

---

9. Professor Louis Finkelstein, Chancellor of JTS.
10. Paul uses the Hebrew expression "כף של חלב בקדירה של חלב," literally, "A spoon of milk in a pot of milk." David Koppel, recognized it from a folkloric *maiseh* (story) his uncle shared when they learned Gemara together.
11. Herschel Vespasian Johnson II (1894–1966), was the acting US ambassador to the United Nations between 1946 and 1947. He was a vocal proponent of the 1947 Palestine Partition Plan.

Jewish spark in his heart leave the Land when our world is about to be born?

True, even in a Jewish kingdom the question of livelihood is a difficult one, still we don't know what the source of your livelihood will be then. I must admit that literature, to my mind, will not be a reliable source of income then either. But I believe that for a young American like you there will be many employment opportunities; it is clear to me that you can fill an important role in the Jewish nation, therefore there's certainly no rush to return to America, wait and see how things turn out. (November 1, 1947)

Part II

The Civil War
(November, 1947 – May, 1948)

Chapter 9

Anticipating the Decision on Partition

The deliberations over the UNSCOP report continued at the UN with the British, Americans and Russians – each with their own interests – intensly jockeying for position. In the end, it was decided that the recommendation for partition would be brought to a vote in the General Assembly of the United Nations at the end of November. For the Zionists it was simultaneously a time of great uncertainty and fervent hope. If the UN were to vote in favor of partition, the Jews could freely return to their homeland after thousands of years of exile. If the vote was against, the Jews of Palestine would remain a vulnerable minority and their brethren in Europe, homeless and adrift. Zionist leaders worked frantically to garner support for the Partition Plan from all the nations of the world.

Although the following letter was written when the vote on partition was still some weeks away, it very much reflects the significance of the time. It contains an editorial for Gershon to use in honor of the sixtieth year since the founding of his synagogue. The editorial is illustrative of how Mordecai, like his father, sees and understands contemporary events within the context of ancient Jewish history and religious destiny.

The concept of the Jubilee year (*yovel*) with which Mordecai frames his editorial is discussed in the Biblical book of Leviticus. It occurred once every fifty years and marked the time that all land and property rights previously given up, for whatever reason, reverted to their original owners:

> You shall count off seven Sabbaths of years, seven times seven years; and there shall be to you the days of seven Sabbaths of years, even forty-nine years. Then you shall sound the loud trumpet on the tenth day of the seventh month. On the Day of Atonement you shall sound the trumpet throughout all your land. You shall make the fiftieth year holy, and proclaim liberty throughout the land to all its inhabitants. It shall be a jubilee to you; and each of you shall return to his own property, and each of you shall return to his family. That fiftieth year shall be a jubilee to you. ... In this Year of Jubilee each of you shall return to his property.[1]

Knowledge of when the actual Jubilee year falls precisely has long been a matter of rabbinical dispute.

Nov. 3, 1947

Dear Gershon – your junk [i.e., writing editorials for you] is coming out of my ears already. Isn't it time you delegated the whole job to one of your geniuses there? I have a number of articles to write, and have to hang fire on them because you pop up every once in a while with some more of this s**t. Nu. Here goes.

THE GREAT JUBILEE

It is a long time since the ram's horn proclaimed "liberty throughout the land" on the eve of the Jubilee Year; a long time since the land, the inalienable possession of the Isra-elite, returned to its original owner. For that was what the

---

1.   Leviticus 25:8–13.

Jubilee Year meant in the old Jewish State. It is a long time since slaves were freed and all men returned to their land-holdings as free men and had a chance to (reprieve their mistakes and) take another lease on life.

About 50 Jubilees have passed us by unsung and uncelebrated, un-noticed by the Jew borne down by the weight of his Exile and the sorrow of living in strange and alien lands. A Jubilee is a long time for suffering and sadness, for persecution and torment, but it gives a people perspective, and seen from the vantage point of those fifty Jubilees the sporadic shedding of blood in Palestine and the seemingly endless procession of commissions and experts (looking for the way to end that bloodshed) can be seen as nothing more serious than birth-pangs.

For they must be birth-pangs – we cannot believe that all the years of suffering have been in vain and all the dead have died in vain. The word from nearby Lake Success hints that these indeed are the pangs of a new world in birth, and some of the things being said in the chambers of the world's representatives at Lake Success sound encouragingly like the practice blasts of a trumpeter long separated from his instrument who takes it up again, confident his skill will soon be required.

Most of us believe that the trumpet will sound again, very soon: some feel it to be a matter of days, some think longer, but few doubt that Israel will be returned to its land, to the land which "cannot be sold forever for it is Mine."[2] Few doubt that Israel will very soon return to its land as free men from the camps at Am Stau and Poppendorf,[3] from the jails of Cyprus and Kenya, from the exiles of Yemen and Arabia and Egypt Africa. Israel all over the world is preparing for the Great Jubilee, confident that it is almost upon us.

---

2.   Leviticus 25:23.
3.   Camps for displaced persons. Some 4,500 passengers bound for Palestine on the *Exodus 1947* and forced by the British to return to Germany were temporarily quartered in these two camps.

Nobody is exempt from that preparation; nobody, whether an individual or a congregation, is free to enclose himself within his seven ells[4] of privacy and let the world go by. (It was with that in mind rather than with any particular interest in architecture that our Rabbis decreed that a Synagogue must be built with windows: neither the synagogue nor those within it may be closed to the world; none is sufficient unto himself.

For us at [blank space for Gershon to fill in the name of his congregation], this year is a Diamond Jubilee year. It signifies our maturity and should remind us of our responsibility. Rather than just observe it as a birthday, albeit it an important one, we must see it, coming as it well may simultaneously with the Great Jubilee of the Jewish People, as a moment of dedication.

It is for us to dedicate ourselves to this double Jubilee: to aid in the full realization of all the possibilities for our people that are inherent in the Great Jubilee; to see our "Diamond" Jubilee as a spur to even greater effort in our task of enlarging the scope of good works we can do within our own community and our own synagogue.

May our own efforts contribute, be it ever so humbly, to the Great Jubilee for which our people have waited so long, and may we be worthy of it when the great day comes.

To quote Uncle Don, as he was heard by his young listeners one day when he spoke up before his mike was turned off – I hope that keeps the little bastards for a while![5]

... That's all for now – write, damn it!

Love,

Mersh

---

4. An ell is a unit of measurement similar to a cubit, here used metaphorically.

5. *Uncle Don* was a children's radio program which aired on WOR radio from 1928 to 1947. The blooper to which Mordecai refers, the host declaiming into a mike that he didn't know was live, "There! That ought to hold the little bastards," is an urban ledgend.

In this letter to Naomi, the saga of Kepi collides with the narrative of Hadassah – with a cameo appearance by Ann.

Sunday, November [unclear], 1947, 2:40 AM

Dear Toots,

You were right. Your last letter got me moving, and I bothered Katznelson in his study for a talk about what happened with Hadassah [Frisch] in Paris. It's straight out of a movie, I swear. Can you imagine her not coming to Palestine because she was loathe to embarrass me, (having heard K's vague references to Kepi and considering him very tactful, she assumed it was a fait accompli and decided to step aside!) I had received an answer to my cable which led me to suspect part of the story, K filled in the blanks. I am now waiting for an answer to my lengthy treatise to her, explaining the true situation. The very possibility of her appearing here thrills me more than Kepi's presence ever did – enough said on that score.

...

Our State is coming along – and here everybody swears that Herschel J.[6] must be Jewish. And I have to explain, patiently, that if he were, the name would be Hank or Hermonides but certainly not Herschel!

But I'm just trying to get my 2 and a half '*grush*' worth – all I have on my mind right now really is Hadassah, and while Ann Strauss is a good kid and a pleasant date, she doesn't rank. She's years behind Hadassah, still has the anti-religious attitude of the adolescent "intellectual." But she's fun anyway.

---

6. Herschel Vespasian Johnson II, US ambassador to the United Nations. See chapter 8, footnote 11.

When are you, the *'giborim'*[7] of the family, coming out here? How about a visit this summer, at least? I know where you can get wonderful meals in Jerusalem...

How the hell did you know so well about Hadassah? Are you psychic – or in touch with her? Oh well, I'm tired enough now to sleep. I just felt like saying hello. Give my best to Munro, Freda, Bob, et al.

love, Mordecai

Mordecai is at his most open and honest in his letters to his sister; he is also arguably at his most self-indulgent. His critique of the women in his life reveals the importance of their religious orientation for him, understandable for an ordained rabbi. There is a plaintive tone to his laments about Hadassah; it seems likely from his phrasing that she had not been on the requisite religious level when they first met but had progressed toward it, unlike Ann, who is a secular intellectual with no interest in religion. At the same time, imagining that Hadassah had "stepped aside" for Kepi is self-delusion on Mordecai's part. In fact, by this time, Hadassah had met her future husband and had no interest in Mordecai.

Sunday, November ??, 1947

Dear Toots,

I know I have been very lax in writing lately, and I won't try to explain why. In part, it was *matzav ruach*,[8] as you might have understood, in part it was being busy – but more of that at some other time.

...GA was finally convinced (after six months of backbreaking work on my part) that with the recent addition of the *AP* service to our news sources I was doing a job for which there should be two men. He decided I should do only editing, and he would find someone to do the

---

7. Hebrew, meaning "courageous ones."
8. Hebrew, meaning "mood."

makeup part of the job. (I'm the only one there, outside of Ted Lurie, who knows makeup). I was delighted. Well, they looked and looked, and finally found a guy – me! So now I cry indeed from "journalism" as Father and I understand it. In brief, overnight it became a job, instead of a lot of fun and excitement. I had decided upon a year's minimum, come what may, and I'll stick to it for a year. But unless there's a change by then in my own particular work I may junk it altogether. It's true it gives me all day to myself, and theoretically, I should get a lot done. But somehow, I haven't been able to keep my mind on serious work, and do a lot of reading and a lot of cafe-sitting.

Your Ann Strauss is quite cute, but her complexion is bad. She works days, of course, and so I shall be able to see her at best at very long intervals. (My one night off a week can not only be used for a "date." Last night I went for a Wizo dinner-dance, which stank with a vengeance. I am now cured of Jerusalem social life, and shall go to Tel Aviv for my next day off, or stay home and go to bed early. They bore me.

I'm all mixed up, on a lot of things, among them the advisability of going back to school for a year and a degree in English lit. The only trouble is – where does it lead? It means a year of fun, of crapping around, if I do go, but at the end of the year, what?

So Herschel[9] came through! We would never have expected it, after Marshall's hemming and hawing. Things are beginning to look up. If some smart Jews in the US would wake up, and recruit a division of ex-servicemen to come here simultaneous with the British withdrawal, it would be a good thing. What do you think?

Mazal Tov on your new apartment – I wish I could say as much for me. The cell I'm in is such that with my bed against one wall and the table against the other, I can

---

9.   Herschel Johnson. See chapter 8, footnote 11.

reach anything on the table while lying in bed. Talk about claustrophobia.

That's all for now – please write, kid, it gets lonely here … and my best to Monroe, I understand he's painting Ohio red and papering the house with $1000 checks.

Love – the brat

P.S. – Since her letter announcing her Zurich trip I haven't heard from Hadassah, although Mother writes a long megillah about phone conversations involving lost and returned letters, which never reached me. Katznelson met the Frischs in London, and brought back enthusiastic reports. She herself never got here though.

Postmarked: Nov 20

Dear Family,

…

A story, before I forget. I was walking down Ben Yehuda one day last week when a tall, angular gentleman accosted (wot a woid) me in the middle of the street. With armored cars, motorcycles and donkeys whizzing by in profusion, he asked whether I would like an interview with a Haganah spokesman, expert on the Arabs (a lot of people here consider me a foreign correspondent because I handle foreign news!). The result of that interview, which took place in a Jerusalem cafe (not the one I frequent) with a fellow I've seen at least a thousand times in the cafe I do frequent, will be mailed to you in a day or three, for forwarding to *PM*,[10] in care of Victor Bernstein or Izzy Stone (I have yet to decide which, I understand Stone is a bit *mefuzar*,[11] and might very easily lose it). I shall send a covering note, telling him of the circumstances of the

10. See chapter 16, footnote 44.
11. Hebrew, meaning "scattered."

piece and reminding him who I am and where and how often we met here. It's a good story, and the approach is a very encouraging one too. So much for that.

I haven't gotten around to [attending classes at] the HU[12] yet — I find reading myself far more interesting and less time-wasting. All I need the HU for, really, is my visa: if you would speed the old passport to me I could dispense with their particular brand of favor. The Joad I read, incidentally, is called *Philosophy for our Times*,[13] and is a fair general survey of philosophical problems and apologia for philo per se: I think there's a good sermon in it too.

Shertok, Dallek, Horowitz, GA, MZR Frank, Pete and Moish are all great men and superb judges of ability, etc. Why not call a meeting of these admirers of mine and have them (in cooperation with another influential admirer — Dan Frisch) decide just how I can best serve the Jewish State. I'm willing to start as No. 2 man in the Political Dep't. I've explored the setup of the Diplomatic (Public-Service) School, and wonder whether it can't be bypassed: a year and a half of monastery life, with a three-year stretch of service at their command seems a bit too much. Further, much of what they learn there I already have behind me. Perhaps Naomi can sound the boys out and find out what's what. In a long session with one of our star reporters last night we agreed that the days of *the Post* — at least as a daily — are numbered; three or four years sound like a fair estimate:[14] I don't think I want to wait until then before changing horses. I definitely intend to round out a full year, but after a rest and a longish *tiyul* I want to get into something a bit more significant for the Jewish State itself. Diplomacy, the political department, seem good fields for a smiling bulls**ter like myself. That I cannot leave Palestine, neither now — as the confinement and birth-pangs get closer

---

12. Hebrew University.
13. C. E. M. Joad, *Philosophy for Our Times* (London, 1940).
14. The *Palestine Post* changed its name to the *Jerusalem Post* in 1950 and continues to publish daily.

and closer – or later, when the infant is bawling lustily for attention and care, is clear enough. I prefer our own brand of corruption and trouble and even evil to the hysteria of a country where Fred Waring[15] tries to cash in on the Communist witch-hunt by refusing to play "Meadowland"[16] because of the "international situation" and relations with Russia. What an ass – non platonic! From his letters, even David[17] is ready to abandon the flesh pots of NY and come to Palestine.

I've sent Gershon, who is a donny boy, a subscription to *B'terem*, probably the best of the periodicals here: a bi-weekly, it deals with internal problems of the Yishuv as well as the political field: it should serve as a goldmine of information and material for lectures and sermonettes. (Who knows – maybe even sermons!)

The Haberdasher[18] interests me: tell me more about this new Christian Revelation in the States (*Time*, incidentally, devotes a good deal of space to religious affairs) – and I could use some material on the number – and names – of recent Jewish traitors to Christianity. Incidentally, Gershon, never fear about me being a dead war correspondent: I

---

15. Fredrick Malcolm Waring (1900–1984) was a popular musician, bandleader, and radio-television personality, sometimes referred to as "America's Singing Master" and "The Man Who Taught America How to Sing."
16. A Soviet Russian song (*Polyushko-polye*), part of Lev Knipper's Fourth Symphony, written in 1934. It was one of the Red Army's marching songs.
17. Probably Mordecai's friend, Rabbi David Greenberg.
18. President Harry S. Truman (1884–1972), owned a haberdashery for a short time before entering public service. He opened the shop with his army buddy, Edward "Eddie" Jacobson in 1919 in Kansas City. Truman tried various business ventures before going into public service. He served as a judge, a senator from Missouri, vice president of the United States under Roosevelt and eventually as president. Jacobson, Truman's friend and business partner, may have been responsible for Truman's openness to Zionism and for ensuring that Weizmann received an audience with Truman at a critical juncture. I don't know how the Chertoffs, in general, or my father, in particular, felt about Truman. The reference to him being a "haberdasher" may be a snide allusion to Truman's early history, or may just be a thoughtless characterization.

love me too much to be a good one, and only the good ones die in harness.

Speaking of passports – they take little time, but visas and PASSAGE take a lot longer to arrange – how about getting started on it? Hurry, or you won't recognize the country.

I saw the Hebrew version of *You Can't Take It With You* – and got quite a kick out of the admittedly amateurish job, particularly the black-face stuff in Hebrew. Tonight, (ahem) I am off, and have a date with Gershon's girlfriend, Ann Strauss. I have no idea what we'll do – the curfew cancelled everything, and while it was lifted this morning, none of the performances have been reinstated. Maybe a movie – even that has become rare enough for me to be something of a treat.

...

Mother – you didn't mean that crack about shutting up when I have nothing to say – it would dry up the correspondence from this end. I took it simply as a figure of speech. Time to dress for my ...."date" good night and all my love,

mersh

Throughout the correspondence there is much discussion about Mordecai's parents coming to Palestine to visit. Their plans change in accordance with the political and security situation. In the following letter it seems that the visit is "on" again.

Monday, Nov. 23, 1947

Dear Family,

That is the best news ever: you're really coming! As soon as I know when to expect you I'll be able to look for a place for you to live. There are a number of possibilities already, but I won't go into them now. However, one thing I would like to know: how do you feel about swapping apartments – ours in NY for one here? It is something to consider, but I must know when you're coming and how long you'll be able to stay. ... I'm in a small room now, and from 2–5 every afternoon the *baal-habayit*[19] sleeps, so that I can't work at home (I am now sitting in someone else's room, to be able to type). After six months we'll see what the situation in Palestine and Jerusalem is, as far as taking a longer lease anyplace is concerned (not as far as whether I'm going to live here or in the States – that was decided back in 1936).

...

What are the chances of Gershon's taking the summer off and coming for a visit? Then he can look into the land situation himself, and not have to rely on me (on the advice of a banker, here in Jerusalem). And I guess Naomi and Monroe are stuck there for the present – soon, though, they may be able to come and settle here too.

I received the passport, and made an attempt to do something with it today, but have so far drawn one blank, I have a few more tricks up my sleeve before I capitulate to the University and really register for this year.

...

By now you should have the passport and visa – what about the reservations? Try not to come on the *Marine Carp* or the *Jumper* – the *Rossia* sounds like a real boat, or the *Vulcania* or *Saturnia* (are they still running?) The most comfortable would be a freighter, if you have the time for it.

But I'd better stop now, I must get some work done.

All my love,

Mordecai

---

19. Hebrew, meaning "owner" or "landlord." Literally, "master of the house."

With apartment mates, left to right: Bernard Katz (Dov Ben Abba), Milt Shulman, Ray Sussman (Ray Noam), Mordecai; 1947, before the UN vote

Chapter 10

The Vote for Partition

As the date scheduled for the vote on partition approached, the details continued to be debated and adjusted in committee. Some countries were clearly in favor, others vehemently against. In a vote of the Palestine Committee on November 25, an amended Partition Plan was approved, twenty-five to thirteen – but it still needed to pass the vote in the General Assembly with a two thirds majority – a result that could not be relied upon.

The amendments to UNSCOP's recommendations favored the Arabs. Britain, the Arabs and the US State Department convinced the UN to reduce the size of the proposed Jewish State from the UNSCOP recommendation, especially in the south. The Partition Plan, formally "Resolution 181 [II]," gave the Jews control of approximately 55 percent of Palestine, consisting of the barren Negev desert (without Beersheba), the central and northern coastal plain between Rehovot and Haifa, and the Jezreel and Jordan valleys. Its population would include 538,000 Jews and 397,000 Arabs. The Arab state would consist of about 42 percent of the land, including the northwestern corner of the Negev, the coastal plain around Gaza, Samaria and Judea as far south as Beersheba, and central and western Galilee. The population would be composed of 804,000 Arabs and 10,000 Jews.[1] The

---

1.   Howard M. Sacher, *A History of Israel* (New York: Knopf, 1991), p. 292.

area of Jerusalem, including outlying villages and Bethlehem, would not be part of either the Jewish or Arab states. Designated a *corpus separatum*, it woul be governed by the UN Trusteeship Council.

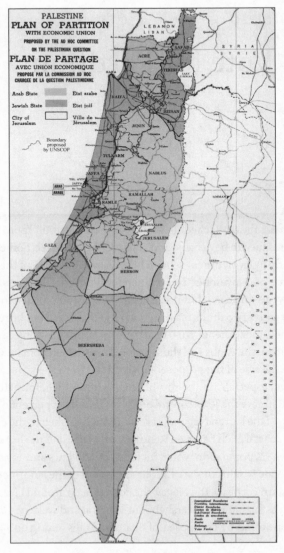

UN Plan for the Partition of Palestine – 1947

In spite of the additional territory, Arab objections to the plan had grown increasingly shrill, to the point where violence was being threatened against Jewish citizens of Arab countries and war promised against the proposed Jewish state. There were hints at an oil embargo and the severing of diplomatic ties with countries supporting partition. The stability of the Middle East was at risk.

A perceptive observation about the differences between the way the Jews and the Arabs addressed these political challenges was offered by General John Glubb ("Glubb Pasha"), the British general who trained and led Jordan's Arab Legion against the Jews. He noted that the Jews accepted every promise or accommodation they could get even if was far less than what they sought. They would pocket, and then leverage, each step in order to gain more. The Arabs did the opposite. They demanded the maximum and would not compromise one iota, thus usually ending up with nothing. The Jews' flexibility and patience strengthened them considerably.[2]

The vote was originally scheduled for November 27. The Yishuv was still concerned that, although there was a UN majority in support of partition, there might not be enough votes to reach the crucial two thirds majority. Supporters were able to delay the vote another day and Zionists in America and Palestine increased their already frantic efforts to round up further support.

After another unexpected and gut-wrenching delay caused by the French delegation, the vote finally took place in Flushing Meadow, New York, late on Saturday afternoon, November 29, 1947. In Palestine, whose fate hung in the balance, the Sabbath had ended and it was approaching midnight.

In a packed hall, the General Assembly presidium at last put draft Resolution 181 on the partition of Palestine to the vote. The proceedings were broadcast live on radio around the world. The vote was conducted in alphabetical order with each country asked whether they were voting for, against, or abstaining. The final result was thirty-three states in

---

2. Lieutenant-General Sir John Bagot Glubb, *A Soldier with the Arabs* (London: Hodder and Stoughton, 1957), pp. 45–46.

favor, thirteen opposed, and ten abstaining. Partition had passed with the requisite two-thirds majority.

Mordecai went to the office after the Sabbath ended in order to monitor the UN vote. The next day, in Hebrew, and apparently in a single sitting, he penned a long, emotional and poetic letter to his family, full of biblical and liturgical allusions – a vivid, powerful and moving account of Jerusalem and its people on the night of the vote and the following day.

What follows is part of the original Hebrew letter, and a translation of the entire letter by Mordecai's granddaughter, Rachel Chertoff Kaminetsky.

November 30, 1947

And so it was – And it came to pass at midnight![3]
And a redeemer will come unto Zion![4]

My dear family – Friday afternoon, before Shabbat, we sat crowded together and fearful around our huge radio in the newspaper office, and heard the proposal to postpone the vote[5] – Our eyes dimmed and our blood froze in our veins: they're "pulling one over on us," as the children say. After the broadcast we walked through the silent and sad streets of Jerusalem, and found no comfort. We envisioned military posts at every corner and machine guns, explosions

---

3. The opening phrase of Exodus 12:29. The verse begins the account of the last of the ten plagues, the smiting of the firstborn, which finally convinced Pharaoh to free the Israelites from slavery in Egypt. Ultimately, that freedom led to the establishment of the first Jewish State. The verse is also the title and refrain of a Passover Seder hymn, each verse of which refers to one of God's miracles on behalf of the Jewish people.

4. Isaiah 59:20. Speaking, as they do, of redemption, they have long been used by rabbis to end sermons, whatever the subject matter. I think Mordecai is using the phrase here to declare the prophecy fulfilled – that redemption has finally come to Zion.

5. The vote was supposed to have taken place on Friday, the 28th, but then the chief of the French delegation, Alexandre Parodi, suddenly proposed that the final vote be postponed one more day to allow for one last attempt at Arab-Jewish reconciliation. His resolution was adopted and the vote was postponed until 4 p.m. on the 29th.

THE PALESTINE
POST

PUBLISHED IN JERUSALEM
BY THE PALESTINE POST LTD.

FIRST ENGLISH DAILY IN PALESTINE, TRANS-JORDAN, SYRIA AND THE LEBANO

and sirens, the terror and suffering renewed. Then comes a clear Shabbat morning under the scalding sun, and the people walk about with some sort of hope and prayer on their lips, and they stream to the Western Wall to pray with the chief rabbis. I visited Rabbi Herzog before going to the office to hear the latest broadcast, and to work with no logical hope of victory but with a great sense that despite all, we will triumph. Friends on the street and at the cafe ask me, the journalist, how the debate will end, what the night will bring and I answer their prayers with a quiet "it will be okay." And until 11:30 [p.m.] I stand hunched over the desk, gloomy and irritable and answer every question with only "It will be okay."

Dr. Aranha begins, and the delegate from Lebanon speaks, and another and yet another after that, and "our Herschel" [Johnson][6] and then Gromyko (hero of the Hebrew state) demands a vote. And suddenly, amid all the chaos, the chairman announces a vote not regarding France's proposal,[7] but on the Partition Plan itself. We sat glued to our seats, each of us with a piece of paper to calculate his prophecy, and pen in hand: [And thus he would count:][8] One, one and two, one and three... thirty-three: a great, joyous cry and silence, the silence of the moment we've awaited for two thousand years. And in the narrow, smoke-filled room, heavy with tension and oppressive concern, one long sigh of relief and fumbling for cigarettes and pipes. As though the Conductor[9] of the dance gave a secret sign – a silent *Mazal Tov* from the depths of the heart.

We left the room, each to his work, and within fifteen minutes the first paper went to print. "*Mazal Tov*"-Cognac bottles are opened and all drink to the Hebrew state. Blessed are we who live in this time and stand on the Holy Land at the time of the great declaration. We embrace and tears of joy glimmer in each eye.

---

6. See chapter 8, footnote 11.
7. To further delay the vote.
8. A reference to the liturgy for the Day of Atonement, which contains a detailed description of the role of the high priest during the Temple service of that day. After slaughtering the sacrificial goat, the high priest took the bowl with the blood into the Holy of Holies, dipped his fingers in the blood and counted each time he sprinkled it on the corner of the altar: "One. One and One. One and Two. One and Three." This dramatic description in the liturgy is introduced with the phrase, "And thus would he count", and the details of the counting are recited responsivly. Mordecai may be suggesting that the vote for Jewish statehood is a kind of "atonement" of the nations for centuries of Jewish suffering.
9. Probably another allusion to the Yom Kippur liturgy in which God is referred to as the "Conductor."

There were those who heard the broadcast and others who called to ask "what's new"- but Jerusalem, dead and deserted by ten at night, was resurrected. We heard a tremendous roar from Ben Yehuda Street *"David Melech Yisrael chai chai vekayam"*[10] and the roar is repeated again and again from the throats of the youth of Jerusalem banding together in a huge hora around an armored police car. I left the office with a young woman who had come to hear the news with me[11] and we raced up the street, we ran and danced and ran and laughed and cried interchangeably without even noticing our tears. We got on a large truck with a great crowd and were like grains of sand – people swarming to the Jewish Agency buildings. And another hora in the building courtyard, men and women in pajamas, half-dressed but completely awake. One young man with a trumpet walked the entire city and people followed him to the Jewish Agency. Police cars drove people to the building, and suddenly they started chanting "get a flag, get a flag..." and suddenly the blue and white appeared on the balcony and a jubilant and fresh "Hatikvah"[12] which we had never dared to hope for and never anticipated, erupted from five thousand mouths.

10. A traditional Jewish (Hebrew) song. The words are: "David, King of Israel, lives eternally." The phrase is found in Tractate *Rosh Hashana*. Yehuda HaNasi was consulting with Rav Chiya with regard to whether to continue the practice of sanctifying the new moon (through which the Jewish calendar was determined), despite the fact that the Romans had prohibited it. The response from Rav Chiya was this enigmatic statement about King David, the implication of it being that despite all difficulties and oppression, present and future, ultimately the Jewish people will be saved – for it is known that the Messiah will be a descendant of King David.

11. In his memoirs, Mordecai says that the young woman was Ann Strauss. He may be misremembering. Had this been true he surely would have named her in the letter.

12. The anthem of the Zionist movement, later adopted as the national anthem of Israel. Its lyrics are derived from a poem written by Naftali Herz Imber (1856–1909), a Jewish poet from Poland who moved to Palestine in 1882. It was set to music by Samuel Cohen in 1888; the melody can be traced back to "La Mantovana," a sixteenth-century Italian song composed by Giuseppe Cenci.

And after that: "Golda, Golda, Golda..." and she appears and speaks simply and touchingly. One old man, tears streaming down, covering his face and disappearing into his white beard, mutters to a six- or seven-year-old grandson "Remember this, remember, this is what I waited forty years for." Tears and laughter intertwine. We sing, we fear to speak, to express what we are feeling.

Now I must get back to the office for the second edition, I approach an armored vehicle with the young woman and ask for a lift, and wishing us, *"Mazal Tov,"* the British policemen in the car lift us on and take us to the door of the building. After the work is done (4:30 AM) we rejoin the singing and dancing and walk through the full, rejoicing streets. Echoes of *"David, Melech Yisrael..."* from the hora circles bounce off every wall. They rise to the heavens and descend like a divine voice, cool and clear and pure and ringing. And all around, the children are climbing up onto every type of vehicle till there is no space, and no way to recognize what kind of vehicle is under them. The little ones shriek with glee and the older ones cry and embrace and run in every direction to see the dancing and the singing and all the people greeting our new state.

We did not sleep. Who could sleep at such a fateful time? I gathered friends at my home and we drank *"L'chaim"*[13] again and again. We returned to the Agency and heard a few lines of Ben Gurion's address and we sang and danced all over again, as if we hadn't run around all night without sleep. All night and all day Jews danced and cried and laughed and repeated *"Mazal Tov,"* and *"L'chaim,"* again and again. And we realized the reason the vote was delayed from Friday to Saturday: The Messiah does not come on Shabbat!

Even now, twenty-four hours after the birth of the State, I sit writing in the office (waiting to finish the second

---

13.   Hebrew, meaning "To life." A toast.

edition) and it is as if a lump is stuck in my throat and I fear I will burst into tears at any moment, unseemly for a hard-hearted journalist.

Only one thing is missing to complete my joy: If only you were here too to "merit seeing the joy of Jerusalem."[14] I see Father's image before me in all the dancing, laughter and tears, and his melancholy words: "Not in my generation – only my children and my children's children will get to see this." Indeed, you were mistaken, and now you must make aliyah and repent. And Mother? You would weep, your face beaming, as it did when I parted from you before making aliyah. And my dear Naomi and Gershon – why did I merit to experience this happiness, while you remain there, in the Diaspora, to read and rejoice from afar? But there is no use complaining: I am representing our family here in Jerusalem, and thank G-d one of us was privileged to witness the first signs of the Redemption and to hear the footsteps of the Messiah – through the feet of Israel's youngsters dancing in the streets – and to feel how close it is.

The People of Israel dwell on its land once more – and we are the last generation of slavery and first generation of redemption.

Who shall sing us the song of this day, without Yehuda HaLevi[15] and Bialik[16] and the prophets, the great poets of

---

14. "All who mourn [the destruction of] Jerusalem will merit to see it in its joy" (Talmud, tractate *Ta'anit* 30b).

15. Yehuda HaLevi (c. 1075–1141), was the most prolific and well known poets of the "Hebrew Golden Age." Born in Spain, he was a doctor and philosopher as well as a poet; his most famous philosophical work is *The Kuzari*. A passionate Zionist, he decided to move to Palestine at the end of his life, despite all the difficulties, but died within a year of his arrival. One of his most famous poems expressed his longing for the Land of Israel and begins with the line, "My heart is in the east, and I in the uttermost west."

16. Chaim Nahman Bialik (1873–1934), was one of the pioneers of modern Hebrew poetry. He ultimately came to be recognized as Israel's national poet.

Israel? Who shall describe this great day and its joy? It is in the heavens...

And we have already paid with our first victims: Seven Jews were murdered today, and who knows how great the number will grow until the day of peace will come to us? But there are no doubts whatsoever. Anyone who heard the *"Ani Ma'amin"*[17] of the celebrating people, and saw the people striding through the streets of Jerusalem, does not fear what is to come. *"David Melech Yisrael, chai, chai, vekayam..."*

Truly, everything will be okay.

Soon I will go to bed, after two days without any sleep at all. But I am not tired: This great miracle stands before me and robs me of sleep- we must be worthy of it!

How was the news received in New York?

And is there not a special blessing, one we have not used for any other event, for any other news, that we can recite now? *"Shehechianu"*[18] is appropriate – but not enough. And yet, until that blessing is found, or that song, that will sing our rebirth: Blessed are You, Lord our God, King of the Universe, who has granted us life, sustained us, and enabled us to reach this occasion. Amen.

Good night.

With much love and great and blinding joy,

Mordecai Shmuel

---

17. The title of a traditional Jewish song based on one of Maimonides' thirteen principles of faith. *Ani Ma'amin* means "I believe." The complete lyrics of the song are: "I believe with perfect faith in the coming of the Messiah, and even though he tarries, I will wait daily for his arrival."
18. Hebrew, literally "who has granted us life." The title of a prayer of thanks usually said to celebrate special occasions, and to mark new and unusual experiences. It is indeed appropriate – and Mordecai goes on to write it out in full in the letter nineteen words latter.

After the UN vote – atop the Jewish Agency building, awaiting Golda, early morning November 30, 1947. (Photo by Judy
Shepard or Alvin Rosenfeld. Used with permission.)

Celebrating the UN vote

Headline: UN Votes for Jewish State. Left to right: Bernard
Katz, Zippy Borowsky, Mordecai, Ray Sussman.

Before receiving his son's description, Paul responds emotionally and
poetically to the UN vote:

> The eve of the eve of Chanukah [December 6, 1947]
>
> > Six days to our Redemption [?]
>
> My dear son Mordecai Shmuel,
>
> First, let me wish you, and us, and all of the nation
> of Israel mazal tov! Mazal tov on the kingdom that is about
> to be built, soon and in our days. In truth, the fact has not
> yet been absorbed in my blood, and has not yet become
> part of my bones, my flesh, my soul. It is hard to believe
> that the same dream that I dreamed all my life has come
> true, it's no longer a dream but a reality. It is hard to get
> used to the idea that the end to the Exile is here, and if
> it's not the full Redemption, at least the "Beginning of
> the Redemption" has arrived. And maybe it's good that I

have not yet fully grasped this event. If I were to feel the full significance of the announcement of the kingdom, my soul would immediately and suddenly expire from an abundance of happiness, my heart would burst from excess joy. Because how could I contain within me this news, the news of the Redemption! Something that fifty generations awaited, hoped for, prayed for and did not merit. What is our merit, the merit of our generation? It is clear to me that these tidings did not come in our merit but in the merit of the thousands upon thousands who were killed and slaughtered and burned in the sanctification of His Name. Their souls filled the hall at the U.N. and castigated the Satans who stood to accuse us, and against their will, all these evil angels answered Amen ...

Overwhelmed by Mordecai's description of the night of the vote, Paul is compelled to write again:

My precious son Mordecai Shmuel,

Your last letter – the description of the celebration of the U.N. declaration of statehood – was superlative. It provided a vivid picture not just of what the Jerusalemites did, but also what they thought and how they felt, and how you felt. I read it the first time and my eyes filled with tears, tears of joy. I tried with all my strength to restrain them, but did not succeed. After that, I had to translate for Mother – I got through the first page with no problem, but when I got to the description of the moment, the moment you heard the announcement, the tears began flowing in a mighty flood and I couldn't utter a single word. And when the river of tears calmed down a bit and Mother heard the translation, she began to cry tears of joy that only a woman can, and thus we sat there, the two of us, crying and had ourselves a "good time."

...

These words also demonstrate to us just how much you are integrated in the land of our forefathers and how much you are connected to our nation, its hopes and its future. I must admit that a feeling of pride, perhaps more than an eighth of an eighth,[19] awakened in our hearts and we say, or we can say, to others, "See the plants we have produced!"[20] You indeed add honor and glory to our family and are worthy of our pride. [Dec. 16, 1947]

In a later letter he adds:

Your description of the joy in response to the declaration is truly excellent... [It] shocks the soul, rattles the heart strings, every detail adds some idea, some point, and the picture emerges whole and clear. It stands, alive, before you and you participate in its happiness, its dances, its songs, and the whole exclaims joy and happiness. [December 30, 1947]

Gershon, too, was full of admiration and compliments. He writes, "So vivid is your account and so easy for us to 'identify.'" In a reference to the Passover Haggadah, which instructs participants at the seder to "feel as though they themselves went out of Egypt," Gershon continues, "Through you we are to regard ourselves as though we were there."

Gershon's English translation of the letter was circulated within the United States and read aloud in synagogues and other venues.

Less than a week after the vote, the British Cabinet decided that Britain would terminate their mandate for Palestine on May 15, 1948 and recommended to the United Nations that the two new countries be established two weeks after that date. Six days later, on December 11th, parliament held a two-day debate on the details of the termination of the mandate. Arthur Creech Jones, the British Colonial Secretary, opened the debate. He referenced the violence that continued between Arabs and Jews and its increasing cost to Great Britain, the Arab refusal to accept partition,

---

19. An eighth of an eighth is the measure of pride suggested in the Talmud (Tractate *Sota* 5a) as permissible, specifically, for Torah scholars.
20. Paraphrased from Tractate *Ketubot* 45a.

and the fact that the United Nation's Partition Plan made little provision for enforcement. [21] Creech Jones was adamant that British troops not be used as instruments of implementing UN policy but only to maintain law and order, "in the area of which they were still in occupation." He reiterated that the British would withdraw their troops by August 1, 1948 and concluded by expressing concern about the increased disturbances since the partition vote. He expressed a hope for an end to the violence and mutual recognition between Arab and Jew: "Palestine and the Arab world, we hope, can now proceed to play a larger part in the general pattern of mankind's march. Under international inspiration, from now on, it is our prayer that the peoples in the Holy Land will co-operate, and find that, while retaining their separate independence, they can join together to mutual advantage in making their country prosperous and happy."

Mordecai's cynical analysis of British behavior is reflected in the following scathing editorial that he wrote for his brother regarding Creech Jones' remarks:

THE MOUNTAIN LABORED

Mr. Creech Jones is to be complimented. In one speech, he has succeeded in putting America on the spot, provoking the Arabs, confounding the U.N. and alienating Russian support for a Jewish State – since Britain is getting out of Palestine anyway, such a state would be unnecessary. In addition, it is meant to placate British public opinion, which has been clamoring for withdrawal in an ever-swelling chorus ever since the hanging of the two sergeants near Netanya.

That Britain will not withdraw, for a long, long time, may already be seen from the qualifications which are being made by British spokesmen on both sides of the Atlantic, their ace-in-the-hole being that the withdrawal must be at such a pace that all the military installations be transferred to North African bases, and not simply abandoned. Since

---

21.   For a full transcript of his remarks, and the debate, see goo.gl/YIuOiK.

the bases are very far from ready, the withdrawal will have to wait...

What appears from the Creech-Jones statement is that Britain has definitely rejected the UNSCOP majority report. For its acquiescence in imposing a solution is premised on the finding of one acceptable to both Jews and Arabs. Since the Jews have indicated, more or less, their acceptance of the report, and the Arabs their refusal to accept it, what we have in effect is the refusal to accept a solution that is unacceptable to the Arabs. Furthermore, the very terms used by Creech Jones, to "impose a solution," is contradictory, since if both sides accept it, it need not be imposed. The implication is, then, (since the British refuse to aid in "imposing" the present suggested solution against Arab wishes) that Britain would agree to the use of force only if a solution acceptable to the Arabs but not the Jews were decided upon.

And so we finally have an official statement, setting forth Britain's motivation and indicating exactly what to expect. Britain is ready to sacrifice what is left of the Jewish people to retain her Arab friendships. That, no more and no less, is the meaning of Creech Jones' appearance before the General Assembly of the United Nations of the World.

Just the other day Britain expressed her certainty, before that body, that the autocratic, totalitarian, oppressive, viciously anti-Semitic Yemen would live up to the "Character of the U.N." That it can hardly do so to any lesser a degree than Britain herself is becoming increasingly obvious.

And to think that it was once poor form to joke about the sun never setting on the British Empire because God wouldn't trust an Englishman in the dark!

Chapter 11

Phase One:
The Civil War Begins

The vote for partition marked the beginning of Israel's War of Independence. The war can be viewed as falling into two distinct phases. The first makes up what Benny Morris and other historians refer to as the "civil" war, which began with the UN partition vote on November 29, and lasted until May 14, 1948, when Ben-Gurion formally declared the establishment of the State of Israel. It is considered a civil war because hostilities took place largely between the Jewish and Arab inhabitants of Palestine, although the Arabs were aided by volunteers from other countries and by Arab irregulars.

The civil war was followed by the "conventional" war, which was initiated by the neighboring Arab states who invaded immediately upon Israel's declaration of statehood. The hostilities ended in the spring of 1949 and armistice agreements were signed that summer.

The first stage of the civil war was characterized by "small scale" fighting and terrorism There were sniper attacks in Jerusalem, Haifa and along the Tel Aviv–Jaffa border, where armed Arabs attacked Jews on the streets. More importantly, there were Arab attacks on Jewish convoys and traffic along various roads throughout Palestine. The constant attacks along the road from Tel-Aviv to Jerusalem and on the road between Hebron and Jerusalem resulted in the siege of Jewish Jerusalem. The first step towards imposing this blockade was the Arab riots in the city, December 1–3, 1947. The use of blockades was an appropriate and effective tactic for the Palestinian Arabs – a fragmented society with no organized or central control – and was highly effective against the Yishuv. The situation on the roads is a major subject in Mordecai's letters going forward.

During December, the *Palestine Post* reported almost daily Arab attacks against Jews, as well as reprisals by the Haganah and Irgun. At the end of December, 1947, the *Post* reported 316 dead and 744 wounded (on both sides) in the twenty-five days since the UN vote.

Until the UN vote for partition, Mordecai's letters were largely focused on personal matters. He reported only sporadically on current events – primarily political developments – but did not describe in great detail the on-going hostilities, the attacks and counter-attacks. But immediately after the vote, as Arab violence exploded, Mordecai offered more details as he sought to reassure his family in the United States that he was not in danger. As part of that process, Mordecai assured them that foreign reporters were exaggerating and sensationalizing events.

December 22, 1947

Dear Family,

Here I had been boasting that my family was the only one which refused to let Carter Davidson's fantasies and Goodwin's lies and Simon's imagination,[1] as printed in the *AP* and *UP* newspaper stories, frighten it, when Ted calls me into the office to show me a letter from Zel, saying that Mother had called him, worried why I hadn't answered your cable. From my answer, which I assume you have by now, you should realize that it may have

---

1. Carter L. Davidson and Joe Goodwin were with the *Associated Press* and Eliav Simon was a correspondent for the *United Press*. They, among others, wrote about the increasing violence in Palestine in the wake of the passage of the Partition Plan.

been a good four or even five days before the cable even
reached me (which was Friday afternoon, when the Rehavia post-office was closed already and the main one a dangerous place to visit and hence un-patronized by me).[2] I
couldn't send my own off until Sunday, and it may have
taken a few days to arrive – all mail is slow as molasses
in winter now, because half of the staff (the Jewish half)
in the main office does not go to work in protest over
the lack of Jewish guards there. All I've received from
you people since the Vote has been one letter from 390[3]
and one from Naomi. By now you have probably heard
from Judy Shepherd and her husband, Al Rosenfeld,[4] of
the NY *Post*, who spent their last night in Palestine in the
Chertoff Pension Pent-House in Rehavia, which strives
to carry out the tradition of hospitality which Father set
forth years ago as an integral part of our planned home
here. In our three rooms we three boys have a sofa, an
air-mattress and a folding bed for spare accommodations,
and can handle all sorts of emergencies. We plan to turn
the "Master bedroom" over to you two when you get here,
and we'll camp in the other rooms. But that's parentheti-
cal. What I wanted to say about them is that they're swell
kids, and they took a picture of me on the roof of the
Agency building the morning after the vote, with crowds

2. The main post office, built by the British and opened in 1938, was at 23 Jaffa Road, where it remains in operation today. It is only a short walk from there to Jaffa Gate and the Old City.
3. The Chertoff family home was at 390 Riverside Drive on the Upper West Side of Manhattan.
4. Alvin Rosenfeld (1919–1992), went on to become a respected journalist, covering nearly all of Israel's wars. He wrote about the War of Independence in 1948 for the *New York Post*, and, together with his journalist wife, the former Judy Shepherd, depicted the difficult early days of mass immigration and austerity in a weekly column, also for the *Post*. He was a correspondent for NBC and was their bureau chief in 1967, when he was the only Western reporter to enter the Old City of Jerusalem with Israeli forces and witnessed the capture of the Western Wall. He was a good friend of Mordecai. Many years later, his son and I worked together in a New York City law firm.

jammed into the court going crazy with joy. I hope you like the picture. They will probably also have reassured you as to the real situation here. I shall not attempt to deny that things are happening, but I do want to emphasize that I am nowhere near them. I live in Rehavia, the heart of Jewish Jerusalem and taboo for Arabs – There hasn't been as much as an Arab vendor or shepherd around in weeks. I never walk home from work at night, but come by car, so even what risk there might be in view of the lateness of the hour is minimized. There is a certain risk – but you've had machine-guns rattling on 42nd Street, and five people were killed recently in gang-warfare in Chicago. Sooo – while I know I can't cable back every time you do – it's expensive and I'm not on a (Junior Hadassah) expense account[5] – nor can I cable to you every time a bullet is fired or a bomb goes off. Mail is necessarily erratic because of the situation, and sometimes more time than I should like elapses between letters: I too must take my turn on the roof looking tough and acting as though I'm doing a job. It's tiring, and at times leads one to neglect even obvious duties. However – please remember that I am not of the stuff of which heroes are made, and prefer to follow the fray from the security of the *Palestine Post* editorial offices and through the confidences of people in the thick of it who must talk to relieve their nerves, and talk to me because they know I am the Fort Knox of information – gold comes in, nothing goes out. I hope I am not asked to reassure you again on this score. Incidentally, we printed both Davidson and Goodwin (*AP*) pieces on the "Battle of Ramleh" ("Knee-deep in stones, barrage of shots." etc.) in the *Post* in parallel columns one day, with our own score of the injured. Davidson had been tipped off that we were going to do it, and the night before, while we were preparing the paper, he came in at midnight, as we were about to go to press, and whined that we were making

---

5.   Like his sister, Naomi.

him look ridiculous and we shouldn't print it: there being two truths, one for foreign consumption and one of what actually happened, and one must not compare the two for fear of looking ridiculous. Of course the stunt did not hinder the guy from continuing with the same junk, after all, NY pays him, not the *Post* in Jerusalem. We're doing the same thing to [Gene] Currivan of the *Times* tonight, though we know it won't help.... They write of every shot fired as a major engagement – it sells more papers, and every time someone looks at them cross-eyed they've been "threatened by a hate maddened mob" and become newspaper heroes of the Battle of Partition....

(I sent Frisch a piece the other day, and am waiting to hear about it.) Meanwhile – we have direct evidence that the British are giving the Arabs arms: a Sten gun (simply-constructed machine-gun of Haganah manufacture, mod-elled after the guns dropped to the partisans in Europe during the war) confiscated from Jews by a British patrol, later found in an Arab's possession. There are more such stories – one is all I can tell at present. ....

My apologies to Gershon for having neglected his editorials lately: I'm so busy with local news and so unin-terested in anything else that I find it almost impossible to keep writing sweet little nothings. I'll try again soon, anyway. It is now 2:12 a.m. – second edition going to press, and so goodnight, and be well. Write – and don't worry overmuch.

Love M.

As Mordecai describes above, the *Post* had an occasional feature called "As Others See Us," in which they contrasted events as experienced in Pal-estine with the way they were portrayed in the foreign press. There was an incident in Ramleh on December 4 which was included in the *Post* on December 7, 1947 as part of a simple round-up of events. It reported that stones were thrown at a convoy of buses carrying Jews. The escort returned fire and at least four people were hurt. This was repeated with another convoy travelling in the other direction. The road was then closed to Jewish traffic.

The *Post* printed exceprts from two Associated Press reporters. At the time, AP was the largest news agency in the world serving over three thousand newspapers, mostly in the US. Their reporter, Carter Davidson, offered a colorful description of the event writing that Ramleh was "knee deep in stones," that shots fired struck his car and wounded his driver. Joe Goodwin reported on Davidson's experience, but with more drama. He wrote that a "violent street battle is raging in the Arab town of Ramleh on the Jerusalem–Tel Aviv road." He called the town a "shambles," and said that "furious mobs beat against the iron wall of encircling British troops and police. ..."

Mordecai may have been dismissive of their tendency toward melodrama, but it is not clear that the foreign reporters were greatly exaggerating the situation. As is apparent from Carter Davidson's article, the Arabs controlled the only road from Tel Aviv leading up to Jerusalem along which all food supplies for Jerusalem were brought by convoys. The winding, narrow road passed close to numerous Arab villages and the many large rocks along its edge provided ample positions from which Arab snipers could shoot at the slow-moving convoys.

The vote for partition had been like a starter's pistol heralding a dramatic acceleration in violence. Mordecai's letter was dated the 22nd of December, by which time casualty figures on both sides were rising dramatically.

But the violence was not confined to Palestine. The almost one million Jews who lived in Arab countries[6] were also at great risk. In Syria, on December 1, there were riots in Aleppo, with dozens of Jewish casualties. In Damascus, thirteen Jews were killed, eight of them children, and twenty-six wounded. Ten synagogues and five Jewish schools were torched and 150 Jewish homes damaged. In the British administered part of Yemen (Aden), during a five day period early in the month, approximately seventy-five Jews were killed and one hundred and twenty were

6.   See Jews Indigenous to the Middle East and North Africa, http://www.jimena.org/jimena-country-by-country, for a country by country census, as well as Arieh Avneri, *The Claim of Dispossession* (Tel Aviv: Hidekel Press, 1982), p. 276.

wounded (thirty-four Arabs were also killed). The *Post* reported on December 21 that Egypt had submitted a draft resolution to the Arab League declaring Jewish citizens of Arab states citizens of the Jewish state and thus enemies of the Arab States. Their bank accounts would be frozen and all Jews would be interned as political prisoners unless they joined the Arab armies to fight against the Zionists.

Beyond the danger of the Arab citizens of Palestine taking it upon themselves to attack Jewish suburbs and settlements, there were organized forces planning the destruction of the Yishuv. Within Palestine, Arab forces were commanded by two men, Abdul Khader al-Husseini[7] and Hasan Salama. They formed "the Army of the Holy War" and started recruiting fighters. Salama took responsibility for the area near Tel Aviv, while al-Husseini established his headquarters at Bir Zeit, near Ramallah, and began attacking the convoys to Jerusalem that carried food, water and fuel to the Jewish inhabitants of the city.

Outside Palestine, Arab nations were determined to act against the Yishuv immediately in order to prevent a Jewish state from ever being declared. While the British were still in Palestine, these forces could not send their own armies in; that would essentially mean declaring war on Britain itself. Instead, on January 1, 1947 the Arab League officially formed the "Arab Liberation Army," the ALA. Headquarters were set up in Damascus, Syria, where the Arab League's military committee was based. Fawzi al-Qawuqji was selected to lead the army and began gathering recruits. Most were Syrian, Lebanese or Palestinian, with some hailing from Iraq, Jordan, Bosnia, Egypt and Turkey, and a few even from Germany and Britain. Benny Morris writes that at its peak in April and October of 1948, the ALA had some four to five thousand troops and access to hundreds of local volunteers in its areas of operation.[8]

Meanwhile, the British authorities were doing little to keep order. In his memoirs, Roy Elston, a British non-Jew who came to Palestine

---

7.   Abdul Khader al-Husseini (1907–1948), nephew of Haj Amin al-Husseini, the grand mufti of Jerusalem, founded the secret militant group, the "Organization for Holy Struggle" in 1933, and commanded its men in its "Army of the Holy War" during both the Arab revolt of 1936–1939 and during the 1948 civil war and War of Independence.

8.   Morris, *1948*, p. 90.

to work for the Mandatory government during World War II, offers a scathing indictment of the British. He became sympathetic to the Jews and wrote a front page column in the *Palestine Post* under the pen name, "David Courtney." In his memoir of the period he laments that, in spite of having fifty thousand troops in Palestine, the British did "nothing" to protect the Jews nor to keep the roads open. He accuses them of leaving the land open to bands of armed marauders who attacked Jews and of allowing the area to descend into anarchy, to be resolved by Arabs of the adjacent countries – some of whom were trained by the British themselves. Like Mordecai, he suggests that the military administration was cowardly, hiding in heavily protected zones and houses from which Jews had been ejected and is outraged by the British treatment of desperate Jewish refugees. He levels specific criticism of the British for "snubbing" the UN commission and for making no effort to stabilize the situation. He concludes by accusing Attlee, Bevin, and the Colonial Secretary of thinking that the Jews "deserved no better than they were about to get."[9]

Indeed, in spite of the passage of the Partition Plan and the inevitability of a worsening military situation, there was still no change in British immigration policy: ships bearing refugees arriving at the Palestine shore were boarded violently by British soldiers, often with loss of life, and turned away. During the month of December, approximately fifteen thousand refugees were denied entry to Palestine and either forced back to Europe or sent to British controlled DP camps in Cyprus.

The situation in Jerusalem was especially grim. In his memoirs, my father wrote, "Food was rationed, and water was brought by a tanker three days a week, one bucket to a family." In December, the Jewish Agency set up the Jerusalem Emergency Committee, which began to stockpile food, fuel and water. Fifty truckloads of goods a week were required to supply the Jewish population of Jerusalem. By the end of 1947, the Jewish section of the city was essentially under siege.

---

9. D. R. Elston, *No Alternative* (London: Hutchinson, 1960), p. 58. Mordecai's thorough indictment of the British, "On the Crimes of the British," was implemented in a long article written in Hebrew for the periodical *Hadoar*.

As the new year dawned, the tension in the country and in Jerusalem in particular, was palpable. There were battles and skirmishes everywhere, marginally sea-worthy ships overloaded with desperate refugees continued to be turned away by the British, and Jerusalem remained under siege. With the city isolated, residents were doubling up on jobs and exhaustion was setting in. The main post office, which had previously been inaccessible to Jews because of its location, was closed completely. Mordecai tells his family to send mail to Tel Aviv instead, confident that he will get it eventually, despite the dangers on the road between the two cities.

During the first phase of the civil war the Jews were largely on the defensive with most of the fighting occurring in areas designated for the Jewish state. There was little fighting in the largely Arab-populated areas such as the central and upper Galilee, Samaria, or the area south of Jerusalem (except the Etzion Bloc). The British were responsible for keeping the peace throughout mandatory Palestine and declared their official policy to be one of impartiality and non-intervention on behalf of either side. In actuality, they intervened frequently during this period, occasionally on behalf of besieged Jewish settlements, and more frequently in support of Arab attacks on Jews.[10] By the end of March, there was such enmity between the Jews and the British that several hundred British servicemen deserted their posts to join the Arab ranks. The British tended to help whichever side was demographically dominant in each area. This ambiguous role is one source of Mordecai's loathing of them and their methods.

---

10.   See Morris, *1948,* p. 79.

Chapter 12

On the Crimes of the British

January 7, 1948

Dear Gershon,

One loses all track of time here: nobody is doing just one job, and 24 hours in the day are not enough, so one sleeps less. After working double and triple time for a while, one collapses: one can do only one full job for a while. Tonight, I have a full night off, all to myself, and if nothing untoward happens (vain hope) I may not be bothered at all, and will go to bed real early. A whole night's sleep! It all comes from there not being enough Jews around – those of us who are here have to double up.

This letter has arrived via very devious channels: with the Jerusalem post office closed and the US telegraphers on strike it is the only way left. You realize, of course, that I have had nothing from you people in about three weeks now – when I think of the pile which must be accumulating and consider the orgy of reading I'll indulge in when the mails are finally resumed it's more than a bit exciting. Write to me not to Jerusalem, but to Tel Aviv: simply *"Palestine Post,* Tel Aviv," and they'll get it to me via our inter-office circuit, which is still open.

... I sympathize with the way your rabinnating keeps you busy, but that's only seven days a week, and never more than 24 hours a day, as people are busy here.

I can't do another description of the celebration — too much has happened since then, too many emotions have gripped the Yishuv, and today, while not completely immersed in other things, we're busy hating our English cousins. You'll never believe what they're doing here, even though you've been here and seen them in action. They've emerged as the biggest group of unmitigated s**ts it has ever been my misfortune to be near. The kindest word for them would be murderers — the proper word has yet to appear. (Perhaps "English" will become an adjective, as "Nazi" has.) Father's letters are still a delight — I could go out and shoot a couple of Arabs if only because they've interrupted the flow, and a few armoured cars, because they haven't prevented the interruption.

Incidentally, the British navy sent out Christmas cards which you would like: [a British ship] (which went refugee-hunting") has as its emblem (on the xmas cards) a frail-looking ship on a stormy sea with the inscription "they shall not pass." I saw one with my own eyes, and had trouble not puking. The lice! They're the same boys who won awards for "gallantry." Perfidious Albion indeed!

Money, as you and Father understand it, is needed here urgently for a special job,[1] and cannot be gotten through the "usual" channels. I want you to pass the sombrero around for a few thousand; I've written to Naomi and to Dan[2] (father of that lovely young lady[3] in Chicago),

---

1. Unfortunately, I do not know to what he is referring.
2. Daniel Frisch, head of the ZOA.
3. Hadassah Frisch.

and asked them to get to work. Before I seal this letter I'll enclose the name and address of the guy who should get the money (in NY): he has the connection to transfer it to us as it should be done. If I forget, I'll cable the address. I may not have it early enough tonight, and I want to get the letter off. All I can tell you is this: many many lives can be saved if certain work is done; it has nothing to do with dissidents, I'm ready to stake what's left of my share of *olam haba*[4] on the propriety of the project and its urgency and worth. Were the money for me I would be shy about asking for it – but *lema'an hamoledet*[5] I have enough chutzpah for a city. I invoke all the *nachas* I've ever earned the family, whatever maturity you consider me to have, any value you attribute to my opinions and judgment, and pray that you don't fail me – us. I'm doing what little I can here – you have no right not to do what you can there. Cast up all the Zionist speeches, sermons and articles which our family has sired and delivered, and God help you if you can resist your own appeal to others!

Aside from this, and my job, and waiting to hear from Hadassah, and all the plotting and counter-plotting around me, I haven't a thing to do but sleep. Sleep – what a precious commodity, ranking higher even than a hot bath! I'm going to eat a long, slow, hot meal now, perhaps take in a movie, then curl up with a book and a bottle of choice old Adom Attic[6] (port wine) at about six cents a glass, and relax. And then to bed. Be good, but above all, be quick.

Love –

Mordecai Shmuel

Mordecai's family is understandably very anxious about the situation in Palestine. Paul writes:

---

4.   Hebrew, meaning literally "world to come," i.e., heaven, eternity.
5.   Hebrew, meaning "for the sake of the homeland."
6.   The words are Hebrew, meaning literally "old red."

Permit me to tell you that until the full Redemption arrives, we here find ourselves in a state of anxiety. First, we fear for your safety, despite your many promises that you are being careful and staying away from dangerous places, and we console ourselves that the difficult battles are far from your home. Even so, we haven't ceased worrying. Even more, though, we fear for the safety of the Yishuv in general. True, our young people demonstrate remarkable courage, theirs does not fall short of the fortitude of our heroes from the distant past, Ehud, Gideon, and the Maccabees, but ultimately, there are casualties among them every day—and until when? Particularly intense is the fear when we know that the "keepers of order"[7] especially protect the adversary.

The first year of our Redemption. (Jan. 9, 1948)

That Mordecai could have imagined that "English," could become a pejorative adjective on par with "Nazi" is a shocking, damning indictment. He explains in detail what leads him to that judgment.

January 11, 1948

Dear folks,

It is now just noon, in the dead of winter, and I'm sitting on our unbelievably spacious balcony here in Ravakia,[8] the Penthouse Paradise of Rehavia, typing with my sleeves rolled up and wearing dark glasses to protect myself from the glare. The sun is full on my face, and I can almost feel the cold I caught in last week's hailstorm drying up. A good feeling. Aside from the woman down the block who is beating her rug and the hoarse cry of a fruit vendor it's

---

7. An allusion to the British authorities.
8. This is a play on words – a mashup between *"ravak,"* which means bachelor, and the name of the Jerusalem neighborhood in which he lives – Rehavia, i.e., "bachelor-neighborhood."

as quiet as the borscht belt[9] probably is now. It is very difficult to believe that just last night Ramat Rachel[10] was attacked by foolishly ambitious Arabs, who had their asses pushed in by some very good friends of mine at the Kibbutz (I've spent some time there lately, since the road to Tel Aviv is a bit too exciting for me, and on a day off one likes to get away from the same streets and restaurants). My old school pal,[11] incidentally, has become something of a gun in the "bloody Jewish Haganah," as your English cousins call it, and after having met some of his pals, I must say I'm glad they're on our side! By chance, I have a few friends who are pretty important too, and so with the magic name I can get into GHQ and pick up military secrets by the earful. Interesting stuff, too, although I still don't know whether or not the Arabs are right in thinking we have the atom bomb — that's one secret they're keeping even from me.

Incidentally, lest I forget to mention it — I hate the British. Even having been here in '36, you can't believe, much less imagine what they're doing from so great a distance. They've fired on Haganah outposts, they continually disarm convoys (Hans Beyt[12] was killed in an attack on a convoy, and he died fighting, literally: he had a licensed pistol, and used it well up to the last minute). When the Haganah has beaten off an attack they [the British] ignore the Arab attackers and search the defenders for arms, which they invariably confiscate when they can, their official news communiques are a tissue of lies, and the official press conference an example

---

9. "Borscht Belt" was the colloquial term for the summer resorts in the Catskill Mountains that catered to a Jewish clientele. Since it is January, those summer resorts would be currently empty.
10. A kibbutz just south of Jerusalem.
11. Unknown.
12. Hans Beyt was the head of the Jewish Agency's youth immigration department. He was killed in an Arab attack on a convoy on the Tel-Aviv–Jerusalem road near the Castel on December 26. Golda Meir was lightly wounded in the attack, and her bodyguard, Haganah Warrant Officer Abraham Filman, was seriously wounded (JTA December 28, 1947).

of the kind of ambiguity of which it seems only the English language is capable – in the mouth of a Britisher. We all feel the same here: let 'er go, fast: we've got the strength to take care of ourselves if we have to fight on only one front. Most guns shoot in one direction only, and so we'd rather not have the British behind us.

But you Jews are letting us down. How can you let them spot the stuff we should be getting with every ship that reaches Palestine? After all the successful bootlegging and rum-running experience garnered during the dry years, why can't you get that stuff out without being stopped! It doesn't help when it gets caught, it's bad for morale and bad from a logistic point of view.

The mail foul up is now over. After having had a few train-loads stolen and the Jerusalem (main) post office closed for almost two weeks, it has finally been included within the zone (security zone, i.e., British area of head-quarters, C.I.D., etc., and the Jews and Arabs are coming back to work, safe from each other's over-zealous friends) and I imagine I should make quite a haul today. I'll be lazy-ing my way downtown in about an hour for my usual full (and expensive) meal, and expect a nice packet of mail at the office. *Halevai*.[13]

Last Friday night Aliza Levin and Zippy Borowsky were over for dinner, which they cooked very nicely indeed. Carmi Charny was with us too, and it was a real Friday night meal, complete with *chaleh*,[14] Kiddush,[15] can-dles and flowers.[16] After it, I went to see "somebody,"[17] and so when we heard heavy firing off in the distance about

---

13. Hebrew, meaning "I hope," or "I wish."
14. Yiddish spelling of challah, the festive loaves of bread served during Shabbat and holiday meals.
15. Prayer recited over wine at a Shabbat or holiday meal.
16. In her published letters from the same period, Zippy Borowsky offers a very similar description of that evening. Zipporah Porath, *Letters from Jerusalem*, pp. 73–74.
17. Presumably someone in the Haganah.

midnight (all our guests always sleep over, rather than have to break up a *mesibah*[18] early) while they all guessed vaguely, I was able to smile smugly and finally tell them just what Arab village was being visited and chastised for just what offense. Chertoff – always in the know! Unhappily, it's just the stuff you'd like to read that I mustn't write: once it's been in the newspapers I'm permitted to talk; until then I mustn't. The result is a very special kind of frustration and an almost perpetual smug, knowing smirk and a permanent worry wrinkle over this or that pending operation and its chances. But what the hell – "*yihiyeh tov*,"[19] as almost every conversation on conditions closes around here.

As you can well understand, I haven't been foolish enough to take a trip to Tel Aviv lately, though I haven't yet seen Untermann.[20] When things quiet down (and only then) I'll do so. For the present I'm shuttling between Rehavia's by-now-famous penthouse and down town (not too far down) and the gorgeous view from the Ravakia *mirpeset*.[21] It sounds terribly limited, but feels so only on rare, nervous occasions.

And now, if you'll be so kindly, I'll retire to the deck chair and read my *B'terem* until Milt[22] gets back, and we

---

18. Hebrew, meaning "party."
19. Hebrew, meaning "It will be okay." A ubiquitous Israeli phrase still used when discussing any problem, including serious ones.
20. Chief Rabbi of Tel Aviv and close friend of Mordecai's father from Volozhin in Russia.
21. Hebrew, meaning "balcony" or "patio."
22. Milton Shulman, a close friend of Mordecai. Born in Chicago, Shulman attended the University of Chicago and obtained a degree in agronomy after serving in the 89th Infantry Division during World War II, in the European Theater. After completing his degree, he did a year of overseas study at the Hebrew University between 1947–1948. While he was there, he volunteered for the Haganah. In later life, he became an early expert in computer science. He was a professor at DePaul University, and then at the University of Illinois. Shulman offers some memories at https://www.dvidshub.net/news/102913/storming-gates-memories.

go out to eat. The sun is so warm, and makes me feel sooooooo lazy! Besides, I want to *chap arein*,[23] I may have to work this afternoon.

    Shalom – and I hope I hear from you tonight. If your lousy telegraphers' strike was over I'd wire!

Love,

Mordecai

Mordecai working from home

It is clear that Mordecai sees the British as an enemy of the promised Jewish state and, judging by their actions, it's hard to disagree. As he describes, they gave active assistance to the Arabs who were attacking Palestinian Jews and continued their draconian policy of refusing entry to Jewish refugees despite the fact that there would soon be a Jewish state.

    Although the British had themselves referred the problem of Palestine to the UN, when it voted for partition, they acted against its implementation. The General Assembly's resolution approving partition had stipulated that a commission be formed to take over the reins of government from the retreating British Mandatory government. Control would

---

23.   Yiddish, literally meaning "catch in," i.e., seize an opportunity.

then be handed over to the new Arab and Jewish states respectively. The first meeting of the commission, which was composed of representatives from five countries – Czechoslovakia, Bolivia, Denmark, Panama and the Philippines – took place on January 9. The commission's members were tasked with familiarizing themselves with the general affairs of the government of Palestine, but their requests to visit the country were refused – the British would not cooperate. Arthur Creech Jones, the colonial secretary, claimed that it would be "undesirable for the Commission to arrive in Palestine until shortly before the termination of the Mandate." The British balked at the idea of an orderly and gradual transfer of power; Sir Alexander Cadogan, the U.K.'s permanent representative to the UN, claimed it would result in "confusion and disorder."[24]

January 12, 1948

Dear Gershon,

Mazal tov – yours is the first letter I've received since the resumption of mail service here. It is the one dated December 18, so you can understand how I've been cut off here lately.

I trust that you've been getting *B'terem* by now, they simply started your subscription a month late. My copies haven't arrived from Tel Aviv because of the transport situation, and I'll be damned if I'll go there for them – I'm not that anxious to see what my share of *olam haba* will be.

Your account of the reception my "victory" description letter received reads strangely these days, with Jews being killed daily and the Syrians getting rambunctious.[25] But I like reading that I did a good job. I'm sending, under separate cover, a story I did on a Haganah girl who was

24. Sources: David Tal, *War in Palestine, 1948: Israeli and Arab Strategy and Diplomacy* (Routledge, 2004), pp. 76–77, and Howard M. Sachar, *A History of Israel: From the Rise of Zionism to Our Time* (NY: Knopf, 1991), p. 295.

25. The "rambunctious Syrians" to whom Mordecai refers are probably the Second Yarmouk Battalion of the Arab Liberation army. The battalion entered Palestine from Syria on January 8 and set up a base in the Galilee. The army was formed

killed a week ago, Hanna Zuta (the writer's daughter). I had seen her here and there around town without knowing who she was, and a blind date was to be arranged for two days after what turned out to be the day of her death. Getting the information on her together I found myself getting to know her and like her, and now I feel as though I lost a real friend – though we had never exchanged two words together! I have the original of the picture we printed with the article – she was quite a girl, all in all. Incidentally, sometime next month a fellow by the name of Yaakov Shapiro ("Shapik") will drop in to see you. He's being sent to study plastics for his *meshek*[26] he'll be able to tell you quite a few interesting stories,[27] and will bring you some mail I'd rather not have opened en route by the wrong people. He's a real good guy, what is known here as *"eisen beton."*[28]

How can I explain my editorial lapse? I could leave it to Shapik when you see him, but this much I can say: I'm working most of the day now too, on extra-curricular activities,[29] which leave me very little room for writing gay little tidbits. Besides, I'm much too preoccupied with current events here to be able to think about other things.... I'll try though, to get back into that editorial habit, though it is really very difficult these days. *Nu* – so I didn't finish the letter last night. I'll try to now.

One of the things bothering me these days is the folk's trip. Unless things quieten down, there is not much point to their coming in April. For them to be limited to Rehavia in Jerusalem and Tel Aviv as the sum total of their travelling here hardly seems to justify the expense and trouble of the trip. I don't want to frighten them – once safely settled in either of

---

with the goal of destroying any potential Jewish state. The Arab League military committee, which was responsible for the army, was headquartered in Damascus, Syria.

26. Hebrew, literally "administration" but usually used to refer to a kibbutz administration, i.e., his kibbutz is sending him for training.
27. Unfortunately, many of these "interesting stories" are lost.
28. Yiddish, meaning "iron and concrete," i.e., a strong person.
29. For the Haganah.

these places it's okay – but it's the getting from one to the other that's fouled up. At the same time, seeing how the kibbutzim have grown these last twelve years is entirely out – they have neither the time nor the patience to be hospitable these days, and going out to them is rather dangerous. While I realize that what I've just written will induce more worry than they've been enjoying on my account, that's far better than leaving them with illusions as to how pleasant a trip they can expect. I believe that by the summer things will have cleared up a good deal, but let them plan on making their trip a little later than they had originally expected. Missing you all as I do it's very unpleasant to have to write these things, but this is no time to crap around. The thought of Mother deciding where she can go and what she can do on the strength of the imagined protection her American passport gives her frightens me more than all the bullets in Palestine and there are plenty of those. And you know that keeping her home (within the safe areas) is a truly Herculean task. It will be far better for her nerves and for Father's ulcers – and for my peace of mind and my work – if both of them keep the ocean between themselves and the "concerts"[30] as we call them. Now that I've written the worst, you can rest assured that when I do write "come" they can come, safely, and not leave an anxious family worrying on both sides of the Atlantic.

I have nothing more to write at present. My own contribution is being made well within the framework of my profession – Shapik will tell you more, with details, when he gets to the States. For the present time, be well, don't worry unduly, and PLEASE WRITE. Mail service has been resumed, and haven't heard from any of you Yankees in a month.

Layla Tov ve'kol Tuv.[31]

Love,

Mordecai Shmuel

---

30. Barrages of gunfire.
31. Hebrew, meaning "good night and all the best."

Following is the article Mordecai mentioned in the letter above. It appeared in the January 12 edition of the *Post*, page 4:

HANNAH ZUTA
By a Staff Correspondent (MSC)

Hannah Zuta was twenty-four when she was killed while trying to bring wounded comrades back to an outpost in Beit Israel during a heavy attack from Sheikh Jarrah Quarter last week.

A Haganah veteran of as many years as her age permitted, she was a platoon commander on leave in Jerusalem; her leave had been spent trying to obtain a transfer to a more active duty than that on which she was actually employed. At the time of her death she was visiting friends in an outpost, and when the attack developed tried to help at least in saving the casualties.

Hannah was born in New York, where her father was studying, and came to Palestine with her parents when she was four. She was educated at the Reali School in Haifa, and then came to Jerusalem, where she graduated from the Rehavia Secondary School, and then attended the teachers' Seminary at Beit Hakerem. Her ambition was to teach, a profession that ran in her family, for her grandfather was the writer and teacher H. A. Zuta,[32] and even in the free time that her service with Haganah left her she was studying at the Hebrew University.

No Time

It was the tragedy of her generation that national service should have left her so little time for study, for Hannah was a good teacher. When she was nineteen she joined the

---

32. A well-respected teacher in Palestine. His memoir, *Darko shel Moreh: Pirkei Zikhronot Sekirot Uma'amarim* (The Path of a Teacher: Memoirs and Articles) was published in 1938 by R. Mas in Jerusalem.

Palmach on the beginning of its expansion programme, and served in Upper Galilee and Samaria.

When the Yishuv was called upon to serve in the British Army, she joined the ATS,[33] and saw service in Cairo and Gaza. In the comparatively placid days of service after the Middle East fighting was over, driver Zuta had no time to waste, vigorous and determined in mind and body, she seemed always to be in several places at once, working, studying and, above all, teaching newcomers Hebrew and Palestinology.

"*Hannah Hayafa*" (beautiful Hannah) even became the subject of a curious – and quite untrue – legend in her lifetime. It appears that one day, during the excitement over the murder of Lord Moyne in Cairo, her uniform was stolen while she was bathing at a pool. About the same time, for a bet, she had cropped her thick fair hair, and promptly the story circulated that her stolen Army clothing had been found in the possession of the youths charged with Lord Moyne's murder, that she had been arrested and returned from the inquisition with her head shaved.

She was not a heroine; she herself would have repudiated the term though she took very seriously all she saw to be her duty. Had you asked her, she would have said that she was no different to every other girl, and youth, who offered himself for service when the need arose, and prepared for this need beforehand by rigorous training. She was not the only one of her stamp, but each such life wasted is a grievous loss.

As it turned out, Mordecai did not get the circumstances of Hannah Zuta's death quite right. The exact details were revealed only relatively recently in an article published on October 30, 2015 in *Haaretz*. Correspondent Ofer Aderet interviewed Yaakov Shafrir who, in 1948, had

---

33. The Auxiliary Territorial Service – the women's branch of the British army. Hannah served as a truck driver.

been an economics student at Hebrew University, a photographer, and a member of the Haganah.[34] The article relates:

> [Shafrir] was sent to photograph the path leading to the mufti's Jerusalem home, in preparation for Husseini's assassination... Just before commencing the operation, Shafrir spent time at a workers restaurant in Jerusalem. When he'd had enough to eat, he met with a twenty-five-year-old female university student, Hana Zuta.

> The two young people spent the evening together, and Shafrir decided to tell Zuta what he was about to do: "I told her about the order I had received and she said, 'I'm coming with you,'" Shafrir recalls... The two devised a plan to pretend that Shafrir was innocently taking pictures of Zuta, the couple a pair of lovers strolling through city neighborhoods. He planned to give the pictures to his commanders so they could get the lay of the land around the mufti's house before setting out to kill him. When they got to the site, though, the two were shot at by snipers. One of the bullets hit and killed Hana.

---

34.   Ofer Aderet, "The Student Sent to Help Kill the Mufti," *Haaretz*, October 30, 2015.

Chapter 13

The Palmach

In Mordecai's article about Hannah Zuta, he mentions the Palmach, an acronym for *plugot machatz*, literal meaning: "strike forces." The Palmach was the elite fighting force of the Haganah. Up to this point, Mordecai has not mentioned them in his letters, but he does so frequently from here on out.

From almost the outset of WWII, the British realized that they needed as much help as possible in blocking a possible invasion of the Middle East by the Germans and, as a result, temporarily eased their previous restrictions on Haganah activity. Thousands of Palestinian Jews volunteered to serve in the British military in order to fight the Nazis. The British employed them for such tasks as identifying bridges and tunnels that could be sabotaged in Lebanon, Syria, Turkey and Iran. With so many Haganah volunteers away fighting with the British,[1] there was a need for an elite, well-trained Jewish "strike force" in Palestine to defend the Yishuv against any invading Axis army and, eventually, to defend the Yishuv from Arab attacks in the event of a future British withdrawal from

---

1. By January 1942, eleven thousand Palestinian Jews were serving with British forces in the Middle East; by August of the same year they numbered eighteen thousand. See Howard M. Sachar, *A History of Israel*, pp. 232–33.

Palestine. The Palmach was established in May, 1941 with the approval of the British who even provided the initial funding. The Palmach fought successfully against Vichy French forces in Lebanon and Syria and were a key element of the British-approved plan for the defense of the Yishuv in the event of an Axis invasion. But when the threat of invasion of Palestine evaporated with the victory of the battle of al-Alamein in July 1942, British support for the Palmach dissolved. They closed Palmach training bases and appropriated their weapons.

Palmach units infiltrated a government arsenal and took back their weapons, at which point the British once again declared them illegal. The Haganah and its strike force simply went underground. They continued to develop their military capabilities and, having lost British support, funded their efforts by living, working and training on kibbutzim. Palmachniks were trained in physical fitness, small arms, hand-to-hand combat, first aid and more. Most received advance training in one or more areas such as sabotage and explosives, reconnaissance, sniping, communications, and operating machine guns or mortars. Great emphasis was placed on training commanders to be independent and broadminded so that they would take the initiative and set an example for their troops. They became the military elite, their motto and battle cry was *"acharai"* – "after me." Palmach commanders led their troops into battle, rather than sending their soldiers ahead.[2] There were approximately three thousand members of the Palmach by the end of 1947.[3]

Mordecai's respect and affection for the Haganah and the Palmach and antipathy for the Irgun and Lehi are recurring themes throughout his letters. In the "editorial" for Gershon in the letter below he argues that the terrorist organizations' methods frustrate rather than further military goals.

2. This ethic of leadership persists until today. In a quip instantly recognized and appreciated by Israeli moviegoers, Israeli actress and Israeli army veteran, Gal Gadot, in the 2017 movie, "Wonder Woman" sneers, "Where I come from generals don't hide in their offices. They stand beside their soldiers. They die with their soldiers."
3. See Jon Kimche, David Kimche, *A Clash of Destinies: The Arab-Jewish War and the Founding of the State of Israel*, p. 77. Note that Bruce Hoffman put the number at five thousand at the end of 1946 (see chapter 2, footnote 7). Benny Morris's estimates accord with those of Kimche.

January 15, 1948
(A year less one month)[4]

Dear Gershon,

Here are two bits for you: a little news story we couldn't print for obvious reasons, and the Dissident-Haganah edit. Use them in good health.

JERUSALEM, Thursday. – Three men in a taxi were over-taken by a plain-clothes police patrol in David Street in the Bukharan Quarter of Jerusalem before noon today. When the policemen got out of their car, with their arms at the ready, the three Haganah men headed for a defense post got out their "*tozeret haaretz*"[5] Sten-guns also at the ready. For a second no one moved. Then one of the men said to the police: "If you shoot, we'll shoot." The police considered for a moment, then lowered their weapons and drove away. The three men did the same.

(Pretty, no? It sounds like Tel Aviv, where the boys are walking around like a bunch of wild-west hombres, Sten-guns on their backs and pistols on their hips. Haganah there is out in the open – and how they love it! You'll never know what a relief it is not to be sneaking through alleys and dark lanes and cutting across fields or with a guy's arms around you as you walk down the street so that there should be no telltale bulges. Nu – to get on to your dissident friends[6] ...)

---

4. Since Mordecai arrived in Palestine, in February, 1947.
5. Hebrew, meaning literally "produce of the land," i.e., locally produced.
6. Mordecai is referring to the members of Irgun and Lehi who are the subject of the next piece he sends to Gershon. It appears from Mordecai's phrasing that Gershon still feels some sympathy for them, despite the vehement condemnations Mordecai has expressed in previous letters.

IRRESPONSIBLE "HEROES"

An Arab spokesman in London told Jon Kimche, *Palestine Post* correspondent, that he was uninterested in how many Arabs were killed in the Battle of Palestine. If Jewish communications could be cut and the everyday life of the Yishuv disrupted to a great enough extent, the Jews would quit by themselves. There are enough Arabs – the Arab Higher Executive is ready to sacrifice "every last Arab in Palestine" to beat the Jews.

From a purely military point of view, then, what the Sternists and Irgunists have been doing these last months is almost worthless: the number of Arab dead will not determine the outcome of the struggle.

Losses in personnel did not beat the English during the blitz, nor did those losses defeat the Germans. Modern warfare – and for purposes of this analysis all warfare since the introduction of the bow and arrow in a society other than purely agriculture can be considered modern – aims to immobilize the enemy, impoverish him, starve him and cut off his supplies. By modern standards, then, the destruction of a fleet of Arab taxis and an Arab gasoline station in Romema[7] a week ago was a far more critical blow than that delivered by I.Z.L. when its "fighters" threw a bomb into a crowd of Arabs at Damascus Gate and killed about eighteen of them. The loss of the taxis and the gasoline meant just that many cars-full less of re-enforcements to the Arabs attacking Mekor Haim[8] on the outskirts of town; the loss of the gasoline meant that many trips less of Arab citrus trucks and consequently that much less money for arms and equipment. The eighteen dead may have included some active Arab fighters, but it also meant the accompanying enlistment of some victim's relatives who otherwise would have remained on the sidelines and limited themselves to

---

7.   A northern neighborhood of Jerusalem.
8.   A Jewish neighborhood in southwest Jerusalem that was surrounded by Arab neighborhoods. It frequently came under attack by residents of nearby Beit Safafa.

throwing stones. When the Haganah saved an innocent Arab's life on Jaffa Road a few days ago they undid the work of a dozen Arab agitators, and the destruction of the flour mill at Beit Safafa[9] resulted in more hungry *fellahin*[10] – and more desertions from terrorist ranks – than the boycott of Zionist goods and Stern-gang murders ever produced.

When the normal human cry for vengeance rises in your throat remember that forty-one Jews died when I.Z.L. [Irgun] tossed a bomb at the Haifa Refineries[11] and killed six Arabs. Did we gain, militarily, by those six deaths? We lost not only forty-one Jewish lives but found our fuel supply drastically reduced as well: the refineries were closed for about a week and kerosene, which is used for cooking and heating, is now being rationed. The I.Z.L. heroes really struck a blow then – for the Arab Higher Executive!

The dissidents are daring – but why shouldn't they be: THEY OPERATE FROM BASES MADE SECURE BY THE HAGANAH! After a bold dash and a heroic gesture they return to streets kept safe from Arab gangs by Haganah patrols, they retire to homes secure only because Haganah men are on the alert guarding them instead of wasting manpower, weapons and hard-to-get explosives on non-military objectives. What is more, they are under no obligation to prevent the reprisals every one of their escapades inspires. After they threw the bomb at Damascus Gate it was the Haganah which withstood the attacks on Beit Israel[12] and

9. An Arab neighborhood in southern Jerusalem.
10. Arabic, meaning "peasant."
11. On December 30, 1947, the Irgun threw grenades at a group of about one hundred Arabs who had gathered at the gate of the Haifa oil refinery in the hopes of finding work. Six were killed and forty-two were wounded. Those Arabs who escaped unscathed immediately turned on the Jewish workers at the refinery, killing thirty-nine (two fewer than Mordecai reports) and injuring forty-nine more before the British arrived and quelled the violence.
12. Beit Israel was a Jewish neighborhood in central Jerusalem.

Shimon HaTzaddik[13] and Mekor Haim. When dissidents killed two Englishmen in the streets of Jerusalem it was the Haganah which was fired upon by a police armored car thirsting for a little Jewish blood in return; the "heroes" were resting from their bold operation in the heart of a Haganah-protected Jewish quarter.

The Sternists and Irgunists sit upon the backs of the Haganah men – and they are a grievous burden indeed.

(Use my name if you care to – I'm not afraid of them: the boys will protect me...)

Love,

Mersh.

---

13. Shimon HaTzaddik was a small Jewish neighborhood in north Jerusalem, named for its proximity to the eponymous tomb. On January 7, three Jews from Shimon HaTzaddik were shot and killed by Arabs from the adjacent neighborhood of Sheikh Jarrah.

Chapter 14

Grievous Losses: Alter Rechnitz and the Lamed Hey ("35")

I
t was inevitable that the growing violence would strike close to home. Mordecai shared details of two tragic attacks on the Jews of the Yishuv. He opens his letter with a moving, elegiac account of the attack on a convoy to Jerusalem – an attack that resulted in three dead, including Ann Strauss's boyfriend, Alter Rechnitz and a fifteen-year-old, as well as eight wounded. The attack occurred on January 18, near the Castel. The *New York Times* mentioned it in an article headlined, "24 Arabs Killed in 'Punitive Action,' Zionists Declare."

Then, within the main body of the letter, Mordecai describes the brutal attack on the "Lamed-Heh,"[1] the thirty-five Haganah fighters

---

1.   Each letter of the aleph-bet represents a numeric value. The Hebrew letter *lamed* represents the number thirty, and the letter *heh* represents the number five. So the "lamed-heh" are the "thirty-five."

(Courtesy of Roy Shenkar)

Alter Rechnitz

who had been dispatched to help relieve the siege of Gush Etzion (the Etzion bloc), south of Bethlehem, on January 15–16.

The Etzion bloc consisted of four kibbutzim – Kfar Etzion, Masu'ot Yitzchak, Ein Tzurim and Revadim. Together, the kibbutzim covered twenty thousand dunams of land and had 450 residents. They were in a strategic location, 'protecting' Jewish Jerusalem from the south, but were within the area that had been allocated to the Arab state under the Partition Plan. The kibbutzim had been under constant attack since the partition vote and their route to Jerusalem had been blocked. Several convoys carrying supplies had been attacked; in December, ten of the eighteen people in a four-vehicle convoy were killed. On January 5, Kfar Etzion and Masu'ot Yitzchak decided to evacuate mothers and children and did so with the help of the British. On January 14, Abdul Khader al-Husseini led the first major coordinated attack against the kibbutzim; the kibbutzim held, but three defenders were killed. The situation was growing critical, and the Haganah decided the Gush had to be resupplied and the siege broken. Since convoys were not able to get through, it was decided that a group would go on foot. During the night of January 15–16, Danny Mass led a group of thirty-eight soldiers, hiking through the night from Har Tuv, near Bet Shemesh, toward Gush Etzion. Three had to turn back because of injuries. The thirty-five hoped to travel under cover of darkness, but the sky started to lighten before they reached their destination. They were never seen alive again.

What happened was pieced together by the Haganah from British reports and Arab testimony. The "35" were spotted near Surif, an Arab village about ten kilometers from Kfar Etzion, and attacked. The battle was long and drawn out, lasting at least ten hours; the last of the thirty-five was reportedly killed around four thirty in the afternoon of the 16th. An Arab training base nearby had sent hundreds of men to assist the local attackers; the British at a nearby police station did nothing to stop the slaughter. Several sources reported that the bodies were mutilated, some beyond recognition.[2]

The eventual fall of the Etzion Bloc and the massacre of its defenders on May 13, the day before the state was declared, is discussed in later letters.

Postmarked January 20, 1948

NO GREATER LOVE

They were not engaged, for theirs was the classic Palestinian problem of a kibbutznik, a member of a settlement, and a city girl. She was an American, from a wealthy family, which made the problem still more acute and the possibilities of a happy ending less than they usually are.

They were *"bachur"* and *"bachura,"*[3] a description which covers all stages of a courtship, and a week before she went out to the kibbutz to visit him she herself could hardly

---

2. Details taken from *Tisha Kabin* (Nine Measures), Tel Aviv: Ma'arachot/Defence Ministry Press, 1986, and the historical materials at Kfar Etzion (http://www.kfar-etzion.co.il, English) and Gush Etzion (http://www.kfar-etzion.co.il, Hebrew).
3. Hebrew, meaning "young man" and "young woman," respectively.

have told you just what stage they had reached. She would phone every week and in a few meager moments try to hint to him what she was doing during her "on duty" hours in the Haganah, and he in turn would try to hide from her what his responsibilities as part of the kibbutz defense unit were.

A convoy was going out to the kibbutz, and she begged a ride. There was a party Friday night, and on Saturday she watched Haganah units in training in the surrounding hills. Her "*bachur*" was the General Secretary of the group, and so was able to take the time to walk in their young forest with her and to help her see what had been added since her last visit two months before.

His "*hofesh*," vacation from the kibbutz, was due, and so on Sunday morning they climbed into one of the three trucks which made up the convoy and found seats for themselves among the crates of fruit and cans of milk the kibbutz was sending to Jerusalem. It was a bright, dry winter's day, a winter "*khamsin*" or hot spell, which burns all the cold and dampness out of one's bones and erases all memory of rain and the mud and Jerusalem's hailstorm. It was a clear day, and the attacking Arabs were in full view as they shot at the convoy from the hills. The driver of the truck they were in was hit and lost control of his vehicle, which skidded into a ditch, breaking the ropes holding the freight and sending it all into a heap on top of the hidden arms. Unable to respond to the Arab fire, the truckload of people tried to take cover behind the bales and boxes which had seemed so big when the vacationers were looking for places to sit down.

With the first shots he pushed her from her precarious seat and stretched out across her body, trying to shield her from the shots. He saved her life – and gave his own. He was hit in the head and chest, and was dead when the Magen David Adom picked him up and put him on a stretcher. She only knew that he had been hit – she had felt his hot blood soaking through her clothing as she lay there on the floor of the truck. She was still pleading to see him and asking how badly he was hurt when an injection put her to sleep and she was taken from the First Aid building to the Hadassah Hospital. She will be told, all too soon.

Tomorrow he will be just one more Jew dead, killed by Arabs on the road. Not Alter, who might have married the pretty American girl, but just a number, a statistic. And it might have been otherwise, had the American government done as much to carry out the Partition Plan as it did to carry it through the U.N.

American arms, instead of assurances, could have beaten off the attack easily, as many attacks have been beaten off: most of the arms on the convoy had been confiscated by British patrols at the very start of the trip; precious little remained, and a malignant fate put even that out of reach.

Grave of Alter Rechnitz, Kibbutz Maaleh Hachamisha.
Note that the tombstone includes the names of his father,
mother, brother, and sister — all murdered by the Nazis.

A young man died a hero's death, but that is slight consolation to the girl who loved him. He might not have died, if... but that is cold comfort to a bereaved sweetheart.

Dear folks,

You know, of course, who I mean in the story on the other side of the page. Anne Strauss (Cleveland) lost her *bachur* that day. (It was this afternoon).[4] I had had a long heart-to-heart talk [with her] just last Friday night, when she was down in the dumps over the city-kibbutz problem, and worrying over whether it would ever be resolved. It was – in a terrible enough fashion.

It's been a terrible week – some of my friends were lost in that group of 35 Haganah men who were wiped out. They fought off two ambushes, and according to reports we later received they killed close to a hundred Arabs before they were finally all killed. They are heroes in the eyes of the Yishuv, and they really did die like heroes. They set out to reinforce Kfar Etzion, on foot (hiding from the British on the roads and the Arabs in the hills as they went), but it seems that *nigzera aleihem mi'Imala*,[5] and they died fighting. One was an ex-Yeshiva boy (Elchanan)[6] who came with Kepi, the others were all Palestinians. And don't you think that some dirty low-down son-of-a-b**ch has already started a rumor that the American kids are all running away? I've already been asked when I'm leaving. Our kids are all over the country now, and did their share when the Arabs attacked Kfar Etzion en masse and suffered such fantastic casualties. I lost friends

---

4. The attack occurred on January 18 and was reported the next day.
5. Hebrew, meaning "it was decreed upon them from On High," a reference to the Yom Kippur liturgy describing the death of the ten martyrs.
6. Moshe Avigdor Perlstein (1925–1948), born in Jersey City, attended the Rabbi Yitzhak Elchanan Yeshiva in New York (now known as Yeshiva University) before moving to Palestine in March 1947. Mordecai wasn't the only Chertoff to have known him; in her letter of January 19, his mother wrote that she had taught him when he was eight years old.

among the 35, but I feel Ann's loss so much more strongly: we had become very friendly, and I know what this will mean to her. Poor kid, she's been working so hard and has had so little *nachas*[7] these last weeks. Knowing her, I'll bet she stays in spite of it: she's got real guts and has already learned to subordinate her own happiness to the common good.

That's all for now,

love,

Mordecai

Ann's "*bachur*," Alter Gershon Rechnitz, was born in 1914, in Poland, and was a founding member of Kibbutz Maaleh Hachamisha, north-west of Jerusalem. He was a farmer known for his strong aesthetic sense. After WWII, he was sent back to Europe as an aliya emissary. Thirty days after his death, the kibbutz published a booklet in his memory, to which Mordecai will make reference in later letters.[8]

This letter, laden as it is with news of death and loss, introduces what becomes a recurring theme in Mordecai's letters – the belief by many Palestinian Jews that their American co-religionists will flee as the situation worsens. This, Mordecai angrily denies. There was considerable parental pressure on young Americans in war-torn Palestine to return home to safety (about which, more later) but while some succumbed and left, many – including Mordecai, and Ann – stayed.

Mordecai remained focused, understandably, on events in Jerusalem and the surrounding area, but there was fighting going on throughout the country. On January 20, a well-armed band of almost four hundred Arabs attacked the western Galilee settlement of Yehiam, killing eight and wounding eleven. The attack began at seven in the morning; British soldiers did not arrive until about five hours later.

In the midst of war and uncertainty, grieving over the loss of friends and furious at the behavior of the British, Mordecai came to the realization that Hadassah Frisch would never accept his proposal

---

7.   Yiddish, meaning "pride, satisfaction."
8.   I had the privilege of sharing Mordecai's story about Ann and Alter with Ann's son, Roy Shenkar.

of marriage. He said as much to his family in an otherwise unimport-ant letter, not included here, postmarked January 27: "I haven't heard a word from Hadassah in a long, long time, and I think there is nothing there, for me." There was something prescient in this, as the very next day Mordecai received a telegram from her, gently but emphatically refus-ing his offer: "TRIED WRITING NUMEROUS TIMES. LONG DISTANCE COURTSHIP IMPOSSIBLE. AM VERY SORRY."

If January had been difficult for the Yishuv, the situation worsened in February. There were invasions by various large, trained groups of Arab guerillas throughout the country; Arab gangs were robbing trains; the British continued to turn back refugee ships; there were frequent bomb-ings and sniper attacks on Jewish civilians in Jerusalem, which remained under siege. On the political front, the American government seemed at a loss as to what to do and even threatened to cancel the passports of American citizens serving in military roles in Palestine. Britain accepted the Palestine Commission as the successor government; as of May 15, it would be responsible for administering the area.

Chapter 15
The Bombing of the *Palestine Post*

Trauma was to pile upon trauma in a shocking week for Mordecai: the day after his rejection by Hadassah, on Sunday evening, February 1, just before 11 p.m., a 5-ton army truck drove up Hassolel Street[1] and parked outside the building housing the *Palestine Post* and several other periodicals and offices. A few minutes later, the truck blew up rocking the city and smashing windows and doors within a mile radius. There was one immediate fatality.[2] Twenty people were hurt, nine seriously, including pressmen Zalman Levin, Shimshon Lifshitz, Aharon Tanadoni, Yitzchal Tawil and Nathan ("Robbie") Rabinovitz. Three buildings were gutted. Glass shards flew in every direction and in the *Post's* press room, lead type became projectiles. Flames engulfed both sides of the street which became impassible. Tenants from nearby buildings had to be helped down from the upper floors due to flames in the stairwells. The fires burned all night and were brought under control by dawn.

---

1. A road off Jaffa Road, near Zion Square, today known as Havatzelet Street.
2. Two more would die later.

At the time of the bombing, Gershon was en route to a church to give a speech. He was given the grim news immediately upon arrival. Knowing that his brother was working that shift, he later wrote, "I felt as though all my strength and blood had been drained." Begging those around him for further information, Gershon nevertheless began his presentation. During the speech, he learned that Mordecai was not on the list of dead or injured. He then called his parents, who were visiting Cleveland at the time, to tell them that Mordecai was fine. They were nonplussed: they had not yet heard about the attack.

Paul writes later:

> You can imagine Gershon's state of mind between hearing and knowing! He was thunderstruck, terrified for your life and for our wellbeing ... As I mentioned, he managed to contact *A.P.*, and thus rescued us not only from worry, whose acuteness would have been indescribable, but also from the catastrophe that would likely have befallen us had we heard such sudden news. And still, we, or at least I, have not returned to equilibrium, to a clear head. The fact that the danger was so close, though thank God you were saved, is enough to rattle my soul unto its foundation ... Every time I think about the danger (and when don't I?) I feel like the person who sees a man falling from a roof, and any minute his limbs will be crushed, and he closes his eyes so as not to see the end ... so I attempt to shut my imagination's eyes but do not always succeed (Feb. 6)....

A few hours later the family received an urgent telegram which read: "Thank God was elsewhere when *Post* bombed, Mordecai." This was untrue; he *had* been in the building when the bomb went off, and in fact acted quickly to help the injured. (Two weeks later he explained that he had had no intention of deceiving them. In the heat of the moment and in his rush to assuage their fear, the word "elsewhere" was simply the first to jump into his head.) Two days later his family cabled back their relief: "We thank God for your deliverance," adding the words of the *"Birkat Hagomel"* blessing, recited publically by someone who has survived a life-threatening event.

Only hours after the attack, the *Post* published a shortened edition which carried a detailed account of the bombing.[3] Mordecai's long letter to his family adds many dramatic details.

Palestine Post, February 2, 1948

February 4, 1948

Dear Everybody,

One of the boys was walking along Princess Mary Avenue[4] Sunday nite when he heard a terrific explosion. He heard somebody shout out in a Police armored car he was just passing "that's the end of the bloody *Palestine Post!*" There was a burst of laughter, and then a harmonica inside the car led the dance. The voice was wrong.

---

3.   A newsreel video about the bombing produced by the British company, Movietone, is available on You Tube: goo.gl/jdwOjw.

4.   Now called Shlomtzion Hamalka Street (Queen Shlomtzion).

Ted[5] and his wife left the office a little before the bang, and saw an army truck drive up our street. They thought it seemed strange for traffic on Hassolel Street that late at night, and looked into the back as it passed them, but could see nothing. They went on to the Atara,[6] and when they heard the bang tried to phone the office to tell us they were Ok: they thought the bomb was outside of the Atara. They were wrong.

Somebody dashed over to Haganah headquarters and reported that a hundred people had been killed. Miraculously, he too was wrong.

I had been sitting in the News Room at the time. It had been a very busy weekend for me, and I was simply too tired to stand on my feet downstairs in the Press room, where I belonged at the time. I was shirking upstairs, nibbling a piece of chocolate and shmoozing with another lazy American there, with my back to the window. When it hit, the last bit of chocolate had already melted in my mouth and was sweet in my throat. I saw Mike,[7] opposite me, crouch low over his desk and then rush across the room to Leah,[8] asking was she all right as he ran. With the blast I remembered all I had been told about hitting the dirt in such occasions, that it's a cardinal rule for self-preservation, etc. As I began to hit, I saw the floor was covered with glass, so I broke the rule. I ran out into the hall, and saw one of the office boys bleeding at the nose. There was a leather easy chair right near him, so I turned it upside down to shake off the glass and made him sit down with his head back. Then I went back in for my Eisenhower jacket, realizing it would be cold outside. I had *Moby Dick* with me, and thought to myself that it would only get in the way, and that I would come back for it later (we did not yet realize the extent of

---

5.   Ted Lurie.
6.   Café Atara was on Ben Yehuda Street. See chapter 4, footnote 41.
7.   Probably Mike Eskolsky.
8.   Probably Leah Ben Dor.

the bang, and thought it had only been a grenade outside the door). Not knowing why, perhaps because it was where I should have been, I ran down to the press and in the dark saw a figure sitting on the floor. I called in *"mi zeh,"*[9] and the fellow with whom I work, and next to whom I invariably stand at 11:00, answered. I ripped down a door to make a path for us (I saw he needed help, how much I couldn't tell) and rushed in. He was dripping wet, and having recognized my voice he kept moaning, "Mordecai, *kach oti leMagen David."*[10] I grabbed him by the shoulders and held on while I yelled for a stretcher, and little Moshe Hai, our ex-IZL office boy, materialized from out of the smoke and glass and flame with a stretcher. Hugh Orgel, of our Foreign News staff, came by, and together we got Robbie onto the stretcher and carried him the hundred yards or so to the clinic and up a flight of steps into the aid room. Then we ran back, and I draped someone's arm around my shoulders and dragged him to the MDA too. A woman found her way out of the building, and was wandering around, stunned and bloody, until I spotted her and brought her in. Somebody, I don't know who, helped me with another stretcher. During the first few minutes of the rescue work we were shot at from beyond the clinic, and one shot hit an ambulance which burst into flames but miraculously did not explode. In the clinic itself all the windows had been shattered and some doors had been ripped off, and with debris all around them the doctors and nurses went to work like automatons. One of them grabbed me, and with some kid at the other end of a stretcher, we brought Shimshon, another of our make-up men, from the aid to the operating room. He too recognized my voice, and kept telling me he was cold. I explained that he was wet, but couldn't tell him it was his own blood all over him.

---

9. Hebrew, meaning "Who is it?"
10. Hebrew, meaning "Take me to Magen David," i.e., Magen David Adom, the emergency medical services.

Out in the street again, an English policeman I had met somewhere dashed up to me, Tommy-gun on his back, to be sure I was alright, and then the two of us tried to move a truck over to the building opposite the *Post* building to bring down the people trapped by the spreading flames. We couldn't move it, and I thought of getting a blanket for people to jump into while we held it, but from nowhere a ladder appeared, and this guy and a few of his buddies braced it against [the] wall under the end of a balcony which was already half ripped off, and brought a number of people down that way. That building was completely emptied out, our building was empty, with flames shooting out of every window and roaring like an enormous furnace, when I remembered the Haganah post in the building and recalled that there was "stuff" in it. I called headquarters from the clinic, but nobody there knew how much, and so I ran around until I found one of the kids from the *Post* and was assured that all but a few rounds of ammunition had been removed. These went off harmlessly when the flames reached them, but had there been any grenades left God knows how many people would have been killed by the wall they'd have blown down in exploding. It wasn't until the following day that we learned that the *U.P.* wireless operator, who sleeps in his office from 10–12 every night (while there's no news coming in on the *U.P.* wire), had awakened, put on his pants and, somewhat dazed by the blast, had calmly walked home to the Bukharan quarter in his stocking feet.

When the Fire Brigade arrived, having had a week of training with them,[11] I was able to help couple hoses and get things going there. By then the buildings were all cleared, and all that was left was the fire to fight. The water pressure was very low, so low that I think with a few glasses of beer

---

11.   In his memoirs, Mordecai wrote: "I had a number of jobs in the Haganah, the first of which was to learn how to fight fires. I learned how to unfold hoses and attach nozzles, and how to detach the nozzles and fold the hoses back onto the truck. We drilled until it occurred to our superiors that there was no water in the hydrants, and so we were disbanded."

I could have almost doubled the volume. The Military fire truck finally arrived, with a pump, and pitched in to help prevent the flames from spreading, and I had the chance to look around. By the light of two burning buildings I saw a street which looked like blitzed London. Pieces of wall, balconies, clothing, a child's doll and shutters were scattered all about. The body of the car which had brought the explosive was blown across the street in one direction, and its motor sat in a crater alongside of the building, under Agronsky's window. Had he been in town, at his office, he would have been killed outright: his office was completely wrecked. Haganah and Mishmar Ha-am[12] patrols took up positions and controlled the crowds. There was no looting, and no panicking either. One guy was a little hysterical, and stood in the yard in his pajamas shouting at me that there were women and children in the building. I smacked him over and over again, until two boys grabbed him and dragged him into the clinic. One of our proof-readers began to crack after the strain of helping was over, and I slapped him once to bring him to. He immediately subsided, and went over to the clinic and sat down on a bed to rest.

There was nothing more I could do, so – I grabbed Ben Abba,[13] from Boston, and we ran to the Post Office where we finally talked them into sending cables home for us. Then we went back to the scene, and I collared Carter Davidson, of *A.P.*, Francis Offner, of the *Christian Science Monitor*, and one of the local reporters and gave them a quick first-hand story, making sure they took my (and Dov's) name and address: I wanted them to make sure you read I was alright in the same story that told you about the explosion.

As I walked away, I heard an English soldier say "I guess it'll be a few weeks now before the *Post* comes out

12. The Civil Guard. A volunteer organization, the Jerusalem branch was founded in September 1947. Members were those above the age of conscription, or those who had not been conscripted for health reasons.
13. Dov Ben Abba, Mordecai's roommate and fellow *Post* employee.

again." I didn't like his tone, so I snapped at him, "not even days. We'll be out tomorrow, if we have to write it long-hand," and then with Dov went up towards the Atara (I don't know why I knew it was open, probably because I felt they should be). When I got there I was mobbed, Tzilah, Ted's wife (with whom I carry on a constant flirtation) took me around and kissed me, and then made me drink her coffee. When I was finished, she said: "Go over to Lifshitz (a print-ing shop), they're trying to put out a paper." I grabbed a guy with a car and told him to take Dov home to my house, giving him the key (Dov had been cut on the temple, and I had brought him into the clinic before, washed his head there, and handed him over for bandaging right after we sent the wires. He had had a nasty shock, and I figured since Milty[14] was home, it was better for Dov not to be alone) and I went over to help with the paper.

With one linotype machine, and heads to be done all by hand, not knowing the shop and its equipment, we went to work. Offner had found the press, and a dozen cor-respondents brought typewriters, everybody pitched in and half asleep on our feet, got a paper together. I jotted down an outline of the Big Story, and one of the boys finished it while I went to work on headlines. The Atara sent us coffee and sandwiches all night, and at six in the morning the *Pal-estine Post* appeared, smaller than usual, but it appeared. And for the morale of the Yishuv it was a great thing. People couldn't believe it, it was too much: to produce a paper from memory, starting at one-thirty in the morning, after a hell such as we'd been through, bordered on the miraculous. But we did it. There was no decision made to do it, no vote taken, it was just in the air. Somebody mumbled something about mimeographing, and Offner suddenly appeared with a press, and so we worked.

---

14. Milt Shulman, another of Mordecai's roommates.

Courtney, our Column One-ist, came in with his mistress, and while he did his column and the editorial, she typed copy. Tzilah and one of the Agency guys came in and read proofs, and Jerusalem's journalists all volunteered to help.

There were people in Jerusalem who did not know the *Post* had been "destroyed" until they read about it – in the *Post*!

One of the linotypers[15] died the following morning. The man I carried in, Robbie, is on the border as I write: if he lives, his three beautiful little children, whom he used to run with in Rehavia on sunny Shabbat afternoons, will have a blind father. You appreciate what a tragedy blindness would be to him only if you could have seen him handle type and work over the page, like a mother chuckling over and dressing her first-born infant. I had been impatient with him one night, it was late, and things were going slowly, and I had picked up the lead myself and put it into its proper place in the page-frame. He had turned to me, his paunch resting on the edge of the table, and said: Let's make a deal; I won't write headlines, you don't handle lead. Robbie incidentally, won LP.300 in the Irish sweepstakes recently.

I walked home after the press was rolling (nu – creaking, with a guy spitting on his thumb to help him put the paper in place) and as I passed the Agency I saw Carmi Charny. He looked, and came running, wondering whether he was seeing things or it was really me, alive. When I got home I got into a bathrobe and a blanket and stretched out in a deck chair on the balcony, in the sun, until a few of the kids came to ask about me. Ann Strauss

---

15.   Haim Farber. In his memoirs, Mordecai reports that another typesetter, Alexander Zvielli, was also wounded but recovered. He is not named in any of the news reports. I met with Zvielli on January 13, 2016, when he was ninety-three years old. He was the *Post*'s longest serving employee, preparing a regular column from the archives as well as occasional special articles right up until his death in May 2017.

also came over, with her broken arm, telling me she hadn't rushed only because the MDA driver, who saw me helping with the rescue work, had told one of her girlfriends that I was ok, and by midnight she had known. People have been congratulating me ever since, and almost perfect strangers have come up to me with their eyes glistening and just shook hands.

All in all, it was quite a bang. A row of bottles as far away as [the] Police Barracks on Mt. Scopus was knocked down, and all the windows up and down Ben Yehuda Street were blasted. At our offices, (from which we prepared to go to press last night and the night before) the news room suffered least: just a few broken windows and shattered lightbulbs, while the accounts department got a bit dusty. Agronsky's office, Ted's office and the business and advertising offices are a shambles, and the ruins in the press room downstairs are still smoking, while the remains of the house across the street have again burst into flames which the fire brigade is wearily battling. Our linotype machines are gone, but the press will be in working order by ten tonight, two hours before press-time.

Hassolel street is digging itself out, and up the street, as far as the building before ours (which is badly burned out) stores are back in business while repair work goes on. One book shop, He'atid, advertised "more open than usual," and kept going without even a day off for repairs. One whole building of people has been left homeless, and taken in by friends and relatives, and *Hayom*, a daily just a few weeks old, sounded the keynote when it wrote about our getting the paper out: "can't be." It holds for everybody on that street, and in the city and the country as well – "can't be?"

As Mike said last night, while we were getting the paper out: I guess we've had our bomb, we don't have to worry anymore. All I want now are all the clippings you can get, from every paper that carried the story. I want to see how they handled it.

And that's all for now. I've got to eat and go to work. I'll hold this until later tonight, so that I can enclose the results of our investigations into the bombing: the names of the British constables who did it.

Laylah tov.

A few days later, Mordecai followed up with some further details about the *Post* bombing.

February 6, 1948 – "Adds, corrections, notes, observations, etc."

I remember back in the States, when the war broke out and all the boys were leaving, worrying how I would react in a moment of crisis were I called out too. I recall the fear I felt then that I would funk. When the bomb hit, I have a sharp recollection of having thought to myself, "do I know what to do?" and a momentary panic at the feeling that I could do nothing to help. It passed much more quickly than it takes to record, and then I knew I'd be alright.

It now appears that the first words spoken in the News room were Mike's alright, but they were not to Leah: he first shouted out "everything is alright," going on the logical assumption that the bomb you hear is not the one which will hurt you – It's already behind, and you're seeing its result.

John Donovan, *C.B.S.*[16] correspondent here, was on the way to give the *U.P.* man hell about a story the latter had written identifying an ex-G.I. as a Haganah man when the bomb hit, and he got there in time to carry the watchman[17] out, on his back. He staggered down the few steps and

16. Probably NBC.
17. Yehoshua Weinberg.

suddenly fell, the weight too much for him, and pitched the watchman forward, like a sack of flour. The poor fellow died at Hadassah yesterday. He had been in the country only a short time, and served as a Partisan during the war. There's been a third death too: a woman of sixty,[18] from across the street, who had a heart attack when it all began. Robbie, my favorite down in the press, will live. I understand that there is even a slight chance for one of his eyes: If you can think of anything but my miraculous escape by now, offer up a prayer for him. He's forty, strong as a bull, and amazingly vital and virile. I really think he would be better off not pulling through than coming out of it blind.

Fitzhugh Turner, of the *N. Y. Herald Tribune*, was caught in the burning building across the street when he went in to try to help bring people out, and had to jump for it. He's a louse Zionistically, but still a mensch...

Last night we put a full paper out — eight columns. It still looks like hell because we haven't the proper headline type, and the text is being prepared from three different magazines, but still it's the *Palestine Post*. After a bomb big enough to have done more damage than was done to the King David, had it been well placed, we put out one two-page job the same night, two small four-page papers, and by the fourth night had it back to normal, in size anyway. Quite a record, I must say. I think it compares rather favorably with the heroic days of the anti-slavery press in the States.

One building was still smoldering this morning, and we've been working in our own building which, from the outside, looks like a corpse — but they just can't stop us.

Last night the Haganah finally came out with the announcement I've been waiting for, and with some of the stuff I helped find: the number of the Police car which took the bastards from the scene after they'd planted the

18. Deborah Daniel.

bomb, the names of the guys – four of them British constables, two Poles and two Arabs, have been given to the
authorities for action. Meanwhile if any of them show their
faces outside of their armored billets – they won't be able
to tell their progeny of how they tried to stop the *Palestine
Post*. I wanted them shot first, but lost in the argument at
H.Q.: the trouble was that if we waited to get them, any
political capital we might make of the outrage now would
be lost, since it may be a long time before they show. We
do know that high Police officials were not involved, as in
the Farran case, and so there is a chance that something
will come of it all.

At any rate, it's over, and with this writing I exorcize
the night and its horror and the hard work of the days that
followed it and turn to more pleasant things: what did Caro-
line name her new daughter?

Unfortunately, Mordecai's hopes for his "favorite" press operator, Robbie, were ultimately dashed. The youngest of Robbie's "three beautiful
children," David Nevo, who was too young at the time to remember
his father, told me that his father had immediately lost sight in one eye
and the other had been damaged. Robbie ultimately succumbed to his
injuries.

The bomb was ordered by Abdul Khader al-Husseini, the leader
of the Arab irregular forces, and constructed by Fawzi al-Kutub. Kutub
was assisted by Abu Khalil Janho, a Christian Arab, and two British
deserters – Corporal Peter Marsden and former police captain, Eddie
Brown. The original plan was apparently to attack the Zion Cinema but
the bombers arrived after the film had ended and the audience had gone.
Instead, they headed toward the nearest building that was still lit up. In
an interview broadcast over Damascus radio in the early 1950s,[19] al-Kutub
detailed how he placed a 1,500 kg. land mine in a truck stolen from the

---

19. David Nevo provided a translation from the Arabic to Hebrew made by his grandson, Assaf Doron, an Arabist, of the relevant parts of the interview. I am grateful
to both of them.

British and driven to the building housing the *Post*. He described the smoke rising from the buildings and the 'cries of the Jews' which could be heard for 'thousands of meters.' And in a gross exaggeration, claimed that 44 buildings were burnt and 50 Jews killed.

Mordecai's confession to his family that he had once worried about how he'd react *in extremis* is revealing. As it turned out, when the bomb hit, he reacted in exemplary fashion. The Associated Press report of the event (probably by Carter Davidson) carried in many US newspapers, reported that Dov Ben Abba and Mordecai Chertoff were unhurt and had rescued seven other employees. The article quoted Mordecai: "I was reading copy when the building suddenly shook like hell…. Glass started flying everywhere. I ran, turned off all the electric switches, walked down a hall to get my coat. Then I heard moans and started carrying those poor fellows out of the fire."

In a later letter, Gershon describes to him the news reports, articles and interviews which reported on his actions. Naomi also expresses amazement at Mordecai's presence of mind during the bombing. Interestingly, she notes that his "service to Israel should more than make up for any discomfort he might feel at not serving in the American army during WWII."

In his memoirs, Mordecai writes: "Reading those first news printings now is very moving. Along with stories of shooting, looting and bombing, there are reports of theater "first nights," one of which was *The Barber of Seville*, in Tel Aviv." He managed to salvage a memento of that horrible night: the six-inch, 2.5-pound mirror-image lead [masthead] "The *Palestine Post*" which was replaced for that first miraculous edition.

Masthead of The *Palestine Post* damaged in the bombing

In this next letter to his sister, Mordecai delves deeply into the issue of what the American Jews in Palestine are doing now that the situation has become so much worse.

February 8, 1948

Dear Toots,

I've just sent off a four-page letter to the folks, telling the story of our bomb, and so I can leave it out of this – and subsequent letters. You probably will receive it from them in due course.

I want you to know how proud I am of my family. Almost all of the kids here have received frantic letters and/or cables to come home, and some have harkened to the tug at the far end of the apron string and left, while others need little more than a few more shots in their neighborhood to take off, coat-tails flying. My family stands firm. You can have no idea what it means to me not to have to withstand a barrage of panicky letters with the usual appeals to filial duty and family obligations. It shows that Zionistically we are a mature family, able to put first things first and withstand the nudging of loneliness and worry and the presence of danger. It also shows that our collective speeches were more than just good; they were sincere as well (and therefore good...) and were not typical of the American Zionist "who collects money to send others to Palestine." Believe me, I know how the folks miss me – it can be compared only to how I miss you all–and how badly I want to see you all. And I also know that no matter how good a case we could make out for the "contribution" I could make in the States, it would be at best a rationalization motivated essentially by our strong family feeling. I imagine I would be publicly ill were I to be called upon to make speeches for "the cause," and I'm sure I would be relatively ineffective: I move in another world, with a different language, with far

247

different realities and reactions the average American could never fathom. I strongly doubt whether I could make myself understood. More than that, however, and far transcending it, is my own conviction that not only is my own greater happiness to be found here but that my greatest contribution can be made from here too. (I wonder whether, were I convinced otherwise, I would have the strength to leave and make my life in the U.S.?) Had I no ability along any lines, were I unable to do no more than serve in the rank-and-file of the Haganah – or even just make sandwiches for them – it would be enough for me to have to stay: the mere fact that an American was doing it and had not run away would be of inestimable psychological value. You remember Shmarya Levin's[20] application of the Moshe midrash to Herzl (why it had to be an outsider, whose dreams would not be the result of suffering and subjective reaction to the conditions of Jewish life, but one who arrived at those conclusions objectively, against the background of an alien culture and a foreign upbringing) – it should be applied to the Americans here. Coming willingly, staying willingly, they strengthen the morale of the Yishuv. We all sneer at those who leave, but it is a kind of whistling one's way past a graveyard, an attempt to hide how much it hurts when they do leave. While not looking for them, the personal losses that we (ex) "outsiders" suffer, and overcome, strengthens morale further. You have no idea how proud people are of Ann, who rejects all pressure to leave and stays despite what for her was a tragic and much-felt personal loss. Some of the Americans here (on their way out) can't understand her remaining; you and I, and our family, certainly do: we were weaned on it. Her own family is still far from appreciating how deeply she feels, and it hurt to see how much Father's few words of approval[21] meant to her (I read that much of his last letter to her).

---

20. Shmaryahu Levin (1867–1935), was a Jewish Zionist activist in the Russian Empire, then in Germany and in the United States.

21. In a letter to his son, Paul writes: "The incident of A. Strauss, as you can imagine,

That I'm still on the job after our little bomb is also good for morale, and the fact that Ted's wife was on duty the very next night (at the Haganah Canteen) was cause for much favorable comment. The steady appearance of the paper itself, of course, and its having been published that very night, went a long way towards obviating the psychological effect of the bomb (while the physical is being erased day by day). That Moshe Pearlstein was killed[22] was a blow to his family and his friends, but his having lied his way into a mission upon which he was killed (he, an American who could have run away) gave some of the weaker Palestinians a little more strength to hold on: it was a token of the solidarity of world Jewry, and the sacrifice was all the more precious having come from an "outsider."

I'm glad you brought our family and Ann's together, particularly since we've become such good friends. She showed me a letter from home, which left me hoping that Father spoke to her people about her staying, despite her loss and the danger. I don't know how the time element of their visit worked out- i.e., whether the folks were there when the bomb hit here – if they were, I'm sure that Father's quiet strength and refusal to be panicked and Mother's certainty of the rightness of my being here, now, must have gone a long way towards reassuring the Strausses. I know how catching Father's faith can be, and I'm sure his own Zionist conviction and certainty [of] the ultimate outcome here would carry over and make things easier not only for Mrs. Strauss but for Ann as well.

---

has become the talk of the town in Cleveland. Some see it positively, others, negatively. Positively, because she wishes to remain in Israel despite everything. And negatively, in the sense of "what is this service to her," as per the question of the Wicked Son in the Haggada of Pesah. In other words, to her and not to them. In any case, the supporters outnumber the naysayers. In truth, it is a wonder how the spirit has so infused a young woman like her! Though according to many here, she is an inspiration" (Jan. 28).

22. The American member of the "Lamed-Heh."

You have no idea what a wonderful girl she is – and somehow it is always the good who suffer most. She loved Alter with the kind of love that few men win and very few deserve, and from all I've heard around Jerusalem about him he was one of the few deserving. I met him once, walking with her along King George Road, but was too wrapped up in a message I had for her to more than take notice of him as I drew her aside. I'm sorry now that I didn't really know him. He was representative of the kibbutznik in the classic mold of quiet devotion and heroic self-sacrifice, without the outward heroics. Any people would be proud of such a man, and it is hard to say that Ann's loss is greater than the Yishuv's. We have so few!

From a cable I've received from Lester it seems that the American press has had a field day with our bomb.... Please send me whatever clippings you can get your hands on.

...

As far as Hadassah goes, I think you're right. I received a cable from her B.B. (Before the Bomb) saying nix, long-distance courtship is N.G.,[23] and it was a wonderful excuse for me to finish off a bottle of Canadian Club all by myself. I talked it out that night with Ann, and we reached substantially the same conclusion, long before your letter reached me. Now I'll have to find other excuses to drink (that expensive) Canadian Club: drinking to my lucky escape That Night was one. *Yihiyeh tov*, as we keep telling each other many hundreds of times a day, and the '*ken, aval matai*'[24] is not at all bitter. An occasional loneliness never killed anybody.

...

love,

mersh

---

23.   Presumably, "no go."
24.   Hebrew, meaning "yes, but when?" i.e., but when will it be ok?

It is clear from Mordecai's letters that the majority of his friends are American Jews, rather than Palestinian Jews; nevertheless, he seems to identify more with the Palestinians. Acutely sensitive to the issue of morale, he does not consider abandoning them, or the homeland, in its hour of need. It is worth noting, however, that as committed as he is, he nevertheless seems to view himself in an "auxiliary" or support capacity. It is perhaps ironic that having professed his relief and pride in his parents that they do not demand his return to America, some of the letters Mordecai receives from his parents from this point *do* suggest, and sometimes urge, that he return home, "at least for a visit" – and bring Ann Strauss with him. Paul writes, "If, in fact, you have any influence on Ann, try, and it will be a great mitzva" (February 6).

By this point, it has been a year since Mordecai has seen or even spoken with his family. While it is hard to imagine someone taking the time to visit the (unknown) parents of a friend nowadays, it was common back then, under such circumstances. This was not only so that Mordecai's friends could bring greetings and pick up various items for him. It also provided an opportunity to fill his parents in on sensitive particulars of his life, especially details of his military activities with the Haganah, something that Mordecai could not commit to writing.

February 12, 1948

Dear Family,

... I had a long letter written to Gershon, (in Hebrew, with the beautiful new pen) but it went up in flames with part of our building. I'll try to cover that ground again.

...

Don't cancel your trip, but don't plan to book passage for before the beginning of June. After May 15 we'll see how things are here. I don't want you sitting next to the radio all day worrying, or jumping every time you hear a shot (even though hours can go by without a sound). I appreciate all the t.l.'s[25] on my Partition letter – but have completely forgotten what I wrote. I couldn't duplicate it now if my literary reputation hung in the balance. How about a copy (English and Hebrew?) There's no question of my looking for Father's relatives now – I simply haven't the time. I intend to write to Haim Eshlagi one of these days, but can't do much more than that. Well well – Mother will soon be able to say that she sponsored a star – Edith Gordon.[26] Is there really hope for her? And Mother's Amer. Jew. Cult. Soc. sounds fine – but what's the "American" for? Red-baiting or anti-Zionism?

Gershon: I'm sorry I missed your public reading of my letter, it sounds as though you did it up brown. As for whatever else I write about the damned English … go ahead, publish it. They know how we feel anyway. They did blow up the *Post*, you know, in spite of the Foreign correspondent[s]… writing from here that "Jewish sources assume the Arabs did it." We have the names of the British constables who pulled it and the number of the car they escaped in afterwards. (In the P.I.O.,[27] the initial reaction of *English* correspondents was: the British did it) They're the bunch who were once in Farran's gang of cutthroats. Another lovely story for you is last night's: A sergeant-major (military) arrested all the boys at an outpost in Beit Israel, confiscated their arms (permitted the girl to remain and overlooked one fellow who hid) and took them down to Damascus Gate (pure Arab stronghold) where the arms were sold to the Arabs and the boys turned out, unarmed, into the arms of the waiting Arabs. They were later found riddled with Sten gun bullets

---

25. Stands for "*toches lik*" – Yiddish, meaning "*tochas* licking," i.e., sucking up, currying favor.
26. An opera singer from Ohio who won a full scholarship to Juilliard as a mezzo soprano. She performed with Leonard Bernstein and appeared as a soloist with the Cleveland symphony, among other accomplishments.
27. Perhaps "Press Information Office."

and very dead.[28] There's your low-livered *mamzerim bnei nidot*[29] who are being so fatally neutral. But that would take a book in itself, I better stop here (now does Father understand my *rogez*?).[30]

...

What Father had to say about the reactions to Ann's staying on did a lot for her morale, particularly since her family has been pressuring her to go home. Did you, Father, talk to her mother about that? I'm sure you could have made her understand why Ann will not leave.

...

Shabbat shalom, and all my love

Mersh

Americans "serving" in Palestine in one capacity or another, were subject to restrictions by the American government. Mordecai argues that there not be any kind of special treatment for the American Jews in Palestine.

---

28. The details Mordecai gives here were also published in the *Post* that day. The Haganah soldiers he describes had been manning a roadblock before the British patrol disarmed them, then "released" them into the arms of an Arab mob. Their bullet-riddled and mutilated bodies were found shortly later. A similar incident occurred barely a fortnight later, in Tel Aviv, reported in the March 1 edition of the *Post*. Nine men, including Haganah guards and workers at the Hayozek Iron Foundry, were shot and stabbed to death by Arabs after they had been disarmed by British military and police. Three others were wounded but survived.

29. This is a double insult, both connected to issues of Jewish law. A *mamzer* is a child born as the result of an adulterous affair (i.e., not simply out of wedlock). *Bnei nidot* refers to the religious status of ritual impurity known as *nidda* that a woman enters when she begins her monthly menstruation and exits after menstruation is over and she has immersed in a ritual bath. According to Jewish law, a married couple is not supposed to be intimate during this time. *Bnei nidot* literally means children conceived when the mother is *nidda* when their parents were forbidden to each other. The implication is that there is something impure about them.

30. Hebrew, meaning "anger."

February 18, 1948

Dear Family,

I'm still trying to catch up on my list, so here goes. Mother — you're breaking my heart over the concerts you're missing! How could you be so cruel as to burden me with such tragedies now, when my life is such a round of carefree parties and dances! Today I indulge — in real meals (they cost a fortune, it's a good thing I don't have to pay rent), and an occasional nap in the afternoon, when the Fate of the Nation permits, is a real luxury. If father thinks me angry — how did he react when news of the four boys turned over to the Arabs by British soldiers reached NY? ...

I met Mrs. Brailove,[31] Gershon, and she was quite excited about a little incident involving you and some stingy son-of-a-b**ch — why don't you tell me such stories? It was a honey! She and her gang had a bunch of Palmachniks as their escort for their stay here, and the kids made a terrific impression, as well they might. I gave her some material, as well as some messages for you (we spent some time at the Eden together, in Jerusalem). For a wealthy American, she made a good impression herself.

Surprise — I suddenly find there is nothing more on my list, so I shall: cue from your last two letters. The American press is full of s**t. I did not save seven — only three, really. I wired that I was "elsewhere" only because in the hurry and confusion of the moment (I still was anxious to get back there and see what I could do) it was the first conclusive worry-palliating word that came to mind. There was no intent to deceive. I was also taking into consideration that the press would go to town, and felt that worry would

---

31. Mathilda F. Brailove (died 2000), a philanthropist from Elizabeth, New Jersey, who crusaded against Hitler and on behalf of Israel. She first visited Palestine in 1948 on a UJA study mission, and became chair of the National Women's Division of UJA in 1950.

be stalled-off at least long enough for you to get the details and be calmed-down. I'm getting tired of the bomb.

Passport: If an American is caught in the act,[32] his passport will be taken away, until such time as he leaves "foreign military service" (i.e., the Haganah or the Nejada[33]) and shows proof of his preparations to leave the country, at which time he gets it back. Does one need a passport at any other time? I'm surprised that all the Talmudists in the family missed the point of the Consulate statement. I'm still here as a student, of course. Passports have not been called in; citizenship is definitely not in danger.

Correction: I came for a year's trial, i.e., I had decided I would stick it out for a year if I did not make good to the extent where I could settle. I believe I've made good. I'm afraid there can be no question of my leaving now either, even for a visit – I assume you've already seen the letter I sent Naomi on the subject. It involves complicated questions of morale and national discipline, etc. Incidentally, the grief of Ann's mother has apparently had its edges blunted, since she's wired Ann to ignore the earlier letters and cables demanding her return, and do as she sees fit.

I won't even ask where you get the idea that Ann is a child, to be "taken with" and brought home at anybody's pleasure. She is an adult with a clear understanding of what she wants and where she wants it. Enough said.

32. Of serving in the Haganah or any other foreign military. Mordecai is responding to his parents' concern about the possible consequences of serving in a foreign army. On February 1, the *Post* reported that the American authorities were threatening to confiscate the passports of any Americans serving in military roles in Palestine and deny them the protections traditionally due to US citizens. In such an eventuality, it would only be possible for them to get a one-way passport to the US after the end of their military service.

33. According to Benny Morris (88), the Najjada was a Palestinian Arab paramilitary organization formed in 1945. It was one of two youth organizations formed to resist implementation of the Partition Plan. The other was the Futuwwa.

Now to re-answer Gershon's itemized letter (the other answer was burnt by the bomb-fire). I'll send you *Iyyun*;[34] there have been no more *kinusim* on *dat*;[35] have not received Gunther; would appreciate Mathiessen[36] (on Melville too, if available); I'm far from being a hero, the American press to the contrary notwithstanding; forget the special funds request, it has all worked out very nicely; Sussman (former apartment-mate) should be there by now with details about me, also Mrs. Brailove; conditions in the States stink, according to what comes in over the wires, and the only peaceful place in the world is the Bahama Islands, the safest — Jerusalem: we can at least get armored cars and armed protection. And the Bahamas have the Duke of Windsor, so even there...; you're right on *Gentlemen's Agreement*[37] — your point was the one I had wanted to make, but lost when I stopped writing in the middle. Bravo. The trouble is that everything you say and I write is just words, and words will stop neither the Arabs nor the British — certainly not mine or yours, as long as they have guns. And speaking of guns — what the hell is this Parents of Kids in Palestine Association, run by Borowsky and Charny and I assume — Chertoff? If you yell for arms for your little boys ok, if you scream for implementation of the UN decision — ok, but if you even whisper for "protection" from the Consulate — s**t NO! We absolutely refuse any consideration differing from that accorded other residents here — besides, we won't

---

34. *The Jerusalem Philosophical Quarterly*, a magazine published by the Hebrew University since 1945.
35. Conferences on religion.
36. He means F. O. Matthiessen (1902–1950), a literary critic and scholar of American literature who wrote a landmark study on Herman Melville. Mordecai mentioned above that he had a copy of *Moby Dick* with him at the time of the bombing of the *Post*. In retellings of the story of the bombing, my father used to suggest that the cover of *Moby Dick* that may have saved his life. He maintained a life-long love of the book, rereading it every few years.
37. A best selling novel by Laura Z. Hobson which explored the problem of anti-Semitism in the United States. It was made into an Oscar-winning film that same year.

get it. I'm serious though – you'll be getting some of the kids in trouble if you keep nagging the consul and he suddenly asks to see everybody – some of them are "out of town,"[38] and can't get back very easily. You take care of the American scene, we'll take care of ourselves.

And that's all for now. I'm going downtown to get my copy of the *Palestine Post* on Bomb-night framed, and get my map of Jerusalem mounted. I also have designs on a good meal. Shalom, and *lehitraot*. Be well.

love, mersh

In this letter to his sister, Mordecai once again returns to the tragic death of the American member of the Lamed-Heh.

February 19, 1948

Dear Toots,

...

Moshe Pearlstein should not have been with that group – he faked his way along. The girl he was sweet on has been on *tafkid*[39] in the Old City – a real hot spot, for a long time (over a month) and he felt he wasn't pulling his share of the burden. So he bluffed experience and was taken along. He had come last April, with Kepi, and Yaakov Herzog received a terrible letter from her over it – she was frightfully upset). He was a good kid.

Talk of the folks' trip must wait until after the commission[40] gets here and we see how things go. That does not mean it's off – just postponed.

---

38. I.e., on duty in the Hagana.
39. Hebrew, meaning "on duty" or "assignment."
40. The UN Commission to assess the situation in Palestine and develop a plan to stem the violence.

...

Tachlis:[41] there is no such thing as a "normal" Palestinian – and here goes for some kind of description of conditions, inadequate as it must be since I've been limited to Jerusalem for some time. – Wait – there's your Last letter first:

Ann has just received a wire from home advising her to ignore previous communications urging her to return, thus closing a very touchy topic. As for the bomb, it was the British, of course. Four constables, two Arabs and two Poles are the names we dug up as being implicated. And there's where it stops: try to get some action against them! I did receive your letter on Ann's "desirability": there is only this to be said: you have no idea how right you are, and how you must of necessity underrate her until you get to know her personally rather than second-hand. How long it will be before she gets over the Alter heartache God only knows – from what I know of her, it will be a long time. As my confidante (which position you have retained, of course, and whose obligations you have admirably discharged) you must understand that I'm not bluffing or sour-grape-ing when I say that the Hadassah cable does not bother me: too much has happened to me, both physically and emotionally, since I last saw her that it seems to be relatively unimportant. At the most "promising" moments of the relationship, her coming to Palestine meant, for the most part, an opportunity to see whether it would work out, not a conclusion. Her not coming, her not feeling the need to be here at all now, is enough evidence of the gap between us and testimony to the improbability of it working out. As we in the Middle East say – *ma'alesh*.[42]

---

41. In this context, the word is best translated as "bottom line."
42. Arabic, meaning "things happen," or "that's life." Mordecai himself translates it in an earlier letter (March 16, 1947) as approximately "what the hell."

Living above Ben Gurion meant extra guards around the house, fellows who used to scare the s**t out of me when I'd come home late at night, I got used to it though, and after a while I'd spent a couple of minutes with them exchanging lies about our adventures. The Sherlock house[43] is now also under special protection, for reasons I can't detail now (even though he himself is away, that is). As for needing an apartment in which to house a wife I don't have and am not likely to have for quite a while – aren't you being more than slightly premature? Let it ride, until I'm ready to.

...

Nobody in Palestine today is "normal," and conditions are radically different from place to place. In Jerusalem only "busy" people go out at night after dark; in Tel Aviv the kids come in from their *emdot*[44] and raise hell all hours of the night, like NY in wartime. There is a different spirit there – they get only the exhilaration of knowing about victories but not the tension of being near a front. We feel we're near a powder keg, and we've adjusted to it, planned what to do should it go off, etc. There's more zest, but nothing to relax with when you're off-duty. My own "social" life is talking shop with my friends here, with Ann and Carmi and Dov, and spending Friday night listening to records. When I have time during the day I read in the sun for a while or have tea in the Atara – it's a gathering-point for all the *chevrah*.[45] My celibacy doesn't even bother me – too much. Hell's bells – this is a war, and it provides plenty of thrills by itself.

---

43. Probably the home of David Tidhar (1897–1970), who was known as the Sherlock Holmes of the Yishuv. Tidhar served in the Palestine Police Force in Jerusalem, but left in 1926 to form his own private investigation office in Tel Aviv. He inspired the author Shlomo Ben-Yisrael to write a series of mystery chapbooks titled *David Tidhar: The First Hebrew Detective* between 1930 and 1932, with Tidhar's picture on the cover.
44. Hebrew, meaning "positions."
45. Hebrew, meaning "gang, group of friends."

How did you like the *mapalah*[46] the [Arabs] got at Tirat Zvi? – They lost 57 dead, scores wounded, 2 prisoners, and we lost 1 dead, 1 wounded (easily worth their 57). They claim 200 Jews dead, 300 wounded, 20 taken prisoner! The Oriental imagination at its best. ..there weren't that many Jews in the whole area!

That's all for now – I'm going to read, and loaf for a while. Laylah tov, and love to Monroe.

Love to you too – the Brat

The *"mapalah"* at Tirat Zvi to which Mordecai refers occurred on February 16. Three hundred Arabs attacked three kibbutzim adjacent to one another in the Beit Shean Valley: Tirat Zvi, Ein Hanatsiv, and Sde Eliyahu. After a ten hour battle, the attackers were beaten back. As Mordecai points out, losses on each side were extremely uneven.[47] This attack came almost exactly ten years after Tirat Zvi beat back a similar attack during the Arab uprising of 1936–39, only months after its establishment.

The victory of Tirat Zvi was a significant morale boost to settlements throughout the country and to the overall war effort but had a devastating effect on Arab morale. A relatively small group of defenders had defeated a large organized military force attacking a civilian agricultural community. Haganah intelligence had picked up word of the impending attack, giving them time to prepare; the kibbutz was reinforced; the Palmach blew up bridges that could be used by the attackers; and the 115 defenders were ready. The decisive win proved that a much smaller force of highly motivated people could defeat an invading horde.

---

46. Hebrew, meaning "defeat, setback."
47. *Palestine Post*, February 17, p. 1: "300 Arab Attackers Routed: Fifty-Seven Killed."

Chapter 16

Ben Yehuda Street Bombing

Over the years, Ben Yehuda Street, one of the most frequented thoroughfares of Jewish Jerusalem, has been a repeated target for terrorism. As of this writing, there have been no fewer than five lethal attacks on this central location. The first took place on February 22, 1948. At six fifteen in the morning, three British army trucks and an armored British police car approached the Romema checkpoint in Jerusalem from the direction of the Arab village of Imwas. The checkpoint was manned by Civil Guard volunteers, Shlomo Cherpi and Moshe Kidmi. When the guards asked the driver of the car where the convoy was headed, he replied that they were on their way to Camp Allenby – a British army barracks in Talpiot, South Jerusalem. When the guards asked if they could check the trucks, the driver screamed at them, in Hebrew, "I said everything is okay! I do not give you permission to do an inspection! I am responsible for this convoy, you worthless Jewish wretch, let us pass!"

The guards noted the number of the car so as to report the officer's rudeness. When they later testified during the Jewish Agency's investigation of the bombing, they explained that the officer's rudeness was not particularly out of the ordinary, and that they had been following instructions not to insist on checking British army or police vehicles.

The convoy arrived at Ben Yehuda Street, stopping at the intersection with Hillel Street. A night guard at a nearby parking lot heard shots, and saw the British officers abandoning the trucks and shooting at passersby before fleeing the area in the armored car. Remembering the explosion outside the *Post* three weeks earlier, caused by a truck rigged with explosives, he ran into the middle of the street, screaming as loud as he could to try and wake those slumbering in the nearby buildings.

At six thirty, a huge explosion rocked the area. Four buildings were demolished, including two hotels – the four-story Atlantic Hotel, and the Amdorsky Hotel. The force of the blast was so strong that windows shattered throughout nearby neighborhoods, including Rehavia, Geula, Mekor Haim and Machane Yehuda. Between forty-nine and fifty-eight people were killed, and hundreds were injured. Although many Palmachniks were quartered in the hotels that were destroyed, most of them were out on operations at the time of the blast, and almost all of the dead were civilians.[1]

The attackers were, once again, British deserters: Eddie Brown, who claimed that the Irgun had killed his brother, and Peter Madison,[2] who had been promised a fee for the attack by Abdul Khader al-Husseini, the mastermind of the *Palestine Post* bombing. With characteristic exaggeration, al-Kutub bragged in a radio interview after the war[3] that there were actually three bombs – the second on Jaffa Road and the third on King George Street – and that over two thousand Jews were killed or injured. The next day the Arab High Command claimed full responsibility for the attack, and said the explosions were in retaliation for an Irgun bomb attack in Ramleh, but later, the Supreme Arab Committee, afraid of international censure, denied responsibility.

Mordecai cabled his parents immediately after the bombing: "MISSED AGAIN NOW ITS OUR TURN, LOVE, MORDECAI." His

---

1. Sources: Ori Milshtein, *Toldot Milchemet HaAtzmaut* ("A History of the War of Independence") vol. 3, pp. 89–91, and Benny Morris, *1948: The First Arab-Israeli War* (Yale University Press, 2008), pp. 107–8.
2. The same British deserters who bombed the *Palestine Post*. See above.
3. See chapter 15, footnote 19.

detailed letter was written two days later. In the meantime, Paul is distraught at the Ben Yehuda bombing. He writes:

> Right now, as I write this letter, I am under the horrifying effect of the tragedy yesterday at Ben Yehuda St.... Naturally, a person is most concerned with those close to him,[4] and my first thought was about you, but I consoled myself with the knowledge that you are usually at home in the mornings, far from the scene of the "adventure." But who wouldn't mourn the great tragedy of the disaster itself ... the dead and wounded and the property that was acquired through immense toil and great suffering ... The press here, English and Yiddish, describe the catastrophe in colors so dark that a deep sigh erupts from my heart, a sigh with a trace of protest against the Heavens, as it were, "Until when, Master of the Universe, Until where!"[5] "How shall Jacob stand? For he is small."[6] But as Naomi always maintains: We must gird ourselves with faith and strengthen ourselves with confidence that even so, and despite it all,[7] triumph will ultimately come ... or as you are wont to say, "It will be good." And in truth, I have never despaired of the Redemption, and now too my heart has not sunk, so what then? I weep for the many victims that we must sacrifice from among our young people, sanctified among our nation, whose light was extinguished before they ever witnessed our victory. (Feb. 23)

While waiting impatiently for a letter from his son, Paul writes:[8]

---

4.   Adapted from *Sanhedrin* 9b, "אדם קרוב אצל עצמו‎," a dictum that explains why a person may not testify against himself.

5.   An allusion to Psalms 94:3, "How long shall the wicked, how long shall the wicked exult?"

6.   Amos 7:2.

7.   From the song by poet David Shimoni. Hebrew is: "ואף על פי כן ולמרות הכל‎."

8.   Although this excerpt is dated March 5, after Mordecai's letter, it was written well before Paul received his son's letter.

...my heart is torn and churning .... The press reports many fatalities, the casualties of the Haganah, who fall daily, and the tension grows until I feel I will explode ... and all I can do is offer a modest prayer to Heaven: "Strengthen your nation's weakened hands, send from on high aid and remedy."[9]

February 24, 1948

Dear Family,

They've done it again, the British. They didn't bother denying the accusations in regard to the bombing of the *Post,* since there were few casualties, but this last job, in which over 50 have died and more than two hundred have received medical aid, is so gruesome a business that the London papers have all screamed that the Arabs did it. I personally would like to know how much the Arabs were paid to claim credit for it – if they were paid at all: as a morale-builder for them, British readiness not to hog the credit is a great thing. Our Jews are wonderful though. Within three minutes they were at work, digging, and have not stopped yet, three days later, having worked all through the evening and nights as well. All but a few of the wrecked stores along King George are open for business, were open within 24 hours; the restaurants and cafe were open by late the same day. The city is digging itself out, quickly, and the rubble of the bombed buildings is being poured along the Jewish-manned roadblocks, making them finally impregnable. The whole length of Ben Yehuda has broken glass and sagging walls to show for itself, and the adjoining streets are slowly beginning to lose the piles of rubble that have covered them for the past few days. I imagine this is what a bombed German city looked like during the war: hard sunlight where once stood an old, stone building; gaping holes where there once were walls and stores and a few trees. The *Palestine*

---

9.   From the *Yotzrot* (special Festival *piyyutim*) of the second day of Rosh Hashana.

Post bomb was a firecracker compared to this; far away, on Radak street in Rehavia, where I now live (with Carmi Charny as a roommate) it woke me up, and the pressure cracked a window. Isn't it time the lousy Americans came with a few bazookas and some M-Is[10] and a few thousand boys to handle them? Money isn't everything – you wear a suit of dollar bills for protection...

The miracle has happened – I'm on a week's leave. So far, I spent last night sleeping, after a long, lingering hot bath, so hot I could just barely sit down in it (a *mechayah*)[11] and today I just walked around slowly, sat in a cafe and drank tea, came home and listened to records for a few hours, and snubbed everybody and everything connected with any and all work. I'm loafing like mad, and refuse to do anything remotely resembling work. I haven't formulated real plans for the rest of the vacation – which lasts all the way up to Sunday night – but I will. It will probably include a movie, a few sun-baths, some light reading.... I hereby promise an article, to be mailed within two weeks. I'll try to make it a good one. Whatever happened to the one on the Arabs (which *The Nation* sent on to the *New Republic*) and to the one I sent to *Commentary*, at their request? You might put in a phone call or two and check on them. Also – Gershon, thank Mrs. Brailove for the lovely hoard of Chesterfields and Tareytons[12] she sent me from Tel Aviv – I'm hoarding them, rationing them to me very slowly and carefully, they should last indefinitely.

And now, since I'm on leave, and have promised me long long rests and complete neglect (almost complete) of duty, this letter will end right here: I'm going to shave, bathe and dress, so that when Ann comes over for dinner, and

---

10. The M1 Garand was a .30 caliber semi-automatic rifle, and the standard US service rifle used during World War II.

11. Yiddish, meaning "life giving," i.e., a pleasure.

12. Chesterfields and Tareytons were both brands of American cigarettes.

Ann, Carmi and I sail outside in the beautiful evening air, I'll look like an ad in an American magazine. That's all for now.

Good afternoon, all, and all my love.

Mordecai in front of bombed-out building, undated

This latest atrocity set off a wave of revenge attacks against the British. Members of the Lehi and the Irgun took to the streets and killed sixteen British troops and policemen. A week later, on 29 February, a Lehi bomb planted near Rehovot derailed a British troop train that had been traveling from Cairo to Haifa, killing twenty-eight.[13]

In addition to the bombings of the *Palestine Post* and Ben Yehuda Street, during February there was heavy fighting in Haifa and Rosh Pina in the north and in Tel Aviv in the central region. By the end of the month, the civil war had been raging for three months. Daily attacks, bombings and shootings continued. In March alone, there were attacks on trains in which over fifty passengers were killed (perpetrators unknown), pitched battles in the Jerusalem hills between Haganah and Arab troops in a failed Jewish attempt to open the road from Tel Aviv, and Arab sniper

---

13.　See Morris, *1948*, p. 108.

attacks in Tel Aviv and Jerusalem. An epic battle between Jews and Arabs was fought in Gush Etzion, south of Jerusalem.

On March 2, the *Post* reported that 1,378 people had been killed over the prior three months as a result of the ongoing violence, including 546 Jews, 666 Arabs and 74 British soldiers. March also brought political setbacks to the Yishuv as the Americans, increasingly dubious about partition, begin to consider the idea of "trusteeship" for Palestine.

In spite of the chaos on the streets, the siege of Jerusalem and the danger involved in travelling between Tel Aviv and Jerusalem, Mordecai is determined to make the most of his brief vacation. Meeting Israeli giants, or soon-to-be giants, of Hebrew literature, was a high priority.

March 1, 1948 [given as "20 Adar 1"]

[translated by Rachel Kaminetsky]

My dear family,

Two kids, each no older than eight, approached us as we walked around on Allenby St, in Tel Aviv (here you can conclude I was in Tel Aviv – I spent six days of vacation there) and they asked us: Where is Abu Kabir?[14] And we: What do you need in Abu Kabir? And they insisted – "Where is Abu Kabir?" And again "What for?" And this time they replied: "We have bullets. We want to carry out an operation there." And we asked "What good are bullets without a 'tool'"? They shook their heads, "We have Stens." (I'm not sure they didn't...) And Abu Kabir, as you know, is a "pure" Arab quarter from which they would shoot at the outskirts of Tel Aviv. Our kids today...

---

14. An area within the municipal boundaries of Jaffa, on the outskirts of Tel Aviv. It had its own distinct character having been an agricultural village. According to the *Post*, the Haganah had repulsed an attack on Tel Aviv from Abu Kabir on February 16 – "T.A. Border Attack Repulsed," *Palestine Post*, 17 February, 1948. It seems these eight-year-olds were planning their own revenge attack!

I got some vacation from the newspaper and I "bluffed" a bit and got time off also from my "position,"[15] and left. Wait, hold on, don't get all stirred up – I traveled in an armored vehicle, with quite an armed escort. Only on our way back did they fire a little, but were not even able to silence our enthusiastic singing, which began as soon as we pulled out of the "Egged"[16] station. Two of the Palmachniks rejoiced at the sound of the shots, and merrily opened fire – fire for the heck of it. Fun times.

Tel Aviv itself is a confusing and utterly "unsympathetic" city. It contains all the noise and alarm of New York, without the convenience or complacency. I was able, over these days, to meet with Lamdan[17] (and I have regards from him to Bavli) and Shlonsky[18] and Lea Goldberg.[19] Lamdan is a man of refreshing simplicity, completely devoted to the homeland and concerned by each and every shortcoming he sees. I found him at a cafe, the day after the horrible brawl with the Etzel hooligans by the Mograbi cinema, and

---

15. In the Haganah.
16. Egged was originally created in 1933 through the merger of four intercity bus companies that served the Tel Aviv area. Today Egged is the largest transit bus company in Israel.
17. Yitzchak Lamdan (1899–1954), born in Ukraine and immigrated to Palestine in 1920, was a Hebrew-language poet, translator, editor and columnist. He was awarded the Israel prize for literature posthumously, in 1955. His epic poem "Masada" (1927), about the Jewish struggle for survival in a world full of enemies, was one of his most famous, and hugely influential.
18. Avraham Shlonsky (1900–1973) was born in Russia and moved to Palestine in 1921. He became a highly acclaimed translator, poet and editor, known for his wit and innovative use of Hebrew. In 1946 he was awarded the Tchernichovsky Prize for his translations of Pushkin and Shakespeare. He was awarded the Bialik Prize for literature in 1959, and the Israel Prize in 1967.
19. Lea Goldberg (1911–1970) was born in Prussia and immigrated to Palestine in 1935. A prolific Hebrew-language poet, novelist, playwright, editor, translator, and literary scholar, her writings are considered classics of Israeli literature. She worked as an editor on two Hebrew newspapers and as a children's book editor before becoming a literature lecturer at Jerusalem's Hebrew University, eventually becoming head of the university's department of comparative literature. She was awarded the Israel Prize in 1970.

he was completely shaken up and upset by it and search-ing for a solution to avoid an inner battle. Shlonsky, whom I found in another cafe, is a whole different character. Crazy mind, a bit of a wild man, loud and lively and jubilant and so aggressively articulates his opinions that there is no room for argument. He is well liked by the people of the Haga-nah, and returns this affection. Leah Goldberg is noticeably not beautiful, but has a grace that is her own. I spent some pleasant hours at her home (along with Sarah and Moshe Ettinger) on Shabbat, in the afternoon.

In my personal life nothing has changed since I last wrote you. In a few moments I will go to a staff meeting, with the hope I can convince "the king" (Agronsky) to place me back at my first job – writing and editing local news: I want, for the sake of change and novelty, to go to bed at midnight rather than at 3 in the morning. Perhaps I'll succeed...

Had you managed to speak with Dolk Horowitz before he left the US, and with Shertok, about a job for me within the Agency or something else related to national work? What does Naomi think of Walter Eytan's[20] school for "dip-lomats"? Should I look into it or is it not of dignity to our family to start from the bottom? Nu?

Joke of the day: A Jew of the Diaspora would like to know how to tell the difference between the Haganah, Etzel, and Lehi. He's told: slap one. If you're slapped back once it's Haganah, twice it's Etzel, three times it's Lehi. He walked down the street, slapped someone, and was not slapped back. He returned and asked for the explanation, and was told: that was Mishmar Ha-am![21]

---

20. Walter Eytan (1910–2001) was an Israeli diplomat. He was Director General of the Israeli Foreign Ministry from 1948 to 1959 and Israeli ambassador to France from 1959 to 1970.
21. Civil Guard. See chapter 15, footnote 12.

And now I must hasten my pace to the meeting. For
now, Shalom to you all – and do not spare work from the
mailmen.

With much love,

Mordecai Shmuel

The determination to at least attempt to lead normal lives during this
period is striking. Mordecai describes attending cultural events and evenings out with friends in the face of sniper attacks and bombs, traveling
to Tel Aviv to meet with literati despite the dangers of the road and, in
the letter below, an evening spent singing folk songs. He even writes to
the famous American poet and folk singer, Carl Sandburg,[22] who had
written a blurb for the cover of the album Mordecai and his friends
were listening to, asking for the bawdy verses which could not be sung
in public. I have not found a reply from Sandburg.

The increasing violence throughout the country rattles Mordecai's
parents. They continue to beg him to come home. Paul's pleas become
increasingly shrill:

Why shouldn't you visit us? True, you don't have that huge
amount [of money to fly], but you can travel by boat. We,
that is Gershon and myself, promise to pay for your travel
expenses here and back, and beyond that, we will send
the whole round trip fare before you even set out. A second promise—Not only will we not try to keep you in our
house, but we also won't entreat you to stay in America
longer than you want to, and not even a few weeks. It's
worth it to us to spend five or six hundred dollars even for
a short meeting. And really, I have a strong claim on you.
We agreed, before you travelled to Eretz Yisrael, that you

---

22. Carl Sandburg (1878–1967) was the winner of three Pulitzer Prizes, two for his
poetry and one for his biography of Lincoln. At his death in 1967, President Lyn-
don B. Johnson observed that "Carl Sandburg was more than the voice of America,
more than the poet of its strength and genius. He was America."

would stay about a year, and after one year decide whether to stay in the Land or return to America. We also agreed that if you remained, we, that is, Mother and I, would visit you in the Land. But with the conditions there now, you also realize that it is impossible for us to visit you in Eretz Yisrael. Therefore, you are obligated to visit us in America. I can't express in words how we long to see you. Only the poet of the Psalms can express this yearning, and I will apply his verse: "My soul thirsts for Thee, my flesh longs for Thee"![23]

The thought that we wouldn't see you for who knows how long terrifies me. Don't forget that someone my age can't plan into the distant future ...

My dear Mordecai, do not think that this is an edict from me and that you must come—I'm merely suggesting, and I think and I am convinced that it's a good suggestion—for you, for your morale, and for me, for my health and peace of mind.

Therefore, my dear one, please do not make light of my suggestion, think about it, study it, because it contains more than I could ever express in words. (Feb. 23)

Similarly, Esther writes:

Sunday night I had the pleasure of hearing a Palestinian string quartet at Temple Rodeph Sholem. It was really thrilling, and I thoroughly enjoyed it. BUT, I thought...Why aren't they in Palestine? They are needed there...Palestinian Jews have to be there at such time as this. There are thousands of Palestinians in this country at this time. What are they doing here? ... [You could come and] go on a speaking tour. You could do good work for the Yishuv, now, in the light of what you went through and people would listen to you..." (Feb. 25)

---

23.   Psalms 63:2.

Esther seemingly sees no contradiction in complaining that there are many Palestinians in the US "when they should be Palestine," while wanting her son to be numbered among them. Both parents implore their son to bring Ann with him. Paul writes that Ann's mother is "forlorn, steeped in deep sorrow… worried about the safety of her daughter in Eretz Yisrael… I would not be exaggerating if I said that, even if there is a need for you to bring her home, that is also worthwhile." (Feb 6.)

Mordecai remains steadfast despite feeling parental pressure and genuinely missing his family. He and Ann seem to reinforce one another's commitment to Zionism.

Wednesday, March 10, 1948

Dear Mother and Father,

I waited a week before writing to give myself a little more time to think, although another week or another month could not change the answer — the only one I could possible give. I also waited in the hope that you would follow your letters with another set cancelling the first.

Remember a few years back when I was supposed to preach in White Plains and Gershon had to pinch-hit for me because I wasn't well enough to go? That whole day before Yom Kippur I couldn't eat, and by morning, when I felt well enough, we were already fasting. Mother, you brought in a steaming bowl of delicious looking soup and offered it to me, and Father said that since I had been ill, there was a "*heter*"[24] and I could eat. I didn't, and Father was both pleased and proud that even though I had wanted to eat I had not exploited a possible excuse and had held out.

That's essentially the way things are now. I want to "eat" — I want to see you all, I want to spend some time with you, and we can find a "*heter*" in that the original year we had planned is up, or in that your planned visit must needs be delayed, but it would be as much of an

---

24. Hebrew, meaning, in this context, "dispensation."

"averah"[25] for me to leave now as it would have been to eat then. Much greater, in fact, since a *"heter"* was always easier granted in cases *"bayn adam lamakom"*[26] than *"bayn adam lehavero,"*[27] and while eating then was the former only, leaving now involves both. I wrote Naomi at length on the role of Americans here at present, and in general on the morale of the Yishuv and what can hurt – or help it. Leaving now would constitute desertion in the face of the enemy, I would never dare show my face here again should I run now, and I would have no right to either. These are the critical months, and I must do what little I can. While I may occasionally be closer to a bomb than I care to be, I am far from the real fighting lines, and comparatively safe.

I don't think I'm being guilty of a breach of confidence if I quote a few lines written home by Ann after her misfortune, they sum things up well:

"...but I'm working and I hope I will have the strength to stick it out. I will have it if my family is strong too – and they must be. There are families here who never know from one night to the next when they will see their sons and daughters. There are a lot of people here who can't run away – and wouldn't even if they could – and I won't either."

Is my Zionist training and devotion to be any less effective than hers, broad and deep as it has been? Before I left NY I was asked "why go" (i.e., why you, when you can propagandize here, etc.) and my answer was: with my background, if I stay, I have no right to preach Zionism to anyone. No, if I go, I have no right to talk or write about Palestine to or before anyone.

Incidentally, leaving now is not simply a matter of packing a bag and paying the fee. One must first obtain leave from

25. Hebrew, meaning "sin."
26. Hebrew, meaning "between man and God."
27. Hebrew, meaning "between man and man."

his superior,[28] then collect 2 passes: one to leave Jerusalem, one to leave the country. Without these, travel companies will not sell tickets. One can get them only if he is being sent to the States on *"tafkid,"* a special assignment of sorts, and since there is no special job I could do that our kids in America already can't, I simply stay put.[29] Of course I could appeal to the US Consulate – and forfeit my right – moral and otherwise – to ever live in Palestine. But you made me as I am, a sort of idealist and something of a Zionist. I don't even feel that I really have a choice in the matter.

I'm afraid this has to be my answer for the present. Should things ease up by the summer, we'll see about a visit home then. Fair enough? And this will have to be all for the present. *Layla tov* – be well, and try not to worry too much.

All my love

Mordecai

P.S. – A possible *tafkid*: contact Harold Manson, Zionist Emergency Council, and ask him what happened to the job he spoke to me about in the Eden the night the U.J.A. people were here. (I can't give you any details about it by mail). If it's a go from his end, I'm willing, under the circumstances. But he has to guarantee a time limit for the job.

Love again.

M

P.P.S. – sending Hebrew article under separate cover, for *Hadoar*. Hope you like it.

It is clear that, under the right circumstances and for a limited amount of time, Mordecai would consider traveling to the United States.

---

28.   In the Haganah, not the *Post.*
29.   Of course Mordecai is searching for just such a *"tafkid."*

Here is the cover letter for the article mentioned above:

Dear Father,

I hope the enclosed[30] speaks for itself, I certainly worked hard enough on it for it to do just that. (You wouldn't believe me if I said I just knocked it off in an odd moment, so why try to fake?) I should add, in all honesty, that Carmi put it through the ringer before he put his seal of approval on it and then with seven of his own dear little fingers typed it out for shipment.

I'm sending two copies, under separate cover, to make sure that if one is begged, borrowed, stolen or otherwise lost you'll get the other. Discuss with Gershon whether you should corner Ribalow[31] yourself or should have Bavli[32] do so – at any rate, I think it should do for the *Hadoar*.[33] If he doesn't like, tell him what I think of his ability as a critic and pass it on to *Bitzaron*[34] (via Shimon Halkin??). I think, though, that *Hadoar* is the best place for it.

This is not a letter, of course, and when I sit down to one later today I shall discuss your latest letter (and Mother's as well) fully. You will probably get all this *chazerai*[35] at the same time – won't you have a reading orgy though!

And that's that for the present. Carmi, you may remember, is my room-mate at Nishry's house, and always available for a 4 a.m. discussion should a word elude me.

30. "On the Crimes of the British" – an article Mordecai wrote in Hebrew.
31. Menachem Ribalow (1895–1953), US Hebrew editor and essayist, editor of the Hebrew language weekly *Hadoar*. Many Hebrew authors in the US made their debut under his guidance.
32. Hillel Bavli (1892–1961), Hebrew poet and professor of Hebrew literature at JTS. Father of the aforementioned Tooltolleh, he was a close family friend. Among his works were *Collected Poems, Mantle of Time* and *Israel, 1955.*
33. A Hebrew language weekly published in the US.
34. A quarterly review of Hebrew letters published in America. It was founded and edited by Chaim Tchernowitz.
35. From the Hebrew word for pig, this means "trash" or "junk" in Yiddish.

He's persecuting me, God bless him, and some day I may emerge as something resembling a Hebrew writer.

Love to all — I got to get back to work.

With love — Mordecai Shmuel

The article was published in Hebrew in *Hadoar*, volume 23, 7 Nisan 5708 (April 16, 1948).[36]

Carmi Charny, later known as T. Carmi, Mordecai's roommate, close friend and, apparently, his Hebrew editor

36. The article is not included here because it is long and summarizes material already presented. The English translation is available at http://www.palestineposts.com.

As an example of the manic existence of Jews in Palestine, in the middle of March, Jerusalem experienced a huge snowstorm. The *Post* carried a headline, "General Winter in Jerusalem." In his memoirs Mordecai relates that the military censor called him to ask "who is this 'General Winter'?" Mordecai suggested he look out the window.

March 16, 1948

Dear Family,

I, Mordecai S. Chertoff, being sound in mind and body, do hereby depose and swear – realizing the damage I might be doing to my status as an objective reporter – that shortly before midnight last night, on the top of Hassolel Street in Jerusalem, Palestine, I took part in a snowball fight. True, it wasn't much of a fight – rain or snow, the *Palestine Post* must appear, and its staff could hardly spend much time away from their posts, but it must be clearly understood that there has been no shortage of the wherewithal for such fighting: as I write, at 1.10 p.m. on March 16, the snow is again falling, having stopped for little more than two or three hours since it began last night, at about eight. Trees, bewildered by the onslaught, bowed low under the weight of the snow, and the crack[ing] sounds the breaking branches gave off brought many a Jerusalem[ite] to the conclusion that "they're shooting again." I personally hit the ground behind a road block as a branch gave in behind me, sure a concert was about to begin. I was wrong. The new Haganah unit – "Hish" (*Heyl sheleg*)[37] was out in force on brand-new skis, and all over the hills of Hebron Arabs huddled around their fires praying for warmth and providing no target at all for our snipers (one of whom caught an Arab with his pants off, literally, his rifle leaning against a

---

37. Mordecai is making a joke. As he explains below, "*Hish*" was really an acronym for "*Heyl Sadeh*" – field army. He pretends the "s" represents "*sheleg*," the Hebrew for snow (there was no snow or alpine brigade in the Haganah).

wall during what he had no doubt planned for a brief inter-
lude. One shot – at close to 400 meters – fine shooting, but
a helluva way to die. Undignified). Somebody is confused
upstairs – it just stopped again, and the sun comes and goes
like a British statesman.

Under separate cover I'm sending you a copy of a new
Hebrew publication called *Mahatz* – a sort of half-hatched
Stars-and-Stripes,[38] which was put out by Hish (really *Heyl
Sadeh*)[39] here in Jerusalem. I'll be helping with subsequent
issues.

Believe me, Gershon, I did not go out of my way
and try to be a hero.[40] I did what anybody else in the same
circumstances would do – and has been doing whenever
necessary. I simply happened to be there.

...

Incidentally, I live on Radak, around a corner and two
blocks away from the zone,[41] with a good three blocks between
me and the outermost row of houses. Since mail service here is
so chaotic, the best thing is to send it to me at Tel Aviv: we have
our own inter-office communication system, and so I know I'll
always get the letter. I've written a number of times since the
Ben Yehuda bomb – twice from here, and once from Tel Aviv
(where I spent my week's leave, which began two days after
the Ben Yehuda bang). My cable was delayed because every
one else had the same idea: in the future I shall not cable. You
know by now that if I am anywhere near a bang the American
press smells a story, so if I'm not in the news you know I'm okay.
Besides, a press cable can go twice around the world in the
time it takes me to get to the post office and get a cable sent.

---

38. An American military magazine.
39. Infantry, literally "field army" in Hebrew.
40. Mordecai is responding to his brother's praise of his behavior after the bombing
    of the *Post*.
41. One of the security zones set up by the British. This one incorporated parts of
    Talbieh and Rehavia.

I wish it were time to write a letter about our Jewish State, so that you people can stop peddling the partition letter (how about sending me one of those printed monstrosities?) By now you should have both copies of the longish Hebrew piece I did for *Hadoar* – I prefer it to the letter. Please let me know as soon as you do whether it's being printed, and airmail me a few copies if it is.

Good for the Rosenfelds. We had a good time here together, and it was very nice having them at "Ravakia." A few days ago, however, my work changed again. With three people having left the staff, I was moved back to the local desk, where I begin a bit earlier, but leave at one, and so get a real night's sleep. Social life is a one-night-a-week affair (a lot really), at home. Carmi and Milt and I are always "at home" then, and some of the kids invariably drop in. Last week, Zippy Borowsky and Aliza Levine cooked a wonderful supper, Ann came, and Barak (an artist and sculptor of sorts) and a sabra, and we sat around all night. Everybody slept over – scattered throughout the house on sofas, chairs, and rugs, and we had a mass breakfast.

I've been getting *B'terem* fitfully – I'll write them and check on your copies. Believe me – I can't write those little editorials anymore. I have neither the patience nor the time nor the frame-of-mind for them. I'm so far from the American scene that I see things differently, and much of what one worries over here would be meaningless to your Jews. How do they see a Jewish State affecting their status now, and what's happening to the philanthropic organization known as the Z.O.A.?) I'll check on the kids[42] in the camps – I think there has been a bit done on them, but I don't know about the psychiatry angle. Ann may know. As for Sammie marrying – I'll believe it when it happens. Brailove was charming – and I finished her American cigarettes a long time ago.

---

42. Holocaust survivors in the displaced persons camps in Cyprus and Europe.

I'll have some pictures taken as soon as I can, and send them on. How about me looking tough, to frighten the Seminary kids with? We'll larn 'em !

No more now – gotta go see a man about a man.

Shalom uvracha,

Mordecai's comments in the penultimate paragraph, about the divergence of opinion and experience between American and Palestinian Jews, are prescient. He feels alienated from American Jews, believes that they cannot comprehend what is going on in Palestine and are more concerned by the impact of events in the Middle East on *their* status in the US. These concerns anticipate what would become a recurring issue between American and Israeli Jews.

March xx?

Dear Gershon,

Front and center – at attention! You are on the carpet – and this is one letter I doubt whether you'll reprint, either in pamphlet form or in your bulletin.

What's all this...about American democracy you hand out in the introduction to my letter? If the present-day witch hunt[43] is at all a continuation of the democracy of Revolutionary days I'm an Arab spy and my name is Mahmud. "It is the same democracy as that of our Founding Fathers" – may I take slight exception to that and quote one of my newspaper colleagues? – "balls," then. At least in Salem they used to hunt witches, and they really believed they were witches. I seriously doubt whether America today is psychologically capable of a Revolution (i.e., whether she has not become so completely lost in her red-phobia and lust for money and world power that any opposition at all could grow and

---

43. Senator Joseph McCarthy's congressional hearings and search for communist sympathizers, which lasted from 1947 to 1956.

flourish in the face of American reaction. For me, the latest blow is the announced death of *PM*.[44] It went in for big headlines, and screamed *"gevalt"* at each and every opportunity, but it was the only paper in the States that had the guts to believe in something other than money and to fight for that something. Marshall Field's idealism was apparently psychoanalyzed away for him, and there is now nobody around with guts enough to show any interest in the "uptown Daily Worker." It's too bad. If Wallace had any sense – since he's been tarred as a red and as being too liberal anyway – he would buy the paper and keep it coming out. It leaves the US, with 144,000,000 people, with the sum total of one almost liberal paper – the *N.Y. Post*, with its many, reservations.

Seeing a letter of mine printed, with footnotes, gives me a funny feeling. Had I guessed, when I wrote it, what would happen, I would have written more of some things, and less of others – I suppose therein lies whatever value the "document" has. I would still like a copy of the original Hebrew, if you think you can spare it.

...

I also received the bulletin[45] with the letter about Davidson and what we did to him and Goodwin in it. It reads well, sounds not at all bad. Send me a copy of what Gordis[46] did with the stuff, I'm curious:

For your information, one does not talk about Haganah operations and long-range plans. The newspapers have mentioned that Haganah has bought two dozen planes. Do you need Technicolor movies of them? The cabinet has not yet been formed, portfolios have not been handed out yet: the

---

44. *PM* was an innovative, left-of-center daily published in New York from 1940 to 1948. It was published without advertising, hence Mordecai's comment that it "believe[d] in something other than money." It was capable of such independence since it was financed by Chicago millionaire Marshall Field III.
45. Issued by Gershon's synagogue, Temple B'nai Israel of Elizabeth, NJ.
46. Robert Gordis (1908–1992), a Conservative rabbi and professor at JTS.

make-up along party lines is not even decided yet. How do the Americans feel about our Communists here participating in the Provisional Council? They're probably scared s**tless! I'll begin sending you the weekly agency summary this week. Okay? It simply means my attending the Friday press-conferences.

...

Has Maurice [Samuel] done any speaking lately, and what line is he taking? Where are the thousands of American ex-G.I.'s who signed pledges to come and fight here – did they lose their nerve? We've got work for them, and let 'em bring their old army toys too – we can use them as well.

Why did you let the folks write urging me to come home now? It's bad for my morale to get such letters ... I have a job to do here, and I'm doing it. Period. Full stop. New paragraph. Incidentally, tell mother her statement of the problem is correct, her solution faulty: I'll be writing more and more in Hebrew – she'll simply have to brush up on it. Tell her to see Mrs. Borowsky[47] on that Parents thing – it should be fun for her, if nothing else, to be able to swap gossip and stories with the parents of other kids here, particularly since the kids see each other here.

Rumba lessons, indeed!

With lots of love

Mordecai Shmuel

P.S. – Where's your doctorate?

---

47. Mother of Zipporah (Zippy), a friend of Mordecai's.

Chapter 17

Partition Plan in Danger

Although the UN had voted in favor of partition, and President Truman had been firmly committed to it, by the middle of March, the escalation of Arab violence was generating doubt within the US State Department as to whether partition was possible. Arab forces, with British support, were succeeding in their efforts to undermine the plan. The north of Palestine was under pressure from seven thousand men of the Arab Liberation Army, under the command of al-Qawuqji. The threat in the central region came mostly from al-Husseini, who led five thousand men, while the south was threatened by two thousand Moslem Brotherhood volunteers from Egypt. The Jewish areas of mixed cities like Haifa and Jerusalem were frequently attacked. Assaults were regularly launched against kibbutzim and isolated settlements across the country. The roads between Tel Aviv and Jerusalem, between Haifa and the Western Galilee, between Tiberias and the Eastern Galilee, and between Afula and the Beit Shean valley had been cut, almost isolating Jewish communities across the country and making their defense very difficult.

As early as January 1948, the US State Department had begun questioning partition. It prepared a document which stated that partition was unworkable and that therefore the US was not obliged to support it. Moreover, the policy planning staff declared that the maintenance of a Jewish state was contrary to the American national interest and its immediate strategic interests. They began to push for America to either cancel or, at the least, postpone partition. Truman himself was wavering. Warren Austin, the US representative to the UN, said that the Security Council was obliged to preserve peace, not force Partition on the Arabs, and on March 17, the US formally broached the possibility of suspending partition and, instead, implement some kind of trusteeship scheme. George Marshall, the US Secretary of State, took the credit for the change in policy. The Arabs were jubilant. The Jewish Agency rejected Austin's proposal and considered it a capitulation to Arab violence. By March 26, Truman had reaffirmed that – in principle – the US was in favor of partition, but asserted that a temporary trusteeship might be necessary. At the same time, Russia reaffirmed its commitment to partition.

The correspondence during this dark period for the Yishuv reflects the despair in the Chertoff household over the possible delay in statehood. In her letter of March 18, Naomi is distraught by the state of the world, the "immorality" and "the UN farce" regarding Palestine, the "Czech thing,"[1] the possibility of "universal military training" – a new draft that would call up those who fought in WWII, including Naomi's husband, Monroe, who had been an officer, and the "beginning of the end of the world." She writes: "I can't ever remember feeling quite so depressed, so without hope, so without faith, as I am today.... God is missing in our lives.... I shall do all in my power to prevent Monroe from being drafted again.... They betrayed us first in Europe and now in Palestine."

Gershon, too, is shocked by Truman's apparent repudiation of partition and recommends that Israel declare the State before the UN meets again. Esther thinks that "the world seems to have gone crazy; and Truman is too tiny for the big job of president of one of the most powerful nations in the world."

As usual, Paul is particularly eloquent:

---

1.   Probably a reference to the coup in Czechoslovakia in which the Communists took control of the country.

I cannot express everything going on in my heart, the depth of my concern for the safety of the Yishuv in general and for your safety in particular. The news coming from Eretz Yisrael does not cheer the heart, and the prospects coming from the U.N. here do not leave room for any serious hope in the near future. And because of this, I am steeped in sorrow these days...my heart is torn and agitated...and I am one big pile of nerves.... I do know how connected you are to the Land and to the fate of the Yishuv, and I also recognize my obligation, the obligation of a Jew to his nation, that "you are not permitted to absolve yourself of it."[2] But, the accounting of the intellect is one thing, and the feelings of the heart another.... (March 19, translation)

Mordecai is no less bitter than his family about what they all consider a betrayal by the United States. He too rages against the Americans but nevertheless manages to conclude his letter with a beautiful, lyrical paragraph that reflects his inextinguishable optimism.

March 21, 48

Dear Family,

Excuse the bitterness – but would you expect cheers from me now? I thank God I don't look like a typical American and I don't have to show an American passport for identification around town, and it's a good thing I don't betray my origin every time I open my mouth. What a bunch of no-good, filthy, scurvy, stinking, bastardly double-crossers! Russia is a threat to world peace, an abrogator of treaties, imperialistic, etc. etc., ad nauseam, while America simply turns around, pushes the knife in gently, and gives it a savage twist. Where are Austin's brave words, and Truman's

---

2.   Pirkei Avot 2:16: "You are not required to finish the task, but neither are you free to absolve yourself of it."

friendliness, and Marshall's understanding, and all the political sagacity of our American Jews, who had done such wonderful work on the political scene they feel themselves exempt from personal service here. What happened to them, took a week off?

Do they begin to understand, now, that the red-hunt was only the beginning, that everything will go, every vestige of personal liberty, as sacrifices upon the shiny altar of political expediency and America's Marshall-plan-imperialism?

The American government will do nothing for us. What about the Jews? Where are the thousands of ex-G.I.s who signed pledges to come and fight with us, where are the arms they've been promising, Where's all the *real* support? The time for speeches has long since passed: you can't debate with a Bren gun, and a six-pounder doesn't understand logic. There was something prophetic in the explosion at the Agency building:³ the fact that it was a US Consular vehicle (albeit stolen, and although it was not sanctioned or planned or aided by the consular officials, of course) was the coincidental, physical expression of a diplomatic aim which is being rapidly realized.

And I'll give you odds that our lousy American Jews vote for Truman again – he'll be saving the country from capitalism – and our little downtown clothing-industry *burjuks* are deathly afraid of communism! Afraid enough to sell themselves down the river. They'll sell cheap, too. As an American I'm deeply ashamed. We, who prided ourselves on our sense of justice and fair play, who spoke so glibly of democratic processes and the will of the majority, have pulled a Bevin.⁴ Remember some weeks back when he said

---

3. The Jewish Agency was bombed on March 11, 1948. Mordecai talks of the bombing in greater detail in a later letter.
4. Presumably, like the British foreign secretary, initially supporting partition and then withdrawing that support.

"the last word has not been said"? He knew what he meant, it seems. But Remez[5] answered nicely, last night: "As long as there's a Jew left alive in Palestine he'll be a free man." And C.-in-C. of the Haganah answered well too, when he said, in the order of the day, that we will never accept any foreign domination, neither in mandatory or trusteeship or any other form. That wasn't just talk. We've been betrayed and we stand alone – Russia, out of her competition with England, may yet help us, but we'll stand...

I doubt if I should ever live down the guilt-feelings I would have were I living in New York now.

Remember "Waiting for Lefty"?[6] The Jews of America are behind us all right, but "how far behind?" They may never catch up, at the rate they seem to be going now.

Nu – let's go on to more pleasant topics: 15 Arabs killed in one attack, 20 killed when they attacked us, 31 hit by our snipers in Haifa, 6 in Jerusalem, beaten back in Abu Kabir, routed at Beit Dajan – not a bad weekend.[7] We lost seven in one battle, and five in another – bad, but we've become hardened to [ILLEGIBLE TEXT]. Palestine is a small country, one knows everybody, and casualty lists are always targets of anxious concern. And what a tremendous country it is: men are lost during an operation and it takes days before they're found – finished. And it's a cruel country, in the way that, traditionally, lovers are cruel – demanding sacrifices nobody could ever accept in theory, and offering them in practice without the slightest hesitation.

When we find potatoes, we're going to roast them over a fire – of American passports.

---

5. David Remez (1886–1951) was the chairman of the Jewish National Council, the main executive institution of the Yishuv. He became minister of transportation in the provisional government.
6. A very successful 1935 play by the American playwright Clifford Odets that was highly critical of profiteering and exploitative economic systems.
7. These engagements are described in the *Palestine Post* of March 21, 1948.

Today is a beautiful spring day, clean-aired, sunny, with just a touch of the cool mountainous air Jerusalem's reputation rests on. A day one feels so much alive, so fit and vigorous; it's a shame to have to work. It's a day made for long walks in the hills, for lying in the grass under a tree, for loafing and physical exercise, for horse-back riding or tennis, for bicycle-riding – for anything but war and work. There'll be more like this, when the war is over, and one will be justified in staying away from work too. There will be days when clear air and sunny skies, followed by a cool night breeze and a bright moon, will not mean a sniper's heaven but a youth's paradise; there'll be many such days, and we here will appreciate them properly, having fought for them and earned them. So much has become unimportant, and right now, sitting in the garden typing, the most important thing I can think of is the sweet smell of the fresh grass all around me. The snow brought it out, lush and fragrant, and we'll have it for a few weeks now, until the summer *khamsinim* begin to scorch the earth and turn everything brown.

"*Yihiyeh tov*"- we really believe it. And until the day it is, completely, we'll take what pleasure we can in the little things. All my love,

Mordecai Shmuel

Paul responds to his son's invective:

... the betrayal – the bitterness that you unleashed in your letter was certainly justified. All of us here, as Zionists or not, recognize that "traitors have dealt very treacherously"[8] with us. Our hearts hurt and our blood boils from restrained anger and our worry for the future fate of the "State" intensifies .... We feel that the last bastion of the world's conscience has fallen ... from now on everyone is deceitful ... I personally have not despaired of good; despite all the

---

8. Isaiah 24:16.

obstacles in our way, I have a strong hope that we will be victorious in the end because "the appointed time has come, the time to be gracious unto her [Zion]."[9] What worries my heart are the many sacrifices that we must make, our precious young people felled by the sword of the enemy ...

I don't understand, however, why you rail so against the Jews of America! What should have we done that we didn't do? We marshalled all our might for the sake of the State, even those Jews who, in the past, remained at a distance, supported our efforts. I bring the testimony of Gedaliah Bublick,[10] may he rest in peace, who was always the toughest prosecutor of these Jews, even he admitted that there was not a single politically influential Jew who was called to help who did not respond favorably .... You ask where are the young men who promised to come ... as far as I know, there are thousands, if not tens of thousands, of volunteers ready and waiting for the signal to be given. But you also know that leaving the Land [of Israel] requires permission from on high, and who knows if that permission will be granted .... And not just the Jews, but the press in general, including the *Times*, yes, the *Times*, the newspaper that always sides with England and opposes Zionism, publicly criticized the betrayal, they protested with all their strength, and still here they are protesting the injustice that has been done to us, but no one is listening, at least for now, and what can we do more than they? Of course, it's not over, and we're still hoping it will end well. In any case, American Jews can't be accused of inaction or negligence. (March 31)

Diplomatic developments plunge the entire Chertoff household into despair. Paul's lament is followed by a bitter missive from Naomi.

---

9. Psalms 102:14.
10. Gedaliah Bublick (1875–1948). Yiddish writer and Zionist leader. He was a well-known religious Zionist activist and was one of the founders of the American Mizrachi, serving as its president from 1928 to 1932.

Despite his own despair, Mordecai takes the time to reassure his sister and attempts to coax her out of *her* anguish.

March 25, 1948

Dearest Toots,

Just received your letter of March 19 – and was shocked beyond words. I never expected such despair from you. I'm surprised that you let "diplomacy" upset you as it has. But then you haven't the source of inspiration there that we have: the kids who are fighting the good fight, and in spite of what the press says – winning it! (Yesterday's stories, for example, of 12 killed and 30 wounded in an attack on the Tel Aviv-Jerusalem convoy, was an outright lie propagated by the P.B.S. (Palestine Broadcasting Service) I'm sure with the intention of panicking the Yishuv. After a 7 hour battle, the casualties were 7 injured, one killed (maybe 3 – we still don't have a full story on it).[11] The foreign correspondents, who had sent a gory story with 12 corpses, didn't want to spoil it by sending a correction, so you probably got the horror picture. We did lose 14 on the way to Atarot[12] (by chance only Yoel was not with them, he was supposed to go to Neve Yaacov[13] that day, and couldn't make it – luck!) but the same day there were more than 35 Arabs killed and a good 50 injured: a bad day for us, but not as bad as

---

11. An attack on a convoy to Jerusalem, pinned down at the narrow ravine of Shaar Hagai (Bab el Wad) lasted for six hours, killing three and wounding seven. Some of the convoy returned to Hulda, some got through to Jerusalem (Itzhak Levy, *Tisha Kabin: Jerusalem in the War of Independence* [Tel Aviv: Ma'arachot/Defence Ministry Press, 1986], p. 444).

12. This was an attack on a convoy to Atarot, a moshav near Ramallah, north of Jerusalem. Mordecai describes this engagement in great detail in his article, "Battle of the Roads," which appeared on the front page of the *Post* on March 25. It is discussed below.

13. A religious settlement near Atarot. Both were ultimately depopulated and destroyed during the 1948 war; both were re-established after 1967, although Atarot is now an industrial zone rather than a moshav.

the press made it sound. Of course the numbers mean nothing when you've known some of the kids (one had been a messenger at the *Post*) and it becomes a personal loss, but we've become hardened to it, and there is no question of giving up. What the American betrayal meant here was a tendency towards a Russian orientation – I saw a wire to Shertok,[14] telling him how the Arab countries were drawing the red herring in front of American noses with the threat of present Arab countries losing out to threatening Arab revolutions should partition go through – if America stands in her betrayal (very unlikely, it seems to have been a tactic to whittle down the partition plan a bit) Russia may get her foothold here anyway, through the Jews. I can think of worse things. In short, we sorrow over every loss and criticize every failure, armchair-general style, and keep going. Remez said the other day that as long as there's a Jew alive in Palestine he'll be a free Jew – and he was right. Most of us have the faith to fight; some fight out of desperation; some because they've been called up; some because they have nothing else to do. The kids I know don't ask why, or how long, or to what end: it is enough that they're fighting for freedom, in the old-fashioned sense of the word, and that off in the horizon there's the image of a Jewish State. It may be a mirage, although we don't think so. Even if it is, and we never reach it, we will have died trying, and we will have gone down convinced that the image is of a real thing. There was one thing missing from that November letter – perhaps I left it out not to worry the folks too soon: we expected what has happened since, and everybody but Magnes[15] was ready to accept the challenge. If we are really living in the kind of world where one must fight for one's place, well and good, we'll fight. And we are. Incidentally, I hope you

14. Mordecai may have seen the wire at the *Post*, or because he was friends with the recipient.
15. Judah Magnes, see chapter 5, footnote 118.

understood your image of us falling with a stone in our hands metaphorically: some of those stones fire a brace of shots almost two kilometers, and some throw mortar bombs a few hundred meters, with real results. From here, all I can tell you is that the Yishuv will never give up; no matter how many we lose we'll keep fighting. If the loss of six million did not take the heart out of the Jews a few more thousand won't do it either.

The reaction that you prophesied for the U.S. a couple of years ago has hit, hard, as I see. We get full coverage of everything...Truman says, but react differently. It doesn't feel as immediate to us, as menacing, since we've come to consider America just another *golah*,[16] and what does one expect from the *golah*? The Jewish insecurity there has not been increased, it has simply been made more obvious. Does the American Jewish Committee[17] still consider Dinaburg's[18] treatment of America as the next stage in the line of diaspora communities as an alarmist exaggeration, as a bit of narrow-minded nationalism? Our only hope is here, small and poor as we may be. The "necessities" of life have become ridiculous luxuries, and on a war basis as we are, we don't even miss them. We may never have as many bathtubs as America and our press may be picayune, by material comparison, but at least we have the dignity of free men. We have our defects, as is to be expected, and it may be

---

16.   Hebrew, meaning "exile, Diaspora."
17.   The American Jewish Committee was founded in 1906. In addition to campaigning for civil liberties for Jews, the organization has a history of fighting against other forms of discrimination in the United States and working on behalf of social equality. It would file a friend-of-the-court brief in the May 1954 case of Brown v. Board of Education and participate in other events in the Civil Rights Movement.
18.   Ben Zion Dinaburg (Dinur) (1884–1973), was a Zionist thinker and educator. In 1948, he was head of the Jewish Teacher's Training College in Jerusalem and lecturer in modern Jewish history at Hebrew University. He later served as Minister of Education and Culture in the Knesset from 1951 to 1955, and was president of Yad Vashem, Israel's Holocaust museum, from 1953 to 1959.

a long time before we get rid of them, if ever, but we're going to live our own lives, or not at all. (I'm afraid all this sounds very poseurish and pseudo-heroic, believe me, it is not meant to.) What is more, if the world is about to go up in flames (which I doubt, you're giving in to a moment of hysteria, despite all the talk, the "great" powers are not ready to fight again, and won't be for a while either. Besides, I think they're too scared of each other's atom bombs).

My own big question mark now is a lovely one: Ann. It is now just two months and one week since,[19] and her arm will be in its cast for another two or three weeks. I have not been *mehutzaf*[20] – or crude – enough to court her directly yet, and I wonder how long I'll have to wait before I can do so safely. Meanwhile, I see a lot of her, almost daily, as a matter of fact, and Friday nights she comes over and usually sleeps over. We've taken a few pictures, which I'll mail soon, and I treat her to the luxury of a steaming bath here when she wants it. I've made some very oblique, extremely vague verbal passes at her, but that's all, although I'm sure she realizes what cooks. (Hmm, mustn't let the personal equation get in the way of the national struggle. Ahem!)

I've got to go to work now – I may write more later tonight during a free stretch. Keep it flying, kid, we still have a long way to go. All my love

Mersh

The March 25 edition of the *Palestine Post* reported on numerous battles on the roads of Palestine. During the last week of March alone, 136 trucks had tried to reach Jerusalem, but only forty-one got through.[21] Mordecai enclosed the article he wrote describing the attack on the convoy to Atarot

---

19. Since the attack in which Ann's boyfriend, Alter, was killed.
20. Hebrew, meaning "brazen, impertinent."
21. Levy, *Tisha Kabin*, p. 137.

in his next letter to his sister. The letter expands on the article, and adds a more personal, emotional element. It also relates the "inside scoop" on the bombing of the Jewish Agency, which had occurred two weeks earlier, and to which Mordecai had until now made only passing reference.

Mordecai with Ann Strauss

Chapter 18

Battle of the Roads and Deir Yassin

MARCH 25, 1948
Palestine Post, Page 1

BATTLE OF THE ROADS

The Battle of the Roads was fought in Palestine yesterday, when the Haganah launched a countrywide campaign against Arab traffic in reprisal for recent attacks on Jewish vehicles. At the same time, Arabs ambushed convoys on roads near Jerusalem and in Emek Jezreel. The death toll in these actions was 36 Arabs and 17 Jews killed.

Their flaming vehicle entangled in coils of barbed wire thrown across the road, a party of young Jews in a convoy from Jerusalem to Atarot shortly before noon yesterday were shot one by one, as they emerged, by a mob of several hundred Arabs pouring out of nearby Shafat village. The vehicle was one of two which had been hit by Arab fire as they raced through the Sheikh Jarrah Quarter. Although the tyres were punctured, the small convoy continued on its way until it encountered heavy fire near Shafat, three kilometres from Jerusalem.

Arabs machine-gunned them from both sides of the road, but the drivers retained control of their vehicles and the escort returned the fire. Near the Municipal Abattoir two mines were electrically detonated and one of the cars caught fire.

The Arab mob converged on the convoy from all sides, firing as they came, and some of the less-seriously wounded Haganah men kept off the attackers with their heavy, concentrated fire. When ten of the attackers had been hit by their fire, the mob gave up its attempts to approach, but maintained a heavy barrage from a distance. Fighting desperately, the trapped men kept them at bay for over an hour.

A first-aid man in the group, although himself hurt, salvaged a kit from the damaged vehicle and crawled to the wounded under fire. By the time the battle was over, fourteen Jews were killed and nine were wounded.

The Arabs are reported to have lost at least twenty in dead and wounded.

Survivors of the massacre reported that there was a police armoured car near the scene throughout the attack, but that at no time did it interrupt its signalling – presumably to Headquarters – to help the stranded party.

About an hour later, however, police and military armoured cars arrived on the scene and engaged the rearguard of the attackers, officially estimated to have numbered close to seven hundred. Most of them had already begun to withdraw.

A Haganah relief party had to fight its way through a barrage of fire laid down by the gangs in control of the Sheikh Jarrah Quarter. From the north, too, Arab gangs kept the road from Neve Yaacov and Atarot under constant fire.

Later, after the men in the convoy had been cut down, an army unit moved towards Neve Yaacov. Soldiers brought the wounded to the Mea Shearim Police Station, from where they were removed to hospitals in the city.

Official reports last night stated that the G.O.C.,[1] Lt.-General MacMillan, and Brigadier Glubb Pasha, Commander of the Arab Legion, who were travelling along the road at the time, prevailed on the Arabs to disperse, and thus saved some of the Haganah men.

The dead are: Moshe Abramovitz, 23; Carmi Eisenberg, 24; Yosef Fichtenfeld; Eliyahu Finkelstein, 35, Yaacov Friedman, 19; Yaacov Goldberger, 56; Yaacov Goldwasser, 20; Eliezer Knoller; Yaakov Meyouhas, 23; David Ben Itzhak Mizrahi, 20; Yosef Shlesinger, 27; Yehiel Steiner, 28; Meir Zandman; and Oved Zemach.

The wounded are: Shmuel Bekman; Haim Carmeli; Arich Einhorn, 20; Shlomo Entebi; Yehoshua Koldre, 18; Shmuel Levi, 25; Moshe David, 18; Michael Shvill, 16; and Yosef Zuri, 22.

One of the men in the ambushed party, David Mizrahi, was a clerk at The *Palestine Post*. He had started four years ago as a messenger.

Four days later, on Monday, March 29, the *Palestine Post* carried the banner headline: "250-man convoy in epic 30-hour battle against 4,000 Arabs. Outnumbered 15 to 1, the Haganah beats back waves of marauders." On the day it rolled off the press, Mordecai wrote to his sister.

Monday, March 29, 1948

Dear Toots,

Their first worried question was *"ma omrim aleinu?"*[2] — after 30 hours of battle against the kind of odds no soldier in a million meets, what worried the boys most was whether

---

1. General Officer Commanding British troops in Palestine.
2. Hebrew, meaning "what are they saying about us?"

they did enough, whether they had fulfilled their "obligations" properly. They carried out the toughest order of their lives there, too – leaving their weapons behind. When they came in last night, tired and hungry and looking fierce behind their matted beards, some of them were able to produce a hand-ful of weapons – grenades and pistols and rounds of ammu-nition from personal "*slicks*" (hiding places). One of the girls turned to the guy next to her, when they reached the Agency building, and handed him a grenade with "take it already, it's giving me a bellyache!" We lost 12 boys, and at least 135 of the 4000 attackers were killed and 200 wounded (that's the British figure, so you can imagine). Of the 12, 9 were not killed in the battle itself: they were in the roadblock-buster truck, and hit a mine after they had burst through seven roadblocks. The car went out of control and into a ditch, and the boys in it maintained a heavy covering fire while everybody else took up positions in the houses of the deserted Arab village nearby and ringed it with their armoured cars as protection. Three of the boys succeeded in getting back to the entrenchments, when a lucky shot apparently touched off the explosives in the vehicle (used to burst through the roadblocks) and the remaining nine were killed. I'm sure Monroe will understand how fantastic a battle it was, then, if only three boys were killed during the fir-ing itself. They held off the Arabs and suffered only superficial wounds themselves: all but three of our wounded were home in bed by last night, and only one needed surgery. The driv-ers of the lorries in the convoy were their usual heroic selves. One of them, telling about it (with gestures) said the Arabs shouted at them to surrender, and across the intervening 20 meters he responded with a Bronx cheer and the gesture you once slapped my face for using when I was about ten years old. When the Arabs shouted "*aleihum*" (at them) this boy shouted back "*ta'alu*" (come on) and threw them a few grenades. At 20 meters, instead of attacking with grenades, the Arabs were firing with Brens (light machine-guns), and hitting nothing but the armoured vehicles, and the boys kept tossing them gre-nades and blowing them up. It was a phenomenal exhibition of discipline and coolness, and I'm ashamed of our leaders who sent a delegation to the [British] army and begged for help. It came, of course, after the army sat by, three kilometers away. For seven hours they negotiated a truce (which provided that only Arab doctors be allowed into the area, and that the boys leave their arms behind). I heard the radio instructions to our boys – I listened all day yesterday – and there was a fubar[3] on whether to relinquish the arms or not. The end of the story was that all the heavy stuff – the Spandau machine guns[4] and the Vickers[5] – were destroyed as the army arrived, and parts of the other weapons smashed as much as possible so that the Arabs shouldn't be able to use them. 20 armoured cars were lost to the Arabs, the others the boys destroyed. Many of us bitterly resent the appeal to the army though, and feel that had an appeal gone out for reinforcements there would have been at least a thousand of us ready, willing and able to go. We could have gone on foot from Ramat Rachel and been there hours before the army. Reinforcements could have gotten them out, and would have prevented the kind of political capital the British will make of this. Now they'll say, and seem to have proof, that without the British army the Jews can't hold on. We could have come out of it with a few more losses in personnel, probably, but a tremendous gain in prestige. And there's the real tragedy of it. The boys themselves are heroes, individually they're great, every one of them, but all is not [ILLEGIBLE TEXT] could – and should – be upstairs. All Jerusalem listened to that short-wave communication with the embattled boys, and I wonder how many wept when the truce order came through, with the statement: "The main thing is to live, to be able to fight again another day." The boys wanted to fight it out, and there are many who agree with me that, with reinforcements, it could have been done successfully. The sight of a thousand men marching on them would have

---

3. Contemporary US army slang. A sanitized version of its meaning is, "fouled up beyond all repair".
4. German-made heavy machine guns.
5. British 7.7 mm machine gun that required a six- to eight-man team to operate.

been enough to scatter most of the Arab "fighters," villagers from miles around who were anxious to get in on an "easy kill." Nu – our strategists decided otherwise, there was nothing to be done from "below," nothing the man in the ranks could have said would have changed things. Go fight City Hall.

Here's the inside story on the bomb at the Agency: The Arab[6] who brought it, in a suitcase on the back seat, had been selling us arms for some time. He was alone in the car, and the guards wouldn't let him in to the courtyard until a Nesher driver, who had been handling the sales, vouched for him. He parked near the entrance to the Agency itself, and the guy who was to do the unloading moved it over to the Keren Hayesod wing, where there was a Palmach base. On top of the suitcase was an automobile jack, wrapped, and looking like a Bren, covered up. A wire connected the jack to a detonator in the suitcase, and it all blew up when the boy lifted it, to hand it in to his Palmach friends, through the window. The Arab had bummed a ride with the Nesher driver[7] on the pretext that he had another bundle of stuff, and they drove off through the zone. The driver waited at a spot in the zone while the Arab – with LP.800 in his pocket in payment – went to "get the rest." Then came the bang. And that's the story.

Haven't heard a word from you people in two weeks. Nu?

Love,

Mordecai

the brat

---

6. Husseini agent and Haganah informer, Anton Daoud Camilio, was not an Arab, but an American-born Armenian. He was supposedly delivering guns to the Haganah and was waved into the Jewish Agency compound. He parked and walked away. Minutes later the car exploded.
7. A taxi company.

Phase one of the civil war resulted in heavy loss of life. The *Palestine Post* summarized the results for the four-month period (November 30–March 31):[8] There were 924 Jews killed and 1,651 injured; 1,762 Arabs dead, 2,591 wounded. In addition, 115 British soldiers were killed.

* * *

The first phase of the civil war, which "ended" in early April, 1948, had been characterized by Arab aggression and Jewish defense. The Haganah had endeavored to support beleaguered communities in Jerusalem and the Galilee, but with the Arabs in control of the roads, Jewish convoys were being annihilated again and again. The last two weeks of March alone saw major disasters at Bab el Wad (Shaar Hagai) and Nebi Daniel during which the Haganah lost most of its armored vehicles. Jerusalem had been under siege since the end of 1947 and, while Mordecai was careful to reassure his parents that he was safe, in reality, the situation had been gradually worsening. The number of trucks reaching Jerusalem with supplies steadily declined. On March 31, yet another convoy was prevented from reaching Jerusalem. The sixty- vehicle convoy was ambushed at Khulda and forced to turn back after losing five vehicles and seventeen men. Food stocks in Jerusalem were dwindling; on March 29: "…the city had on hand a five-day supply of margarine, four days of macaroni, ten days of dried meat. There was no fresh meat, fruit or vegetables available in its markets. If eggs could be found, they were sold for twenty cents apiece.[9] The city was living off its slender reserves of canned and packaged food: sardines, macaroni and dried beans."[10] Food rationing was announced for the 100,000 Jewish inhabitants of Jerusalem that same day. The draconian system that Dov Yosef,[11] military governor of Jerusalem and head of its Emergency Committee, had to introduce

---

8. In the edition of April 4, 1948.
9. Exorbitant for those days.
10. Larry Collins and Dominique Lapierre, *O Jerusalem!* (Simon & Schuster, 1988), p. 242.
11. Dov Yosef (1899–1980), born Bernard Joseph in Montreal, Canada. Served in Palestine during WWI in the Canadian contingent of the Jewish Legion. He returned to Canada to study economics and politics and then law and, after qualifying, moved to Jerusalem. He entered politics in the 1930s and was appointed legal adviser and

allowed a bread ration of two hundred grams per person; about four slices a day. Children were given an 'extra' ration of one egg and fifty grams of margarine per *week*. Something had to be done.

The next day, a meeting took place whose outcome would mark the beginning of the second phase of the civil war – and determine the fate of the Yishuv. On April 1, the commander of operations of the Haganah, Yigael Yadin, met with David Ben-Gurion to report that Arab forces were strangling the Yishuv. Yadin declared that it was impossible to keep relying on passive defense. If they wanted to survive they would have to go on the offensive and seize control of the country's roads and heights. The Haganah would have to capture any and all Arab towns of strategic importance. This would be a huge risk. Beyond their severe shortage of weapons and ammunition, the Haganah could not know how the British would respond. The cabinet debated the merits of changing strategy for hours before acquiescing to Ben-Gurion's position. The Zionists would go on the offensive.[12]

The first step in the offensive was Operation Nahshon whose goal was to open the road from Tel Aviv to Jerusalem. This involved taking Al-Qastal, an Arab village on the road to Jerusalem named for its proximity to the Castel – the ruins of a crusader castle. The Castel (from the Latin '*castilium*,' fortress) was situated eight km west of Jerusalem, on the road to Tel Aviv. The village, Al-Qastal, was used as a base by Abdul Khader al-Husseini's "Army of the Holy War," and was instrumental in the attacks on Jewish convoys from Tel Aviv to Jerusalem. It was a vital strategic location that had to be taken if the road to Jerusalem was to be opened. Mordecai mentions the operation in this next letter.

April 4, 1948

Dear Family,

Since [this] is being delivered by a special red-headed carrier pigeon: one of the Americans, flying back tomorrow, will mail this when he gets to NY, and so you'll probably get

---

deputy head of the Jewish Agency's political department in 1936. He was appointed military governor of Jerusalem during the siege. He was a member of Knesset until 1959 and served as a minister in nine different capacities.

12.   For more, see Howard M. Sachar, *A History of Israel*, pp. 304–5.

it long before all the other mail stacked up in the office waiting for the Jerusalem-Tel Aviv road to be opened up again.
For two weeks it's been closed, and so all your mail for me
has been sitting in Tel Aviv, and mine for you in Jerusalem.
I tried to call twice, but the goddamned Arabs said "lines
down" and the calls were cancelled. I won't try again, me
noives[13] won't stand it: to sit around for hours and wait,
maybe, to plan what subjects to cover so nothing important
is left out, and then to be left absolutely speechless – it's a
fate worse than death!

Being a mobilized Jew, food is no problem,[14] I have
special protekzia,[15] so that regardless of Jerusalem shortages I can also gorge myself in the "*Mitbach Hish*"[16] to which,
through a clerical lapses, I am still permitted admittance. I
seldom go there though, until now there's been no need
for it. And I have a damned good idea there won't be any
need either: the boys moved into Castel yesterday morning,
early, and threw the Arabs out. They are camping there now,
and have thus rendered harmless one of the worst spots
on the road from Tel Aviv. According to my strategy (hear
that, Gershon, can you sense the inflection with which I say
that, the cock of the eyebrow and the waggle of the omni-
scient finger?) they'll push on, leaving a garrison there, to
Abu Ghosh and Bab el Wad, and then the convoys will start
roaring through with food for Jerusalem and mail for me.
Morale here hit the ceiling when the striking PBS,[17] against
its will, announced the least it could: that Jewish forces
"have occupied the Arab village of Castel." We military men,
of course, understand what is involved, and I take exception to the great Major George Fielding Eliot,[18] who told me

---

13. "My nerves," in a stereotypical New York accent.
14. It was, however, a huge problem for most residents of Jerusalem.
15. "Privileges" or "connections."
16. Field corps army kitchen.
17. Palestine Broadcasting Service.
18. The Major George Fielding Eliot to whom Mordecai refers was a major in the
     military intelligence reserve of the United States army. He authored fifteen books

(ahem) that we need ten thousand men to keep that road open. (I met him at GA's[19] Friday night, and he's full of the old proverbial s**t, *zolt mir excusen*.[20] He knows as much as my elbow – the right one, and you'll recall I'm a lefty. He did scare me, though, he said he thinks we'll win – and as I recall, he's a lousy prophet. Just imagine, a prophet in Jerusalem again, after two thousand years! In brief, he didn't impress me, and I showed off a bit sparring with him and egging him on. I even got him sore, somewhat, just for the hell of it. (Just the old *enfant terrible* in me getting in its licks) I suppose I was showing off for Ann too – the eternal male, proving himself. Feh. But it was fun.

Carmi and I are composing a child's letter to David[21] now, in Hebrew, *menukad*[22] – we'll shame him into writing us!

And that's all for the moment – I just want to get this to the travel office for Phil so's it gets out in time. The main thing is – don't worry too much – things are going much better than we'd anticipated. I've still got a note to dash off to Naomi for the same mail – so *laylah tov*,[23] and be well. And I'm waiting to hear from you – oh boy, will I have an orgy when that packet of mail comes from Tel Aviv!

love from the brat

P.S. – This month write me direct to Jerusalem – or at least until I tell you to change...

---

on military and political topics and was the military analyst on radio and television for CBS News during World War II.

19. Gershon Agronsky.
20. Yiddish, meaning "excuse the expression."
21. Probably David Greenberg.
22. Hebrew, meaning "punctuated," i.e., with vowels.
23. Hebrew, meaning "good night."

On April 4, the Jews took Al-Qastal easily, finding it nearly empty and meeting little resistance; this ease is reflected in the tone of Mordecai's letter of the same day. However, when word of the fall reached Arab leaders, they ordered Abdul Kader al-Husseini, commander of the forces of the Army of the Holy War in the Jerusalem region, to take it back. Thousands answered Husseini's call to arms, ascending the hill to Al-Qastal in waves, attacking with knives, rifles, and explosives. The Jewish defenders ran very low on food and ammunition but continued to hold the village. After several days of fighting, on April 8, two Jewish guards spotted three unidentified figures walking up the slopes and opened fire. Two fled, one was killed.

The dead man was Abdul Kader al-Husseini. The three must have thought they were walking into Arab-held territory. When the Arabs realized that their hero had been slain, they attacked again, opening fire on three fronts. Many of the Jewish fighters were killed and the Castel was recaptured by the Arabs. Ever determined, Palmach commandos returned the next day, the morning of April 9, and were amazed to find the village almost empty once again. The Arabs had recovered al-Husseini's body and gone to bury him. (Thirty thousand people attended his funeral.) The Palmach company then recaptured the Castel.

Thirty-nine Jews had been killed in the battle for Castel, along with thirty-one Arabs. All were combatants.

April 8, 1948

Dear Gershon,

You write with as little evidence of your vocation as I have feeling for it. However, it was a rare treat for me to be able to detect signs of your disapproval of Truman and his policy in your last letter. ... Being so far from the scene you wonder, a bit fearfully, as Naomi does, whether the Yishuv can stand in the face of betrayal after betrayal. By now it should be clear that it can. The reaction here to American double-dealing was the fatalistic middle-eastern shrug accompanied by the almost inevitable "nu, goyim," and the realization that we are indeed alone.

...

Instead of quitting, the Jews, those historical illiter-
ates and political boors, keep doing what can't be done:
they occupy Castel village, and then Khulda and then Deir
[Muh]eisin,²⁴ beat off attacks on Mishmar Ha'emek²⁵ for 4
days. Being ignorant of modern warfare and the logic of
comparative strength and possibilities of outside support
they presume to model themselves on their forebears, and
instead of the answer to *"mi atem damay rothim bi"* being
"dam kdoshey tah vetat" it is not, *"dam hamakabim."*²⁶ But
do not imagine that we are heading for a Masada or, that if
we are, we alone will meet it. It is not egocentrism which
leads me to say that if the Yishuv goes down to defeat it will
be the defeat of Jews wherever they are, and it will impose
the futile unity of destruction upon American Jewry as well,
with Finky²⁷ and Wise,²⁸ Silver²⁹ and Proskauer,³⁰ Hecht³¹

---

24. Khulda and Deir Muheizin were small Arab villages situated along the Tel Aviv–Jerusalem road.
25. A kibbutz in the Jezreel Valley, in the north of the country.
26. Mordecai is quoting from a poem by Shaul Tchernichovsky, "My Melody," written in 1916. The poem is a defiant battle cry that rejects the idea of the Jew as victim. Mordecai quotes the poet, who asks throughout the poem, *"Mi atem damay rothim bi?"* – Who are you, my blood, boiling within me? – i.e., Whose blood is coursing through my veins? The poet rejects *"dam kdoshei tah vetat"* – the blood of the martyrs of the Chmielnicki massacres. He also rejects *"dam hamakabim"* – the blood of the Maccabees. Ultimately the blood he accepts as his, is that of the generation of the Exodus – those who conquered Canaan.
27. Louis Finkelstein (1895–1991) was chancellor of the JTS at the time.
28. Stephen Samuel Wise (1874–1949), born in Budapest, was an American Reform rabbi and Zionist leader, and president of the World Jewish Congress.
29. Abba Hillel Silver. See chapter 4, footnote 6.
30. Joseph M. Proskauer (1877–1971), was a lawyer, judge, philanthropist, and political activist. He was president of the American Jewish Committee from 1943 to 1949.
31. Ben Hecht (1894–1964) was an Academy-award winning screenwriter and playwright. He was a civil rights activist and an ardent Zionist who supported the Irgun politically and financially – so much so that the British boycotted his work and he had to write many of his screenplays anonymously. See Mordecai's letter of March 23, 1947, in which he discusses ships carrying refugees to Palestine, one of which had been financed and therefore named for Ben Hecht.

and Rosenwald[32] and the rest of American Jewry all in one big, bloody bed. The big difference between us is that you don't have much hope, while I do. You haven't the reassurance of the visible stand of the Yishuv to reassure you, you haven't the physical aspect of the struggle to give you strength. If you could see one kid here handling a Sten or a Bren, if you could see the "farmers" at isolated Maaleh Hahamisha deciding not to evacuate their children from the kibbutz to a place of "safety," you would understand a good deal more. I dare say if you yourself could throw one grenade or fire one round you would feel immeasurably better – and more confident.

As for proclaiming the Jewish State now – it is not practical. As long as we adhere to the official time-table our money in the U.S. can buy things, and what we buy can be gotten out of the country. Were we to rear up and say "this is it, we s**t on you," they would do likewise, and our benevolent Uncle Sam would manifest all of his already apparent malevolence and simply freeze our funds. How long would we last? It will be a while before we can declare war on the U.S.

...

Incidentally, "Jerusalem's Jews" were not "reduced to eating weeds," if that line evokes a picture of gaunt, starving people frantically digging in their gardens for a little nourishment. Some people did use some of the garden greens for soup, and spinach-style, but it was to supplement the cans, etc., which were being devoured. There are food stocks in the city. I myself have been eating well from stocks in the

---

32. William Rosenwald (1903–1996), son of Julius Rosenwald, part-owner and leader of Sears, Roebuck and Company. Both father and son were dedicated philanthropists. In 1939, William Rosenwald organized the National Refugee Service, and in 1939 was one of the co-founders of the United Jewish Appeal, serving as one of its national chairmen from 1942–1946. He also served on the executive committee of the American Jewish Joint Distribution Committee for five decades and was a leader of the American Jewish Committee and the Council of Jewish Federations.

house on the one hand and the "Mitbach Hish" on the other, so that you need not worry on that score.

And that's about all I have to say for the present. Keep writing – all I've had from home is a letter from each of you in more than three weeks. Surely you can do better. Remember all the propaganda for mail to the soldiers during the war? Well, now it's your turn to be a morale-builder. And now I'm off for a meal.

All my love,

Mordecai

Meal coupons

Mordecai again minimizes reports that Jerusalem was starving, and makes no mention of the rationing in force. He does admit that people were collecting *khubeiza*, the Arabic name for mallow, a spinach-like plant that grows wild all over Israel and is rich in iron and vitamins, though he downplays its importance. Recipes for cooking the plant were broadcast over the radio; even Hotel Eden began serving "spinach croquettes" made with it. In her *Jerusalem War Diary* (1950) Devora Hyrkans-Ginzburg reports a very grim situation, at odds with Mordecai's blasé description; she struggles to find enough to eat. Mordecai's friend, Zippy Borowsky, also describes a bleak situation:

There is absolutely NOTHING to be obtained in the food shops – especially if your ration card clearly states that you do not have three children, a husband and elderly parents to feed. The only place to get food is in the restaurants, where there isn't much – thin "potato" soup and mock "sausage," and no way of knowing what they are made of. After two days of stomach upsets I gave up eating out and have gone back to concocting. You'd be surprised what powdered milk and powdered eggs can do to revive each other when you slip in some foreign agent, a great deal of love, and mix well. Tonight, three of us had a feast, some noodles in powdered milk soup, a sardine salad and hot water with a pinch of coffee. So your packages have literally saved the day. (letter of April 7)

* * *

The Castel was just one of the Arab villages that had been controlling access to the road to Jerusalem. In the previous letter, Mordecai mentions two others that were taken by the Haganah: Khulda and Deir Muheizin. A day after he writes the letter, the day on which Abdul Kader al-Husseini, commander of Arab forces in Jerusalem, was buried, another village was taken – but not by the Haganah.

Deir Yassin was a village of approximately one thousand residents which stood at the entrance to Jerusalem, across from the Jewish village of Givat Shaul (today part of Jerusalem).[33]

Wanting greater authority in the struggle for Jerusalem, the Irgun and Lehi undertook (with the acquiescence of the Haganah) a joint mission to attack and take an Arab village. They chose Deir Yassin. There were numerous reasons for their choice. First of all, the village was strategically located: it commanded approximately 5 kilometers of the Jerusalem–Tel Aviv highway and connected Arab Har Hebron to the Castel via Bethlehem. Second, it was the source of frequent sniper attacks on Jewish traffic as well on Jewish suburbs of Jerusalem. Third, it was thought to have substantial food stocks and other supplies, desperately needed in besieged Jerusalem.

---

33.   The events of April 9, 1948 remain in dispute through today. To reiterate a principle expressed in the preface, in an effort to avoid privileging any particular point of view, the following summary account is drawn from multiple sources, most of which are listed in the bibliography.

There were operational problems from the start. Hoping to avoid a fight entirely, the attackers had intended to warn the residents of Deir Yassin of their approach, causing them to flee the village. But the truck equipped with loudspeakers brought for that purpose fell into a ditch and its broadcasts were too faint to hear. When the attackers – more than a hundred of them – entered the village, they were met with unexpectedly strong resistance. There were no foreign Iraqi fighters housed in the village as the attackers expected, but most Arab men had weapons and were more than ready to use them. The attackers had little experience in house to house fighting and few arms but substantial explosives. A primary tactic was to blow an opening into each house, throw in hand grenades and then enter shooting. This resulted in substantial casualties – of both the defenders and their families. The Irgun and Lehi ultimately succeeded in taking the village but at a very high cost to both sides.

When the Haganah arrived on the scene after the battle, they were aghast at what they saw. Eliyahu Arieli, who led the Gadna, was the first to enter the village and called what he saw "absolutely barbaric." His report was called in to David Shaltiel, Jerusalem commander of the Haganah. Shaltiel was so incensed he told his adjutant to disarm the remaining members of the Lehi and Irgun in the village and to open fire on them if they refused to lay down their arms. The adjutant insisted that this would be disastrous for the Jews. Shaltiel relented and, instead, ordered them to clean up the village.

The attack was roundly condemned worldwide, as well as by the Jewish Agency and the Haganah who asserted that it was contrary to Zionist ideals. The Chief Rabbi of Jerusalem went so far as to excommunicate those who had been involved.

News of the events spread quickly and generated great fear among Arab Palestinians, causing many villagers in other locations to flee approaching Jewish soldiers on sight. It is undeniable that this helped the Jewish war effort but also led to reprisal attacks against Jewish targets. The attack proved to be a pivotal event in the war.

The received wisdom is that the Irgun and Lehi perpetrated a massacre which included rape and mutilation but the two Revisionist groups claimed that the reports of atrocities were false or exaggerated. In his book, *The Revolt*, written three years after the event, Menachem

Begin, commander of the Irgun at the time, said that there were fighters in the village, not just residents, and that they had hung white flags and pretended to surrender, but attacked as the Irgun fighters approached. He confirmed that the fighting was fierce and asserted that any women and children who died were inadvertent casualties of that fighting.

A recent, meticulously researched analysis[34] of the event, including archival information and interviews with survivors on both sides, reconstructs the events of the day on an almost minute by minute basis. Its author, Professor Eliezer Tauber, emphasizes the consistency of testimony of both the Jewish and Arab combatants and concludes that, while there were substantial civilian casualties, there was no massacre and no rape. No doubt his will not be the last word on the matter. To this day, Deir Yassin is invoked by critics of Israel as *the* example of Israeli military cruelty.

---

34. Eliezer Tauber, *Deir Yassin: The End of the Myth* [Hebrew] (Kinneret, Zmora-Bitan, Dvir, 2017). Forthcoming in English by Toby Press.

Chapter 19
The Attack on the Doctors' Convoy

On April 13, in retaliation for Deir Yassin and the death of al-Husseini at Castel, Arabs attacked a medical convoy on the way to Hadassah Hospital. The hospital, as well as the campus of Hebrew University, stood on Mount Scopus, an isolated Jewish area in northeast Jerusalem, whose only access was via a narrow road through the Arab neighborhood of Sheikh Jarrah. Jewish convoys made regular visits to the hospital. Arab troops had blockaded the road immediately after the vote for partition and convoys taking supplies to the hospital often had to deal with sniper fire – despite British guarantees that they would be protected. The Hadassah organization had started looking for an alternative site for its medical activities in downtown Jerusalem but nothing had yet been found. In the meantime, the hospital was in dire need of fresh personnel and supplies.

The convoy that left for Hadassah on April 13 comprised ten vehicles. When it was attacked, six of the vehicles managed to turn back, but the remaining vehicles were pinned on the road after an explosion stopped the lead vehicle. Gunmen lying in wait in the houses along the road strafed the pinned vehicles with continuous gunfire. Although those guarding the vehicles tried to defend them, they were severely outnumbered and waited for hours for help that didn't come. The one British officer who tried to help, Major Jack Churchill, was inexplicably forbidden from using effective weaponry against the Arab attackers by his superiors. Tragically, when he offered to evacuate some of those pinned down, they refused, preferring to stay within the shelter of the vehicles to wait for a Haganah rescue. But Haganah reinforcements were also slow to arrive and were then denied permission to approach by the British in charge of the area. Seventy-eight Jews were murdered that day – doctors, nurses, students, patients, faculty members and drivers, as well as the fighters guarding the convoy. Many of the bodies were burned beyond recognition. Among those killed was Dr. Chaim Yassky, director of the Hadassah Medical Organization and one of the driving spirits behind the establishment of the Rothschild-Hadassah University Hospital on Mount Scopus (which had opened in 1939). Yassky was a close personal friend of the Chertoff family. He was also Ann Strauss's boss. Ann was supposed to have accompanied Yassky on the convoy, but Yassky had asked her to remain behind in order to finish up some paperwork for him.[1]

Eyewitness accounts of the massacre are appalling. On April 21, The *Post* published a long and detailed account from a doctor, one of only twenty-eight survivors of the massacre. He described how the shooting started at ten fifteen in the morning after the ambulance in which he was riding was disabled by a landmine. He believed that Dr. Yassky was a particular target since so much of the shooting was directed at the ambulance in which he rode. Sometime after one in the afternoon, British vehicles passing nearby were signaled for help, but ignored the pleas. At two a second British army convoy passed by, which also ignored the attack. At three p.m., "two army ambulances passed by the stranded cars, help was asked for, and again was not given." Waves of Arabs approached the crippled vehicles, shooting at the terrified doctors and nurses within. Some preferred to make a run for it and be shot rather than just wait to be burned alive or butchered. "The ordeal lasted seven hours and then, at four thirty PM, British help arrived."[2] (Of course this eyewitness would not have been aware of Major Churchill's earlier attempt to help.)

---

1.   Told to me by Ann's son, Roy Shenkar.
2.   *Palestine Post*, April 21, 1948, p. 4.

In an article published in 2015,[3] Iris Yassky, granddaughter of Chaim Yassky, recounted what she knew of the fateful day. She said that her grandmother rarely spoke about the events of that day. It was simply too painful. She reported that Dr. Yassky was shot in the liver, said good-by to his wife and died. Mrs. Yassky used her blouse in a vain effort to stem the bleeing. She then walked home from the scene without her blouse. Apparently, British soldiers who used to have tea with the Yasskys, offered her a ride and a shirt but she refused.

April 15, 1948

Dear Toots,

What a country! I need a television typewriter with a soundtrack to begin to do it justice, but will try without it. What the hell – you have an imagination, and if I really try hard maybe your imagination and my attempts will produce some kind of picture…

There's one fellow whose sister was just killed at the Castel: his normal abnormality has been aggravated by the blow, and he came over this afternoon for me to hold his hand.

Down in the press one linotyper wails about Robbie (the fellow blinded by our bomb), another whines about the situation in general, and the foreman… complains that we "upstairs" are sabotaging the paper and making him work very late. One guy sidles up to me with a tight-lipped "what's new," eyes cast down, and I mimic the pose exactly and say "nothing" and he thinks I'm another plotter. Carmi's worried about his girl coming now, and over not getting letters from her, Jack Cohen worries about getting shot, and cries about it…

---

3. March 23, 2015, http://www.hadassah.org/news-stories/remembering-the-67th.html.

And that's not all. Ephraim (Kepi had a room at his house when she just came) lost his sister: she was killed at the Castel a few days ago. I know her, and so he came to talk about her, and ask me to write about her for the *Post*... One Haganah macher, whom I know by chance and who became a friend before he became a general and still talks to me in spite of his brass, b**ches on higher levels, while his wife gripes about the b price and general unavailability of eggs and the intrigue in her department.

I'm considered on the in around Haganah up at the *Post*, and so the other day GA called me in with his "Come, Motel,[4] confide in me. Who's in control of the Castel now." With the barest hint of a wink and a slow confidential smile, I tell him "as far as you're concerned, we are." After he recovered from his stroke of hysterics he said "no, really," and I simply nodded back at him, "really." He took it as gospel. He saw a piece in a Hebrew paper signed by "Our Military Correspondent," and immediately yelled for me to get him the "original, uncut version" of the analysis every day, from my general I gotta produce now too!

In short, I sometimes get the feeling that all the aches and pains in Jewish Jerusalem are being brought to Dr. Chertoff. An agency guy, who does public relations, treated me to a two-hour performance of the "oy, what they're doing" routine (I ask "where," and he nods knowingly, as much as to say you know, I don't have to give you details just remind you of it), with the pout and the despairing, upward-lifted hands. The *AP* photographer cries about [getting] out of this "goddamned country," where if the British say he can take a picture the Jews say no, if the Jews let him, the Arabs say no, and if all three agree that he can, it's not worth taking anyway. He does take one, and gets it printed in a NY paper, and the bureau chief here, playful, tears it up for him.

---

4. A Yiddish nickname for Mordecai.

The guard at the Agency building b**ches to me about his hours and lack of protection from the sun, and one of the road-block guards informs me, with curses and gestures, that he hates the "bloody bastards" and would get the hell out if he could, but he can't – his wife is a Palestinian[5] (he's Scotch) and refuses to budge.

All of this serves to distract me somewhat from my own private little headaches. I think I'll hire me out as a baby-sitter.

What a country! Looking up – what a letter! Before I spoil you I'd better quit. And don't hog it, see? It's for the whole family. Love to Cleveland and New York, from me.

I'm back.

What a country!

I saw something really beautiful today – I don't mean in the feminine pulchritude line either: after the Jewish Agency press conference today I was invited along on a press trip to see the convoy from Tel Aviv, which had just arrived, and was being unloaded.[6] I jumped at the chance, and went along with a few of the photographers, to Schneller. 170 trucks were scattered about the streets in lines of fifteen and twenty, most of them not even armoured. In each caboose there was a driver and a dirty, unshaven, unkempt, hungry, tired little man with a nice, new, fresh, beautiful 1948 Czech rifle, right from the factory. One of the escorts gave me his rifle to handle – a thing of beauty and a joy for as long as we'll need the little toys. He said "look how light it is, a toy – and what a lovely toy," and kissed it lightly

---

5. I.e., Jewish resident of Palestine.
6. Between the 16th and 21st of April, three convoys totaling seven hundred trucks reached Jerusalem thanks to the clearing of villages along the Tel Aviv-Jerusalem road. This didn't last; most of the Haganah forces that had operated along the road were moved into Jerusalem to address the situation within the city; those left behind weren't sufficient to hold the territory they'd cleared, and the road soon closed again. See Morris, *1948*, p. 130.

on its bright stock, "Not a shot from Tel Aviv to Jerusalem!" The whole road was practically lined by Palmach, some of 'em learned to sight a rifle long before a razor meant anything to them.

There was one girl, 18, a mere slip of a lass, all dressed up in blue-jeans and a sloppy blue shirt open at the bottom, refusing to stay tucked into her jeans. Two shiny new grenades hung from the belt, and she cradled a Sten the way Kathy Hepburn carries flowers. She had a *bachur* on each arm, carrying a rifle as she pranced down the street towards Zion Square, drawing admiring gasps from the crowd of cheering Jerusalemites. Photographers took miles of pictures of the little girl – by tomorrow they'll probably be in the American papers. Just a little pisherke.[7] She can probably handle a gun better than a guy. Then there was a little swarthy Sepharadi, with a gun on one arm and a *bachura* on the other collecting the traditional tribute of the warrior before the envious gaze of his buddies. One of them sported a red *tarbush*,[8] bullet hole and all, jauntily cocked over one ear: a one-man army, *behayai*![9]

One of the drivers told me you can now go from Jerusalem to Bab el Wad by bicycle, the road is so clean of Arabs. All along the way they saw deserted Arab villages, with lonely wooden plows studding their fields and deserted cows eating themselves sick. One of the boys came riding into town with a banana stuck in his face, for effect. And the finishing touch was the chalked inscription on at least a dozen of the trucks – "*Im eshkaheh Yerushalayim*."[10] We eat tomorrow! What a country! All the way from Tel Aviv without a shot – and the Hadassah

---

7.   Derived from Yiddish – "young squirt".
8.   Arabic name for a fez – a traditional felt headdress worn throughout the Ottoman Empire. There were two types: a truncated cone or a short cylinder, usually made of red felt, with a tassel attached to the top.
9.   Hebrew, literally "in my life" – accepted meaning, "wow."
10. Hebrew, "If I forget thee, Jerusalem," the beginning of the fifth verse of Psalm 137, it continues with "let my right hand forget its skill." The line, together with the next

convoy runs into hell just 100 yards from its goal. After a four hour battle which all Jerusalem heard we got the sad news: about 30 dead,[11] among them your old friend Yassky. I shudder to think of Ann tomorrow, they were such good friends. And I shudder to think of the hospital without him. What luck. The only bright spot there is that Edward Joseph, our only surgeon, came through okay. The old boys were right when they called Palestine *"eretz ohelet yoshveha."*[12] What an appetite. The whole story isn't in yet, but it was certainly clear to the Arabs what was going in those Magen-David marked and flagged ambulances and busses. This whole business of "civilized warfare" is damned stupid. Is a man any less a target because he's wounded, from the enemies' point of view? Why should he be, logically speaking? Wars are won in all sorts of ways, they aren't games, to be played according to set rules. If by killing doctors the Arabs can indirectly kill hundreds of later-to-be-wounded fighters, why shouldn't they? If we're being realistic about it, any killing and any destruction which weakens the enemy is a contribution, and strengthens his opponent. The attack on the hospital convoy is a blow to us, but for the life of me I can't feel "shocked" at it, in the accepted sense. From a military point of view the death of a doctor, a commander-in-chief, and a political leader are all understandable and no reason for outraged sensibilities. The man with the gun is as great an enemy as the fellow who tells him where to use the gun, the nurse who patches him up so that he can hold [it], and the political leader whose pep-talks give him the will to use it. It seems to me the Arabs are much more realistic in that they consider all and every Jew fair prey, and see all of them as fair targets. They don't understand the "rules," and provide themselves

---

line, "May my tongue cling to the roof of my mouth if I do not remember you, if I do not set Jerusalem above my highest joy," is recited at Jewish weddings, where the groom breaks a glass, in commemoration of the destruction of the Temple.

11. Mordecai had not yet heard that the death toll was closer to eighty.

12. Hebrew, meaning "a land that devours its inhabitants." It is a quote from Numbers 13:32, and was said by the spies whom Moses sent to spy out the land. A similar sentiment, although not the same wording, also appears in Ezekiel 36:13.

with what protective devices they can regardless of whether they're sending doctors or nurses or mobsters. We, Europeans, who have accepted the "Rule" of International Warfare, too often act under the assumption that the Arab also has – and so we lose our doctors and nurses and expose our ambulance drivers in a criminally neglectful way. Someday we'll learn that there's no room for sentiment in war – I hope it isn't too late.

And now I really quit.

Love – Mersh

RESTRICTED[13] – of course.

From the preceding pages you can judge what kind of day it's been here in Jerusalem. By now, as I sit on our charming little balcony, with its drapes and desk, after having come home from work, this morning's convoy is all but forgotten, and we're fighting, over and over again, today's battle at Sheikh Jarrah,[14] on the way to the University and Hadassah Hospital. The Police blocked our reinforcements from reaching the area, and tonight they have tremendous floodlights all over the area to prevent us from taking any reprisal action. Our f....cousins!

Ann suddenly appeared in the office, a little after midnight. She had spent a good part of the afternoon with Mrs. Yassky, who was in the armoured car with him when he died, and watched him die in her arms. Ann wanted to know about something from Haifa, ("security" says say no more on that) and she waited for me at the Magen David Adom clinic (across the street) while I finished up and got ready to go home. I took her home in our station wagon, sat talking to her a while, and then walked the block over to Nishry's, where I'm now typing listening to the background of machine-gun fire from the hills. Yassky was her boss – she came to Palestine as his

---

13.   This is a continuation of the same letter, but intended only for Naomi's eyes. Unlike the first part, it was not to be shared with the rest of the family.

14.   Where the doctors' convoy was ambushed.

secretary, and worked for him until she joined up. They were good friends, and for her this is another real loss. In addition, she really believes that without him the hospital will collapse – I don't know how right she is, although she should know. Perhaps you yourself know better than I do. But all this is the kind of tangent the normal individual goes off on much later in a letter, having once tentatively touched on what's bothering him.

You really opened the flood-gates, hit the jackpot, when you invited my brotherly confidences. I'm very much afraid you won't be able to turn me off now until something finally happens to my problem. Unfortunately, I studied Talmud once upon a time and I've been making matters worse by reading philosophy lately, plus Stuart Chase on semantics. All this logical foolishness, coupled with the air of Palestine which, the Rabbis tell us, is enlightening, has resulted in a new form of masochism, which expresses itself in a question: Naomi may be 100 percent right in her analysis of why I hark back to Kepi from time to time (and there is a good deal of pleasure and devotion [?] to which to hark back) – but perhaps those very reasons – the *ga'agu'im*[15] and the empty bed – also explain my feeling or apparent feeling for Ann? I've been doing a few pages a day of the booklet they wrote at Maaleh Hahamisha about Alter, translating it for her into English at her request. The person his friends describe simply never existed, but they believe he did – and she does too: I wonder will I ever overcome that image? It isn't that I'm faced with a "choice" between somebody else now and her at some mysterious future date; the question is whether I'm kidding myself into thinking that there will be such [a] date, and that I should be waiting for it. That is, whether from her point of view that date will – or can – come. When I see how she lights up when she meets anybody from Maaleh I mentally push the date off another six months. It isn't a very cheering prospect. What makes it worse is the waste of hours and days and weeks and months, the waste of opportunities

---

15. Hebrew, meaning "longings" or "yearnings."

for being alone together which would make an American wolf go crazy with jealousy: our empty house, with Nishry away (still in Tel Aviv) and Milty at a camp and Carmi away all day and dead to the world all night. Empty rooms, empty beds, loneliness – it all reminds me of the letter Tommie, that Chicago nymphomaniac once wrote me (before I met her) imagining me sitting in my room of a Saturday night writing, faced by an empty bed. For her, of course, bed means one thing – you realize I'm using it more as a symbol than anything else. I've matured somewhat since "those" days.

(No more machine-guns, now it's mortars.) Oops, I was wrong – a Spandau just sounded off, and a *chutzpedik*[16] pistol barked a snotty answer.

Right now she's sitting in bed mourning for Yassky and I'm sitting here just a few hundred feet away feeling sorry for her – and for me too. On top of it all, this afternoon I could have sworn I saw my old flame – Elaine. Of course it was somebody else, but it gave me a start, and set me wondering all over again whether you can ever know when you've made the right decision, and whether I'm not being a Palestinian Don Quixote tilting at non-existent windmills for an equally non-existent Dulcinea. I envy you people who have resolved that question and settled, for better or worse, that particular question. Right now I don't even know which of all the girls I've known I really want – maybe it is Ann, if so, it seems criminal to have let so much time go by.

Love –

the brat

Later in the month, a "special" ration was allocated to the hungry residents of Jerusalem for the week of Passover: per person, they were allotted two pounds of potatoes, two eggs, half a pound of fish, four pounds of matza, forty-two grams of dried fruit, half a pound of meat and half

16. Yiddish, meaning "audacious, cheeky."

a pound of matza meal. Meat cost one pound per pound.[17] Following is Zippy Borowsky's description of how she was able to cope with the "generous" Pesach rations:

> The herbs were truly bitter, plucked from the fields, like the greens we now eat with our daily fare. The *charoset* tasted every bit like the Egyptian bricks it was supposed to represent, although in these times there's no way of knowing what it was made of... Despite the terrible food shortage, a meal of sorts was served, simple but plentiful, with kneidlach [matzah balls] made from something that tasted like nuts... This morning, Alizah and I made a matzah omelette from our special Passover ration of one egg each. (April 24)

Translated from the Hebrew:

April 19, 1948

10 Nisan 5708

My dear Father,

Your words about a visit home did not embitter my spirit, but they did cause me worry that perhaps you wouldn't withstand the test of time and perhaps would weaken my will and ability to withstand it. Happily, both you and Mother, in explaining your suggestion at greater length, proved that your desire to do everything possible to speed the establishment of our state does not fall short of mine. Indeed, I'm proud of you, and though I am used to Mother's eternal "youth," the very fact that she hasn't made peace with the thought that she must wait in the Diaspora until the generation that is younger than she in years only, but not in energy, was a very pleasant surprise

---

17. Harry Levin, *Jerusalem Embattled: A Diary of the City under Siege* (Cassels, 1997). One British pound in 1948 would be worth approximately 34 pounds or 44 dollars today, an exhorbitant price indeed for a pound of meat.

[sic].[18] I hope that by the summer, the situation will improve and the war will subside, and I will be able to visit you with a clean conscience, without feeling as though I have fled the battle.

I should note that my resentment comes not as a reaction to the negligence or lack of interest of American Jews, and not even their lack of success in preventing the betrayal — I fully understand the power of our opponents — but to the fact that apparently they didn't see a need to recruit more than money to help us. Now we need people, hands. To hold the villages that the Palmach is conquering, to help secure the road to Tel Aviv, to go out to the battle-field, and acquire with their blood, if necessary, the right of the nation and of the individual to dwell in our land. I know what is involved in this demand, and I also know that if those who have fought as part of every army in the world are unprepared to fight in their own, they are unworthy to be among the returnees to Zion. For two thousand years, we built cities and countries for others; have we already wearied, so that we cannot accomplish the building of our land? It is possible for a Jewish army to leave today from the United States to Eretz Yisrael via Canada (the Canadian government has already announced that it would not inter-fere and would not prevent these trips) — was there any appeal to American youth to enlist? We opened the road to Tel Aviv, we chased Qawuqji out of Mishmar Ha'emek while conquering five villages in the area, we conquered Hulda, Wadi Sarar, Saris, the Castel, and other places that, for security reasons, no one talks about: Do our fighters not deserve some kind of rest, some kind of assistance? We must leave an army in every place we conquer. Whence will we find so many people? So? — it'll be good. ... I hope

---

18. This is exactly as the Hebrew reads, a somewhat poetic way of saying that he is happy that his mother has not made peace with the fact that she must remain passive while the younger generation does the work of creating the State.

to spend Seder night on our army base – perhaps I'll have time to arrange that – and I will record some details for you.

I will stop now for a while, and before I leave for work I will add a few lines in English, lest Mother grow angry with me and spread slander that I neglect her. Farewell–and for God's sake, pressure Gershon to finish his paper, finally, and get his degree. Does he intend to be a religious functionary in the Diaspora all his life?

I wrote a long letter to Naomi – I'm sure she's already forwarded it to you …

And now, I will switch typewriters and turn to Mother …

[switches to English from Hebrew]

If we're not careful we'll go too far, one of these days: now the bloody Haganah has gone and chased all the Arabs out of Tiberias – what chutzpah! (If we could only do the same for Jerusalem!)

I tried to phone Redelheim[19] a number of times, but couldn't get him. Last night, however, taking a story down from our Tel Aviv office, I asked them to get hold of him and take for me what he has: cigarettes are worth their weight in gold these days, and as for American tobacco…! If he gives it to our office I'll get it, sooner or later. If it isn't too much trouble, some cans of real salmon and tuna would be nice, but don't go to any lengths to send it. Now if you could send a few thousand machine guns and a couple of hundred bombers to help us finish the job off in a matter of days – that's something worth taking trouble over! (You

---

19. Abraham Redelheim (1897–1965), president of Bnai Zion, the oldest Zionist fraternal organization in the United States. He later became president of the Zionist Organization of America, from 1958 to 1960, as well as of the Histadrut Ivrit of America, and served on the boards of the Jewish National Fund and the United Israel Appeal (Keren Hayesod).

could send some packages in each of the planes – double gift, bargain package)...

Jerusalem is now in full bloom, and walking through the Haganah-infested streets at night there are spots where the blossoms are simply intoxicating. Everything is green, a luscious, fresh, soothing green; it's the time of year just begging for trips around the country, for real walking through – and they'll have to wait until next year. Damned nuisance, this war, it takes up so much time...

Nu – *Ich muss*[20] you-know-what and I want this to be mailed out. So – be well, and keep writing.

All my love – mersh.

Mordecai is anxious to know if the Hebrew language article he submitted to *Hadoar,* on the perfidious behavior of the British in Palestine, has been published. In a letter written on April 20, Paul informs his son that "the cover of the 7 Nisan issue of *Hadoar*, Volume 23, featured, in large letters: "Mordecai S. Chertoff – 'On the Crimes of the British.'" As proud as he is of his son's success as an English-language journalist, Paul's dream, apparently, is to see his son as a "man of *Hebrew* letters." He writes:

This is the first time that an article of yours in Hebrew was printed, and this is your first Hebrew article! And it was accepted immediately.... What can I say, Mordecai, your article brought me much *nachat*. I am proud of it and of its author. For this I prayed, for this I waited, and, as you know, this was the purpose for which you made aliyah to Eretz Yisrael, which means that my hope is slowly becoming fulfilled; it's consolation for the sorrow and worry that have been filling our hearts recently.... Your article is lying here before me, and I've been staring at it for minutes. I read it just to read it, look at it for the pleasure of it, a glance that

---

20.   Yiddish, meaning "I must."

nourishes a father's pride that his son, yes, his son, is one of the speakers about the issues of our nation, and soon will be one of its primary spokespeople.... Only a father can experience such delight.

Paul also comments on the political and military situation:

Particularly, we were happy about you, that is, your state of mind which is full of hope for the future. We had already read about our military's victories in the press as they occurred, and by the time we received your letters, we could already attribute to them Safed, Jaffa, and what they did in Jerusalem. These actions are testimony that your hopes and ours are not false. Just today, we read that the British are re-sending an army to Eretz Yisrael, because the "situation has deteriorated" badly. We understand that all the nations understand that the meaning of "deteriorated" is for the Arabs; the entire time that the Arabs were attacking, the situation wasn't bad ... "Yet thou hadst a harlot's forehead, thou refusedst to be ashamed."[21] But I am convinced that the British, as well as our government, will, perforce, answer "Amen"!

---

21.   A quote from Jeremiah 3:3; the full verse reads: "Therefore the showers have been withheld, and there hath been no latter rain; yet thou hadst a harlot's forehead, thou refusedst to be ashamed."

Chapter 20

The British Withdraw and Turmoil Ensues

Although not mentioned in the following letter, on May 7 the worst fear of Jerusalem's governor was realized – water rationing became necessary. Most of Jerusalem's water flowed in from a spring far to the west of the city and the pipe used to get the water across the country and up three thousand feet to the city passed through Arab territory. The only water that did not come from that source came from King Solomon's Pools, *also* in Arab-controlled territory to the south. It would be very easy for the Arabs to deprive Jerusalem of water once the British left. Dov Yosef had prepared for this eventuality. He had surveyed the cisterns within the Jewish neighborhoods and when he judged it necessary, confiscated them all. A portion of the incoming water to Jerusalem was diverted to the cisterns, and as they were filled, they were sealed.

As it turned out, the Arabs didn't wait for the British to leave. On May 7, they cut the city's water line. Suddenly, there was no water in Jerusalem's faucets. At this point, the cisterns held 115,000 cubic meters of water. Yosef's water expert, Zvi Leibowitz, had determined people could survive a hot Jerusalem summer on two gallons of water a day – four pints to drink, the rest for laundry, cooking, flushing toilets and hygiene. They had enough water to last 115 days. Immediately, Yosef mobilized his team of volunteers and sent out donkey and horse-towed water tanks. Every three days, Jerusalemites received their water ration.[1]

There is growing excitement over the impending declaration of the state scheduled for May 14 but some of Mordecai's enthusiasm and choice of language is difficult to read.

May 9, 1948

Six days to freedom.

Dear Family,

I have just a few minutes to write – one of the guys is flying to Haifa in a little while, with the R.A.F., and will take this letter with him for mailing there. Our own mail system will be cracking in a few days (stamps are already for sale today) and I won't need special channels. Keep writing to me, but write directly to Jerusalem now. I think it will be okay.

I'm delighted that the article[2] was printed. Of course, I would like to see it – I wonder how much they cut. ... Of course since the thing was written so much has already happened that a piece on the British as allies of the Arabs could be written with almost no need to use newspaper files. But then the time for all that is past.... The fact is that a few hundred thousand lousy kikes in Palestine have defeated the high and mighty British Empire! I've toured Jerusalem, been in almost every post – and believe me, we have the city sewn up in a little water-tight bag. The minute the British get out, we take over, unless they shove in an international force during the week. As for the rest of the country – in 40 years of Zionist settlement not an Arab fled the country and not an Arab village was abandoned. In four months of war, which they started, more than 100,000 Arabs have hit the road, and at least 100

---

1.   Details of the water situation in Jerusalem sourced from, among other places, Collins and Lapierre, *O Jerusalem!*, pp. 147, 324.
2.   "On the Perfidy of the British," in Hebrew.

villages are clean – but really clean! Haifa, Tiberias and Safed are what they should be – Jewish; Jaffa is dying, it will never recover from the evacuation, because we'll let it rot without lifting a finger. The new part of Jerusalem, outside of the Old City, has "lost" a tremendous portion of its Arabs – they're scared s**tless. All their shooting now is a whistling in the dark, a frantic attempt to convince themselves that they're still in it. The "truce" talks are silly, they're down on their knees, and without the British army Jerusalem too would be without an Arab in it. All talk about the Jewish State arising is crap – it's here already. We have an army – god bless it – one of the best in the Middle East (Montgomery said we could handle all the combined Arab states could throw in against us), we have a government, we even have a national debt. (The new loan – I'm buying a L.P. 10 bond, for the sentiment attached – if I had the money I'd buy one for each member of the family.)

There will be a convoy from Tel Aviv either today or tomorrow, and I hope my tobacco and cigarettes come with it. If anybody leaves for here from now on, make 'em take some of my records and a couple of vacuum-packed salamis, they would come in handy.

There will be some more action in Jerusalem – there are a couple of buildings we simply must have, if we have to knock down a few people to get them, but don't worry, *yihiyeh tov*. I'm still eating, for the most part, in the Haganah kitchens, except for when I feel rich and go in for a black-market steak. It happens a couple of times a week.

Item: I just heard from Dov (the sick boy who lived with me here) and he tells me you still think there's work I can do in the States. Maybe. I know that Kolodny[3] (in Tel Aviv)

---

3. Possibly Moshe Kolodny, later known as Moshe Kol (1911–1989). He was an executive with the Histadrut and a director of the Jewish Agency who was one of the signatories of the Declaration of Independence and served on the Provisional State Council, later founding the Progressive Party and serving as an MK.

wanted Nat Cohen to go back to recruit Americans for the Haganah (what Manson had mentioned to me), but Nat refused. I have no contact with Kolodny, and can't get to him. If Naomi uses her drag for me to be sent, okay. Otherwise I stay put until the war is over and I can come with a clear conscience. Besides, this is the best place to be now! This week and the one following – our first in independence in 2,000 years, I wouldn't miss for that many dollars.

Gotta quit now – the mails must go out. I'll be writing again soon, less hurriedly and more at length and in greater detail. ...

all my love,

mersh

The Yishuv was hard at work preparing for "the day after" the British withdrawal and Mordecai had several important tasks to perform. That he had "toured Jerusalem, been in almost every post..." was not idle curiosity, but reconnaissance. It was critical that the Haganah move into every position vacated by a British soldier as quickly as possible. Mordecai's press pass gave him freedom to move about the city and unfettered access to almost every location. He told me, and my sons, that he used this freedom to visit and sketch such positions, especially within the area known as Bevingrad. In a recent visit to the Haganah archives,[4] my son David and I found several such sketches. Of course we cannot know whether these drawings are his or are based upon his intelligence reports, but they are examples of one of his activities.

Another aspect of the Yishuv's preparation was to have Jewish workers with jobs in key installations remain at their posts as the British withdrew and to hold those positions until Jewish troops could arrive. But for this to happen, it was necessary to supply the Jewish workers with some kind of weapon – camouflaged explosives. In his memoirs, Mordecai writes:

---

4.   July 23, 2017, with warm thanks to Shimri Salomon, Haganah Archives.

...the four of us (who shared a bachelor apartment on Ben Maimon Street in Rehavia: Carmi Charny, Milt Shulman, and Dov Ben Abba) were delegated to manufacture defense bombs. We filled toothpaste tubes and cigarette boxes with dynamite and made percussion caps for fountain pens. We even duplicated the sticks Jewish policemen were permitted by the British to carry, but with some changes: the body was hollowed out and stuffed with dynamite and a detonator was fitted into the handle. A twist of the handle and in ten seconds the thing went off with a lovely bang. ...

The explosives were taken from land-mines, smuggled across the Egyptian border by Jewish soldiers serving in the British army in World War II. One of them was the son of "T. Z." Miller.... The explosives were hidden in Miller's

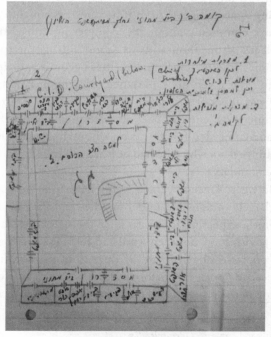

(Haganah Historical Archives)

Sketch of Jerusalem building (courtesy of the
Haganah Historical Archives)

orange grove. By one of those strange quirks of fate, Miller and my father had stolen across the Russian border together just around the turn of the century.

This memory, with some minor variances, is corroborated by Collins and Lapierre. They describe how Carmi Charny and some others prepared explosive devices hidden inside of ordinary objects, on a rooftop on Ben Yehuda Street. The devices were to be used by Jewish workers waiting to be reinforced by Jewish soldiers.[5]

* * *

Most of Mordecai's focus in the letters covering this period is on the Yishuv's preparations for the British withdrawal. However, he also makes disturbingly gleeful mention of the growing phenomenon of the fleeing Arab refugees. Even if he does first qualify his remarks, Mordecai's comments about the conquering and clearing out of Arab villages, about thousands of Arabs "hitting the road," and his satisfaction with previously mixed cities becoming solely Jewish, are distasteful. But given his experience of living in Palestine through the civil war, it is not surprising that he saw every Arab in Palestine at that time as an enemy. They were responsible for the deaths of friends and comrades, for attacks on kibbutzim and settlements, and for bombings from which he had only narrowly escaped. His feelings are understandable.

Between December 1947 and March 1948, approximately 100,000 largely middle and upper-middle-class Palestinian Arabs left their homes, expecting to return after the quick destruction of the nascent Jewish state. Between April and July 1948, another 250,000 to 300,000 poorer Arabs fled, and by the end of the war, July 1949, the total exceeded 700,000.[6] Historians have not been able to determine how many of the refugees fled of their own accord, how many left on

5.   Collins and Lapierre, *O Jerusalem!*, p. 314.

6.   Benny Morris, *The Birth of the Palestinian Refugee Problem Revisited* (Cambridge University Press, 2004). The total number of Palestinian Arab refugees as a result

orders from their leaders, how many fled through fear of approaching Jewish forces, and how many were actually driven out. There are many well-documented examples of Jews pleading with the Arabs to remain. For example, three days after the Haganah captured Haifa, on April 23, a British police report from the city stated that "every effort is being made by the Jews to persuade the Arab populace to stay and carry on with their normal lives, to get their shops and businesses open and to be assured that their lives and interests will be safe."[7] A few days later, the Jewish labor organization, the Histadrut, issued a similar plea, in Arabic and Hebrew, begging the Arab population to remain in their homes and return to their businesses.[8]

Several months later *The Economist* reported that

...[O]f the 62,000 Arabs who formerly lived in Haifa, not more than 5,000 or 6,000 remained.... Various factors influenced their decision to seek safety in flight. There is but little doubt that far the most potent of these factors was the announcements made over the air by the Arab Higher Executive, urging all Arabs in Haifa to quit.[9]

This is well documented by Morris and others.

There were, of course, instances of Arabs being forced out. In many cases, such as the villages abutting the Tel Aviv–Jerusalem highway, the evacuations were strategically necessary for ensuring the survival of Jerusalem. Still, some of these "forced evacuations" were harsh. The most extreme example was in July 1948, when fifty to seventy thousand

---

of the 1948 war continues to be a source of dispute. Arab officials speak of 900,000 or one million, Israeli officials claim 520,000–530,000, and UNRWA puts the figure at a precise 726,000 (p. 602).

7. Memorandum: "Subject – General Situation – Haifa District." By A. J. Bidmead, for Superintendent of Police, District Police Headquarters, Haifa, 26 April, 1948. http://www.ijs.org.au/British-Police-Memo/default.aspx.

8. "An Appeal by the Haifa Workers Council," 28 Apr. 1948, IDFA 48149\62

9. "The Arab Refugees" © The Economist Newspaper Limited, London 2 October 1948.

Arabs from Lydda and Ramleh were forced from their homes, and many died.

Mordecai's surviving letters from this period are strangely silent about other critical events that occurred during the second phase of the civil war: there was frantic political activity surrounding the proposed trusteeship plan and truce for Palestine and extensive fighting throughout the country; King Abdullah of Jordan "declared war" on Zionism and Arab planning for a three-front campaign began in earnest; fighting took place in Mishmar Ha'emek, where Arab irregulars and volunteers fought the Haganah and Irgun; Syrian and Lebanese members of the ALA and irregulars crossed the border in armored cars and tanks and attacked five settlements in Upper Galilee; the Haganah wrested Safed from the Iraqis and Syrians in bitter fighting; and the city of Jaffa surrendered to the Jews. The British continued with their obstructionism; they intercepted three more refugee ships; the *Tirat Zvi*, (eight hundred refugees), the *Mishmar Ha'am* (eight hundred refugees), and the *Nahshon* (six hundred refugees), and deported their passengers. They turned over key positions in territory assigned to the future Jewish state to the Arabs. Mail was piling up as postal service was suspended and the airport was closed.

On May 6, the *Palestine Post* published casualty figures for the period covering most of the civil war (November 30, 1947 – April 30, 1948): 1,047 Jews killed, 2,032 wounded; 1,141 Arabs killed, 2,649 wounded; 144 Britons killed and 450 wounded.

Part III

The Declaration of the State and the Conventional War (May 14, 1948 – Spring, 1949)

Chapter 21

Introduction to the Conventional War

On May 14, 1948, in a ceremony lasting barely thirty-two minutes, David Ben-Gurion formally declared the establishment of the State of Israel:

> We ... are here assembled on the day of the termination of the British mandate over Eretz Yisrael and, by virtue of our natural and historic right and on the basis of the resolution of the United Nations General Assembly, hereby declare the establishment of a Jewish State in Eretz Yisrael, to be known as the state of Israel ...

The declaration was like a starter's pistol for the "conventional" war: Egypt, Jordan, Syria and Iraq immediately declared war and invaded. The civil war, which had begun with the UN vote for partition and prosecuted by volunteers and Arab irregulars led by Fawzi al-Qawuqji's forces, was instantly transformed into a full-fledged clash of armies.

The conventional war consisted of three phases and two truces:

- Phase I: May 15 – June 11
  The first truce: June 11 – July 8
- Phase II (the "ten days of fighting"): July 8 – July 18
  The second truce: July 18 – October 15
- Phase III: October 15 – March 10, 1949

The Arab decision to invade had been made a month earlier. The Arab League claimed their goals were to restore order, protect their Palestinian Arab brothers, and eradicate Zionism. Their goals did not include midwifing the birth of an independent Arab Palestinian state. There was also a religious imperative at work – Islam had to prevail over Judaism. Although there was very little actual planning done, a young Jordanian officer did produce a coherent battle plan in which Jordanian, Syrian, Iraqi, Lebanese and Egyptian armies would work in concert. According to his plan, the combined Arab armies would win the war within eleven days. But then Lebanon backed out of the invasion and Jordan announced it would only go after the west bank, i.e., the land that had been allocated to the Arab Palestinians for a state, and East Jerusalem. What was briefly a coherent plan to abort the birth of a Jewish state turned into an uncoordinated land grab by the surrounding Arab countries. Those countries saw no role for the local Palestinian Arabs, did not acknowledge local political aspirations and never accepted the idea of an independent, Arab Palestine.[1]

General John Bagot Glubb, commander of the Jordanian Arab Legion came to a similar conclusion but for different reasons. Although he believed that the creation of the State of Israel was unjust, he saw no reason to create a separate, independent Arab state of Palestine. He wanted to preserve Britain's long investment in, and friendship with, the Arab countries in the area. He believed it would better if each country would simply absorb the area allocated under partition nearest their borders, i.e., Lebanon would absorb the Galilee, Jordan would annex Judea and Samaria and Egypt would control the area of Gaza and Beersheba.[2] Indeed, Egypt's goal was to take the Negev and a significant part of cen-

---

1. That would change after Israel's victory in the Six-Day War of June, 1967.
2. Glubb, *A Soldier with the Arabs*, p. 59.

tral Palestine, including the southern part of the West Bank, Hebron and Bethlehem. In secret meetings, Jordan's King Abdullah told Golda Meir, acting head of the Jewish Agency's political department, of Jordan's intention to take over the West Bank, and not territory earmarked for the Jewish state. Abdullah later reneged and there was heavy fighting between Israel and the well-trained Jordanian Arab Legion.

From the north, the Iraqis apparently intended to take the area along both sides of the Iraq Petroleum Company pipeline, which ran from Mosul in northern Iraq, through Jordan,[3] all the way to Haifa. Syria had no articulated military goals, but was interested in reaching Afula and connecting with the Iraqi army in order to cut the Jewish state in two. It is also possible that they coveted Tiberias. Lebanon did not participate in the invasion but did deploy its troops defensively and offered support to the volunteer Arab Liberation Army.

Late on the fourteenth of May, King Abdullah of Jordan and members of his personal staff stood on the eastern side of the Allenby Bridge, which spanned the Jordan River and marked the international boundary between Jordan and the West Bank. At midnight, precisely, he drew a revolver and fired a shot into the air symbolizing the start of the Jordanian attack.[4] A few hours later an Egyptian expeditionary force consisting of some six thousand men crossed the border between Egypt and the Gaza Strip, at Rafah. At the same time, Iraq's Second Brigade Group forded the Jordan River in the Galilee and approached Kibbutz Gesher, about ten kilometers from the Sea of Galilee, while Syria's First Brigade attacked Ein Gev, a kibbutz on its eastern shore. This was a diversion for their larger forces, moving from the southern end of the lake into the lower Jordan valley.

The newborn Jewish state was forced to simultaneously confront this four-pronged assault while continuing to protect Jewish Jerusalem and working to lift the siege.

During the invasion period there is a larger-than-usual gap in the family correspondence. I have only two letters. Of course there were severe disruptions in mail service and it is likely that letters are missing.

---

3. The pipeline was in use from 1935 to 1948.
4. Morris, *1948*, p. 209.

Mordecai's family complained that their letters are being returned marked, "Return to sender. Service suspended." On May 17, however, the Chertoffs were able to get a cable through: "Congratulating Yishuv and you representing us in Israel."

During this period, Mordecai wrote many articles for the *Post*, several with his by-line. He sent them to his family and they serve here as letter substitutes.

Unlike his beautiful description of the vote for partition, there is no poetic, sweeping essay from Mordecai describing the declaration of the State. A retrospective account written a year later recalls the emotions and experiences of Jerusalemites at the time:

29 April 1949

THE NEW PALESTINE[5]
Jerusalem Did Not Celebrate

By Mordecai S. Chertoff

The writer, a noted newspaperman, is a young American who has just returned from a two-year stay in Israel, where he witnessed the siege of Jerusalem and the battle to open the lifeline from that beleaguered city to Tel Aviv. – Ed.

Jerusalem did not celebrate the declaration of the State of Israel last May 14. There were no parades and no banquets: all manpower not essential to the city's vital industries had been mobilized; there was little enough food in the city to keep real hunger away, let alone for celebrations. And Jerusalem had already been at war for four-and-a-half months. There was no fuel, and no water beyond the pails-full doled out by truck every day, under fire. Jerusalem was a desolate

---

5. *The New Palestine* was published by the Zionist Organization of America. It started as a newspaper but in 1946 became a monthly magazine.

city,[6] bristling with road-blocks and dragon's teeth,[7] remembering the night and day and night of wild rejoicing that followed the historic UN vote on November 29 and the destruction of the old Commercial Center near the Old City that followed it; remembering the battles fought in and around the city; remembering that "Bevingrad," the British Police compound and security zone, had to be taken to secure the New City against Arab attack, and wondering how it would "go."

Jerusalem was a tense city that Thursday night, May 13, and few slept in their beds. Every Jew in the city was alerted, and fronting every zone – every potential vacuum or battleground. Men were lined up, ready to fill the vacuum – or to fight.

Haganah Took Over

As dawn broke over the city, the last of the British soldiers began to move out. They backed out of "Bevingrad" towards the Old City, moving along the only road open to them there (Haganah had the others heavily barricaded) and incidentally – and inadvertently – blocking any proposed Arab advance. As they moved out, the Haganah moved in, and anxious citizens "off-duty" early that morning made their way down to the area to cheer the Blue-and-White fluttering from the top of the imposing Generali Building, commanding all of Jaffa Road and most of the New City, a building from which British machine guns had swept Jaffa Road more than once, and cut the city in half while British police reacted to an I.Z.L. bomb or a Sternist hand-grenade. They were gone now, and the Arabs hadn't replaced them.

---

6.   An allusion to the Biblical book of Lamentations, attributed to Jeremiah, which opens with a description of the desolation of Jerusalem following the destruction of the First Temple.

7.   Small reinforced concrete pyramids used to impede tanks and other traffic.

All through the day young men and boys were to be seen leaving a certain compound, dressed in as much of the abandoned British police uniforms as they could get on – and as many. Three tunics and two pair of pants, pockets stuffed with socks and extra shoes hanging from the shoulder tabs was the order of day. But more serious work was being done at the compound that morning. Bren gun parts were being salvaged from the storerooms, and the hunt was on for overlooked weapons, sorely needed in poorly-equipped Jewish Jerusalem. In one room we found weapons – countless hundreds of rifles and pistols, and all worthless: the British had smashed the barrels and operating mechanisms of each and every weapon. It was only then that I fully appreciated why one of the police officers had been so sure a few days before that the Arabs would take the city: he had an idea of how much we had, and what the Arabs had – and he knew what we could expect to find in "Bevingrad." After a heartbreaking rummage around, the day's "loot" in the area was one case of forty brand-new Colts and Mausers, overlooked by the British and inadvertently left behind.

The Etzion Heroes

But there was no Arab Sweep, no attempt at real infiltration into the Jewish areas. Down in the Jaffa Gate section, near Notre Dame and opposite Mt. Zion, the fighting raged all that day and the next, but the brunt of the onslaught was born by the Kfar Etzion bloc, which fought off sixteen consecutive attacks by eighteen [Jordanian] Legion tanks and stood up to the Legion's cannon. Kfar Etzion itself fell on the 13th, but Mas'uot Yitzhak, Revadim and Ein Tzurim fought on until late on the 14th, when their ammunition failed completely. Sixty men constituted the entire fighting force still fit for action when headquarters ordered their

surrender to avert needless loss of life. The Etzion bloc fell –
but Jerusalem was saved.

While the heroes of the Etzion bloc – and they
earned for themselves a special niche in Israel's Hall of
Fame – held the Legion, the Haganah was able to seize
most of the strategic points in New Jerusalem, and so
morale was high when the Legion tanks swept in a wide
arc around Jerusalem and tried to break through from the
north, only to be repulsed again and again.

That Friday night, on guard behind a lone olive tree in
a field in Talbieh, on the eastern edge of the city, one of the
men paid the only tribute he could to the hours-old state:
he squeezed-off a burst from his Sten gun, and watched the
bullets go straight to Heaven, much like the spark from the
whip of the Jewish wagon-driver, the illiterate Hassid, who
had cracked his whip to the greater glory of God.

Tel Aviv had its celebration. The historic proclama-
tion was read in the Municipal Museum there and people
wept in the streets as the new prime minister and the members of the provisional government – the first free Jewish
government in two thousand years – came walking down
the steps of the museum.

The Third Commonwealth

Jaffa had formally surrendered the day before, and Tel Aviv
was secure – by land. But Tel Aviv's first day as capital of
the provisional government was marked by three air raids.
Battle-hardened Jerusalem worried for Tel Aviv, for its "soft"
citizens who had had only their border-warfare with Jaffa
to look back on. But hard-pressed Jerusalem stopped worrying when word came that Tel Aviv had shot down two
enemy raiders.

Morale soared still higher when American and Soviet
recognition followed each other in rapid succession. Today

only collective world recognition by the UN is lacking, but even the die-hard Arabs realize it to be a foregone conclusion.[8]

The Third Commonwealth has been established and the country is being rebuilt. Paid for with the blood of our best young men and women, the third redemption has come, and after this redemption *ein tza'ar veshibud malhuyot* – there will be no further enslavement to a foreign power. This time the Jewish people will rebuild the age-old new land, there to live the lives their prophets dreamed of, and of which their poets sang.

---

8. Less than two weeks after this article was first published, on May 11, 1949, the UN approved Israel's membership by the requisite two-thirds majority.

Chapter 22

The Fall of the Etzion Bloc

The fall of the Etzion Bloc and the massacre of its defenders and inhabitants is among the most dramatic and painful episodes of the war, unfolding over a period of almost six months. The four settlements comprising the bloc, located between Jerusalem and Hebron, were in an area earmarked for the Arab Palestinian state. The Arabs besieged them as soon as the UN voted for partition on November 29, 1947. After the unsuccessful attempt to relieve the siege by the "35" soldiers in January, 1948 (recounted above), there were numerous further attempts to support the defenders and families living in the bloc.

General Glubb was concerned that the Jewish communities in the area which controlled the southern approach to Jerusalem could disrupt Arab traffic between Hebron and Jerusalem. He believed they had to be removed. As a result, two days before British rule over Palestine was to end, the Arab Legion attacked and captured Kfar Etzion and the other communities in the bloc.[1]

---

1. Glubb, *A Soldier with the Arabs*, p. 78. Note that Glubb was "jumping the gun." The Jewish state had not yet been declared and this was technically an area being attacked by an officer holding the King's commission.

The final assault was mounted on May 12 and Kfar Etzion fell the following day. The precise details of the final hours of the battle are in dispute, but it is clear that the remaining defenders, men and women, surrendered and assembled in the open. Almost all of them were shot, and the kibbutz destroyed. Most sources claim that the death toll was around 127, but it is unclear how many died in battle and how many were murdered in the slaughter that followed. After the fall of Kfar Etzion, the other three settlements belonging to the Etzion Bloc surrendered and their inhabitants were taken prisoner. Today, the rebuilt Kfar Etzion[2] offers a sound and light show of its history which concludes in the bunker within which twenty women were said to have been murdered after the surrender. Glubb claims that the Arab Legion treated the Jewish survivors as proper prisoners of war and that, only after they withdrew, did the local villagers loot and demolish the Jewish communities.[3] Indeed, there are reports of Legionnaires protecting Jews and even shooting Arabs who were attempting to rape and attack survivors. In a rather macabre footnote to this battle, the bodies of the murdered defenders of the Etzion Bloc were left exposed at the site for a year and a half before Jordan eventually allowed Israel to retrieve them for internment at the military cemetery on Mount Herzl.[4]

Ben-Gurion is reported to have said that the Etzion Bloc was critical to the defense of Jerusalem, a point Mordecai makes in his article. The valiant defense of the Bloc prevented the Jordanians from immediately overrunning Jerusalem, and gave the Haganah the time they needed to establish themselves there.

Immediately upon the declaration of the state and the withdrawal of the British, the Haganah moved into positions in Jerusalem that the

---

2. Nineteen years later, after Israel captured the area during the Six-Day War, descendants of the defenders returned and reestablished Kfar Etzion. As of 2016, there are many communities in the Etzion Bloc (Gush Etzion). Its Jewish population is estimated at approximately seventy-five thousand residents.
3. Glubb, *A Soldier with the Arabs*, p. 78.
4. By the time Jordan permitted the bodies to be recovered, many could no longer be identified. In a recent article ("Gone but not Forgotten," *Jerusalem Post*, January 19, 2018, p. 15), the *Post* staff describes the medieval ritual used by revered Rabbi Arye Levin, in which heavenly advice is obtained, in order to identify the bodies.

British had abandoned. This operation was called *Mivtza Kilshon* – Operation Pitchfork. It was part of "Plan Dalet" ("D")[5] the goal of which was to connect the isolated Jewish neighborhoods of Jerusalem and to take over abandoned British positions. The Haganah succeeded in taking sections of the southern part of the city – Baka, the German Colony, the Greek colony, Camp Allenby in Talpiot, Defense Area B,[6] the David Building on Jabotinsky Street, the train station and electric power plant, and the neighborhood of Abu Tor. Israeli forces were also able to capture positions in the downtown area including the "Bevingrad" compound, the Italian hospital, the post office, the Russian compound, the Arab neighborhood of Sheikh Jarrah, the monastery of Notre Dame and a section of Musrara, next to the Old City walls. Forces assigned to the northern areas failed to take Jaffa Gate but did take Zion Gate and broke the siege of the Old City's Jewish Quarter, at least temporarily. The Jordanians responded by unleashing indiscriminate artillery barrages into the Jewish Quarter. Eyewitness reports described extensive Jewish civilian casualties.

Between May 19 and 24 there was a fierce battle over Kibbutz Ramat Rachel, just past the southern edge of Jerusalem, which controlled the Jerusalem–Bethlehem highway. The Palmach Harel Brigade prevailed and the Jews were able to secure the southern entrance to the city.

Although there was fighting all over Palestine, Mordecai naturally followed events in and around Jerusalem most closely as they unfolded. He also observed several operations first hand, and wrote about them. Below is an article he wrote for the *Palestine Post* describing the (temporary) Palmach success in taking Zion Gate. The article had a significant impact on his career as a journalist.

---

5.   The introduction to Plan Dalet includes among its objectives: gaining control of the areas of the Jewish state and defending its borders; gaining control of areas of Jewish settlement and concentration located beyond the borders, against the various armed forces – regular, semi-regular, and others – operating from bases outside or inside the state. (See Walid Khalidi in *Journal of Palestine Studies*. V XVIII *Number 1*, 1988, from *Sefer Toldot Hahaganah* [History of the Haganah], vol. 3, ed. Yehuda Slutsky [Tel Aviv: Zionist Library, 1972], Appendix 48, pp. 1955–60.)

6.   Defense Area B included the King David Hotel and the YMCA across the street from it, Terra Sancta College, and parts of Talbieh and Rehavia.

May 20, 1948

HOW PALMACH TOOK ZION GATE

By Mordecai S. Chertoff

Battle-hardened Palmach soldiers stormed Zion Gate in fifteen minutes during the pre-dawn hours yesterday, bringing food to the 1,500 residents of the Jewish Quarter and reinforcements to the small Jewish garrison and ending the five-and-a-half month siege. Instead of breaking their spirit, the siege had turned the residents of the Quarter into soldiers.

In one hour, a handful of men, many of whom were engaged in the capture of Katamon and the Battle of the Roads, did what it took the mighty Roman legions three years to do: penetrate one of the massive ramparts guarding the city. The Palmach Commander's orders to his troops telescoped nearly 1,900 years of Jewish history in the words: "You stand before the walls of Jerusalem. For 1870 years no Jew has climbed them. Tonight you will mount them."

They did.

One Palmach soldier fell in the battle.

Escorted by a Staff Officer who has been with Palmach since its inception just seven years ago, a small group of correspondents were privileged to watch Palmach in action. We drove down to Operational Headquarters and were briefed by the Officer-in-charge, a twenty-five-year-old Palestinian-born youth who identified himself only as "Uzi."

He was in command of the Jewish forces when Kfar Etzion was first attacked, (more than 130 of the attacking Arabs were killed), and he later commanded the Palmach forces that took the Castel after three days of bitter see-saw fighting.

Objective

The main drive would be through Zion Gate, he said, with diversionary attacks on Jaffa Gate and Damascus Gate. The object was to bring to the Jews of the Old City what they needed, and take out their twelve dead and fifty wounded, casualties of a week's fighting which brought Arab Legionnaires[7] and Iraqis to within thirty metres of the defenders' posts. This object was to serve as the answer to the terms of surrender offered the Old City Jews, through the Truce Commission, a day or two before.

When we arrived at Operational H.Q. at 1.30 on Tuesday night, there had been some shelling from Jewish lines. An Arab vehicle which had apparently tried to run the gauntlet to Jaffa Gate had been hit, and its horn wailed on a high sustained note.

There was the background murmur of the radio operator making his last-minute check as Uzi explained to us that all of Mt. Zion was in Jewish hands; we could see an occasional flash from the signals post opposite. What we could not see were Ra'anana's men, crouched fifteen metres from the gate, ready to break through the minute the sappers completed their work.

From the candle-lit, two-room H.Q. we crawled along a trench to a stone wall and made ourselves as comfortable as we could for the long wait until the break-through. The heavy rumble of a Browning machine gun nearby was answered by a Spandau further down the line, while the crash of the heavy mortars was pointed up by the lesser whoosh of their little brothers. Rifles cracked all around us and tracers arched overhead, while some disappointed soldier assigned to "peaceful" H.Q. added his "me-too" pistol pop to the growing din.

A bright red flash lit up the sky over the Old City at 2.20 in the morning, and a second later there was a tremendous explosion. A mushroom of a dense black smoke rose over the Armenian Quarter, and a bewhiskered Palmachnik next to me hummed as the softening-up barrage reached a pitch it was destined to maintain, with brief eerie lulls, for almost an hour.

---

7. Of the Jordanian Arab Legion.

We began to count the shells as they exploded, but soon lost count. The columns of smoke indicated where some of them had struck: where Iraqis had been reported in great numbers in the Armenian Quarter; along the wall west of Zion Gate; near the Kishleh – the old Police Station near the Citadel at Jaffa Gate.

An anguished shout to "Allah, Allah," rising and falling as it came to us across the wadi, indicated one Arab hit: we were later told that at least seventy-eight Arabs had been killed and scores more of the massed Arab Legionnaires and Iraqis wounded.

(Through all the racket, we could hear the thin wail of the stuck motor horn.)

Moonlit Attack

At exactly 3.15 two young Palmach sappers crawled across the faintly moonlit field to Zion Gate itself, planted their charge and crawled back under cover of the heavy softening-up fire their comrades maintained. This operation is laconically referred to as "withdrawing" but was, in this case at least, a full military operation demanding the utmost training and steel nerves if it is to be carried out without exposing oneself to the enemy's return fire.

Within five minutes, when the smoke had cleared enough for the men to see that the Arabs' sand-bags and towering curtain of barbed wire blocking the gate had been properly blasted away, members of Palmach, the "Portzim" (those who break through), stormed into the walled area, and within fifteen minutes had tossed their grenades into the ring of Arab defence posts opposite them and cleared the path to the Jewish Quarter, 150 metres away. Seconds later, when the wireless operator shouted up to us "they're inside," we heard the rumble of an armoured car as it toiled up the steep Mt. Zion road, bringing supplies.

Skirting mines and jumping hedges, we worked our way from Yemin Moshe down the hill, across the rock-and-thorn strewn wadi and up to Mt. Zion, where Ra'anana, who commanded the attack on Katamon a little over two weeks ago, assigned a man to take us to Zion Gate itself. We had lost precious time threading our way up the hill, and it was growing light as we crawled along a wall, hoping the snipers on David's Citadel would miss us. We raced along an open stretch, and found ourselves in the shadow of the Gate, close enough to see where its massive masonry had sagged, and where the once-straight lines of its mammoth courses now curved and zigzagged.

The last man to leave the engagement was a seventeen-year-old Palmachnik who didn't bother to duck as he ambled along, chewing his helmet-strap. I asked him whether he was too tired to bother, and he shrugged contemptuously. He had been running despatches all night through the heaviest fire the Arabs could muster; a couple of snipers were not going to bother him now.

Linking-Up

An excited redhead told me how he was received by the defenders within the Quarter, who had attacked positions lost to the Arabs only a few days before with their pitiful collection of small-arms and grenades – all that British Army searches had left them with which to hold off the British-equipped Legion. His shouted *"Ze anahnu"* – it's us – reassured the weary defender coming towards him with finger in the ring of his last grenade. The grenade dropped into a ragged pocket, and at 3.40 the link between the Jews outside the city and those within the walls was made real with the embrace of a grey-haired old man and a red-haired young one.

The road was open. The operation had been another of the phenomenal Palmach "jobs" the Yishuv has learned to expect.

Instead of breaking their spirit, as their would-be overlords hoped, the siege seemed to have turned every one of the residents of the Quarter into a seasoned soldier.

Heavy damage had been done by the Arabs to the houses they had briefly occupied, but the Quarter was saved, and the link firmly welded.

As we left the area along a circuitous route to avoid the increasingly heavy sniping, we could hear the high thin wail of the auto-horn.

The article endeared Mordecai to the Palmach who subsequently adopted him as "their reporter" and invited him to accompany them on other operations. It also impressed Gershon Agronsky, editor-in-chief of the *Post*, who wrote:

I don't think it is necessary to tell you that the fact that you have turned yourself into a war correspondent has not escaped the notice either of the staff or of the paper's readers. More power to you. GA (May 31, 1948)

May 24, 1948

Dear Family,

Well, I was wrong. It isn't that I put too much trust in Palmach, but that the on-the-spot conditions were such that all four plans they had prepared had to be abandoned. I saw them in a moment of great success, and I was with them on Friday night when they did not get through. They took it like real soldiers. They weighed the chances of each plan, tried one, and then another, and then decided that they would rather live to fight again than try to pull a suicide job. That even the high command, which for heart-breaking political reasons has not provided the proper supplies to Palmach — they still have no uniforms, and are not overly supplied with arms — realizes they alone can save Jerusalem is attested to by the fact that they have been given the command here in the city, and now have all the say. I rely on them so completely that I feel I could obey any order a Palmach commander gave me without the slightest doubt or hesitancy, regardless of how cracked it seemed to me. In short, they're the greatest bunch on earth, and I feel so proud and cocky that my story pleased them you have no idea.

I had written it for Thursday's paper, and when I went back to Mt. Zion for Friday night's attack with Azariah[8] (more about him some other time – he's my companion on these junkets) and we were challenged by the sentries our answer – "Azariah u'Mordochai" was enough. The next question was: "did you write that long *chizbat*[9] (a Palmach slang word for s**t-story) about us?" "Yes" brought a laugh and *"tayib"* (swell, fine) from them, and we were in again. I didn't do a piece on it for the paper because it didn't work, and I didn't want a negative story about them published. This afternoon I was alerted – Azariah and I have priority on all Palmach operations now – he for *Haaretz*, me for the *Post* – and we expect to go out again with the boys tomorrow morning. It will be a big job – so big I have a damned fine idea it will finish this messy war up, with the Legion and the wogs[10] from Egypt running as fast as their black legs will carry them.

Nu, enough of that, I could rave about my pets for hours. About me, there is nothing new. I'm working hard, and loving it. My Zion Gate story put me on the journalistic map, and gave me status overnight, and now an operation

---

8. Azariah Rapoport (1924–1997), was born in Tel Aviv. He volunteered and fought with the British during WWII, then joined the Haganah and was also a reporter for *Haaretz* during the period of Israel's War of Independence. After the war, he acted in both plays and movies, was a newscaster for the radio station Kol Yisrael, and became the film critic for the newspaper *Maariv*. He served as a communications officer for Israeli UN and consular officials. His father was among the leaders of the Irgun.

9. From the Arabic, it means 'tall tales' told especially by soldiers. Derived from the Arab custom of sitting around a campfire telling heavily-embroidered but essentially true stories.

10. Derogotary British slang for colored people.

is not pulled off without me getting a tip so that I can cover it if I want to.

For a pleasant change, I took Ann to lunch today, and we sat and swapped military secrets for a couple of hours. When this war slows up I intend to give that young lady the time and attention she deserves.

...

Regards to everybody – by the time you get this the war will be little more than a grim memory. Boy, have I got a *tiyul* planned – if I can only get the right company for it!

That's all for now – all my love,

Mersh

Unfortunately, Mordecai was being far too optimistic about the progress of the war.

A second article with his by-line appearing in the May 30 edition of the *Post* concerned the fight for the Old City from the vantage point of Notre Dame, which played a key role in the efforts to defend the Jewish Quarter. Strangely, he does not mention that many of the defenders of Notre Dame were members of the Gadna youth corp, an organization he deeply admired. One of the defenders was only fourteen years old.

May 30, 1948

MONASTERY BATTLE

By Mordecai S. Chertoff

It was just 4.15 on Monday afternoon when we walked into the high-ceilinged library of Notre Dame, near the New Gate of the Old City, built in 1882 by the French and now occupied by Jewish troops after a one-hour battle of conquest and uncounted hours of defence against the Arab Legion.

The building consists of a monastery and a church, a school and a chapel, a museum and a dining room, but for the conqueror-commander of the building, it is far more important that it dominates the Old City, Musrara, Sheikh Jarrah, Mt. Scopus and sections of the Old City Wall, including both Damascus Gate and New Gate, and which in Iraqi hands was a menace to Jewish sections of the city.

Itzhak, a twenty-two-year-old Haganah man, explained to us that his troops had blown up a building just in front of Notre Dame, and thereby effectively sealed off the New Gate, while his guns cover Damascus Gate: in pivot, he showed us an Arab Legion armoured car, burnt and stripped of its weapons by his men.

The labyrinthine basement served as barracks for the British troops which evacuated on May 14, leaving it to the Iraqis to take over. When he was ordered to take the building on May 20, his men had to machine-gun their way across the stretch of yard from Darouti's Hotel and wipe out the Iraqi post at the entrance. The rest was fairly easy, he said, and it took little more than an hour for his men to work their way down from the third floor to the basement, and clear out the more than one hundred rooms in the building.

The operation began at 4 a.m., but it was hardly over when the Arabs showed their unwillingness to relinquish their snipers' heaven and to let the inhabitants of Mea Shearim and other parts of Jerusalem live in peace. They counter-attacked in force, and in a fierce eight-hour battle the toll of Arab dead mounted to at least twenty, while two armoured vehicles belonging to the Legion were completely destroyed.

Prisoners Taken

One prisoner was taken that first day, and seventeen more during the counter-attack. There were eighty wounded in the adjacent French Hospital, Itzhak said, and it was expected that another twenty of these would be taken as prisoners of war as soon as their condition warranted it. Since the occupation, Jewish losses totalled six killed and fifteen wounded.

Walking through the halls laden with dust made deeper by every shell the Arabs fired at the building – and several hit while we were there – we saw a corner of the New Gate, blocked by the wrecked house, and from a heap of rubble in a corner we could see the Iraqi flag flying over a building just twenty metres away. Mt. Scopus, green in the distance and with its scars blurred by the shimmering heat-waves rising under the khamsin sun, provided a startlingly peaceful contrast to the battered shell of the chapel rose [sic] through which we could see it. It was here that a shell from a Legion twenty-five-pounder killed Pere Mamert.[11]

Scroll of the Law

We looked in at the Museum of Biblical Antiquities, completely untouched by the battles which had raged over and around it, one as late as yesterday morning, when the Legion was again repulsed with heavy losses.

Open on a table was an ancient parchment Scroll of the Law, open as it would be for use in a synagogue today as it had been years ago, when it was first found. A verse from the dusty scroll leaped to the eye: "And should a man sin …"

Coughing from the dust, we made our way upstairs, past a kitchen in which water dripped slowly from a leaky faucet into a bucket, and out through the library again. Outside, two Stern Group officers[12] from a nearby post were comparing notes with Itzhak's deputy.

Although we had been on our tour a little over an hour, the library clock which had come through the

---

11. An Assumptionist priest killed during the fighting.
12. The Lehi ("Stern Group") was formally dissolved and integrated into the Israeli army on May 31, 1948.

fighting unscathed and was running smoothly, read only a little past 3.15.

Jerusalem was still cut off and besieged, its population suffering hunger and thirst and living with strict rationing – all while under attack by the Jordanians. Latrun dominated the road to Jerusalem occupied by the Arab Legion since May 18. The Haganah's first attempt to take it, during Operation Bin Nun Alef, May 24–25, failed.

Bayt Susin was a small village on a strategic hilltop less than three kilometers from Latrun. It, too, had been occupied by the Arab Legion and was used to launch attacks on Jewish forces during the operation. The village was near a network of roads that led to several urban centers and was linked by a secondary road to the main highway to Jerusalem. On May 28, Israeli soldiers from the 72nd Battalion of the Sheva Brigade succeeded in clearing the village. Immediately afterwards, Mordecai traveled with the Palmach into the Judean Hills.

Sunday, May 30, 1948

STEADY SWEEP EAST ON ROAD
With the Palmach Forces in the Judean Hills

The Arab village of Beit Susin, straddling a mountain 360 metres high just two-and-a-half kilometres south of Latrun, was conquered and occupied by forces of the Jewish Army this morning in their slow but steady sweep eastward. Beit Jiz, three kilometres southwest of the Latrun battlefield, was taken by these same forces early yesterday morning.

Despite heavy shelling from Yalu village, three kilometres north of Dir Ayoub, Palmach's control of the heights dominating the road from Jerusalem all the way to Bab el Wad has remained unshaken, and one can drive down the road past the upper and lower Pumping Stations – with the unit names and numbers of the victorious Palmach units painted on their greyish-green walls – as far as the now-Jewish roadblocks.

The Sector's Edge

That is still not the end of the road, though. The edge of the Latrun sector, where the real battle for Jerusalem is being fought, is marked by the old "Half-Way" cafe almost two kilometres further down the road, and by the remains of the petrol station, destroyed by Palmach soldiers three days before they wrested complete control of the Bab el Wad area from the Arabs on May 11.

You can walk it unarmed, as we did this afternoon when we went to visit one of the posts dominating the area. We climbed a narrow, winding, hardly discernible path up the steep mountainside where a young sentinel greeted us with a bombardment of questions. Not about us – we were all right, since we had obviously passed through the road-blocks and been directed to the post by a guard whom we had satisfied as to our identity. What he wanted to know was what was happening in the "wide world;" back at Kiryat Anavim and way, way back, in Jerusalem. Himself battle-tried and accustomed to measuring out his bread and water, he was amazed at the heroic stand of the Jews in the Old City.

Three men on guard at the post did not turn their heads once all the time we were there: they were waiting for something to come from the west, and couldn't risk its being the wrong thing and letting it come too close.

Settlements Shelled

Both Kiryat Anavim and Maaleh Hachamisha have been subjected to heavy shelling from Arab guns on the radar station hill opposite this, causing some damage to buildings in Maaleh.

At the same time, most of the Arab guns at Nebi Samwil, some five kilometres north-west of Jerusalem, have been turned away from the city and concentrated on the stretch of road within their range and at the famous Castel, where Palmach forces have rebuilt and re-fortified the positions they had to destroy in capturing almost two months ago.

Two of them have just come from a little picnic in Gan Zilah – where they waded in the still well-kept pool and smoked their day's issue of cigarettes in the shade of the monument to Zilah, first daughter of Kiryat Anavim, who died there just two years ago.

Legion troops, frustrated in their frontal attacks on Jerusalem, have again moved forces up in an attempt to cut the Jerusalem-Tel Aviv lifeline.

Advancing along the only roads still open to it, the Legion yesterday put out two armoured columns: one from Sha'afat to Bidu, through Nebi Samwil, and to the former British Army Radar Station; and from Ramallah along the main road through Imwas to the crucial Latrun crossroads, where a battle is now raging.

While Arab forces from the Triangle[13] were engaged by troops of the Jewish Army around Latrun, Jewish fighters of the Palmach and Haganah field troops ("Hish") in the Kiryat Anavim–Maaleh Hahamisha sector were battling an Arab drive to take the Radar Station – only metres distant from the most advanced Palmach post – and sweep on to the twin settlements, Jewish islands in an entirely Arab area.

From Biddu, three kilometres east of the Radar Station, Arab Legionnaires with 2- and 6-pounders brought their armoured column around in a wide sweep, working their way from the south over to quiet Abu Ghosh, and attacking the Radar Station from the west.

The onslaught began with a barrage from the Arab cannon and heavy machine guns before the cold dawn came up over the still-green hills, and lasted forty-five minutes, until at 5 a.m. Arab infantry then tried to storm the heights,

---

13. A concentration of Arab towns and villages in the eastern Sharon plain among the Samarian foothills. It includes, among other places, Kafr Qara, Ar'ara, Baqr al-Gharbiyye, Umm al-Fahm, Tayibe, and Kafr Qasim.

but was met by the withering fire of the defenders. The battle raged until the defense posts, riddled by six-pounder shells, were no longer tenable, and it was decided to evacuate the Station itself and withdraw to positions closer to Kiryat Anavim

Arab Armour at Bay

Slowly the Haganah forces withdrew towards the Jewish positions, which sent out a unit to provide covering fire and hold four Legion armoured cars at bay, preventing them from continuing their planned advance upon the settlement itself.

Late last night, Palmach forces launched a counter-attack against the newly entrenched Arab positions, and effectively prevented Arab reinforcements from moving on to Ramallah.

Jewish forces here are awaiting another Arab attempt to break through. Looking at the men resting at ease, stretched out on the grass all around me, a few steps from headquarters, one would hardly expect them to be waiting for anything more exciting than lunch – which is due in fifteen minutes.

But the battle for Latrun and control of the Tel Aviv–Jerusalem road was far from over. Israel launched no fewer than three operations to try to control the choke point at Bab el Wad (now called Shaar Hagai): Operation Bin Nun 1, on May 25, Operation Bin Nun 2, from May 30–31, and Operation Yoram, from June 8–9. All were met with defeat.

Chapter 23

The Fall of the Jewish Quarter of the Old City

As Israeli troops were taking Bayt Susin, tragedy was befalling the Old City's Jewish Quarter. After two weeks of hard house-to house fighting in the warren-like lanes, the Jewish defenders had reached their limits. They were vastly outnumbered and exhausted, fighting an enemy with fresh troops and superior weapons. A Haganah officer quoted in the *Palestine Post* on May 30 explained:

> Our fighting men were too few – our arms were too few – finally our position was hopeless and our casualties very heavy. We kept hoping for a new linkup with our people outside Zion Gate. We had this link on the evening of May 17, and brought in new fighters and ammunition. But when the Legion came into the Old City on May 18, the link-up was broken and never restored. We surrendered yesterday because we were at the end of our resources. We were finished.[1]

---

1.   From "Held Out Until Ammo Ran Out," by Daniel de Luce, *Palestine Post*, May 30, 1948. All the details of the surrender and expulsion are taken from the May 30 edition of the *Post*.

On Friday morning, two residents of the Jewish Quarter, seventy-year-old Rabbi Reuven Hazan and eighty-three-year-old Rabbi Israel Mintzberg, approached an Arab position carrying a white flag fashioned from a tablecloth. The Arabs sent one of them away to fetch a Haganah representative and when he returned they presented their terms for surrender. All able-bodied men between the ages of fifteen and fifty would be taken captive and all other Jews were to be expelled from their homes. The Legion guaranteed they would protect these civilians from the Arab mob as they left their homes. The terms were accepted. The Jewish Quarter fell to the Arab Legion; thousands of years of Jewish presence in the Old City ended. Sixty-four Jewish defenders had been killed in the battle.

Close to three hundred Haganah defenders were sent to Jordan as prisoners of war. Approximately twelve hundred civilian inhabitants of the Old City were expelled from their homes and sent through the gates to West Jerusalem. The Legion threw a strong protective cordon around them to protect them from the wrath of a lynch mob, also bringing in the Red Cross to provide them with food and water. Evacuation of the civilians took more than six hours. With all the able-bodied men taken prisoner, the evacuees were old men, women and children, carrying small bundles of belongings. Afterwards, one reporter ventured into the Jewish Quarter and described the remains of walls that were once homes, and piles of rubble that were once a synagogue. He compared the scene to World War II Bergen Belsen, Stalingrad or Berlin. Roofless walls were askew and passageways were waist-high with debris. Once the Jews were gone, the destruction continued. The entire quarter, including almost all of its twenty-seven synagogues, was demolished by the Arab mob.

Mordecai's next dispatch to his family is written from Tel Aviv. He cannot reveal to his family – yet – how he was able to get there from besieged Jerusalem.

June 2, 1948

Dear Family,

The enclosed *Palestine Post*s will explain fully what I'm doing these days. Running around in the headquarters

Palmach armoured car is really something for the books, and were it not for our preposterous censorship on every-thing interesting I would have a lovely series of articles on it. However, I shove through what I can, the boys like and keep inviting me out to do more... I'm in Tel Aviv now, sneering at people living off the fat of the land almost unaware of the war while Jerusalem pulls its belt tighter and tighter, and I'm anxious to get back. How I got here is a military secret I can't go into here and now, but at some future date certainly will. After some swimming and a show, and an orgy of fresh fruit and vegetables, I'll be going back to the Palmach base near Jerusalem, where I spend a good deal of my time, and from which I occasionally deign to go to the office to work of a night. Usually, I pretend to be doing a story which is invari-ably "censored" through no fault of mine, of course, and so I'm having my cake and eating it as well.

Give letters for me to Moshe Ettenberg,[2] he'll be fly-ing back here in a few days (from when you get this) – and I insist that each and every one of you write. Hell, the pre-rogative of every soldier is to scream for mail, and even though I'm only a soldier theoretically, I'll scream for it any-way. Send it to our Tel Aviv office, they'll forward it.

This is important: write to the Cleveland Strausses, and tell them that Ann is fine. She's even lost a little weight, and I've never seen her looking better. You may know she's doing a very

---

2. Moshe Ettenberg (c. 1917–1991), a professor of electrical engineering appointed to teach at the Weizmann Institute, arrived in Palestine in 1947 with his wife, Sylvia. When the War of Independence broke out Moshe could not assume his position and instead was drafted into the newly formed Israeli Air Force. He founded the 505 Squadron, the IAF's first radar unit, and commanded a group of forty overseas volunteers with radar experience. Only a few people knew of the existence of the unit. All the radar operators were women who had been trained by two female volunteers, one from England and the other from South Africa. The Ettenbergs returned to America in 1949. Moshe was professor of electrical engineering at CCNY. I had the privilege of knowing him. He was a true gentleman. His wife, Sylvia, was a prominent Jewish educator, and one of the founders of Camp Ramah.

important job, highly hush-hush,[3] of course, and is living a few blocks from me, in Rehavia, where the only noise is women threatening kids with a whipping every time they hear rumours of a shelling and the kid is not in the house. I wish there were more I could write about her at present – *insh'allah*,[4] I will soon. Meanwhile, let her people know she's okay.

...

And that's all for now – ... and tell Shertok I refuse to be called an Israelite.

With love and hope for a rapid victory – Mordecai Shmuel

Mordecai's dismissive opinion of Tel Avivians as "unaware of the war" is unfair. The Egyptians had initiated war by, among other things, bombing Tel Aviv. From May 15–21 they pounded the city, killing dozens of civilians. On May 18 they attacked the central bus station, killing forty-two and wounding dozens. Still, unlike Jerusalem, Tel-Aviv was not enduring extreme food and water shortages.

June 7, 1948
THE PALESTINE POST NEWS
INSIDE JERUSALEM

By Mordecai S. Chertoff
Palestine Post Correspondent

In Jerusalem, people picture Tel Aviv's "cardboard" houses collapsing in neat rows as enemy planes fly overhead, while after only a few hours in Tel Aviv the barrage of questions

---

3. Ann's son, Roy, told me that, with her degree in geology, his mother read maps and interpreted aerial photographs for the army.
4. Arabic, meaning "God willing."

as to what it's like in the Jerusalem "Diaspora" is almost enough to frighten one out of going back.

A full-time resident of the "besieged" city takes it for granted that Tel Avivians are simply expressing their sense of guilt over still having plenty of cigarettes to smoke and all the ice cream they can eat. With no phone communication between the two cities, and with wireless facilities overtaxed, the disparity between the real and the imagined situation is easy enough to understand, but still does not go far towards making a "recent arrival" from Jerusalem feel guiltless over his not betraying a gnawing hunger by breaking into grocery stores as he walks along Tel Aviv's busy streets.

There is still powdered milk for Jerusalem's children and fresh eggs are still included in their diets. Most food supplies have been rationed, but before the children go to school in the mornings they have had their breakfasts, as often with bread and butter or margarine as not. Almost all food is rationed – which is not so important in itself as is the fact that it is there to be rationed. Adults eat less, of course, but don't seem to mind particularly. They take comfort in talk about "Palmach," the commando striking force, and "summations" of the military situation invariably end with the unanswerable, "Well, another (any figure will do) 'Palmachniks' have just arrived. Just watch now."

Shelling Damage

Hardly any damage has been done to fashionable Rehavia, and Zion Square. The main targets of the Arab Legion's shelling show little wear-and-tear. In most of the areas that Tel Avivians believe "destroyed" by the shelling, one must look hard to find the damage.

A case in point is the building of the *Palestine Post*, which was bracketed by shells for an uncomfortable three hours one night. Some of the windows went and most of the electric cables went, but "Single Shot Charlie" helped the nerves from going. Nobody knows who posted him, wherever it is he's posted. All we know is that he squeezes one shot out of his pistol every time he sees the guns flash, and we have an average of fifteen seconds in which to prepare ourselves for the bang. When there is none, somebody or other in the office invariably mutters "dud," and everybody keeps working. People too impatient to wait out a shelling in a shelter have learned to count and time the bangs which occur usually in groups of six, with ten minute intervals, and manage to flit from shelter to shelter without losing too much time.

The really serious damage has been inflicted on the Hadassah Hospital on Mt. Scopus, where the X-ray, radium and surgery departments have been almost completely demolished, and on the former English Mission Hospital in Prophets Street, now used by Hadassah.

Morale High

Fuel is the biggest problem in Jerusalem. There was no Butagas for cooking long before the Mandate's final disappearance, and soon after oil supplies also gave out. With inadequate solar[5] fuel available for the electric generators, current has been severely rationed. Rather than rely on the skimpy supply and risk a cut cable, leaving the tea just half-boiled, many Jerusalemites have taken to cooking on open fires in their backyards.

Nobody questions Jewish ability to hold the New City. The two big questions monopolizing most conversations are: "What's happening at Latrun?" (which means "When will the road be really open") and "Will a truce be proclaimed before we beat the Legion to its knees?" Popular opinion seems to say "soon" to the first, and "let's hope not" to the second.

---

5.   Local Israeli term for diesel.

> Morale is high, and people would be sorry for Tel
> Aviv, cowering under a cloud of airplanes raining bombs
> from the skies, were it not for the theatres and concerts, the
> cinema and swimming also available under those same skies.

Perhaps in this upbeat article Mordecai wanted to convey – or was
encouraged to convey – an image of a confident, thriving Jewish Jerusalem to the public. It's easy to see how that would have bolstered the
new Israelis and dimmed the confidence of their attackers. But in truth,
the situation in Jerusalem had become desperate. There was constant
shelling and gunfire and Jews from outlying neighborhoods such as
Talpiot and Malha had to take refuge in more northern parts of the city.
Morale was not high and Ben-Gurion was afraid that Jerusalem would
surrender to the Arab Legion once ammunition ran out.

One of Mordecai's friends, Zippy Borowsky, a fellow 'student' at
Hebrew University turned medic for the Haganah, described the situation to her family in a letter sent during a cease-fire:

> ...there was hardly a single day or night, barely a single
> hour without an ever-present barrage of shooting, inces-
> sant explosions, merciless shelling, shrieking cries for help,
> without somebody being killed or wounded. Never a letup
> from constant fear and terror, never a moment's respite.
> There was little you could do to protect yourself – cower
> in a corner, drop to the ground, cover your head with your
> arms, hold your breath...hope that the whining of the mis-
> sile you heard wasn't meant for you.[6]

The food situation remained bleak, despite the few jeeps that had been
able to make the trip. The daily bread ration at the beginning of June
had been reduced to 160g per person, and the weekly ration of dried
foodstuffs was down to 100g wheat, 100g beans, 40g cheese, 100g coffee or 100g powdered milk, and 50g margarine, with one or two eggs
for the sick. In his letters, Mordecai does not complain much about the

---

6.   Zipporah Porath, *Letters from Jerusalem*, p. 176.

lack of food, probably in order to spare his family from worry but in his memoirs, he was more frank and less sanguine:

> There was black bread available, rationed at four slices per person per day. Those of us who had jobs to do in the Jewish Agency building on King George Road had a little halvah, since the boys had "liberated" an Arab halvah factory. I don't know whether the nine hundred calories we were reported to be getting during the siege was accurate; I do know that I lost twenty-five pounds, and the panels of my single-breasted jacket overlapped to make it double-breasted.

The siege was real. "No food" was not an exaggeration, but a literal description. As noted earlier, people harvested khubeiza, a weed that grew all over Jerusalem. They made soup and croquettes out of it – cooking over wood fires in the gardens because there was no fuel for the stoves.

Chapter 24

The Burma Road

With the situation in Jerusalem becoming ever more desperate, something had to be done. On May 21, Ben-Gurion instructed his commanders to find a different route from Tel Aviv to Jerusalem, to relieve the siege. After the capture of Bayt Susin, the Harel Brigade and the Seventh Brigade were only separated by a narrow strip of very mountainous territory. If a way through that territory could be found – a way out of reach of the guns of Latrun – a new route to Jerusalem might be opened.

Mordecai writes to his family from Tel-Aviv but does not explain how he made the periolous journey. That explanation comes later.

June 12, 1948

Dear Family,

I'm afraid I have to surprise you again: I'm in Tel Aviv. I don't know how long I'll stay, it depends on how soon the Arabs break the truce and there are more good fighting stories for me to cover for the paper. You see, that story I sent you "How Palmach Took Zion Gate" developed into quite a sensation in these parts, and the boys themselves were quite pleased. As a result, I was invited along on other jobs, one of which brought me to Tel Aviv this morning just in time to hear about the truce. When we left the firing was still fast and furious.

Let me tell you something about "my" unit — "Haportzim."[1] They are heroes, every last one of them. I would obey an order from their lowest officer telling me to walk upright into machine-gun cross-fire feeling safer than if any other outfit's top-man told me to hide behind a three-foot wall of steel plate. They know the business, they don't go in for splash, and they value each life very highly. The result is that every job is well-planned and carefully executed, and almost invariably successful. They are probably the most famous unit in the country by now, and you can't begin to imagine how proud I am that they've taken me in and see fit to consider me okay. Last night Azariah (my traveling-mate on these things) and I were given a note by Itzhak Rabin,[2] 27-year-old commander of "Harel" (Har-el) — Palmach, in all of the Jerusalem sector, saying simply: take these two men to Tel Aviv, they're okay, and they help us." Result — we're here. We usually travel in the staff armoured car, and are right up there with the boss when a job is under way. I don't know whether this information will make you worry more or less — after all, generals always die in bed — but it certainly is no more dangerous than Jerusalem when the shells begin to fly around.

My big surprise was when I got here, to Tel Aviv. After a wonderful hot bath at Fish's (remember there's precious little water in Jerusalem these days) and a luxurious barbershop shave and a real breakfast, I trotted over to the office

---

1.   The 4th Battalion of the Palmach (lit. "those who break through").

2.   Yitzchak Rabin (1922–1995) joined the Palmach as a teenager and rose through the ranks to become its chief of operations during the War of Independence. He was Chief of the General Staff during the Six-Day War in 1967 and served as Israel's ambassador to the United States from 1968–1973, during a period of deepening U.S.–Israel ties. He served two terms as prime minister. The second ended when he was assassinated on November 4, 1995. Unfortuantely, I did not find the note Rabin wrote.

to say hello, and found the letter you had given Sidorsky, with my article.... Air mail does go to Tel Aviv, and from here office stuff gets to Jerusalem a few times a week. One must be patient, I guess.

Understanding how you feel, I can also understand how the parents of my friends feel, and so I insist upon your doing a little phoning. Call Mrs. Borowsky, tell her Zippy is fine, I saw her just before I left Jerusalem. Call Rabbi B. Charny, 1244 e. 13 Street, Brooklyn, tell him that I was with Carmi most of the night before I left Jerusalem, we're living together, you know. He's written some good poetry since he's here too. Call Efros, tell him his wife and kid are okay (pains in the arse, but that's incidental). And last, but by far most important, drop a line to the Strausses in Cleveland, tell them Ann looks wonderful, is fine, working hard and well (for the Haganah, of course) and is one reason I refuse to remain in Tel Aviv more than a few days. One worries so about one's friends at the front! That finishes the agony column.

Here's a little news which will be stale by the time you get it, so that my divulging it and prophesying is really putting me out on a limb. Palmach is being given control over the Battle of the Roads again,[3] which includes the vicious Latrun area. I believe that by the end of the week I'll be able to go back to Jerusalem over the main highway in a simple taxi. *Um gottes willen!*[4]

I may add that I've just spent a wonderful week at the Palmach camp in Kiryat Anavim, where I had three cubic (that's more than square) meals a day, and plenty of sunshine. I feel like a million bucks, and people claim that I'm thriving on the war. Nu nu.

---

3.   Although there is a truce and the Burma Road is operating, the Arabs still control the main highway between Tel Aviv and Jerusalem via their stranglehold at Latrun.
4.   German, meaning "God willing."

You'll have to forgive me now – I'm going shopping for my Jerusalem friends, for cigarettes and such things, and I want to see Izzy Stone too. I'll write you again before I leave Tel Aviv.

That's all for now – and write.

All my love –

the Brat (P.P. Military Correspondent, if you please)

While in Tel Aviv, Mordecai wrote about life in Tel Aviv – a dramatic contrast to his description of life in Jersualem.

June 14, 1948

TEL AVIV AND BACK

By Mordecai S. Chertoff

TEL AVIV, Thursday – There are people here who don't really believe that Jerusalem still stands. Those who do – who know the difference between the New and Old cities, assume that what is left is held together by bits of wire and tape. Some of them actually seem upset that I don't look gaunt and haggard, as though Jerusalem has been the object of sympathy evoked under false pretences.

It might be something of a mass-masochism that inspires the kind of questions they ask here:

"Nobody walks in the streets, of course....?"

"Where have they sent the children?"

"Isn't anything at all open?"

It is more likely the compulsion to know the worst immediately. When after hesitant questioning they learn that Rehavia hasn't suffered particularly and that the Jewish Agency building is still there, there is inevitably a barrage of personal questions.

Genuine Concern

Tel Aviv, barely feeling the war and showing hardly any scars in the city proper, is genuinely worried about Jerusalem, and while offers to send back a bar or two of chocolate are hardly either realistic or practical, they are sincere and heart-felt enough to render a Jerusalemite anxious to allay their fears and almost automatically provoke him into insisting that nobody in our beleaguered city needs anything.

Tel Aviv itself has everything, of course. From regular bus service to strawberries-and-cream, from constant electricity, concerts, theatre and cinema to taps running water, some of it hot, and fountains playing in the sunlight in the public gardens.

There are far fewer uniforms around than one would expect, although a seemingly endless stream of vehicles bear the "Army" label, some with the special Air Force or Navy insignia. Although arms have been banned within the city limits, there are as many pistols – all shapes and sizes – being worn in hotel lobbies and bars as there are in Jerusalem's streets.

Total Blackout

The most immediate signs of the war are the uniformly dirty-brown "Dan" buses and the automobiles wearing hats of twig-bearing netting, camouflaged against low-flying Egyptian raiders. And the most depressing sign of the war is the total blackout in Tel Aviv homes and streets, a blackout which cuts visibility to almost nothing, but cuts traffic – both velocity and quantity – almost by nothing. To walk the dark streets dodging traffic and pedestrians simultaneously calls for "Tel Aviv eyes," which I won't be here long enough to acquire.

After a command appearance – or performance – on [radio program] "Kol Israel," in an attempt to tell Tel Aviv what Jerusalem is like in five minutes, all there is left for me to do here is pack for the return trip – not forgetting the 27 letters I have already been asked to deliver.

In his letter to his family, Mordecai did not explain that he had been staying with the Palmach unit tasked with finding a new route between Tel Aviv and Jerusalem. On May 31 he embarked with them on a dangerous adventure through the Jerusalem hills to Tel Aviv, just as Operation Bin Nun Bet – the second attempt to take Latrun – was underway nearby.

Once the operation was declassified, this dramatic journey would become the focus of several articles, each revealing more details than the last. I am including only his most detailed, published account.[5]

The road that Mordecai describes in his article below was called the Burma Road, after the road linking Burma with the southwest of China. The Asian original was built during the Second Sino-Japanese War in 1937–1938, and was then used by the British during World War II to transport material to China. One of the British Royal Engineers who worked on the Burma Road during the Second World War was George Trenter, a German Jew who had escaped Germany in 1939 and joined the British army. He became expert at building roads under difficult conditions. Trenter had long been involved in Zionist activities and willingly came to Israel to help with the road. He met with Mickey Marcus,[6] the American commander of the force responsible for freeing Jerusalem and recommended several changes and techniques for completing the project. The road had originally been called Road Seven, after the Seventh Brigade whose men built it, but was then renamed the Burma Road.[7]

---

5. See also "Led by Pillar of Dust by Night" Mordecai's shorter account published in the *Post* on June 18, 1948, p. 4. Available online via http://web.nli.org.il/sites/JPress/English/Pages/Palestine-Post.aspx.

6. David Daniel "Mickey" Marcus (Feb. 22, 1901 – June 10, 1948) was a United States Army colonel who assisted Israel during the war. He became Israel's first modern general. He was killed by friendly fire when he was mistaken for an enemy infiltrator while returning to Israeli positions at night.

7. Most of the information for this paragraph comes from an article concerning the British Zionist Federation, "The ZF Burma Connection" by Dr. Zvi Han, *Zionist Review* (April 1983), and was brought to my attention by my cousin, Joe Sofair.

By June 10, just before the first cease-fire, the Burma road was open and convoys could finally reach the starving city. Mordecai's account was published almost two weeks later.

June 22, 1948

THE "BURMA ROAD" STORY

By Mordecai S. Chertoff

It began with three men on foot, moving down through the Judean hills in the darkness to the thunder of cannon and crack of rifles at Latrun. Today it is an unpaved road over which lorries climb towards Jerusalem from Tel Aviv with their load of supplies and solidarity.

The three were picked from Palmach's "Haportzim," the unit which had learned every inch of the way during the original road-clearing operations, "Nahshon" and "Maccabi." They were assigned by Palmach brigade headquarters "Har-el" (Mt. of God, the name defining the area of operations – Jerusalem and its vicinity) to find a new route through to the coast, to determine whether it was at all possible to skirt the Latrun battlefield, to by-pass the few hundred metres of road the Arab Legion was so convinced could control all traffic to Jerusalem.

We watched the three leave their base somewhere in the hills, and kept the night-long vigil at headquarters, waiting for the radio message from their goal – the advanced Israel Defence Army[8] post – that they had-arrived. The dawn shelling from the nearby Legion mortars went unheeded as the field radio came to life: along a goat's trail, threading their way between towering boulders and thick brambles, with flares from the Latrun area forcing them to take cover

---

8.   It seems that what is now the standard translation of *Tzava leHaganah leYisrael* as "Israel Defense Forces" had not yet become established.

every few moments, they had arrived. For two hours they had crouched in the lee of a bare rock-formation barely a hundred metres from a Jewish post, waiting for the light of morning to reveal them as friends.

The following night we went out to meet the three scouts, now returning with reinforcements for Jerusalem's Palmach brigade. The tense silence of the night was suddenly shattered by an excited babble from the wireless operator, cut off by the commander's wry observation: "use the radio, Itzhakele, it's easier on the lungs."

They were back. We stood out on the road watching the clouds scud by, listening for the tread of marching men. It came, faint at first and then strong and sure as they came closer and passed in nocturnal review before a handful of tired hosts.

Following the Trail

Two correspondents and three men on leave decided to follow the trail when the next night fell, planning to return to the advanced Jerusalem base with the escort due to arrive with the first jeep convoy to try out the road.

We crawled along the thorny floor of the wadi until the moon ducked behind a cloud, giving us a chance to run until a contrary wind bared it once again. It was flop and run, flop and run, until something warned me to flop again out of turn: as I hit the now dusty stretch and my musette bag[9] bounced to a rest beside my head a mortar bomb exploded what must have been inches away. The explosion covered me with earth, and a fragment ripped through the musette bag, tore into the front of my camera case within it, and scored a bulls-eye on the lens. I lost a good camera, but nothing more.

---

9.   A small leather or canvas bag issued by the US military, with shoulder strap, used during hiking or marching.

First Jeeps

We stood on the road again the following night, and watched the first jeep convoy slither up the last few metres of the gravel track and climb onto the stretch of main road this side of Latrun, a stretch that has been in Jewish hands all along. And the night after that we set out with the first convoy of jeeps to go down to Tel Aviv. They were going empty, to bring another load of supplies to "beleaguered" Jerusalem.

This time we got through without incident, without unexpected incident, that is. But we got down to Tel Aviv only after we had taken our places along the stonier stretches of road to help coax the jeeps just so many inches to the left and so many to the right, to help them thread their way between the rocks. We got through after we had slid down a gulley alongside the jeeps, which had to be brought down one at a time at that particular point, and seemed to take to the air in the descent.

We were in Tel Aviv for a week, a week during which work on the road night after night made it easy for our jeeps on the return trip. During that week "meat-on-the-hoof" was driven to Jerusalem along that road; supplies were brought in, on trucks as far as the trucks could take them, then carried on the backs of men and borne over the few hundred metres of still-difficult road, and finally loaded onto jeeps again for the last stages of the trip. During that trip fuel was brought to Jerusalem: the petrol tanks could not be carried across that stretch of the rocky route, so they were set up in one wagon and tanks from Jerusalem were set up in the next, and the precious fuel was siphoned across the intervening rocks.

Customs Post

We passed a new customs control point as we left Israel, winding our way through a series of road-blocks and barricades. We drove through a deserted Arab village – deserted except for our own patrols, men of our regular army who cheered as we passed in the gathering darkness, men who cheered because they had seen the traffic grow from three lone meagre convoys of jeeps, and from jeeps to the lorries that were with us a good part of the trip.

The mountain we crossed driving down was much easier – squads of men had worked at it, blasting away with dynamite and nosing boulders away with bulldozers under cover of diversionary attacks in the Latrun sector nearby. But the stretch of improvised road, before the sweep onto the "Jerusalem section" of the old main road is within range of distant Arab mortars at Latrun, and as we raced by in the chalky ground a flare lit up the hilltops over the tree to our right, the well near it – and the line of jeeps, and mortar bombs exploded around us, spurring drivers to greater speed making us cling to the sacks of powdered milk under us, lest we be jolted off the bouncing jeeps. From the surrounding hilltops Israeli Army and Palmach units provided heavy answering fire, and within five minutes after the flare we were on the main road, protected by the towering hills on both sides.

Last Lap

A few minutes later the jeep jolted to a stop, and their supplies were loaded onto trucks for the last stage of the journey – the straight, quiet run up to Jerusalem itself.

For us, the trip was over. For the jeeps, and their amazing drivers, it was only half the trip. Within half an hour they would be on their way back to Israel to bring another modest shipment of supplies.

The existence of the route is no longer secret – it is now a matter of pride, a source of infinite satisfaction to the men of "Haportzim" who first established it as a possibility, and to the Israeli Army and the Palmach units who protected them and brought through the early convoys.

Three men went walking on a cloudy summer's night down the hills of Judea, and the siege of Jerusalem was broken. Whatever the diplomatic or fighting war may bring, Jerusalem has its own lifeline to the coast.

Gershon Agronsky liked Mordecai's story and wrote: "I am glad that in the end you wrote your own rather than re-write the Magen story on the 'Burma Road.' It's vivid, readable, and has an authentic ring to it: What more can one expect?" (June 22, 1948).

By the end of the first month of the conventional war, Jordan had succeeded in taking much of the area now known as the West Bank, including the Etzion Bloc. They also controlled East Jerusalem and the Old City, and had completely destroyed the Jewish Quarter and all of its synagogues. The Jews managed to maintain control over West Jerusalem, had reestablished travel between Jerusalem and Tel Aviv, and had acquitted themselves well against the professional, British-led Arab Legion.

Mordecai does not address the situation on other fronts, but this, in brief, was what was happening elsewhere:

As previously noted, Egypt entered the war by bombing Tel Aviv. The aerial attacks went on for six days. On land, their expeditionary troops crossed into Israel and began moving north. They reached the southern border of the land allocated to the Palestinians, cutting off and isolating more than twenty Israeli settlements. A decisive battle was fought at Isdud (later, Ashdod), where an Israeli airborne attack halted the Egyptian advance, inflicting significant psychological damage on the poorly-motivated Egyptians. By the end of May, the Egyptians had lost most of their Spitfire[10] squadron based in El Arish (in Sinai) and had abandoned their plans to drive toward Tel Aviv.

In the north, the Iraqis had entered Palestine via Jordan and acted as their "junior partner," operating primarily in the northern West Bank area of Samaria. There were major battles in the Jenin area, which the Jews lost, but the Iraqis hunkered down in the Triangle and did not press their advantage.

---

10. It should be noted that, in an ironic twist of fate, the Egyptians were flying British-made Spitfires, while the Jews were flying German-made Messerschmitts (pointed out by David Olesker).

The Syrians had entered Palestine via the Golan, with only vague military objectives. On May 15 some of their forces attacked kibbutz Ein Gev, on the eastern shore of the Sea of Galilee, but this was only a diversion – another force pushed further south, toward Samekh, at the southern tip of the sea. They continued westwards but were stopped at the perimeter gates of Kibbutzim Degania Aleph and Bet. The Jews were able to drive the Syrians back, almost to the previously recognized border of Palestine at Tel-al-Qasir, and reoccupied Samekh. As a result of this defeat, the senior Syrian military establishment resigned. The second prong of their attack was more successful; the Syrians managed to advance up to Kibbutz Ayelet Hashachar in the Northern Galilee, acquiring a toehold west of the Jordan River.

As noted earlier, the Lebanese did not invade. They had a small, weak army and a large Maronite Christian population which had a positive relationship with the Jews of the Yishuv and supported the establishment of the Jewish State. Nevertheless, in order to claim that it had participated, Lebanon deployed its army defensively and offered its support to the Arab Liberation Army. The main battle on this front was fought at the abandoned village of al-Malkiyya, on the Lebanese border. The village changed hands several times, but by June 8 was held by the ALA.

After four weeks of fighting, Israel had beaten back the four-pronged Arab attack and was in a surprisingly strong position in terms of territory. They held much of the land earmarked for the Jewish State and in some areas, had added to it – Jaffa, the Western Galilee and the Jerusalem Corridor were theirs.[11] Most importantly, the strategic initiative rested with the Jews. In addition, the Israelis enjoyed a measure of international political support since the Arabs were widely viewed as the aggressors.

---

11.   Morris, *1948*, p. 263.

Chapter 25

The First Truce:
June 11 – July 8, 1948

Hard on the heels of the declaration of the State and the subsequent Arab invasion, the UN began efforts to stop the fighting. On the twentieth of May, Count Folke Bernadotte[1] was appointed UN mediator in the conflict. Two days later the Security Council called urgently for a truce to be implemented. The Israelis agreed but the Arabs did not. To do so would expose the lie they were telling their people – that they were beating the Jews and driving them out. The Arab leaders were afraid of the Arab "street." A week later, the Security Council again called on both sides to cease hostilities for a period of four weeks. This time both sides agreed. The four-week truce was set to begin on June 11. One of the conditions of the truce was an arms embargo on both sides.

---

1. Folke Bernadotte, Count of Wisborg (1895–1948) was a Swedish diplomat and nobleman. During World War II he negotiated the release of about 31,000 prisoners from German concentration camps, including 450 Danish Jews from Theresienstadt.

June 22, 1948

Dear Family,

...

    Gershon – Judy Avrunin[2] told me last night that she spoke to mother over the phone, and that mother's message included an injunction to me to be a good Zionist and a good soldier. The first I can fulfill, the second I'm afraid is no longer possible. I've left active service in the Haganah,[3] and am now an accredited war correspondent for the *Palestine Post*. It means a chance to go places and see things, to write and have the stuff printed, and to wear a blue-and-white shoulder flash with "War Correspondent" on its lower border and *"Katav Zvai"*[4] along the top. It also means being stopped by every Jew in Jerusalem and being asked what's "really happening." Frankly, I enjoy the degree of notoriety and publicity it affords. You know I'm essentially an exhibitionist! It has also meant something else. After my story about the Mt. Zion shindig, run by Palmach, and my stories about that same group in a number of other places, I am now an honorary member of "Haportzim," the famous Gdud IV[5] which fought throughout Jerusalem and twice opened the main Jerusalem-Tel Aviv highway, besides their part in the famous Castel fighting. I'm crazy about the boys, and I would unhesitatingly obey any order, regardless

---

2.   A *Palestine Post* representative in Haifa.
3.   There are no letters describing his initial induction because, under the British, the Haganah was illegal and Mordecai did not want any written evidence of his membership. He only describes his military career after the state is declared. It is not clear how he could just "leave" active service. He had joined the Haganah when he first arrived in Palestine in a clandestine position that afforded him much flexibility and the freedom to work for the *Post*. He will be formally drafted in July to a position that affords him no independence. It is possible that this difference reflects the evolution of the Haganah from an underground, "loose" organization to an established one with a more formal structure.
4.   Hebrew, meaning "military correspondent."
5.   Fourth Battalion.

of how distorted the judgment behind it seemed to me. And that, I'm sure, is the secret of Palmach's success: the men rely on their officers, they know they can be trusted, there is a real camaraderie, a real bond, between all ranks. They're indescribable. They come from all the world, but they have this in common, in addition to their love for the country and their real hope to be able to return to their jobs as farmers or seamen: they were trained together, they lived together for two years, working and drilling together, and they understand each other. Of late something of this common history has been lost through the replacement of fallen comrades by new recruits, who have not had time to absorb the Palmach spirit. Of "my" *gdud*, which began with 800 men, less than one fourth are still alive, of them only about 100 of the original group still fit for combat duty. Heavy losses, but for every man gone there are vast areas of New Jerusalem safely Jewish, and many, many civilians alive who otherwise would not be. But I better stop – I'll have me in tears soon. Pray for them, that all their heroism and sacrifice be not wasted and made futile by petty statesmen and mean diplomats.

I'm well, as you've probably heard from chubby, charming Izzy Stone by now. I spent a few days and a few of his pounds with him in Tel Aviv, and got along well with him. I'm waiting to hear from him now, and if it comes in the form I anticipate I'll have good news for you.

With this letter are a number of clippings from the *Post*, evidence of what I've been doing and where I've been during the past few weeks. I hope you like them. GA is pleased with my having had me appointed war correspondent, and shows it by continually asking for more stories. As long as paper stocks in Jerusalem hold out I'll be able to oblige – and then I'll run down to Tel Aviv for more!

...David Goldberg and his wife, Ida, are leaving for the US in a few days, and I've bought their beautiful radio-phonograph combination (with automatic record-changer) and about a dozen albums of records. So – when David hands you a note from me asking for the paltry sum of $100 (one hundred dollars) you'll know why. Pay it, of course, and simply debit my account with you that much. All we need now is some electricity here in Jerusalem! (We'll have it by the time you get this letter.) If you still needed it, the purchase should obviate any doubts you might have had about where this scion of the Chertoff family plans to make his home. This does not, of course, preclude the visit I've mentioned in other letters. When peace comes to Palestine I propose to make the trip. Now, I can't very well leave.

…During the worst part of the Great Hunger I was part of the time in Tel Aviv – where everything is to be had – and part of the time with the Palmach, at their camp, where there was not much variety, but what there was was damned good: Why complain about varying a diet of egg and coffee for breakfast and meat and potatoes for lunch, with the usual bread and jam or margarine, and tea or coffee! Which is why I look as though I haven't been in Jerusalem long, and people still ask me about the State, as though I'd arrived here in Jerusalem only yesterday.

And that's about all there is for the present. It's about all I'll write for the present anyway – until I hear from you. There's more, of course, lots, lots more, but it will keep.

…

lehitraot,

The brat.

Mordecai's father is not pleased with his son's job of war correspondent. In a long objection written on July 9 he describes his worries about the personal risks the job entails:

You wrote that you have attained the title of "military reporter," and that your current job is different than what it was previously. What is now your arrangement regarding salary with the *P.P.*? You say that this job has many advantages and that you are thrilled about it. I must admit that for myself, I'm not thrilled about it. I read the piece you wrote in the *P.P.* about the new road, and I see that you were in a truly dangerous place ... even after you attributed the clash resulting from the bombing in [?] to the fertile imagination of a military reporter, the road was still very dangerous in any event ... And especially now that the fighting has resumed, you will need to be at the fighting front ... these thoughts will not give me peace and it's impossible to put them out of my mind for even one minute. To my many worries about the situation in Israel in general, have now been added pressing worries about my son, whose soul is bound to my soul ...[6]

Despite his concern about the dangers inherent in the job, Paul nevertheless does not forget to ask about salary!

During the truce, the *Post* carried several stories about the improving situation in Jerusalem. Food rations were increasing, yet on June 23, the *Post* still deemed it newsworthy that eggs, poultry and kerosene were available in Jerusalem and, on the 25th, that there was fresh fish in the market. Over the next few weeks, the *Post* will continue to report on which foodstuffs are available.

June 25, 1948

Dearest Toots, my favorite sister;

...

I hope Izzy Stone has phoned the folks by now – I spent a few days with him in Tel Aviv, and was enchanted with the guy. As far as I can judge – and from what he seems to have told Ann when he got to Jerusalem for a few hours one day subsequently – his impression of me is not all bad. Be that as it may – and I'll get back to Izzy and

6.   Evoking Gen. 44:30.

Ann anon – he was excellent company, and we took a run to Rishon Lezion together to see the results of the air raid there[7] (horrible!) and interview Ostershinsky.[8] The old boy was quite pleasantly surprised when I unmasked as a relative at the end of the interview, and invited me to come over "socially" and spend some time with him, etc. He was very pleasant indeed.

Comment on the Haifa campaign, or what the British did in Jaffa, both of which you mention in your letters, would of course be out of date now. It all seems so long ago that we cleaned Haifa and took over Jaffa, so long ago that the Etzion bloc fell, that Neve Shaanan and Atarot fell, that the Old City of Jerusalem fell, that we cleaned up almost all of the New City and suddenly found ourselves in "*Galut* Jerusalem"[9] far far from the state. The big stuff now is the Egyptian bombing of the Negev convoy,[10] in spite of the truce, and the I.Z.L. show in Tel Aviv.[11] On the former, all I can say is that I do not think it means the end of the truce, I think the bastards are just chiseling, trying to get all they can militarily until they're stopped by the UN. Bernadotte knows whether the truce will last out the month or be extended, but I'm afraid he won't tell me. If the truce does die, the Holy City, as the *trefa goyim*[12] insist on calling it, will be in for another pasting. But I don't think it will last 28 days, or even that many hours: what I just heard about the Israel

7. In addition to the six days of aerial bombardment of Tel Aviv by the Egyptians at the start of the war, on May 30, the Egyptians hit Eqron Airfield (now the site of the Israel Air Force Tel Nof Airbase) and the center of the town of Rehovot, killing seven and wounding thirty. Rishon Lezion must have been another of the areas hit, although I have not found any reports on it beyond this letter.

8. The Ostershinskys lived in Rishon Lezion. They were related to the Chertoffs, but I do not know how. Esther mentions him in the correspondence of 1935–36.

9. *Galut* means exile in Hebrew.

10. The Egyptians violated the truce several times. Mordecai is probably referring to the Egyptian attack at Isdud in the Gaza district.

11. A reference to the *Altalena* affair, described further below.

12. Hebrew, meaning "non-kosher non-Jews" – obviously an insult.

Air Force from one who should know just yesterday leaves me rather hopeful that the blacks will get a few nice little air-mail packages which may well discourage them from continuing. I do think that Tel Aviv will get the worst of it, since it is the seat of Government and the military H.Q. as well – as far as the blacks know.

Jerusalem is known as a *"bardak"* (Arabic for whore-house) as far as Haganah goes; we seem to always draw the s**ts for commanders. The Hadassah convoy is a case in point. For over seven hours the slaughter went on while men under arms in a base within spitting distance practically sat on their haunches: the C.O.[13] was busy considering how sending men there would affect the position vis-a-vis I.Z.L., he was wary because of unspecified political considerations, etc. In brief, nothing was done, and many good men died, needlessly. (Dov arrived in Haifa the day his father, Yassky, died!) If the O.C. was right, that there was nothing he could do, he should have demanded a public investigation, to clear himself of very nasty charges; if wrong, there should be a public inquiry to prove it, and pay him his just desserts. The same thing had happened before, with a convoy to Atarot,[14] when 17 were killed who might have been saved had he done his military job and sent the men – available men – to the spot. On May 15 we could have over-run the Old City and taken it, easily: all the blacks were busy at Etzion. A number of Sternists had actually climbed the wall, and asked for covering fire from Haganah men. Haganah on the spot radioed to H.Q. for two platoons of reinforcements (about 20 men) and permission to advance. They were ignored, and the opportunity was lost. When Palmach broke through Zion Gate (see my story in *Palpost*, mailed ages ago and again yesterday) we could have taken over again: our "secret weapon" was used for the first time in this

13. David Shaltiel, C.O. of the Jerusalem sector. He will be discussed later in connection with the failed final attempt to take the Old City, July 16–17.
14. March 24, 1948. Described above.

area, and induced such a panic among the Arabs that the Armenian Quarter was ours for the asking. Palmach needed men to hold a number of points within the Quarter, points dominating the area, which would have put the Arabs in the Old City on the defensive. None were forthcoming, and so another great opportunity was lost. (We've got enough heroes, not enough top-leaders!) There were other things, too, but this is enough for the present. Mickey Marcus (who was known here by the nickname "Stone")[15] was to be the C.O.'s superior, he was to be in charge of all military operations: he died accidentally. And there are those who are not sure it was an accident, and others who claim that if there had been none, one would have been arranged by interested people: the Jerusalem C.O., for one, and a number of commanders of the Latrun debacle whom Stone was to bring up before a military court for another. How true these charges are nobody knows, and probably never will, but they are not at all impossible. This C.O. is now out, and we're waiting for the new man to show up. All three possibilities named for the job are good men, as far as we now know. We'll wait and see what happens.

...Which brings me to the Ann question again...

There is the other, more usual question: is (Miss) Barkis a'willin'?[16] I've given up at least part of my self-analyses, and readily admit that at the drop of a syllable I would marry her, the syllable being "yes," of course, I display all the symptoms: nervousness as I type, waiting for her with half an ear cocked for her voice; fits of jealousy upon seeing her with another guy; envy of the people in the office where she does her bit for the war-effort, since they have the pleasure of her company without any need for planning meetings, etc.; butterflies when chance brings us together in

---

15. Colonel "Mickey" Marcus. See chapter 24, footnote 6.
16. A reference to the stagecoach driver, Mr. Barkis, in Charles Dickens' *David Copperfield*. Persistent in his courtship of David Copperfield's nurse, Peggotty, he asks David to tell her that "Barkis is willin'" – to marry her.

the street; worried figuring-up of the latest odds every time we exchange a few sentences and the usual preoccupation with the eternal "what does she think of me?" heightened more than is usual by the constant doubt as to her opinion over every bit of Chertoffiana appearing in the *Palpost*. She almost never says anything about the pieces, and of course I find me trying to provoke something by showing her the little chits[17] of t.l.[18] I occasionally get from Agronsky (that's to impress you too, incidentally!).

...

Jeezuz, I hate wimmen! Before going on to the "naughty Jew,"[19] I may point out that Ann has had more than a little to do with it, whereas with Kepi there never was any question at all, and no need for rationalization or analysis, neither in regard to observance or to the lack of it. She enjoyed ritual the way you do, and took pleasure in it the way any of "our" kind of Jew would. Would, incidentally, is something I can't help but remembering every time I decide "to hell with it" and begin thinking of alternatives...[R]eligiously [Hadassah Frisch] ... was about half-way between Kepi and Ann... Like the insect in Titus' ear[20] a couple of centuries back, the three gals keep chasing each other around in a circle – in my head. (Although Hadassah may have retained her place in it primarily as a result of her being somewhat in the nature of "unfinished business," me feeling sure I could have swung it had I been there, and still believing, deep down, that were I there now, I could overcome all competition and sweep the prize off [on] my white horse – or dust-covered jeep (I've ridden both).)

...

---

17. A short note or receipt for a small debt, typically a small sum of money or food.
18. Stands for "*tochas* licking," i.e., sucking up.
19. Probably a reference to the fact he is becoming less religiously observant.
20. The Talmud (*Gittin* 56b) recounts how the Emperor Titus, responsible for the destruction of the Second Temple in Jerusalem, was tormented for many years by a buzzing sound caused by a gnat or some other insect entering his ear.

Slight change in plan: I'm going to defer the "naughty Jew" letter[21] for a few days, because if I start it now it will take more hours than there are between now and Varda's departure for Tel Aviv.

For the present, then, Shabbat Shalom, and all my love.

mersh.

P.S., Write, kid, care of the Tel Aviv office. Our contact with them is now good, and I'll get it within two days after it arrives in the country. And don't wait too long before you write – not hearing is worse than not eating, and I've had to do both.

---

21. Unfortunately, never found, and perhaps never written.

Chapter 26

The *Altalena*

Before his sorry description of the state of his love life, Mordecai refers to the *Altalena* incident, which came to a head on the 20th and 21st of June. After the State was declared, in May, agreements were reached with the Irgun and the Lehi to integrate their fighters into the Haganah, which would then become the new army of Israel. This was a complicated process, made more so by the outbreak of the war and the fact that many of the Irgun fighters were in besieged Jerusalem. As the headline of Mordecai's article (below) implies, the new IDF was viewed as a continuation of the Haganah.

Before the declaration of the State, the Irgun had procured arms and ammunition abroad and were bringing them – together with nine hundred volunteer fighters – into the country on board the *Altalena*. The ship was initially scheduled to arrive before the State was declared but a series of delays caused it to arrive much later – after the Irgun was already part of, and subordinate to, the Israel Defense Forces (IDF). Menachem Begin, head of the Irgun, informed David Ben-Gurion of the ship's movements and the two men agreed upon where it should land. But when Begin requested that the arms be sent specifically to Irgun men within the IDF, Ben-Gurion refused; the government had to be in control of all fighting men. There could be no "army within an army," or the country could descend into chaos.

Ben-Gurion ordered the Irgun to hand over the ship but the Irgun refused. A gun fight erupted at Kfar Vitkin between Irgunists sent to unload the ship and IDF soldiers sent to prevent its landing. Two soldiers and six Irgunists were killed before the Irgunists on shore surrendered. In the meantime, the boat continued on toward Tel Aviv. Ben-Gurion had declared the Irgun's actions traitorous: "Jewish independence will not endure if every individual group is free to establish its own military force and to determine political facts affecting the future of the State."[1]

The IDF forces that were assembling on the Tel Aviv beach were soldiers of the Palmach, whose own integration into the IDF was not yet complete when they were fired on by men on the *Altalena*. IDF officers refused orders to sink the ship. The soldier who finally did agree was apparently Hillel Daleski,[2] a South African immigrant who later became a prominent scholar of English literature at the Hebrew University. The ship was set ablaze. Those still on board jumped off and swam to shore where IDF soldiers were instructed to help them to safety. Ten Irgunists were killed in the gunfight.

The *Altalena* affair was a turning point for Israeli defense organizations. By ordering his people to stand down, Menachem Begin avoided civil war. The IDF took over the Irgun's headquarters in Tel Aviv and arrested many of the Irgun's leaders but released most of them relatively quickly. Ironically, the IDF troops enforcing the unity of Israeli forces was an as yet unabsorbed unit of the Palmach, fighting what was to be that organization's final action.

The Irgun fighters were eventually integrated into the regular Israeli army. In an article published on June 28, Mordecai described the formalization of the army including a detailed description of the new, formal military ranks:

---

1. From a Government Press Office bulletin issued on June 21, 1948, quoted in Martin Gilbert, *Israel: A History* (New York, 1998), p. 211.
2. Hillel Daleski (1926–2010) was born in South Africa and fought with the South African army in Italy during WWII.

Monday, June 28, 1948

Jerusalem

HAGANAH BECOMES ISRAEL ARMY

At the Israel Army General Staff Headquarters somewhere in Palestine, a number of top staff officers yesterday pledged allegiance to the State of Israel and to its Army as the Minister of Defence, Mr. D. Ben Gurion, administered the oath.

At Army services today officers and men will take the oath. The names of the Commanders and Staffs, which have long been kept secret, will be disclosed, thus marking the complete emergence of the "Haganah" from the underground as the Defence Army of Israel.[3]

At the ceremony yesterday, the Chief of the General Staff, Jacob Dostrowsky, was absent because of illness. The Defence Minister addressed the men, stressing the privilege of being able to serve the Jewish State in the Jewish Army in its own homeland – a privilege, he said, which had been denied to hundreds of thousands of Jewish soldiers in all lands throughout the centuries.

The Pledge

Following the ceremony, Area Commanders returned to their commands, and administered the oath to their staff officers who, today, will in turn give the oath to their men. The ceremony will take place in all Army camps in Israel, and by day's end every soldier will have pledged himself to dedicate his life to "the defence of the homeland and the freedom of Israel."

The Chief Rabbinate here has prepared a special prayer for the occasion to be recited at Army services

---

3. *Tzava Hagana leYisrael* is now routinely referred to in English as the Israel Defense Forces (IDF). When used in the Hebrew Bible, *tzava* is sometimes translated as "host," meaning a large body of men, or even angels.

today for the first time. The pledge which every member of the Army will take is:

> I pledge allegiance to the State of Israel; to its laws and duly constituted authorities; and I undertake to accept without condition or reservation the authority of the Israel Defence Army; to obey the orders and instructions issued by its authorized commanders and officers; and to dedicate my strength and my life to the defence of the homeland and the freedom of Israel.

Immediately following the ceremony in Tel Aviv the Commander of the Jerusalem District returned to Jerusalem where last night he gave the oath to the representatives of the Second Echelon. In turn the battalion commanders and staff officers were administered the oath.

The officers were paraded, and after the pledge was read, names were called out alphabetically. After each officer was called, he replied, "I Swear." A large Zionist flag used for the occasion was the same which was hoisted by a Company of the Jewish Brigade over its H.Q. in Benghazi in 1943. As a result of the action, the Company, which was then part of the Palestine Regiment, was disarmed and confined to barracks. Later the flag was flown in Austria and Antwerp.

Biblical Ranks

Officers of the Israel Army will have ranks with terminology adopted from designations used in biblical times. Equivalent ranks in foreign armies are only approximate since the Israel Army is not modelled after any of them. Some of the ranks are:

Rav Aloof (Brigadier) – originally indicated the commander of more than a thousand men, and in a later biblical period signified a ruler or commander (approximately equivalent to Brigadier).

Aloof (similar to Colonel);
Rav Seren (Lieut.-Col.);
Seren (Major) – a rank of Philistine noblemen;
Rav Sagan, Sagan Rishon, and **Sagan** (Captain, 1st Lieutenant, 2nd Lieutenant) – honorary titles used during the Babylonian exile.[4]

Non-commissioned officers are called after the unit which they command, such as "Section Commander." Men without rank are *"turaim."*

Order of the Day

The Chief of Staff of the Israel Defence Army had issued the following Order of the Day on the occasion of the swearing-in of the men and women of the security forces:

Conscious of our duty, and in a spirit of dedication, we pledge allegiance to the State of Israel which has arisen and been fashioned in our day and sanctified by the blood of thousands of our people and springing from the yearning of generations thirsting for freedom, deliverance and liberty.

Let us remember at this moment those from among us who did not grudge lives – young and precious – and bequeathed to us, and our children after us, a life of liberty and self-reliance in our liberated homeland.

May their pure blood serve as an eternal monument for us, a source of self-sacrifice and a heritage or courage, for us to follow until our State arises, a sturdy bulwark and sure refuge for the people of Israel.

With this our oath of allegiance to our State, we proclaim this day before the world that we have sworn not to lay down our arms; to spare ourselves neither burden nor toil, to flinch from no sacrifice until the treacherous enemy is crushed and lasting peace is vouchsafed our people in its country, its homeland.

---

4.   The Hebrew names of the ranks have changed since then.

Today, we close a glorious chapter in the history of the Haganah, the nameless army of the Jewish people in its battle for liberation and public stature. We begin a new chapter in the history of the Defence Army of Israel.

May the unsullied arms, loyalty and dedication to our national interest and consecration to Israel's teachings which marked the Haganah be the pillar of fire leading the hosts of the Israel Army, Heyeh Hazak!

In a letter written eleven days after his last letter to his sister, Mordecai is resigned. He accepts the fact that nothing is going to happen with Ann. Perhaps it is this resolution that allows him to talk of her in critical, cynical tones that he hasn't used until now.

July 6, 1948

Dear Toots,

I'm afraid I have to disappoint you — and me too, as well as the folks, Carolyn[5] and Dick, if what you said about their attitude is true: I'm afraid it's simply no dice with Ann. No, I haven't tried talking to her again, nor have I made any other premature fruitless overtures.... It's simply that I'm no Don Quixote, and I don't stand a chance against windmills — or dead men.

...

In a letter written on what was supposed to be the last day of the truce, Mordecai provides some clarity on his military career and counsels his brother-in-law on whether or not to come to Israel himself.

July 8, 1948

Dear Brother-of-a-war-correspondent, Mother, Father, Naomi and anybody else who cares to listen;

---

5.   Ann Strauss's sister in Cleveland.

I take strong and violent exception to what I consider a very dirty crack, implying that suggestions of personal danger in my dispatches are, as Pooh-Bah put it,
"merely corroborative detail, intended to give verisimili-
tude to an otherwise bald and unconvincing narrative."[6]
I've writhed too much from the fake of other correspondents to dare be guilty of it myself. When you finally
received my account of the "Burma Road" beginnings –
in which there is no invention, but straight recording
(and slight omissions for what are ingenuously known as
"security reasons") you may understand why I've been
given an honourary membership in Palmach, 4th Battalion, known as the "Portzim" – that's right, the boys who
broke through Zion Gate that famous night. They've just
returned to Jerusalem, and my most precious war souve-
nir will be neither the dress-swords nor the silver Turkish
coffee set (property of the Inspector General of Police) nor
even the beautiful double-barreled shotgun I picked out
for myself when we moved into the Russian Compound
on May 14 .... It will be the emblem of the battalion, which
I am being authorized to wear. So – a little more respect,
please. As you were, Chaplain.

Mother's question re my status tickles me. Yes, I am
a civilian. It seems I just can't get into a good war, fulltime,
for the life of me. I joined Haganah soon after I got here,
with Yoel Malkoff (commander on Mt. Scopus up to now)
as my induction-contact.[7] After taking regular field-training
with Hish (*heyl sadeh*)[8] at once-beautiful Ramat Rachel I was
shifted to Intelligence, where I did work I still don't care to
write about – I'll give you all an earful someday. With the

6.   Another reference to Gilbert and Sullivan's *The Mikado* (1885), Mordecai got the
      quote exactly right.
7.   Mordecai's induction into the Haganah probably took place in April, 1947. His
      description of the event, from his memoirs, was quoted above. See chapter 4.
8.   Field troops.

Pin of the Palmach: Note the name "Haportzim" (in Hebrew) along the sword in the middle. This is a special version of the more general Palmach pin just for Haportzim. It is easy to understand why Mordecai treasured it and his right to wear it.

exit of the British my work changed somewhat, and by May 20 I was more or less fed-up, and bored. The draft didn't touch me, since the *Post* is considered essential, and I was given a full deferment. I worked, voluntarily for a while, until food in Jerusalem became critical. My superior wouldn't arrange for me to eat at the Haganah kitchens, and so I told him to go soak his head, and dropped out. I got the meal tickets, instead, from a female quarter-mistress, a friend of Ann's. Then came Zion Gate, and then Notre Dame, and then the trip out to camp, where I spent almost a week, and ate like a horse. Then came the fantastic trip to Tel Aviv, where I acquired (adopted) war-correspondent status, shoulder-flash and all. Agronsky was pleased as punch, and I have carte blanche to goof off whenever I smell a story. And so, Mother, the Boro Park call, with its reference to me as a "civilian," was accurate. And I was the first, too. I was the first correspondent and/or civilian on that road, and all these reporters who claim firsts are being slightly inaccurate. I taxed one with it, and he said I was a local correspondent, so it didn't count!... But – wasn't there a *U.P.* story with my name from the first week in June, telling the story and giving a picture of Jerusalem? The *U.P.* guy in Tel Aviv sent it, I saw the carbon copy! As for Father – I know this will not allay your concern over danger I have or may be in, but you must understand the situation: my job, as correspondent, requires that I visit battle-fields, before, after, and/or during an operation. It gives a story the authentic ring that makes all the difference. It is also, and this is most important, a big morale-booster for the boys. They need company, they need somebody from the outside to "*chizbat*" with, they need someone to bring them the latest news, and they love to see the stories about them in the papers. Little English as some of them know, it's a big thing when they can spell-out "Palmach or "Haportzim" on a printed page. My *gdud* lost 3/4 of its original complement, and has been built up to strength with Cyprus refugees: the oldsters (from point of view of experience only, certainly not of age) need the encouragement they get from stories about them. (After the big convoy to Etzion, when 200 held off 4,000 Arabs and they were finally taken out under surrender terms arranged by Herzog, et al, and had to leave their weapons behind, their first question was "*ma omrim aleinu?*"[9] They were afraid that after a heroic two-day stand against frightful odds they would be thought of as having failed. Being exempt from the shooting, can I do less? In addition, Father, there is no real safety anywhere, unless one goes down into a shelter and remains there until it's all over. And believe me, it's easier to protect yourself when you know from what direction the shells are coming than when you're in the city and they can come from any side. I don't know, yet, whether there'll be an extended truce or not, either in Jerusalem or the rest of the country, but I can only go on doing what I've been doing – or demand leave

---

9.　Hebrew, meaning "What are they saying about us?"

from Agronsky and join as a soldier. I think I can do more this way – especially with my vision.[10]

I met Eban,[11] vaguely, at Herzog's house once, months ago. His sister-in-law is married to Victor Herzog.[12] The son I know is Yaacov, a bachelor. Both Eban and his wife impressed me, but I never had the chance to really get to know them. He is a brilliant son-of-a-b**ch, isn't he?

...As for my writing about Marcus[13] – I never got to meet him! I was always about a day behind. Besides, what I know about him, and what is suggested about his death,[14] would not look very nice in an American publication. I'm thinking of a piece about "my" battalion, though, and may do it one of these days. They're a terrific bunch, and have suffered heavily. They did almost all the fighting around Jerusalem and opened the highway twice, before they got around to pulling-off the Burma road job. (see my second *Hadoar* article, sent off some weeks ago)[15]... There are a lot of things one mustn't write about, too, unfortunately, for both morale and security reasons. We'll see what I can *qvech*[16] out one of these days. Incidentally, a lot better stuff has been written than my Beyt Susin story, and not by me either. Remember gentlemen by the names of Pyle, Hershey, etc.?[17]

---

10. Mordecai was plagued with poor eyesight his whole life.
11. Abba Eban. See chapter 5, footnote 1.
12. This is a reference to Chaim Herzog (1918–1997), who held many civil and military positions in Israel, eventually becoming president in 1983. During his career in the British army in WWII he was known as Vivian (the English translation of Chaim) because the British had difficulty pronouncing his Hebrew name. Perhaps Mordecai confused "Victor" and "Vivian".
13. Mickey Marcus. See chapter 24, footnote 6.
14. Marcus was killed in a friendly fire accident on June 10, 1948, but some conspiracy theorists suggest that it was not an accident.
15. Not found.
16. Yiddish, meaning "push."
17. Ernest Taylor Pyle (1900–1945) and John Richard Hersey (1914–1993) were famous war correspondents.

...As a member of the Journalists Assoc. I just came into almost LP.10 worth of food, and about twice that as a member of the *Post* staff – both outfits arranged special trucks from Tel Aviv, so that come what may, I have enough to eat for at least six months (honest, I doubt if I'll ever finish the stuff. I even got 5 gallons of neft,[18] for cooking, since there's no steady current in the city – except where I live now: Van Vriesland. We're between two Consulates and next door to a Haganah headquarters, in addition to being on the same line as the Electric Corp. boss's lady-friend. Nuf sed. For a few hours a day only we don't have current (in the rest of the city each area get it once in three days, with luck).

...

Incidentally, Marion's[19] letter was very sweet. It feels good being able to do a little good occasionally. I visited Mrs. Yassky[20] this afternoon, during the break in this letter, and she gave me hell for not having come in to eat there during the Great Hunger, when, as she put it, a lonely bachelor has a hard time, while for a family one more or less can be easily managed. I promised if I get into that kind of trouble again (now impossible, with the stores I have) I'll come in. She's an amazing women, and has taken the whole business amazingly well. I extended Naomi's sincerest, and she specifically asked that Naomi write her. So, Toots, you got no choice but to sit down and write now. She understands how difficult it is to send condolences, and if you put in one brief line on him it will be enough; I already extended our whole family's sympathy. She is interested in you as a friend, and was very thrilled to hear that Naomi and Monroe talk about coming, eventually. And about that I have something to say.

---

18. Kerosene.
19. Probably Marion Strauss, mother of Ann.
20. Widow of Dr. Chaim Yassky, killed in the Hadassah convoy attack.

As a soldier (Battalion 4, etc...) I know what the military situation is, as a war correspondent I know what problems will face the country when it's all over: and in both my capacities I say don't dare come for more than a flying trip now, if that much. One more gun means little – one hundred does not mean very much right now, not enough for Monroe to give up a far greater source of benefit to Israel: greasy old American dollars. Every cent he banks now will help buy what's needed, commercially, when it's all over. In other words, (and I spoke to the manager of Barclays[21] about this last night, on the way home from work) yours is no rationalization. I know. Monroe, it's a "good" war to get into, but "he also serves who"[22] etc. And I mean it. You're big, and you'd make too damned big a target, you don't know the language, your experience is in the navy, how much good could the few hundred rounds you would have time to squeeze off in this shindig do, compared to what the few hundred dollars will be able to do to help stabilize our economy after the war.... And I make probably the best Turkish coffee in the country. In brief, I'd love for you to be here, but I'm convinced you should wait. Have I been obscure enough? Your job for the present is to amass the shekalim and take care of the little Sioux (or is she Iroquois; she has a tendency to hide her origin[23]) until you both come, or I get there for a visit. (I expect a real steak when I do come though, so you'd better start saving up right now, and don't say later that I didn't warn you.)

...

All my love,

the brat.

---

21. Barclays Bank is a British bank that operated in Palestine from 1918. Its Israel activities were eventually absorbed into Bank Discount.
22. The original quote from Milton's sonnet is, "They also serve who only stand and wait." It was used in both World War I and World War II to refer to the loved ones at home, waiting for their soldier sons/husbands/brothers/friends to come home from the war.
23. Naomi had somewhat dark skin.

Chapter 27

Phase Two: The "Ten Days," July 8–18, 1948

The UN had hoped to use the four-week truce to achieve a political settlement. Their mediator, Count Folke Bernadotte, viewed the Arab world's rejection of the existence of a Jewish state, of any size, in any borders, as the main impediment to a peaceful final resolution. By the end of the first month of fighting, Bernadotte acknowledged that the Partition Plan borders were no longer relevant and accepted the Jordanian conquest of the West Bank. On June 27, he had proposed[1] that Jordan and Israel be re-formed as two states, one Arab, one Jewish, with a "union" between them. He suggested that the Arab state retain control of Jerusalem, and be given the Negev, and that Israel be compensated with the Western Galilee. Both Israel and the Arabs rejected the proposal. Israel would not agree to giving up all of Jerusalem, and the Arabs would not acquiesce to the establishment of the Jewish state.

Jordan, which had achieved its military goals, did not want to return to the battlefield, but the Arab League decided unanimously

---

1.   Letter S/863 [7] to the UN Secretary General, June 27, 1948.

against extending the truce. The Egyptian foreign minister, Ahmed Muhammad Khashaba explained, "It was a matter of life and death for [the Arab leaders] that there should be no Jewish state."[2]

Both sides had violated the truce. The Arabs reinforced their lines with fresh units and prevented supplies from reaching isolated Jewish settlements. The unity of the Arab aggressors was marred by continual bickering over the future division of the anticipated spoils of war. The British aided the Arab effort by continuing to sell arms to Arab countries. The Israelis used the truce to move troops to the front and to bring in arms and military personnel to the country. They accelerated military training and transformed the Haganah from an underground militia into a formal army. Their efforts were undercut by the British, however, who continued to impede immigration, preventing fighting-age Jewish men in their displaced persons camps on Cyprus from leaving.

The Egyptians ended the first truce prematurely by attacking in the south the day before the truce was to end. The following day, Israeli forces launched simultaneous large-scale offensives on all fronts. As a result of its military successes and increasing military strength, and the absolute Arab refusal to accept a Jewish state, Israel went from merely trying to consolidate their holdings to the more offensive posture of fighting to add to its territory. It was also not averse to reducing the number of Arabs living in areas controlled by the Jews.

The fighting during the "Ten Days" was intense on all fronts. There were several important Israeli military operations, with significant Jewish gains. They will be discussed below.

Until the formal establishment of the state, the Haganah was an illegal, underground army – at least according to the British. There was little formality, and scant record-keeping. As described above, Mordecai worked in an intelligence capacity. The arrangement was loose enough to allow him to continue working for the *Post*. In fact, his newspaper credentials were invaluable to the Haganah. But his intelligence work essentially ended once the British left, and as for combat, as he put it, he "couldn't get into a good war for the life of him." This was about to change. Having declared his civilian status in his last letter, Mordecai,

---

2.   Campbell to British Foreign Office, 7 July 1948, PRO FO 371–68375.

who had become an Israeli citizen, was formally drafted a mere three days later – although not into a combat role. His new position necessitated leaving the *Post*. Gershon Agronsky sent him a note (July 11, 1948), more dramatic than usual and in Hebrew, wishing him the best and assuring him that "all [your] friends at the editorial board will accompany you on the path of bravery and glory upon which walk the nation's best in the land." He also asked that Mordecai view himself as "connected to the newspaper and continue to contribute to it to your best abilities as you did as a member of the editorial board…. Strength!"

Mordecai in uniform

Mordecai took advantage of his departure from the *Post* to write to two love interests: Hadassah Frisch and Kepi. Although the letters contain similar summaries[3] of his recent activities, there are also significant differences between them. His letter to Hadassah seems more "distant," which is perhaps strange, considering he had hoped to marry her, while his letter to Kepi suggests an intimate relationship, mentioning his loneliness and his "empty bed." He also confesses the privation he experienced when Jerusalem was under siege, something he never fully communicated to his family in the US.

There are few letters to his family and only one newspaper article from the *Post* from the period of the ten days.

It is interesting that Mordecai gives his address as "Jerusalem, Palestine," rather than "Israel." It may be an acknowledgment that Jerusalem was not supposed to be part of Israel, or a reflection of the situation; that it is still embattled and cut off.

July 15, 1948

Dear Kepi,

Tonight the Security Council votes on the American truce resolution;[4] planes (presumably Egyptian, not clear yet) dropped a few bombs in Jewish Jerusalem; the shelling from Arab 100-pounders, which was about a city-block away an hour ago, has stopped, and I'm taking advantage of the electricity to write to you. For the first time since the war began I was frightened tonight. It wasn't the shelling, no worse than on other nights, or the shooting or anything, but simply a sudden funk. For the last few hours I had an unaccountable feeling that all the shells were looking for me, and would go around corners to get me. They didn't, of course, otherwise I wouldn't be sitting here on the rug on the floor of Hadassah Van Vriesland's room (opening onto the back garden, you remember, where we once sat with

---

3.   I include only the letter to Kepi.
4.   The resolution for a second truce was passed by the UN on July 15, but was not to come into effect until July 18. It was never accepted by the Arabs.

Mrs. V.V.) where I now live, typing. I suppose I wouldn't feel lonely; but then would that be much of a way to get over loneliness?

This is my first free night since I left the *Post*. (You read that correctly.) Knowing me, and my bloodthirsty nature, what I'm doing must be fairly obvious. It is no less than you would expect, perhaps even a bit more. (The shelling has started again, heavily, and it's close. But this room is an excellent shelter, and the funk has passed, and all my reaction now is to cuss, subconsciously, in my best Arabic.) Security being what it is, all I can say is that my assignment is in Jerusalem, I continue to live in my own room and not at camp, and I draw a (meager) subsistence allowance to boot. The room, itself, is lovely, well furnished, and very comfortable. It suffers from the same thing every room I've had has suffered from since September 1947: The Empty Bed. This room is the worst, though, because it almost always has electricity, and as I type now the new radio-phonograph combination with the automatic changer which I bought from some fleeing Americans is delivering Bach, 5–6 Brandenburgs, which inevitably recall you. And Carmi's wonderful Vatican choir recordings (à la Fauré Requiem, which I'm dying to hear again) left with me when he went off to Tel Aviv, have the same effect. In fact, I have never yet been able to listen to music anywhere in Palestine without thinking of you.

I can't review what I've been through. Besides the *Palestine Post* bombing, I've been shelled, ambushed (with 4 other guys, trying to get to Tel Aviv on foot one night) sniped at (missed, of course) and gone with absolutely nothing to eat and only warmish water to drink for three days. I've also had a Jeep "shot" (mined) from under me. In retrospect everything seems to fit in under the general heading of "War Experiences," and I just can't see anybody really being interested. I've taken a liberty – I'm sending you some clippings I think you might enjoy reading, I'm proudest of the Mt. Zion story and "my" battalion (by adoption), and I like the Burma Road story too. In spite of all the bunk thrown by U.S. correspondents, including Izzy Stone, I was first on it: I was there when the three went out to see if it was possible, I went out to meet the first convoy that tried to come up to Jerusalem and failed, I met the first that succeeded, and I went down with the first to go. So there.

And that's about all, I have a full day's work ahead of me tomorrow, and if I don't get some sleep the pistol I wear (a lovely – gives me cowboy slouch) will be too much to carry. Please write – tell me what you're doing, where, what about school, what you're thinking about Palestine, how you feel, and what, if anything, do you hear about or from David [Greenberg]. As a soldier, I invoke my inalienable right to ask you to write. Won't you? Care of the *Post* in Jerusalem, I still collect mail there... You know what they say about soldier's morale and the war effort – won't you contribute? Did you get to Tanglewood this summer?

Laylah tov.

Mordecai

In many locations, Israel's War of Independence was an "intimate" affair, not a clash of armies on an open battlefield where the strongest army wins. Rather, it was a war fought strategic point by strategic point. It was prosecuted in villages, towns and cities, often house to house, in vineyards and through schools. With their villages often used as bases and battlefields, it is hardly surprising that so many Arab Palestinians fled. This reality is reflected in Mordecai's article on the battle for al Maliha (Malha[5]), one of the villages south of Jerusalem taken during July 13–14. He will explain the genesis and evolution of the piece in the letter that follows.

---

5.   Malha, along with many of the other villages mentioned in the article, are now well within the city limits of Jerusalem.

Thursday, July 15, 1948

MALHA TAKEN

By Mordecai Chertoff

In a perfectly coordinated three-pronged attack, Israel Defence Army forces and IZL troops conquered Malha village about a mile-and-a-half to the south-west of Jerusalem on Tuesday night.

The operation began with the heavy shelling of Ein Karem and Beit Safafa to the west and east respectively, while heavy machine-guns in newly-won positions at Khirbet Masmil and Khirbet el-Hamama poured heavy fire at Legionnaires in the valley below.

Maliha itself was silent in the bright moonlight, and not a shot was fired at it until the moon was low and the three columns had advanced upon their unsuspecting objective. To the west, one long silent column took the height dominating the road leading from Ein Karem, to ensure against help coming from that quarter, while the eastern column headed for the outskirts of the village, its objective: the schoolhouse.

Combined Assault

From there, it was to swing around and meet the central column for a combined onslaught on the main base in the village, the mosque, surrounded by four concrete-fortified buildings.

Beit Safafa was shelled by a Sixth Brigade Mortar Company in Jerusalem, and Mar Elias was pounded from Jewish gun positions further east. By the time Jewish forces stormed their objective, the Arabs were completely bewildered as to just what point was being attacked – and their spotty opposition was ineffectual. It was concentrated in the mosque and in the school. The two buildings clearly

showed signs of the heavy fighting as dawn broke upon the
Jewish forces in full occupation of the village and entrench-
ing themselves for the counter-attack, which never came.

A kilometre away from the village itself, an Arab
Legion armoured car fired burst after burst from its
machine-gun in an attempt to break up the western column
advancing on the height, but Jewish mortar bombs, probing
the area, kept it in check.

Garrison in Fight

Earlier, one of the three advancing columns had turned
south to capture Er Ras, a strategic height south of Malha.
The Arab garrison of Malha, which consisted of one company of Trans-Jordan irregulars, was soon put to flight, but
some stayed behind to fight a rear-guard action. By 9.30 in
the morning, the village and a good deal of military equipment were in Jewish hands.

Jewish casualties were relatively light – one killed and
five wounded. Enemy losses are unknown.

With the conquest of Malha and the isolation of Ein
Karem – and the advance of Jewish positions a kilometre
closer to the Egyptian lines – Israel forces are in a position
to consolidate the entire southern front. Malha, now Jewish, prevents any flanking attempt on the part of the Arabs
against Tzuba which was taken on Monday. And any plan
the Arabs had to choke off the Jerusalem-Tel Aviv roads by
sealing the way at Tzuba has been nipped in the bud. At the
same time one more Arab battery emplacement has been
eliminated from the Beit Hakerem–Bait Vegan front.

It was from Malha, too, that the Egyptians supplied
reinforcements during the Kfar Etzion battle in the middle
of May, and to the Latrun front at the beginning of June.

A second village which has fallen to Israel forces is
Sar'a, a kilometre-and-a-half west of Hartuf, an important
strongpoint on the Hartuf – Beit Jibrin road. This village,

which was captured on Tuesday, had constituted a threat to the Jewish supply line to Jerusalem.

Following the capture of Sar'a and various other Arab villages in the area, the few places still left in Arab hands are now being evacuated by the enemy, a Haganah spokesman in Jerusalem said yesterday.

Chapter 28

Battle for the Old City: Operation Kedem

July 16, 1948

Dear Family,

At 5.30 tomorrow morning, local time, another damned truce goes into effect.[1] I phrase it so indelicately only because I mean it that way. Given a few more days we could take the Old City, clean out what's left of the Legion in Latrun and Beit Naballa .... Seriously, our military position now is such that the man in the street will tell you the truce is another dirty British trick to prevent us from rolling up a few more military victories.

As a soldier – you heard me[2] – as a soldier I feel more than a bit peed-off, as the boys say, about the truce. But perhaps I'd better explain my status at present. The Army here decided that I was invaluable, and sent me greetings.

---

1. It did not come into effect until two days later.
2. Mordecai's letter of July 8 had informed his family that he was a civilian. Furthermore, with the declaration of the state, Mordecai is free to admit that he is in the army.

Always a good patriot and a show-off at heart, I reported to the draft office, wangled a four day extension, and invited one of my armchair general friends to offer me an armchair. He did, and so now I am a member of the Israel Defense Army, as it is cumbersomely called, and wear a beautiful par (parabellum to you, Gershon), in a rich leather holster. Since I always do things in style, this holster rides a belt studded with extra cartridges and as it hangs low on the right hip gives just the swagger the girls fall for. Unfortunately, there are no girls here to fall. But just imagine, were I to show up in Times Square dressed in khaki shorts and shirt, sandals – and pistol. I would stop traffic for miles around. People would probably think it was an initiation to a fraternity! I may add, by the way, that this information is not for the ears – or eyes – of the American State Department, which might look askance at my serving in any other army: professional jealousy, you know! What really gripes me about the job, though, is that I gotta take orders,[3] and this afternoon, as I casually let slip to my boss that he dare not give me a job for the night, since I want to go down and watch the Jews chase the Arabs, he nearly hit the ceiling – and me too. No, he explained, urgently. My people do not go to battle, neither as observers nor as participants. I need them, he elaborated, and I'm not taking any chances. In short, if you ever do sneak off to watch an operation, I personally will take you out in the back yard and fill your balding head with bullets. Furthermore, you are working tonight (Friday night – I screamed in unavailing fury). When I had settled down a little, he explained my job: you'll sit near me, and be nervous with me! Go fight city hall! And lest I get any ideas about sneaking off, he quietly informed me that he has the authority to put me in solitary confinement for three days. As if his order was not enough! Nu, after the brief information about the three days detention, I changed – nay, dropped, my slowly-developing plan to

---

3.   Mordecai's previous military tenure was far "looser" than this new posting.

sneak off and watch the fight, and submitted to fate. What a fate! I guess I'll have to do what I did about the conquest of Malha: I got hold of Azariah, my former travelling mate, who has not been drafted, and he told me his story, following which I read the official report and wrote a piece as though I had been there. It appeared the following day under my name, and left people who are not supposed to know I'm in the army with the impression that I'm not. But it really is ridiculous, to be so much safer and more protected in the army than I ever was as a civilian! Still, I'll have some good inside stories to tell when this whole business is over. All I have to worry about now is getting leave, when the shootin's over, to drop in on you for a visit. What I was so anxious to watch tonight, by the way, is the attack planned on the Old City. By the time you get this – by the time I mail it, in fact, you'll know how it went. It will be a tough nut to crack, but I think it can be done. For me it will be a pretty anxious night, since where I sit we'll know every moment how it's going. The only indiscretion I've been guilty of in connection with the job was my warning to two people not to go out for air tonight, but to go to bed – they won't be able to sleep – early. It's gonna be so wonderfully noisy – and the trouble is that we can't announce to the Jews of Jerusalem that most of the noise will be ours, for them not to worry and not to dash for shelter every time they hear a bang. In some areas, near the Old City, it will be unhealthy to move around (Gershon: explain to the folks something about ballistics, angles of fire, mortar and cannon range, etc.). In those areas people will have to keep their heads down. I'll bet there won't be a street in the whole city in which at least a few spent bullets will not drop. But *yihiyeh tov*, don't worry. I hope to walk home sometime tomorrow morning with the knowledge that should I so desire, I can go to the Kotel for *shahrit*.[4]

---

4.   Morning prayers.

... Dear Mother – you rate a book, all by yourself. If I were to try to shop for a rug now they would send me out to Beit Hakerem – to the booby hatch. There is no Old City in which to shop – the Jewish area has been reduced to rubble, all the Arab civilians have fled, and at the moment – I hope not for long – there are Legionnaires within, Jews about to break in. The only other place is one fancy store in town – you know what that would cost – or Tel Aviv, and you can't guess what it would cost there. I think it would be cheaper in New York – and much easier shopping. Incidentally, you didn't have to tell me you wrote that letter on your "yap" – the resulting eye-strain (*zolt mir excusen*)[5] was proof enough. The inference from your remarks on Father's health as it fluctuates with the postal services is easily drawn. Believe me, if I could, – or could have at any time since this began – I would have flown home, and felt a week with you all well worth the expense involved. But it is absolutely impossible for the present. Up to last Friday I planned to come home as soon as some kind of peace were established; now I must wait to be discharged from the army. Unfortunately, I'm responsible for a network of people, and must keep them working – I can't just drop out and let somebody else keep turning a handle – it isn't that kind of job. It takes time to ease into it, and will take longer to get released from it. But Father needn't worry anymore – the truce begins tomorrow, and it will not end in war, since the damned British-American axis is determined to foul us politically this time, since they've failed militarily. In short, I'm under orders – I'll come when I can, and let you know when it will be just as soon as I do. Meanwhile, the best I can promise is that as soon as I get a day's leave and can run down to Tel Aviv I'll try to phone you from there. Fair enough? I'll also get back to my old habit of writing every week, But Jeezuz – stop worrying. By the time you get this

---

5.   Yiddish, meaning "excuse the expression."

far in the letter my pistol will be a museum piece, neatly oiled – and hanging on a wall....

Wow – what a war! All three "Wacs"[6] in the office are busy as hell – flirting. Every time a shell lands anywhere near the city, they jump. A helluva a way to make love, I must say....

(I'll break off now, and wait to finish this letter tomorrow night, when this night's action is over and we can look back on it – I hope with satisfaction. Shabbat Shalom.)

Nu, it didn't take. Despite all press stories to the effect that there was no serious attempt to take the Old City but rather a demonstration of the possibility alone, believe me: it was a "puncture."[7] I'm ashamed that we haven't the grace to admit it as such. There should have been no I.Z.L.-Sternist participation in the attempt, it should have been just Palmach, rather than no P at all. But there's no point in hashing it over – we did all last night and into the wee wee hours of the morning. As compensation is the capture of Nazareth.[8] *Hatzi nehama.*[9]

We're having a quiet evening "at home." Asher and his wife came over – she brought a cake. I made Turkish coffee. During the evening Barak got on with his painting of Leah, I typed, Asher tried to take a pistol apart (not mine) and ended up with a few extra pieces (really, he did!) and Ilani[10] took a few indoor pictures, copies of which I'll send as soon as I have them. Right now, Barak is painting, Schubert's Great Symphony is coming in fine over the automatic phonograph,

---

6. Acronym for "Women's Army Corps" – a unit in the US army created for women during WWII. It was discontinued in the 1970s. Mordecai is referring to female Israeli soldiers with a term that would be familiar to his parents.

7. In Israel "puncture" means not only a flat tire, but any failure, particularly an unexpected one.

8. Completed on the evening of July 16.

9. Hebrew, meaning "half a consolation."

10. Photographer Ephraim Ilani (1910–1999).

Ilani is kibitzing the painting, and Asher and his wife have gone home with the dog (who usually comes flying in in the morning and kisses me awake with a long, pink tongue and continually gives queer endings to my dreams. I have to be up at nine tomorrow morning, so I'll quit now and make the necessary preparations for the evening's retirement. I hope to remember to enclose the clippings.

Laylah tov, and be well. Take care of yourself, Father – it should be easy now, with no worry on my account anymore.

love to all, I miss you all!

Mersh

(Photo by Ephraim Ilani, courtesy of Peter Ilani)

Mordecai and friends. Note the pistol hanging
on the wall.

The effort to take the Old City to which Mordecai refers was Operation Kedem (July 16–17), the last Israeli attempt to take the Old City before the second truce was to come into effect. It was masterminded by David Shaltiel,[11] the Haganah commander in Jerusalem. A force consisting of

---

11.   David Shaltiel (1903–1969) was born in Berlin. He moved to Palestine in 1923 but
      returned to Europe two years later where he enlisted in the French Foreign Legion. In

Haganah and former Irgun and Lehi fighters, now integrated into the IDF, aimed to break through in a frontal attack, using an experimental shaped charge explosive called a "conus" (cone), which was to blow holes in the walls of Jerusalem. The conus was devised by a professor of physics at Hebrew University, Giulio Racah,[12] who came upon the design in an Italian textbook. A prototype was built in a Bet Hakerem laundry. It weighed 335 pounds, and rested upon a metal tripod. To be effective, it had to be exploded precisely six inches from its target. The Israelis were utterly sure that they would succeed, but the Conus failed to breach the walls in two attempts.[13] The attack started late and Jordanian soldiers poured murderous fire on the attackers. As a result of the failure, bitter recriminations were issued against David Shaltiel for the botched operation, which cost eighty-three dead and eighty-four wounded.[14] Shaltiel was relieved of command and replaced by Moshe Dayan.

As usual, Mordecai does not describe the battles going on outside of the central region but, once again, it is worth summarizing some of the action. On the southern front, there was little change during the Ten Days. The Egyptians were poorly motivated and low on ammunition. After intense fighting, Israel emerged with a slight edge. Nevertheless, on July 13 the Egyptians again bombed Tel Aviv, killing fourteen and injuring forty. In the north, along the coastal strip of the western Galilee and eastward toward Nazareth, Israel successfully prosecuted Operation Dekel against the Arab Liberation Army, which resulted in

---

1934 he returned to Palestine and joined the Haganah. While seeking arms in Europe, he was captured by the Gestapo and spent three years in prisons/concentration camps, including Dachau and Buchenwald, until the Haganah succeeded in freeing him. From 1942–3, he was the Haganah commander in Haifa. He was also the coordinator between the Haganah and the Jewish underground groups, the Irgun and Lehi.

12. Giulio (Yoel) Racah (1909–1965) was born in Florence, Italy, and by 1937 was professor of physics at the University of Pisa. He immigrated to Palestine in 1939, and became a professor of theoretical physics at Hebrew University, later becoming dean of the faculty of sciences, then rector, and then president. He was awarded the Israel Prize in 1958. There is a crater on the moon named for him. During the War of Independence, he served as deputy commander of the forces defending Mount Scopus.

13. Collins and Lapierre, *O Jerusalem!*, p. 554.

14. Levy, *Tisha Kabin*, pp. 313–19.

the Jewish capture of Nazareth.[15] In the northeast, the IDF battled the Syrians, and while successful in reducing the size of the Syrian holdings, failed to completely erase the Syrian bridgehead.

Of critical importance were the battles in the central region. Mordecai describes the battle for Malha, some of the battles which occurred during July 13–14, and the failed attempt to take the Old City on July 16–17, but does not mention Operation Dani, Israel's successful campaign to take the Arab cities of Lydda and Ramleh, nor does he discuss Israel's unsuccessful strategic effort to secure the Tel Aviv–Jerusalem highway. Latrun and the surrounding villages remained in Arab hands and would remain so through the end of the war.

---

15. The Arab residents of Nazareth were not forced to evacuate.

Chapter 29

The Second Truce:
July 18 – October 15

The second truce began on July 18 and was in effect until October 15. It was a period of introspection for the combatants, and for Mordecai. Benny Morris describes the period as one dominated by UN efforts to mediate a permanent solution to the conflict and to the refugee problem. After the fierce fighting of "the ten days," Israel wanted time to improve its strategic position. The Arabs had no appetite for continuing the war but continued to violate the truce. Arab snipers in Jerusalem shot Jews on an almost daily basis, and the city was shelled "night and day."[1] The water pumping station at Latrun was blown up and water rationing reintroduced on August 11. On August 8, the *Post* reported twenty-five breaches of the truce within five days. Both sides rearmed, re-positioning their forces and "probing" each other's positions.

At the same time, Israel continued to build the organs of a modern state. It introduced its own currency, completed the integration and

---

1. According to the *Palestine Post*, September 1, 1948.

organization of the army and started the process of drafting a constitution (which has still not been completed).

UN mediator in Palestine, Swedish nobleman and diplomat
Count Bernadotte's first proposal to resolve the conflict, submitted on
June 27 during the first truce, had been swiftly rejected. His second plan,[2]
submitted on September 16, was intended to acknowledge the realities
on the ground and "update" the Partition Plan. In it, he recommended,
among other things: that the current truce be changed into a formal
peace or at the least an armistice; that there should be geographic homo-
geneity and integration among areas allocated to Jews and to Arabs; that
refugees should be allowed to return to their homes as soon as possible
or receive adequate compensation; that the City of Jerusalem receive
separate treatment with free access to all holy sites; that Haifa be a free
port and Lydda a free airport; and that the Negev should go to the Arabs
and the Galilee to the Jews.

In recognition of the reality, the report asserted that: "A Jewish
State called Israel exists in Palestine and there are no sound reasons for
assuming that it will not continue to do so." He also made a surprising
recommendation:

> The disposition of the territory of Palestine not included within
> the boundaries of the Jewish State should be left to the Gov-
> ernments of the Arab States in full consultation with the Arab
> inhabitants of Palestine, with the recommendation, however,
> that in view of the historical connexion and common interests
> of Transjordan and Palestine there would be compelling reasons
> for merging the Arab territory of Palestine with the territory of
> Transjordan, subject to such frontier rectifications regarding other
> Arab States as may be found practicable and desirable.

In other words, the UN mediator's second proposal envisioned a Jewish
state but no separate Arab Palestinian state. Arab portions of Palestine
would be allocated among the Arab countries, chiefly Jordan – exactly

---

2.   "Progress Report of the United Nations Mediator on Palestine Submitted to the
      Secretary-General for Transmission to the Members of the United Nations."

as those countries intended. Again, there would be no separate state for Palestinian Arabs.

This second proposal was immediately rejected by all parties.[3]

The day after the publication of the second proposal, as Bernadotte's motorcade traveled through Jerusalem, four Lehi gunmen approached his car, and shot and killed Bernadotte and an officer sitting next to him. The world, and the Israeli government, were outraged. The Lehi was finally fully disarmed and dismantled.

During this truce period, Mordecai seems to have enough time to write almost every day. The letters he writes are personal and include little about the war or politics.

August 1, 1948

Dear Toots,

I began writing this letter on July 26, with a blow-by-blow description of my tactics, hopeful that I could climax the recitation with a terse "prepare the fatted calf,"[4] but the fates have decreed otherwise, and so I've scuttled the original letter, and here's the summary-sequel.

I made all the arrangements[5] – got me a substitute for my work, fixed things so they would go without me, finagled a seat on a jeep, got permission not to report for work for two days – and then the big-shot boss of my outfit in Jerusalem, Top Man, Second-only-to-God, he thinks, said no. Very meekly, I remembered he was my superior officer, and spent the two days sleeping. But I didn't get to Tel Aviv, where I hoped to arrange for my inclusion among those who are to

---

3.   This aspect of the proposal was ultimately one of the final results of the war; Jordan annexed the West Bank.

4.   I.e., for his visit home to New York. A slight misquote of a phrase from the Parable of the Prodigal son found in Luke 15:11–3.

5.   To get leave to go home to New York for a visit.

be sent on a mission to the States. I feel it's time I took the trip, since I've been away so long[6], haven't seen the family, etc. In addition, Al and Judy (Shepherd) Rosenfeld of the *N.Y. Post* showed-up suddenly, and read through my file. They're sure I could get correspondent status (and salary) from the new *N.Y. Star*, if I get to N.Y. It would mean a real chance, to write and to see, and to live an almost normal life, not chained to a night-desk as at the *Palpost*. I'm very much afraid, though, that by the time I get to make the trip my stuff will be so out-dated it will make no impression, and I'll be out of luck. That's what they mean by "war is hell," huh toots? Haven't given up, though. I'm trying to have Dallek or Moish[7] in Tel Aviv "order" me to appear there – they outrank my boss of course, and he'd have to say go. Once there, by invoking your name and my own bluff-ability, I should be able to swing the trip with orders for my boss to release me. What occurs to me as a brilliant alternative is for you to get on to Elias Epstein[8] in Washington, have him demand me there for a while...think it would work? Tell him how terrific I am, etc., maybe he'll want me for a month or two. It would be a real vacation... and I could get that job lined up. Just between us Chertoffs, kid, this business of being a cog stinks, you're too dependent on the wheel. You've got to roll with it. And for a guy like me, it's no good. I get awfully impatient with the whole business. See what you can do with your connections.

Your Hadassah is back in Palestine, "somewhere in the State, with our Wacs. Her address is …. And according to Ray Sussman, "my" Hadassah is engaged to some guy[9] from the U. of Chi., and will be married this month....

---

6. Mordecai has been away for a year and a half at this point.
7. Moshe Sharett (Shertok).
8. Eliahu Epstein (later Elath) (1903–1990), was Israel's first ambassador to the United States. He was later Israel's ambassador to the United Kingdom and, from 1962–1968, president of Hebrew University.
9. Marvin Bacaner.

My own army job is going fairly okay, with the usual ups and downs. It's a quiet job, demands more *toches* than anything else. I'm ready to drop out whenever they let me, and take that trip home for a visit.

Mordecai asked his sister for help in finding a position that would allow him to return to America because he saw her as a "big shot" due to her large network of contacts and position as national head of Junior Hadassah. There is a family story that when Ben-Gurion was in the US, she called him and said that it was urgent that he receive her. He agreed and then asked her what was so important. "Nothing," she replied. "I just wanted to meet you." Naomi remained in some contact with Ben-Gurion.

Mordecai's family continues to press him to return home for a visit. His father, not yet understanding that his son has been drafted, writes on July 19: "It is difficult for me to understand what or who is holding you back. You are not subject to military discipline; as a military correspondent you are free to do as you like."

August 3, 1948

Dear Family,

To begin with, let me explain that my saying nothing about coming back to visit is not a result of unwillingness or filial disobedience. I've reached the point where I feel I can come – and have been trying to arrange things. Unfortunately, the army is a sticky affair, and chances right now look very slim indeed. Methinks I'll be able to go skiing by the time I do get back. You see, the truce is a very vague sort of thing, accompanied by a perpetual series of "incidents." As a result, Jerusalem is on a war footing, and no army personnel may leave unless Tel Aviv orders them to appear there. I'm trying to have such an order pushed through by my Tel Aviv friends. Once there I'll see what I can do about getting myself sent – there's no other way of getting permission to leave the country now, since it would be desertion or draft-dodging (really physically impossible now, unless one goes crying to the American

Consulate and waves the green passport – hardly the way for me to leave!). I'm doing what I can. If you can convince Elias Epstein in Washington or some Israel government representative in the States that he must have me there for a couple of months, okay: it would go very smoothly – and inexpensively – for the Chertoffs. Otherwise, we'll just have to sit and wait.

...

You should understand by now that I no longer work for the *Palpost*,[10] the army is rather narrow-minded about serving two bosses. The advantages I had in mind when I wrote that my new job (then, as war correspondent) was better revolved around the fact that I could buzz off (and not work at night in the office) whenever I smelled a story, and I had acquired permission to leave whenever and for wherever I pleased when moved by the spirit. It was a real reporting job, where there was a chance to do original writing, based on my own observation. Now, of course, that's out of the question. If I do get to NY, I'll be in a position to get me status with one of the NY papers (perhaps the *Star*) as its Palestine correspondent when I go back, so there's that to be considered too. For the present, of course, that is also out....

And that's about all for now. I have a date with a little blond soldierette, we'll probably go to the movies (*Jesse James* tonight!) – I'm even developing soldier's taste! (In movies, not women...).

Love, from me, the brat

August 4, 1948

Dear Toots,

Just got yours of July 23, and hasten to round out this letter by answering it immediately, even at the cost of an

---

10.   Nevertheless, Mordecai has several articles in the *Post* in August.

extra envelope – I had already addressed and sealed the letter. Oh well, you can do a lot on LP.2 a month.

Don't be too shocked about the intrigue, and don't imagine that being Jewish is a *zchut*[11] which is enough to compensate for all evils. I heard part of Begin's fulminations in Zion Square last night,[12] and believe me, I was ashamed to think that he too is Jewish. He spoke à la Hitler. Standing on the balcony of a hotel, with his disciples filling the square, he screamed and cried into the microphone and used all the tricks dear to demagogues the world over. His mates had a few Bren guns set up here and there to make an impression and served to remind everyone there that the score with IZL has not yet been settled. It will be some day, and it will be a bitter, but unavoidable day – if our State is to grow and be healthy.

The Jerusalem commander, Shaltiel, the one I wrote about, is gone. Instead, there's Moshe Dayan, veteran Palmachnik, one-eyed hero of the Litani Bridge (held by our kids for the Aussies' invasion into Syria, an invasion which never came off), and member of the United Workers Party.[13] My conviction is that he was given the job because 1) no more chance for anti-Arab military heroism in Jerusalem; 2) let him be stuck with the dirty work against IZL and Sternists and make the U.W.P. unpopular – as long as Mapai keeps "clean." I think they picked the wrong guy – he'll do a good job here. Incidentally, tone down some of the anti-Shaltiel

---

11. Hebrew, meaning "privilege."

12. Mordecai is referring to the speech Menachem Begin gave on August 3, 1948, from the balcony of the Jerusalem Hostel on Jaffa Road (formerly the Tel Aviv Hotel and later, the Ron Hotel), in which he announced the official dissolution of the Irgun and the sign-up of his soldiers with the Israel Defense Forces. Aviva Bar-Am, Shmuel Bar-Am, "Haman's Hat: Life in the Jerusalem Triangle," *Times of Israel*, August 24, 2013.

13. The United Workers Party was usually known by its acronym, "Mapai." It was a center-left political party, and the dominant force in Israeli politics until the 1960s, when it merged with the Labor party.

accusations I made; it has subsequently developed that in some of the cases (some, not all, by any means) he was not at fault. Did you Jews hear about our famous spy, caught, tried and properly executed?[14] It touched off a real spy scare which lasted for some time – until the truce, as matter of fact.

...

I think I'm going to move again. There's an enormous house in Talbieh, formerly occupied by wealthy Arabs, which has been liberated. It has about ten rooms, in two of which one of my friends is living with his wife. My superior officer is taking a room, and I'm thinking of taking one. It will leave us with a tremendous living room, a big reception hall, three johns, a big kitchen. There's a telephone and a well, so water will be no problem, and with us brass there the electric lines will be fixed as well. Sounds fine – and is rent free. The only trouble is distance from town. To take advantage of our office transport I would have to be up sort of earliest – about 7 – instead of being able to sleep until nine. It will bear thinking over. The room I'm in now costs LP. 12 a month, for two of us, and one is leaving soon, so there'll be a bill of LP.10 per month. I think I'll have to move – my salary is LP.2 per month!

Incidentally, I don't know whether I've mentioned it – but immortality does not interest me in the least, and I'm doing my unsuccessful best to avoid it. Nu – one lives in hope.

And that's all for how. Gotta stop and go eat, so I can get to work on time. Keep writing, kid, we soldiers need it badly. shalom, and all my love,

the brat

P.s. pictures in next letter.

---

14. Mordecai seems to be referring to the case of Meir Tobianski (1904–1948), who was an IDF officer who had been convicted at an impromptu court martial on June 30. Without legal representation or a right to appeal, he was executed the same day. A year later a reexamination of his case led to his posthumous acquittal and a formal apology to his widow from David Ben-Gurion.

Mordecai's father seems to think that his son has enlisted voluntarily in the army and writes an unusually harsh criticism. Though Paul later apologizes for not understanding, I include parts of his tirade because of the insights it offers into his thinking.

> My Dear Mordecai,
>
> Your letter of 16 July reached us yesterday.... Naturally, we are always delighted when we get a letter from you, though we don't always enjoy its content. And the content of this letter, the main part, in other words, did not please me at all. I can't understand why you've burdened yourself with an iron yoke on your shoulders when you could be free ... Now you are an indentured servant[15] to someone and you must nullify your will for his. It's possible that in your surroundings, this is considered a big honor for a person, and especially since you speak with such enthusiasm about your friends, but for my part, I do not see in this great importance or great honor. Especially, as it seems to me, you are not bringing any great benefit with this. Your particular strength lies in writing, and you should use this strength and not waste it on things that any simple person can do. And in addition, you seem to have forgotten that you are a product of America and you owe a great debt to that country. I don't want to talk about it too much, but it's not smart on your part to lend a hand to the suspicious ... enough said.[16]
>
> I said what I said from an objective point of view, but I won't conceal from you that I was sorely disappointed by what you did. I had genuinely hoped that you would come to visit us this summer still, at least for the High Holy Days, but now all hope is lost. You know that the affairs in Israel

---

15. Hebrew is עֶבֶד נִרְצָע, "*eved nirtze*," literally, "pierced servant," from Exodus 21:6. The implication is of a somewhat shameful rejection of freedom.
16. The Hebrew expression והמשכיל יבין, "*hamaskil yaven*," literally, "and the wise one will understand."

are wearying, and who knows when peace will come. And now, we must wait and hope, with no assurance when this hope will be fulfilled ... I will not conceal from you as well that this disappointment affects me badly, and I am often in a difficult frame of mind. Every small suggestion of worry, whatever it is, casts me down into despondency. I am not, God forbid, sick with a particular illness, but as I wrote you in my last letter, I am approaching the "days of our years,"[17] and at this age, the body weakens and our strength diminishes and every trouble and worry has a negative impact. Naturally, what's done is done, and there's no crying over spilt milk,[18] but I want you to understand why we so yearn for you to come home. (August 4, 1948)

August 19, 1948.

Dear Family,

Let's get a few things straight before I go on: your Star Lake letter from August 4 was waiting for me this afternoon when I got in from Tel Aviv, and it upset me a good deal, mainly because of the misunderstanding which inspired it. I did not, Father, go to HQ, sink gracefully down on both knees, and beg to be admitted into the army. I simply received my "greetings," which in this case was notification that my exemption had been cancelled, and I was to report for assignment within 24 hours. I spoke to some army friends and as a result was assigned to a special job in Jerusalem, at a desk. That job has now been completed, and I'm waiting to be given a new one. There has been talk of

---

17. A reference to Psalms 90:10, which puts the lifespan of humans at seventy years.
18. The Hebrew, "אין צועקים על העבר" (*"Ein tzo'akim al ha'avar,"* meaning, "don't shout at the past,") included here in quotation marks, is cited (on several internet sites, though I could not find it in the original) as a rabbinic statement. It is based, apparently, on the Mishnaic dictate in Mishna *Berakhot* 9:3: "הצועק לשעבר הרי זו תפילת שוא," *"Hatzo'ak leshe'avar harei zu tefilat shav"* – one who shouts about the past, this is a wasted prayer.

making me a war correspondent again, with the army. (That is, much as before, but in uniform and drawing army pay rather than from the *Palpost.*) I'll know tomorrow whether there's anything to the talk or not. But please understand that I did not and do not consider myself a soldier or anything remotely resembling one; I have no urge to have my name inscribed in honor rolls and my picture in halls of fame. Would you really have preferred me to hide behind my American passport and lose all and any moral right to ever settle here, or should I have gone to jail as a shirker and draft-dodger? Enough of that.

Much more interesting is this: I spent my leave – 5 days – in Tel Aviv, swimming, seeing a play, taking showers, and sounding people out about... a trip home. I saw Dallek Horowitz, and he sends his love. (I was there when the Russians presented their credentials, it certainly was impressive. This guy Yershov,[19] incidentally, is 34, and looks like 20.) I won't drag you through the whole long list of people seen and discussions held, but there is the possibility that it will work out and I'll be able to get a month's leave for a special mission. I'm making no promises, but simply pointing out that the possibility exists, it is not remote, and I'll try – am trying – my best to bring it to fruition. Fair enough? I give fair and ample warning, though, that it's going to cost Gershon the kind of money it will take me a long time to pay back on my current army salary: $450[20] one way. (I can't go by boat, it would take too long, and the whole leave-mission may not be for more than a month.) I'll try to arrange for Berlin to give me the money here and for you people to pay it in dollars there (since the pound is down to 3 dollars, it represents a saving of $150, no mean sum). I'm assuming this will meet with no objections.

19. Pavel Yershov (1914–1981) was the USSR's first ambassador to Israel.
20. Equivalent to about $4,690 in 2018.

Glad the Jerusalem-and-road story has been printed, it was a real labour of love, and weighed like a stone until I did it. I'm having a third story retyped for me now, and will mail it within a couple of days. It's about the Gadna, the kid's army (I've enclosed a vaguely parallel English version which appeared in the *Palpost*, with less stuff in it though.)

...

As for you, Gershon, where do you, a Rabbi, get off taking such a tone with almost-a-general? (I figure I must have some rank, 'cause privates get 2 LP a month while top-guts draw about 6, and I'm somewhere in the middle with LP.3.500 (that's 3-and-a-half). I'll explain the Old City campaign to you when we sit down over a *glezzel*[21] [tea] and discuss our wars, O Veteran Brother....

Haven't heard from Naomi in some time, guess she's busy having a good vacation. Nu, be well, all of you, and maybe we'll have a reunion in New York one of these fine wet, foggy days.

laylah tov, and all my love,

The brat

In his memoirs, Mordecai writes how, around September 8, he took leave in Tel Aviv before assuming his new assignment as army liaison for Central Front Combat Headquarters. While there, he met up with his former roommate, Carmi Charny, who had been transferred to the air force to debrief pilots after flight operations. Since there were few planes and few flights, Carmi had plenty of free time. His former roommate took one look at his friend and invited him for a "black-market" dinner, for what he said would be Mordecai's last decent meal for a long time.

---

21.   Yiddish, meaning "glass of."

"Why?" Mordecai asked.

"Look in the mirror! Your skin is yellow; your eyes are yellow... you have yellow jaundice!"

Mordecai ate very well indeed that night, and then reported to the army hospital at Tel Litwinsky.

In the following letter[22] to his father, Mordecai gives his location as, "an army base 'somewhere' in Israel" when, in fact, he is in the hospital. The Chertoffs had a long history of "sparing" each other news that might be distressing. Mordecai is especially sensitive to his father's nerves and ulcer.

September 13, 1948

My Dear Father,

I'm writing from an army base "somewhere" in Israel, and since I have yet to find myself a typewriter here – and I have mercy on you all and the deciphering work needed to understand my English handwriting – I am shortchanging Mother a bit and writing in Hebrew. No matter, she needs to advance her Hebrew anyway.

Regarding the draft to the American army – have no fear. First, I was not required to register here, as the American consul did not officially announce it (and also knew no details when we asked him). Second, because I passed the registration age during the registration period (ok, by one day, but nevertheless) the draft order does not apply to me at all. And so, this issue is off the agenda.

There is nothing "to forgive," and my "anger" was not anger but merely correcting an error. Obviously, I have not yet mastered the language sufficiently, and the proper subtlety and exactness are beyond me.

One possibility of travelling, for vacation, has already been disappointed, and a second is unravelling: I spoke here

---

22. The next few letters are not in precise chronological order for the sake of continuity.

to Israel Goldstein, and he telegrammed Henry Montor[23] in New York, to invite me there to do publicity for the UJA. Montor responded in the negative because "the program is full at the moment." Goldstein himself promised that he would check into the situation when he got back to New York, and if he found an opportunity, he would take advantage of it. I suggest that someone who knows Montor or has access to him – perhaps Gershon or Naomi – could influence him to telegram me to come and help them. A telegram, and a follow-up letter to Mr. Harold Jaffe, Officer, Israeli Manpower Directorate, General Staff, Israel Defense Forces, will suffice to arrange the matter. The letter should be sent directly to me, for transfer accompanied by another letter and documents from him....

I sent a third article to Ribalow. I'll leave the question of money for a personal conversation in New York. For now, I'm satisfied with the fact that I'm writing and publishing in Hebrew....

Continue sending letters directly to Tel Aviv, since I'm not far from there, and it's easier for me to get there or to send to there than to change my address every so often. My job, at the moment, is "Journalism Officer" for the headquarters of a well-known brigade, but I have not yet figured out the work itself. I got the job just a few days ago, and until now, I've been spending my time reading and walking around the base. We'll see what happens. We'll see what comes first – getting into the job or travelling!...

Did you get Moshe Shamir's[24] book, *He Walked through the Fields* there? The Cameri Theater put it on as

23. Henry Montor (1905–1982), was involved in the establishment of the United Jewish Appeal and at that point was its executive vice president. He was also the chief architect and founder of the Israel Bond Organization.
24. Moshe Shamir (1921–2004) was an Israeli journalist, author, poet and playwright noted for his independent views. His career included editing the IDF newspaper *Bamahane* and editing the literature section of the newspaper *Maariv*. His account of his brother's life, *With his Own Hands*, is an icon of Israeli writing. The play Mordecai refers to was adapted into a film by the same name in 1967.

a play, very successfully. If not, I'll send you my copy. It's interesting for several reasons, first and foremost because it shows the point of view of Israeli youth. But from a literary perspective, it's weak.

So – mealtime has arrived. If you can push Montor (I can come for a month – two if he's satisfied – and suggest that we're prepared to pay the travel expenses if that's the determining factor) you'll succeed in hurrying up the trip. Seems to me that we can't rely on – or wait for – Goldstein.

With much love and longing,

Mordecai Shmuel

* * *

September 22, 1948

Dear Gershon,

Sitting on a beautiful balcony overlooking the sea I'm taking time out to bring you up to date on my history: this morning I left the hospital at Tel Litwinsky, where I boarded for two weeks with yellow jaundice! This evening I go to Givat Brenner, to the *Beit Havra'a*,[25] for another two weeks, to swim, play ball, eat like a horse, and have me a real vacation. Milty, who is mailing this letter for me in NY, will tell you the whole story. It was a real nice stay, in the hospital, and I made some new friends. I'm looking forward to the *Beit Havra'a* now to make some more. Then, we'll see. I'll have another shot at getting a *shlihut*.[26]

Son, there is no town by the name of Dein Mheisen,[27] as you misquote in one of my letters. It is either Deir Yassin

---

25. Hebrew, meaning "recuperation/rehabilitation home."
26. Hebrew, meaning "mission abroad."
27. Mordecai is wrong. In his letter of April 8, he mentions Deir Muheisin, which must be the place to which Gershon refers.

(which was the infamous I.Z.L. slaughter) or Beit Mahsir, a Palmach cleanout which was beautifully done. What I can contribute to your sermon now is a wet rag: all the trappings of a police state are being developed here: the iron curtain (tough as hell to get out of the country), censorship of mail, delay of newspaper cables, and now, in the new Emergency Regulations, ex post facto provisions. It makes me sick to see such things here, but I'm in no position to do anything or say anything about it....

Have you seen Ilya Ehrenburg's[28] "stand" on Israel and Zionism? The old radical s**t-line – only universal improvements will aid the Jew, Zionism is mystic, bourgeois, we're being tools of imperialism, etc. What it boils down to is we've got Russian support because we're of necessity in the anti-English camp....

And that's all for now – (still haven't heard from Naomi in ages, she must be having some vacation... too bad yours bore no fruit) – I have to eat and catch a bus. Ann, incidentally, should have called the folks by now, she left here a week ago. If the chance comes, I'll grab it. Meanwhile, don't worry, Milty will tell you more about my work (what I'll be doing when I go back to work, that is). Meanwhile, happy New Year to everybody, and keep well. In spite of it all, *yihiyeh tov*. And don't worry about me, I'm well, and getting a wonderful – and much-needed – rest right now. As soon as I get hold of a decent machine I'll type out a real shmoozy letter.

Bye now....

all my love,

Mordecai

---

28.   Ilya Ehrenburg (1891–1967), was a Soviet writer, journalist and translator. He was most known for his reportage for three wars – World War I, the Spanish Civil War and World War II. He considered himself Russian and a Soviet, but left all his papers to Yad Vashem. He took strong public positions against antisemitism.

Mordecai's article describing his hospital stay is an interesting glimpse into the world of immigrant Jews that made up a large part of the fighting forces during the War of Independence.

October 24, 1948
IMPATIENT PATIENTS

By M. S. Chertoff

All 40 of us knew all the details of each other's aches and pains: we watched temperature charts, spied on blood test reports and jealously observed the changes in diet and treatment, but we never did learn anything about the patient in bed number 38.

The "walking" patients took turns helping the hard-pressed nurses' aides with the food trays for the bed patients, and the personal histories of this hospital cross-section of the world Jewry was common property: all except the story of bed number 38. We didn't even know what hurt him.

It was a Palmach sapper with too many white blood corpuscles who first noticed that there always seemed to be a nurse hovering near that particular bed; that its occupant never received visitors; that he was never addressed by name by the ward doctor; during visits by the doctors the bed was generally almost hidden by the swarming physicians who, it was assumed, prodded and poked its occupant just as they did to us less secret mortals.

The revolver one of the boys spotted under the pillow simply highlighted the mystery without offering any lead to a solution, and it wasn't until weeks later that I learned part of the answer. Retailers of military secrets were whispering about "so-and-so, from GHQ" who spent some time with the rank-and-file without his identity being even guessed at.

The secret of that 38 was beyond us all at the time, but Uri's 7 1/2 inch knife wound, memento of the battle for Haifa, was something we could see – and measure – and talk about, and Menachem's blood tests were the common concern for days.

Secret Weapon

Since ours was a military hospital every man had his story to tell. The tall gangling fellow in bed 17 had fought at Negba back in the days when the Molotov cocktail was an untried secret weapon against Egyptian tanks, before Baruch had gone through officer's training school and learned that according to all the rules of modern warfare it was impossible to defend Negba. But in the bunkers at Negba nobody had ever heard of the rules, and so they beat back the best the St. Cyr-trained Egyptian commanders could throw at them.

The hulking Bulgar, who had acquired a few words of half a dozen European languages on his way to Palestine, began his own fighting career before the war was officially declared when an Arab picked a fight with him on board ship. That particular Arab, if he made it, will be able to tell his cronies about how he swam halfway across the Mediterranean.

My immediate neighbor to the left was from Abyssinia, more recently from Mishmar Hayarden, while across the aisle was a Jew from Syria, a Halabi (with a distinguished hospital record in the British army,) and a friendly Druse who played a good game of checkers. He was picking up Hebrew fast, but always retreated behind a musical "*Aineni mevin*" (I don't understand) whenever asked about his fellow-tribesmen or Druse life and customs.

"My" Yemenite was always anxious to talk though, and always about America and the power of the Jewish vote there. Since I've been away from the US almost 2 years now he scornfully dismissed anything I had to say on the subject, and I was in near-despair at the profound contempt he displayed as he quoted from the daily press. I finally persuaded him that I had also worked for a newspaper, and he grudgingly conceded that one reporter's word was as good as another's, even though he gave the printed word the slight edge.

Leave from Jaundice

With Benyamin I had another kind of feud, a race to see whose golden yellow coloring would fade back to normal first. I beat him out by a nose – he took two days leave (from jaundice) to meet his parents who were arriving from France after two years of separation. The high Tel Aviv living did him no good...

My favorite patient though was Uri. Massively built sabra son of a sabra, he couldn't make his peace with being ill. The knife-wound was different, and the bullet in his thigh with something else again; these were things he could see, he could watch them heal, feel the hurt gradually melt away and the old suppleness come back; he could see the long, ugly welt fine down to a thin, angry red line and the jagged rip shrink down to a small, round 5-mil piece scar. But internal aches were beyond him.

Being bedridden was the one thing Uri couldn't take, and when his pain eased up for more than a few hours he invariably announced himself cured and went chasing around the camp in his white pajamas, heckling the girls drilling in a nearby field or visiting acquaintances in other wards.

The agony which invariably followed each breach of hospital regulations he would attribute to some vague, malicious agency – a mysterious something referred to for fuller identification as "they" – assigned to torment one Uri, Palmachnik veteran of the Galilee and Negev fighting.

"Malaria is no illness," the early *halutzim* used to say, and today any nurse will add that regardless of the ailment, a Palmachnik is no patient. Rather than wait for the results of the X-rays and tests, Uri insisted upon being sent to a convalescent centre. I had by then "faded" enough to be discharged from hospital and we left together. But I found that we weren't to be together long; while I sunbathed and swam, frightened by illness into obedient convalescence, Uri ran wild.

We were close to town, and a holiday without cinema was unthinkable, so Uri, who had learned how to sneak up behind Arab sentries and had led silent Palmach raiders into Syria and the Lebanon, would steal away for a little entertainment.

Opera Flight

When the opera came to town, Uri decided we were going. We clambered through a ground floor window without difficulty, but it took a lot of arguing and the baring of Uri's knife wound to get us in without tickets. I tried looking ill but it was Uri who turned the trick.

That he suffered for every escapade was painfully obvious to me, since we were roommates, but there was no stopping him. His stock rejoinder took the form of swashbuckling, accompanied by a derisive twirling of the sweeping mustaches, a slap at the powerful barrel-chest and the conclusive "look at me, yaaaa, do I look sick?"

When life became too dull and there were no more gullible victims to believe Uri's stories about his "flying roommate," with the 5,000 hours flying time to his credit who had been shot down three times and who had bombed every Arab capital (and I've never been higher off the ground than I could climb); and when people stopped following us about respectfully across the beautiful green lawns, Uri decided to leave.

Nobody knew he had gone until the dietitian found his dinner still standing on the table one Sunday noon. I did my best to seem surprised when questioned about the disappearance, but I don't think I fooled anyone: before he left, Uri had told me he was going back, down to the Negev. His brother had been killed there while commanding the garrison forces at Nirim: Uri had an account to settle with Egyptians.

While continuing to recover from jaundice and waiting for a new assignment from the army, Mordecai looks ahead, from the need to fight for the state to the challenge of building it. He responds to an anxious letter from his sister with a forward-looking analysis of Israel's future needs. Here is the portion of Naomi's letter to which Mordecai responds:

September 13, 1948

Dearest Mersh,

I am almost ashamed to admit this toots, but I find that since the recognition of the State of Israel, my own emotional involvement in Israel has changed. I feel more like a spectator now...you've no idea what the creation of a new flag (instead of the Magen David) did to me. It was the most concrete manifestation of the change in status of the Israeli Jew. I honestly feel that only those who live there have the right and obligation to determine Israel's destiny. Although we must continue with economic support (even our moral support is questionable) I feel, (since I don't have ... [plenty of] dough to set up a castor bean corporation for plastics) pretty much left out. Maybe, once I'm there again, I'll feel different. This is the first time in my life that I feel remote (perhaps too strong a word, but you get the idea.) It's almost as though I know that Israel will get along without my speech making, etc. Perhaps this is a reaction to living in Cleveland, away from the national board and the hub. Perhaps it's a reaction to no longer being a "big shot" on things in Israel etc. I hope so, for if it's not so, if it's not colored by this last consideration, and it can happen to me, I dread the change in the masses of Americans. Although, on second thought, this worry is foolish, since most American Jews climb on the bandwagon only when the band is playing loud and strong. They weren't in on the building and planning and fighting etc., and so don't have the finished feeling. I have hesitated even to admit this to myself. What do you think? Am I a renegade?

* * *

[Late September, 1948?]

Dear Toots,

... By now I hope Ann has explained to you why it is NOT so simple for me to just drop in for a visit. ... Right now, it would be a good deal easier for the whole family to make the trip here than for me to go to America. Nuf sed.

Where did you get that flag stuff? We still fly the Magen David; I haven't seen any other! Of course the navy and the air force – and the army – have their own insignia, just as the American forces do, but that does not change the State flag. As for your feeling about the country – its needs have suddenly changed, and you're in the position of the guy with the perfect mouse-trap – confronted with DDT. You developed an approach and a technique adequate for the potential state, now that's no longer needed, and we need other techniques, to meet other problems. We will always need people to do public relations, though (the job done with the Anglo-Saxon recruits stinks, and we're making enemies of some of the boys we've brought over to help us fight!) and there you certainly have a job. In addition, within the state, and granted its safe existence, we'll need psychiatrists and social workers and analysts to deal with the emotional and psychological wrecks this war is producing, we'll need people to work with the cripples and aid in their rehabilitation; we need all the services America needed – and still needs – for her discharged serviceman, as well as something America never had to worry about – someone to handle the tremendous aliyah, from the psychological aspect. Remember the problems of the Teheran kids?[29] We have all of that magnified a thousand fold now.

---

29. The "Tehran Children" were a group of Polish Jewish children, mainly orphans, who escaped the Nazi German occupation of Poland. They found temporary refuge in

Your let-down feeling is natural; I felt very much the same when the underground vanished and the army emerged. As a non-soldier, as one qualified to be no more than a pair of hands, to contribute no more, after having been here so long and learned the country, than a kid here three days, hurt. I felt left out. I finally found an assignment suitable to my abilities, and felt useful again. Now, having been sick, (and that first job having been completed) I'm again hoping. Within a day or two I'll know where I'm going to fit myself in, and I'll again feel like a mensch. Right now I'm still on leave in Tel Aviv....

Army salary, dear child, is only £2 per month, regardless of the glamor of the job...I've had a commission offered me, but it's to do a job I don't care for, so I said no. As I said a few lines higher, something is brewing, and I'll know soon. There may be rank involved (since you seem so anxious to have brass in the family. Wasn't Gershon's captaincy enough for you?)

As for writing – has the Eternal Light[30] had a script on the Burma Road yet? I've been thinking of trying one... you did not tell me about the new job. You mentioned there was one on the horizon, but that's all. What gives? Mrs. Yassky got the letter. Keep using the Tel post address.

I don't know how to break this, since I don't know how the American press handled the story – but you'd better write to Hadassah Van Vriesland too. Mrs. V.V. was murdered,[31] along with three others, travelling on the main Tel Aviv highway to Jerusalem. It was near Latrun, and they were shot at an almost two yard range. I haven't been in to see Hadassah yet, but I hope to be able to do so soon....

---

orphanages and shelters in the Soviet Union, and were later evacuated, along with several hundred adults, to Tehran, Iran, before finally reaching Palestine in 1943.

30.   Possibly a radio program.
31.   Jeanette Van Vriesland. The attack occurred on September 22, 1948.

That's all for now – keep writing, Toots, *Leshana tova*,[32] happy birthday and happy anniversary. All my love to everybody.

The brat

---

32. Hebrew, meaning "to a happy (Jewish) new year." In 1948, Rosh HaShana coincided with October 4 and 5.

Chapter 30

Phase Three: October, 1948 – January, 1949

Israel had performed well and made some important gains during the intense period of the Ten Days that preceded the truce. But if unchanged, the situation on the ground, in both the north and the south, would leave Israel without large sections of the land allocated to it under partition and with borders that could not be defended. While the UN was working to end the fighting permanently, Israel was planning its next campaigns to address these issues.

In the south of the country, most of which had been allocated to the Jews under partition, Israel held only two areas, one of which was completely encircled by the Egyptians. The Egyptians were entrenched along the coast all the way up to Isdud,[1] just twenty miles from Tel Aviv, and held a strategic corridor of land in the Negev which bisected Israel's holdings. They also held Beersheba and were on the outskirts of Jerusalem.

With the resumption of fighting, Israel's strategy was to rout the Egyptians by waging a war of attrition, i.e., to cut enemy supply and communication lines, isolate specific brigades, and erode them gradually.

---

1. Renamed "Ashdod" in 1956.

The Israelis launched the campaign with an effective surprise attack on Egypt's airfields in el-Arish. They also intercepted and deciphered, in real time, Egyptian radio transmissions and used naval commandos to sink the Egyptian flagship, *Amir Farouk*, lying off the coast.[2] Israel eventually succeeded in halting invading Egyptian forces and encircling them in the area of Faluja but did not gain possession of the Gaza strip.

In the north, the Partition Plan had awarded the Central and Western Galilee to the Arabs, but after the first two phases of the war, the Western Galilee was in Jewish hands. The central portion, however, was held by the Arab Liberation Army and constituted a threat to the Jews' ability to maintain their hold on the western portion. In anticipation of a resumption of the fighting, Israel prepared Operation Hiram, whose goal was to take the entire Galilee and establish a defensible northern border.

On October 22, the Arab Liberation Army attacked Kibbutz Manara, in the Upper Galilee on the border with Lebanon. The Syrians also participated in the battle. The Jews launched a counter-attack, Operation Hiram, on October 28 with an air raid designed for psychological impact – on both the Arab and the Israeli forces. As with the campaign in the south, Israel used wedges and pincer movements to isolate and disrupt enemy troops. It was effective: the ALA was caught completely off guard. Israel's campaign required barely sixty hours and resulted in complete Jewish control of the Galilee.

---

2. These are all military tactics which Israel would use again, with great success, in subsequent wars with Egypt in 1967 and 1973.

Chapter 31
Frontline Magazine

Most of Mordecai's letters written during this period are personal and introspective. By the time he was well enough to leave the convalescent home, the post of liaison officer had been filled. The army could not wait for him. Instead, he was assigned to a new magazine to be published in English, called *Frontline* – for the volunteers from Anglo-Saxon countries. He was issued *Frontline* Magazine Press Card #1. He describes the magazine and his work there below. In addition to the new job, Mordecai also moves from Jerusalem to Tel Aviv.

Oct. 20, 1948

Dear Family,

You amaze me, individually and collectively. For what perverse, malicious reasons do you imagine that I refuse to make the trip home when I might?...

I had to accept a job or find myself up on charges of desertion or something like it. Besides, one must live, and on what? If your papers aren't in order you don't stand a

449

chance in this country. So, I took this job – war correspondent, assigned to help get out an English weekly[1] for our Anglo-Saxons, and to be its roving reporter. True, I'm getting a lot less money than I did before, but then it's the army, after all. At present, the only chance for an exit from the army (first requirement) and then from the country is if I'm designated by an American paper as its correspondent here. I've sent Izzy Stone all my clippings; if he's still there maybe he can do something. A cable from a NY paper asking me to cover events here for them and granting cable rights would get me the army release. It would then be a matter of a month and I would be able to leave for consultations with the paper, etc. I'll see Weisgal as soon as I get settled here in Tel Aviv (I just got in from Jerusalem, where I had to move from the Van Vreisland place because Hadassah is going to rent the whole house, now that her mother is gone – you might have written her a note, you know, both you, Mother, and Naomi, who were such good friends.) But please, please, don't make of my life a goddammit with blind insistence that I just "drop in" for a while. Believe me, it is a bit more complicated than a trip to the Bronx! The people who are making the trip are of all kinds, and most are not to be envied: at the cost of an arm or a leg, or eyes, it would be easy to get home, but hardly worthwhile. Please remember that it is not a matter of choice at present, and I shall continue to do my best. But don't push so hard, you simply aggravate things

[The rest of the letter is missing.]

Although he is now a soldier assigned to *Frontline* magazine, Mordecai still manages to send articles to the *Palestine Post*. In the following he describes his visit to Nir Am, one of the settlements cut off by the Egyptians during the Ten Days. It is located close to the current northern border of the Gaza strip. Battles raged in the corridor between the two Jewish-held enclaves of the Negev from October 15 to 20. Mordecai must have visited the area shortly after.

---

1.   I.e., *Frontline*.

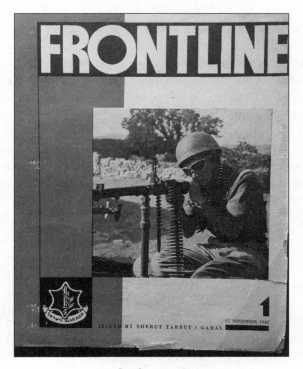

Frontline magazine

Oct. 27, 1948

THE OPEN ROAD

By Mordecai S. Chertoff

The dining-room-bunker at Nir Am, isolated since the Jewish State was declared and kept supplied by the Israel Air Force air lift, is barely large enough to hold three tables. Grouped around those tables, the besieged defenders listened to recordings of symphony concerts and sat in three shifts to see *The Hunchback of Notre Dame* when they weren't on guard duty or when Egyptian shelling let up enough for gardening-by-night.

Nir Am's own pretty little dining room, where the UNSCOP delegates were received after their tour of Jewish settlements in the Negev, is now a weather-beaten, shell-riddled hulk, but Hanna, two-year veteran of the settlement, refused to discuss material loss when she met with journalists after units of the Israel Negev Army had swept past on their triumphant drive south to Beersheba.

After the fall of Huleikat, where the Egyptian army lost one of its three Negev battalions, the Israel drive picked up such speed that the defenders of Nir Am could only wave happily as it swept by, leaving journalists to bring the first eye-witness reports from the new State to its long-isolated citizens.

Certified Violation

We crossed the Egyptian east-west line between Majdal and Iraq Suweidan, near the Tegart Fortress[2] above which we could see the green Egyptian flag fluttering in the breeze. But there was no sign of life there: Hill 113, retaken after the Egyptians had seized it in a certified violation of the truce, dominates the eastern side of the fortress and keeps the occupying Egyptians away from the windows.

To our right, as we crossed the Faluja-Majdal line without let or hindrance, Israel soldiers manned a barbed-wire roadblock. The tables were turned: the Jewish supply route to the Negev settlements is no longer at the mercy of the Egyptians, who now find their own east-west road closed.

There are no fortifications to be seen on Hill 113, and we could only guess at underground bunkers as we passed far in the wake of the Israel army. There weren't

---

2. A type of militarized police fort constructed throughout Palestine during the Mandate as a measure against the 1936–39 Arab Revolt, named for its designer, Sir Charles Tegart. Since the time of this article, the name has come to be incorrectly rendered in Israel as "Taggart."

even evidences of the bitter fighting that raged there. The only sign of victory to be seen – aside from the empty Arab villages of Kaukaba, Huleikat and Bureir, was the lone Egyptian tank parked under a tree by side of the road. And the soldier sitting on its back was an Israeli.

It was around Huleikat, for the heights dominating the village, that one of the bitterest battles of the war was fought. For more than four hours it raged, and when the Egyptians finally took to their heels they had lost some 500 men in casualties as well as tens of prisoners and 31 tanks, four six-pounder cannon, two two-pounders, 20 Vickers machine guns and 100 others, including hundreds of rifles, PIATs, mortars, a 37 mm cannon and arms and clothing stores. The Egyptians had held Kaukaba and Huleikat and with them a ten-kilometer stretch of the now-open highway.

At the same time, the early Egyptian drive eastward, from Majdal to Faluja, had cut Israel's bypass route to the Negev through Hatta and Karatiya which were taken on the eve of the second truce.

And the Egyptians refused to abide by the U.N. decision to open the route.

The Israel drive, besides opening the Negev road, chopped the Egyptian lines at the crossroads just south of Hill 113, on the Majdal-Gaza road near Beit Hanun, and east of Iraq-el-Manshiyeh, at Khirbet Massarah.

Israel forces crashing down from the north fought their way to a junction with other units coming up from the south; the fall of Huleikat on October 19 saw the union of these forces, which had made full use of Israel artillery with the superb cooperation of the Israel Air Force. Planes bombed the main Egyptian bases at Gaza, Majdal, Faluja and Beersheba night after night. The first night Beersheba was spared after a week of such bombing was the night of October 20, when Israeli army units were already swarming around it and bringing up their forces for the drive, which was to bring about the initial fall of the city by dawn and the wiping out of its last resisting pockets by noon.

Historical Interest

The Egyptian drive on Negba, at the beginning of the war, had been brought to a dead stop by Sten-guns and Molotov cocktails. Now the whole Negev block is clear, and the run southward from Rehovot to Negba and Nir Am across the rolling, rich farmland of the northern Negev is of interest to news-thirsty correspondents only from a "historical" point of view.

The defenders of Nir Am are anxious for a trip in to Tel Aviv – to see the fifty children evacuated early in the war, and to see "what the State is like."

And then they plan to return home, to the settlement, to what Jews all over Israel are doing when the truce in the area permits: rebuild what has been destroyed, replant what has been uprooted.

On November 16 the UN Security Council passed a resolution to begin talks. A truce was in effect from the middle of November through most of December. The Israeli cabinet was conflicted about continuing the war but there was a consensus to get the Egyptians out of areas designated for the Jews and encourage them to sue for peace and encourage the other Arab countries to follow suit. Mordecai does not discuss any of these developments in his letters.

November 24, 1948

Dear Folks,

First of all, let me reassure Father that what he took to be *yeush*[3] must be understood in context – disgust with the blank walls I kept meeting in all my attempts to

---

3.   Hebrew, meaning "despair."

arrange a *shlihut*. A week or two ago I thought I had one all arranged, but in my haste I overlooked the catch: finding a replacement to do my job before the army will release me. Find me somebody who's been here almost two years, knows the country and the language, has had newspaper and magazine experience – and is neither in the army nor in a good civilian job, and is willing to step in. (We couldn't get another army guy, because no unit is going to hand out releases, especially of guys with any ability.) SOOOooooo – it looks as though I'll be here a while.

My job, at the moment, takes me back to college days – I'm editing an army magazine for the Anglo-Saxons. It is called *Frontline*, and it is a bi-weekly which will probably appear every three weeks. At the moment, a boy from Canada is giving me a hand on it. He's a navigator who was in a little flying difficulty one day and has been grounded. Until he leaves he'll be working with me. Since he's had some experience in the field he's a big help. When he gets to New York he'll drop in to see you.

...

I can't get too broken up about Magnes.[4] At least he died quietly, without earning himself martyrdom. Just imagine if some hothead had knocked him off!

The Anglo-Saxons, Father, are the boys who have come from America, Canada, England, South Africa, Australia, Ireland, Scotland – both Jews and Gentiles – to help in the good fight. How many is a lovely military secret, but enough to warrant a special magazine for them. The magazine is like any army job, with pictures, stories of battles, and a sprinkling of light stuff and a bit of political education and orientation stuff thrown in for good measure. Our first issue will be off the press tomorrow, and I hope to send you a copy during the next few days.

---

4. Judah Leon Magnes died on October 27, 1948. See chapter 5, footnote 118, for more about him.

What boredom is, and from what it derives, I don't have to explain. This fear business is very complicated, though. It has a way of working like a delayed-action fuse. Things I went through months ago sometimes come back vividly, and while during the incident itself the demands made upon me and the effort I had to expend drove all fear away, in retrospect, with the need for action on my part removed, I can savour more fully of the danger-content of the moment, and suddenly, in the absolute safety of my bed, feel an unreasonable fear. I lived through days and days of intense shelling in Jerusalem without being afraid, or at least without being conscious of being afraid. Yet there are times when I feel my flesh beginning to crawl as I try to explain to a newcomer to Israel what those days were like. With the body relaxed, the emotion repressed at the time of the adventure has a chance to come to the surface. And it does. But not for long, and not in a way to cause any real or lasting discomfort. [ends]

Mordecai describes what is obviously post-traumatic stress disorder honestly, candidly and clearly. He may not have been a soldier on active duty during the war, but he was a member of the Haganah, in a besieged city, and he is finally able to be honest with his family about the consequences of his experiences, no longer needing to protect them from that difficult reality. As an embedded journalist, he was an eyewitness to battle, with all the stress that entails; as a civilian, he suffered privation and repeated attacks on his home city. Lucky enough to not be harmed physically, he knew many who were, and many who died.

Mordecai's new job was not without drama. In his memoirs, he describes how he neglected to check the budget for the new magazine. He simply told the *Haaretz* printers to bill the army:

When they did, I was nearly court-martialed. I had spent as much on one issue as all the other foreign-language papers spent together (they were all mimeographed). But Ben Gurion said it was just the thing for the '*Englo-Sexim*,' and I was saved.

In early December, Israel launched Operation Asaf, the successful effort to take control of the western Negev Desert.

Sunday, Dec. 19, 1948

Dear Family,

I am, to use an army phrase, pissed off. For the last three months I've been negotiating for leave, missions and what have you, and suddenly, pop! Another friend is going to America for six weeks, all expenses paid, to speak for the new U.J.A. youth arrival [?]. He met Morgenthau here, who liked him, Bernstein, with whom the guy traveled as press man for a month, pushed a little, and on Tuesday Azariah flies out to Paris, then on to N.Y. He'll call you when he gets there. For closer identification, he's the guy from my Burma Road story, the other correspondent. Be nice to him – we almost got killed together. He's a good-looking boy, very vain, superficial, but with talent. He needs editing, he should work under a tough boss for a while and he'd really develop into a writer. But that's neither here nor there;

...

Before I forget – you should read the "Israeli Diary" every Shabbat in the *New York Post* "Home News." My very good friend Al Rosenfeld writes it, and I generally read the man-uscripts here either after they're written or while still in the process. Yesterday, for example, I sat there listening to music and fighting with Judy who was doing one part of the diary – over a few words. I had my way, and it changed the whole tone of the piece. I imagine you'll get this letter before that diary appears, so make sure you read it; it's an honest account of one of the local dangers: the lack of understanding on the part of the yishuv of the democratic processes, or the need for them. Some of them feel that if it's "neat" – *mesudar*[5] – it's okay. It's a touchy subject, I'd rather not go into it now.

---

5. Hebrew, meaning "organized" or "orderly."

...

That's all for now – I want to get this letter off without undue delay.

Shalom, and, "Insh'Allah,"[6] lehitraot bekarov.[7]

love,

mersh

* * *

Dec. 1948[8]

Dear Family,

The second issue of *Frontline* has just come off the press, and you will be getting both issues in about a week – Perry, whom I've mentioned before, is leaving on Sunday, by plane, and he'll bring them both....

Jeeezuz, Maw, if you ever shake hands with that lousy...Begin without spitting in his eye simultaneously I'll never forgive you.[9] How my own mother should so let her political intelligence slip I can't imagine. To save me the trouble of a long lecture, won't somebody there remind mother what...Begin is?...

I'm planning to be in Rehovot on Sunday to do a story for the magazine on the Institute,[10] ...

I did not read about opening night at the opera, and as I re-read this letter of yours and see that bit about Begin[11] I begin to see red, so I'd better get on to something else. ...

---

6. Arabic, meaning "God willing."
7. Hebrew, meaning "See you soon."
8. Probably around Dec 20.
9. Later in life, Mordecai came to admire Begin as a statesman and man of integrity.
10. The Weizmann Institute of Science.
11. After the opera, Esther went to a fundraiser for Begin at the Waldorf Hotel.

After the appearance of the first issue we found a guy to take my place. I'm breaking him in now, he helped with the second and I'll have him do most of the third. Meanwhile, bright and early Sunday morning my application for two months compassionate leave – without tricks, without protektzia, without what is known as *foyleh schtick*[12] – will be put on the proper desks. My. C. O. has agreed that I may leave, and now I just have to convince the board. As I understand it, the chances of my being home by the end of January are pretty good indeed. So there.

I wrote to George a long time ago, thanking him for his help.

[letter continues to Gershon]

Dear Gershon,

I'm trying to duplicate my letter to you which I lost, but I'm afraid it's no go. You see, it opened with exclamations of surprise and delight over finally getting a letter from you, and then went on to comment very brightly over each and every line. I'm simply awe-struck at the way you turn out sermons, week after week, *hag* after *hag*,[13] each one better than the one before. I would run dry in half an hour. As a matter of fact, when I think of being called upon to speak when I get back to the States, I shudder. I have nothing to tell them. Really nothing. They'll never understand what we went through here, they can't possibly. Hunger, thirst, fear, sleeplessness, constant danger, are just words to them. In addition, I have a sneaking contempt for most of the young Jews in America who didn't find it necessary to come and help, I hardly share language and feeling with them. But you're doing fine – you'll have to let me come and listen someday....

---

12. Yiddish, meaning "pulling off something sneaky, underhanded."
13. Hebrew, meaning "(Jewish) holiday after holiday."

In view of the possibility of my return soon, don't send me any books for the present. Furthermore, I have no room for anything now. Some things have accumulated at the hotel, where I never feel that they are secure. The less I have kicking around the better I'll like it. Incidentally, Zippy was not in Sheikh Jarrah when I visited her, but in Deir Yassin. And she's not a full nurse, but a *hoveshet*.[14] You'll be able to read the story in *Frontline*, I reprinted it. (It just occurred to me, in the first issue I wrote pages 2, 4, 9, 10, 11, and re-wrote page 5, besides picking and captioning the pictures, planning the layout and doing the back-cover story as well.

...By the way, *bocher*,[15] you can't expect to think of a job here, and then plan your future accordingly. The only thing to do is come. I suggest that you plan to spend next summer vacation here, at least, and look around then. You must visit the state anyway, I'll be here too, and it should be very pleasant indeed. We'll talk about it when I get home.

That's all for now. Next time you'll get a letter all for yourself. But right now I have to get back to work and get some stuff ready for the next issue. (Even a bi-weekly takes work.)

Shabbat shalom, and all my love,

Mordecai

Israel launched Operation Horev, a large-scale offensive against the Egyptians, on December 22. By December 27, they were attacking the Egyptian army at al-Auja, on the Egyptian border, about sixty km south of Gaza. The Egyptians would effectively surrender a little over a week later. But Mordecai's attitude to the progress of the war has become somewhat detached.

14. Hebrew, meaning "medic."
15. Yiddish, meaning "young man."

December 27, 1948

Dear Family,

There's been another break in the stream of letters from you, but I assume the mail system is at fault. What with the censorship and the general lack of respect for speed in these matters I'm not surprised that it takes time.

...To date, three issues of *Frontline* have appeared. I assume that you've seen the first two already – Perry took copies for you. He should be in New York by now. (I just received a card from him, in Paris, dated Dec. l6, and he was about to leave for the States.) Sooooo. Like it? I bet you can't pick out the stuff I wrote...

Last night I got back to Tel Aviv after a very restful, lazy weekend in Jerusalem. The weather was fine, Moshe Sachs (JTS boy) was a gracious host, and his wife is a good cook. In brief – it was fine all around.

You know as much about our war here as I do, I guess. I'm too busy with the magazine to pay much attention to the war. Incidentally, do you ever listen to Arthur Holzman's nightly (5 nights a week) program from Tel Aviv, over WMCA? It should be good, he's a good man. And do you like the stuff Al Rosenfeld has been writing in the *NY Post*? Most of it, I think, is good....

On Thursday, December 30, I appear before a committee which will decide whether I rate a trip home – at my expense – for a couple of months. There is every chance of success – but you know how these things are. At any rate, I'll let you know as soon as I do.

That's about all for now – I'm going out for supper, and then I shall either take in a movie or go visiting.

Laylah tov – and lehitraot.

All my love,

Mersh

The last article Mordecai files with the *Post* in 1948 is a timely and conve-
nient summary of his thoughts about the role of American volunteers in
Israel and their expectations. Mordecai was not a volunteer but a drafted,
regular citizen-soldier. In later life he was involved with the Organization
of American Veterans in Israel and was active in MAHAL,[16] the umbrella
organization for foreigners serving in Israel's army.

Dec. 29, 1948

MAHAL FOUND THE
BATTLE HALF DONE

From a Mahal Correspondent

Three American students at the Hebrew University, wearing the remnants of their American army uniforms, nearly
touched off a local celebration when they went into a Jerusalem café for a bite to eat. That was in December of last year,
soon after the war had begun and every American here was
being held personally responsible for what the U.S. State
Department said and did. It was before the volunteers had
arrived from overseas and the very possibility of their arrival
was a matter for conjecture and debate.

It was "ah, you're America" when Austin voted for
Partition, but it was "you and your America!" when the
embargo remained in force even after the Arab invasion.
And all over the country American ex-soldiers met the same
challenge: "when are your friends coming?"

We didn't know. All we did know was that many of
the Americans already here had been in the Haganah long
before the trouble started, had had their training and were
being sent to posts in Jerusalem and its environs, were taking
part in the defence of the city both in special Yankee Units
and alongside of the Sabras in mixed units as well. Among

---

16.   MAHAL is the acronym for "*Mitnadvei Hutz LaAretz*" – "Volunteers from Abroad."

ourselves we groused over the absence of our friends and wondered not only when, but much more, whether, they would come at all. We weren't too sure.

Bits of information filtered up to Jerusalem from Tel Aviv, and we shared the excitement with everybody else when we heard that the "Americans" were coming, wondered which of them we knew, how they had come and what they had brought with them.

Saving the State

One of the things they brought was a mistaken conception of why they were coming. Many of them felt they were coming to "save" the Jewish State, to win the war for the natives – after which they would pack their bags and go back to the fleshpots until they were "needed" again.

Initially, then, albeit subconsciously, they resented the accomplishments of the meagre forces who not only held against the invaders but took city after city, town after town, and had complete control of Haifa, Safed, Tiberias, Jaffa and most of New Jerusalem before many of the would-be saviours had one foot off the boat – or plane. And because they had come to fight, they resented the unexpected periods of idleness resulting from the truces and the string of sub-truces and cease-fires. And even if only subconsciously, they were jealous of the plethora of "heroes" they found when they arrived, local boys and girls who had gone from battle to battle, from campaign to campaign, translating the paper recognition of the U.N. into a material fact built on the bodies of those who asked for no recognition and rebelled against all early attempts at the formation of a regular army, with rank, insignium and medals.

Part of the guilt for the basic misunderstanding involved lies in the recruiting offices overseas, which exaggerated the need, in the eagerness to raise a volunteer army, and in so doing prepared these volunteers for the kind of reception the liberators of the Nazi concentration camps met when they brought freedom and food to the victims of the world war.

Over Persuasive

Part of the guilt lies with the authorities here, both civil and military, who forgot their own early days as immigrants to Palestine and looked upon the English-speaking volunteers as a new aliyah – and nothing more. We took it for granted these "*olim*" would want to fight, would take every trial that came their way with understanding and appreciation of the newness and rawness of the administration and not be personally discouraged by the apparent indifference to their presence and assistance manifested by the Yishuv.

But this was not a new aliyah, not another wave of immigrants coming because the balance of factors in the scale determining whether a given Jewish community stays put or strikes out for Palestine had shifted in favour of the latter.

Disappointment

True, there was a resurgence of Zionist feeling overseas. But these men and women had been sold a bill of goods that they were "essential" to the salvation of the Jewish State. Feeling very much like liberators and saviours, then, they came. To their shocked surprise the rugs were not rolled out to greet them, nor were the trumpets sounded in their honour. They were put through the army routine of Transit Camp, training an assignment without fuss of feathers. And because of it they felt slighted. They had come as fighters, not settlers, and they expected special recognition, special status.

Some did, that is. One must of course, distinguish between the kinds of people who came or, more properly, between their reasons for coming.

There were those who were attracted by the fighting itself because, as veterans, they had difficulty in readjusting to American civilian life. And there were, of course those who had been planning to come "ultimately" and advanced their plans because they felt they were needed here and could contribute more by coming immediately.

There were non-Jews among them too, men who came to fight for a just cause, the scores who went to Spain in its time. There were those who came out of an unconscious need to atone for the wrongs done to the Jew through the ages by the non-Jew.

We've already lost a number of these men, among them many who had much to contribute to the peace-time building of our state. And we've lost most of them not because they were poor material or unfit for life in Israel, not because they hadn't what a pioneering country needs and couldn't meet the challenge of the rising young state, but because we forgot they were not a real aliya, we forgot that they needed a special approach and a special orientation. Not the "old" Zionists among them – they need little but demobilization for them to take their place alongside the immigrants of the earlier aliyoth – but the fledgling Zionists, those who came from a need, little-understood even by them, to identify actively with the Jewish state, to fight for it and help it become safely and strongly established.

Democratic Traditions

Numerically, this potential aliyah – and it is still only potential – is a small one. But it is basically a healthy one, physically and emotionally, without the years of con-centration-camp living and oppression which inform so many European immigrants. If only because of this, it is potentially a very important factor in the development of the state.

What is more, it brings with it a democratic tradition and experience of personal liberty and human dignity alien to large segments of the European aliyah. Whether this tradition becomes part of the fabric of the state will depend in part on how many of these English-speaking volunteers remain when their term of service is up, and will, in turn, determine whether many of them ultimately decide to settle or pack up and leave when the fighting is over.

Israel has met the physical challenge of the Arabs; will it meet the intellectual and ideological challenge of its own soldiers and potential settlers?

Mordecai's article reflects the increasing ambivalence he felt as an American in Israel. Throughout the correspondence he oscillated between feeling total commitment to Israel and a desire to return to New York to pursue a life of the mind. His use of "We" at the beginning of the third paragraph demonstrates his clear self-identification as an American in Israel, despite the fact that he was not an overseas volunteer, but an Israeli citizen and a regular soldier. As staunch a Zionist as he was, he treasured American democracy and press freedoms.

As it turned out, the article was heavily edited, and Mordecai's byline removed, making it anonymous. He was furious and sent the following tirade to *Post* editor, Leah Ben Dor. I include the letter because it touches on Mordecai's increasing concerns about the health of democracy and press freedoms in Israel, frustrations previously expressed in his letters to his family.

December 29, 1948

Dear Leah,

For once I must take violent exception to the manner in which my article, printed in today's *Post*, was cut. Space could hardly have been the reason for your omission of every reference to the Yishuv or to the Government containing any kind of criticism, direct or even implied. As a result the piece does not say what I wanted it to say, and leaves unexplained a good deal of what was printed.

Mention of the "democratic tradition," for example, is meaningless as it stands in the article: I had referred to specific violations of that tradition, were they cut lest someone, somewhere, be offended? Was mention of the undemocratic element in the Yishuv cut out of deference to that element or out of a fear that "outsiders" would find something to which to object in the young state?

The article was not intended as a bit of harmless reportage, not something to amuse the reader for the moment. I fully realized, when I wrote it, that there would be no lack of zealots to object to this or that item, and for that reason it never occurred to me to take refuge behind an anonymous "mahal correspondent." I signed the article, embodying my views, because I was quite willing to be held responsible for those views; I did not expect the Post to assume the responsibility – and cut the piece accordingly. That *Post* responsibility for any article would entail cutting out criticism is hardly to the credit of the paper, and leaves the box at the head of the leader column a rather pathetic bleat, particularly coming from a publication that once had the energy – and the nerve – to fight.

I would be much obliged to you if you would kindly send the complete manuscript on to me, care of the Tel Aviv office – I still feel that what I said had to be said and still bears saving, if the *Post* is afraid to print it I'm sure I can find someone who is not.

Sincerely,

[Mordecai S. Chertoff]

Copy to G.A.

Chapter 32

Going Home

January 2, 1949

Dear Family,

So Perry spilled the beans. I was going to wire just before leaving, but it's just as well this way, since borrowing from Miller will save me a lot of running around.

I went in to appear before the special Leave Board, and found it to consist of two people – Kieve Skiddel, ex. Habonim, etc., whom I know well from NY, and Lee Harris, an American (civilian) with whom I am on good terms (the day before, he had moved into a new apartment, where Al and Judy Rosenfeld live, and Judy and I helped him push furniture around. It was a good deed that paid off). I had with me a picture of four kids at Kfar Blum, bare buttocks flashing in the sun, as they played in the Jordan (a picture we're running in *Frontline*). Both Kieve and Lee knew what I wanted, of course, so the interview was, in effect, staged for the recording secretary.

It went like this:

Lee and K: *Shalom*, sit down.

Me: *Shalom*. Before we get started, Kieve, here's your picture.

Everybody: Ooh, ah, my my my!

Lee: Can you tell which is yours, even from behind?

Kieve: Of course!

Lee: How long you here, Chertoff?

Me: Almost two years.

Lee: You came to study at the University (nodding vigorously at me).

Me: Yes, then I got into the Haganah and then...

Lee: (Waving a hand at me) Okay, okay, we've got a lot to do today.

Kieve: (Who's been writing all this time) You're asking for two months, correct?

Me: Yes.

Kieve: Maybe we better make it three?

Me: No objections at all!

Lee: You'll have to pay your own way, of course.

Me: (Gulp gulp) That's all right.

Kieve: Let's see you before you go, *ken*?[1]

Me: Of course. *Todah rabbah*.[2] *Shalom*.

Kieve: Next case – *shalom*.

Secretary: Here's a leave paper, come in on January 14, we'll have all the rest for you. *Shalom*.

At which point I floated out and wandered around in the street, somewhat drunk and most unbelieving. I was at Peltours[3] this morning, and I'm planning to leave on January 20, via Trans-Caribbean Airways, to Paris. I'll be there anywheres from two days to a week, depending on the weather. So – let's just say that I'll be home this month. Gee – no skiing until February!

---

1.   Hebrew, meaning "yes."
2.   Hebrew, meaning "many thanks."
3.   The travel agency, whose name is an acronym of "Palestine, Egypt and Lebanon Tours," is still active today in Jerusalem.

I make only one request before I come home: please, don't ever try to feed me sardines. My stomach begins to turn over when I even think of them. And you needn't write me after the tenth of January, 'cause I won't be here to get it.

Gershon – I humbly suggest that you call the *New Yorker* and ask them to change the mailing address from *Palpost*, Jerusalem, to 390 Riverside. Better do it immediately, too, 'cause copies are going to waste this way

And that's all for now – I have things to do before I go out on a date tonight. Tomorrow morning I'm off to Jerusalem to get my clothes for the trip. So – *shalom* for the present, and *lehitraot*[4] – really soon!

love to all,

the brat

In the middle of January 1949, as Mordecai was on his way home, via Paris, armistice talks got under way. They were concluded with Egypt on February 24; with Lebanon on March 23; with Jordan on April 3 and with Syria on July 20. Iraq refused to enter into negotiations.

Israel had significantly expanded its borders from those envisioned by the Partition Plan. In the south, it had control of the cities of Beersheba and Gat, and a wide swath of territory along the Egyptian border; in the central region it now had an "insulating ring" around the West Bank; and in the north it had taken Naharia, Acre and Nazareth. Israel had established geographical contiguity, albeit with borders that were difficult to defend. Among the defense challenges were the narrowness of Israel's "waist," only nine miles wide at its narrowest point, and the Syrian threat from the Golan Heights.

As per UN Mediator Count Bernadotte's recommendation, no Arab Palestinian state was declared or created. There were no demands for one. Much of the land that had been allocated for that theoretical state in the Partition Plan was simply annexed by Jordan, a move

---

4.   Hebrew, meaning "Bye for now, see you soon."

recognized only by Britain and (perhaps) Pakistan. The Gaza Strip was occupied by Egypt.

Unfortunately, the agreements that ended the War of Independence were little more than detailed cease-fires. Although tired of fighting, the Arab countries remained steadfast in their rejection of a Jewish state in any borders. The region entered into a situation, which still persists, of "no war and no peace," although several full scale wars and numerous smaller-scale engagements would be fought in the years that followed. Eventually, Egypt and Jordan signed peace agreements with Israel in 1979 and 1994 respectively. But relations remain chilly. Over time, the conflict has metamorphosed from the "Arab-Israeli conflict" to the "Palestine-Israel" conflict, with all its attendant political complications.

Chapter 33

Brief Return to Israel

Mordecai returned to the United States on February 3, 1949, almost exactly two years after he had left. He remained there for about ten months – far in excess of the three months' leave he had obtained from the army. He was technically AWOL (absent without official leave), or was at least an "administrative deserter" – something he had to resolve with the army when he returned. During his sojourn in New York he became the UN and Foreign News correspondent for *Hador*,[1] a Hebrew daily published in Tel Aviv between 1948 and 1955. He covered the news of Israel's acceptance as a member of the UN, and foreign news generally. I do not know what else he did, or where he lived. There is no written record of that year, nor did he and I ever discuss it.

In November 1949 Mordecai sailed back to Israel to take up his new post as public relations officer for the Palestine Economic Corporation. His first letters home virtually reprise those of his previous trip, which began in 1947. His job at PEC included writing brochures and promotional articles and creating posters for the New York office. His salary

---

1.   This is Hebrew for "the generation." Not to be confused with the periodical, *Hadoar*, "the post."

was low and he struggled to collect money owed him by some of the journals for which he wrote. Many of his letters home include "income statements," reviews of salary, expenses, and the like. It is clear that he did not enjoy his job and took it merely to pay (at least some of) the bills. He talks of wanting to write his own "stuff" including, apparently, a novel. Like many early American residents of Israel, he was dependent on care packages from home. Many of his letters include lists of things for his family to send.

Mordecai continued to believe he was irresistible to women. In reference to Louise, his counterpart in the New York office of PEC, he writes (December 20, 1949), "she's been subjected to the fatal Chertoff charm..." Yet, apparently, she did not succumb. And there are at least two letters in the correspondence listing all the women he could have had, including Ann Strauss, who never responded to his romantic overtures, and Hadassah Frisch, who unambiguously rejected him.

The post-war economic situation in Israel was difficult. Food was scarce; rationed, and unobtainable without a ration book. Meat was available only a couple of times per week. Housing in Tel Aviv and Jerusalem was, according to Mordecai, "frightful," with nothing available at a reasonable rate. The mails remained unreliable and subject to censorship. The unbearable bureaucracy for which Israel is still justly famous was already formidable.[2]

Mordecai's efforts to prepare for his parents impending visit in the spring of 1950 throws all of these matters into stark relief – he struggles to find housing for them, tells them to bring substantial food stocks and, worrying about satisfying his mother's wanderlust, warns her that kibbutzim can no longer host guests as they did in 1935.[3]

The surviving nineteen letters from this period paint a depressing picture of post-war life in Israel and reflect the moods of someone who is clearly not happy nor excited to be back. There is a real post-event,

2. On a lighter note, in 1950 there was only one traffic light in the whole of Israel, in Haifa.
3. Mordecai's parents apparently came to Israel in the early summer of 1950. There is only one brief reference to the visit in a letter to Naomi in which Mordecai describes their mother's frenetic activity and her "perpetually *shlepping* to get Father to run wild with her" (July 7, 1950). I can find no other descriptions or details of the visit.

let-down feel to them. Mordecai is frustrated by work and unrealistic about prospects. By the spring of 1950 he is clearly disengaging both from work and from Israel. His letters to his sister reflect these frustrations. This dissatisfaction notwithstanding, Mordecai remains determined not to enter the rabbinate, despite his certainty that he would be very successful. In January, he writes:

> This little boy gave up the rabbinate because he wanted to live in Palestine-Israel. In so doing he gave up what would have been a comparatively easy job, particularly considering training, speaking ability, writing talent and a good appearance, not to mention the tremendous help both Father and Gershon could provide to make things easy. To have remained in the rabbinate and rationalized so doing would have been easy...

By June, when he is already clear about his return to America, he writes:

> I would hate the rabbinate and feel as though I were prostituting myself in either the rabbinate or a Hillel job... As for being a "horse's ass" or not being one, we are what we are, and must make the best of it. I'm not worried about what I'll do when I get back either – but I'm pretty damned sure it won't be the rabbinate – for the reasons you gave. Whether or not I can really write I don't know, but I don't expect to find out standing on a pulpit in Ass Hole Creek, Kansas. (June 13, 1950)

In one of his last letters from Israel, written on July 7, 1950, Mordecai tells his sister that he has "been running around with an English girl here these last few months, and of course mother is being belligerently 'neutral.'" I assume he means his first wife, my mother, Lilli Sefton.

Born in London, to Polish parents, Lilli had served in the British navy during World War II and then went to Marseille for several months to help with refugee relief efforts and to look for survivors from our Polish family. She found none. She sailed to Israel in 1950 and started working for Palestine Films Co. Ltd. One of her colleagues was photographer Efraim Ilani who also did work for the *Palestine Post* and was a friend of Mordecai. It was he who introduced them. Unfortunately, I have not found any letters describing their courtship nor did either ever discuss it with me. I regret not knowing more about the process.

They married in 1951, in London, and moved to New York.

Lilli Sefton

Chapter 34

Epilogue

Shortly after returning to the United States, my father began his unsuccessful career as a pulpit rabbi, serving only several years in a string of congregations. My understanding is that although he gave interesting sermons, and was dignified and knowledgeable, he was a poor pastor, insensitive to the concerns of his congregants. He eventually settled on a mid-level position at the Jewish Agency, then the Histadrut (Israel Labor Federation), and finally, the Herzl Press. While not especially fulfilling, these positions at least allowed him to remain engaged with Israel-oriented activities.

My parents had a bad marriage but nevertheless stayed together for twenty-six years. They both had relatively successful second marriages. Three years after the death of his second wife, my father agreed to move to Israel. He lived in Jerusalem for six years until his death at the end of 2013.

Even though he did not return to Israel until the end of his life, my father remained utterly devoted to the state. His work revolved around helping and promoting Israel and his moods typically reflected what was happening in, and to, Israel. One of my most vivid memories is of waking up on the morning of June 6, 1967, the start of the Six-Day War, and finding my father in the kitchen, glued to the radio, crying. By the next day, he was elated.

Part IV
Reflections

Chapter 35

My Father, My Grandfather, Myself

The writer and poet Grace Paley was reported[1] to have once said, "Every story is two stories, the one on the surface and the one bubbling beneath. The climax is when they collide." There are two stories contained within these letters – the story of the birth of the State of Israel as seen through the eyes of a young, idealistic American participant, and the story of the inner life of a young man far away from his family, trying to make his way in the world. The two are bound up together.

I started this project determined to be an objective observer and researcher, editing and adding context to a series of letters that document a historic time. I understood that there would be an emotional component to confronting my father as a young man, but did not fully anticipate or understand the overwhelming personal stake I have, not only in my relationship to my father and the rest of his family, but in

---

1.   By Ann Hood in a short vignette, "Every Story Is Two Stories," *The American Scholar*, January 12, 2015.

the story of the creation of the State of Israel. The two are, indeed, inextricably bound up with one another, and their collision gives rise to a host of questions.

Given his extreme dedication and determination to remain in Israel, why did my father leave, not resettling there until the end of his life? Having left the State so soon after its establishment, how did his relationship with and feelings toward Israel evolve? Why did no one else in his immediate family, all passionate Zionists, ever fulfill their dream of moving to Israel? Why did Mordecai abandon journalism and a life of letters? How could he go into the rabbinate after dismissing it so definitively? What kind of woman did he finally marry, and why? What kind of man did he evolve into? Am I, his son, entitled to judge or even speculate? How has this project influenced my feelings for him? What impact will it have on my memory of him? I can only guess the answers to some of these questions, and others will have to remain unanswered.

* * *

The letters reflect someone familiar to me and shed light on how he became the man I knew. They show critical aspects of his character, made all the more dramatic and honest by their context. As I observe my twenty-five-year-old father through my sixty-four-year-old eyes, it is impossible for me not to see him as an authority figure. And while it may seem unfair to draw broad conclusions and judgments based upon such a small window of time, some clear observations can be made, especially as they are confirmed by later events.

The Mordecai Chertoff who emerges from the letters was articulate, observant, witty, energetic, academically successful, and idealistic. It also seems that he felt entitled and superior. In addition, he was judgmental, sarcastic, and racist – even for that time. These contradictions reflect a certain immaturity and insecurity.

Like all humans, he was complex and contradictory. In his letters, he assures his family more than once that he is no hero, avoids risks, and takes good care of himself. But his response to the bombing of the offices of the *Post* was certainly heroic and his determination to be among the first to travel between Tel Aviv and Jerusalem at the end of the siege is more than a little reckless. He was at risk living in Jerusalem, in close proximity to many attacks, and seemed to have handled them well. Only much later did he suffer from PTSD, something he acknowledged, addressed, and overcame.

Mordecai was the beloved youngest child, the golden boy, and, for better or worse, every other member of his family seemed to see him as the embodiment of the dreams and aspirations of all of them; he had the rabbinic learning his father cherished, along with a deep appreciation of literature, both Hebrew and English; the social skills, connections, and handsome physical appearance his mother valued; the "golden pen" and way with words that his brother coveted; and the active social life his sister experienced vicariously and was eager to manage and coach. Both older siblings called him the favored son, "THE source of family *nachas.*" Their praise is lavish and unselfish.

He naturally had a different kind of relationship with each of them. He venerated his father, with whom he exchanged beautiful, poetic, and personal letters. He was impatient and frustrated with his mother, often criticizing her and needing to "set her straight." It is true that her neverending list of tasks for him, especially her request that he venture into the Old City during perilous times to buy a "good, large Persian rug," was comically unrealistic, as was her assumption, communicated during a period of particularly intense fighting, that Mordecai had "probably read all about the opening night of the opera" in New York. With his brother, Gershon, Mordecai mostly discussed scholarly matters and ideas which could generate material for sermons and speeches. His most intimate relationship was clearly with his sister, Naomi. Their letters are mostly about his social life, often venturing into exchanges about love and intimacy, although more often about his successes and disappointments.

The family believed themselves to be superior. They considered themselves upper class but had significant financial limitations and wanted their children to marry "well," i.e., for money and position. I am particularly struck by how involved the parents were in all aspects of their children's lives, even once the children were adults living thousands of miles away. This is clear from the correspondence in general, but also finds expression directly in an exchange between Mordecai and his father in which Paul encourages his son to move on from the *Post.*

In an attempt to address Mordecai's depression at working there, Paul writes: "I'm not sure that what you did until now was a mistake. And if you erred, we all did, that is, the entire family, because we all agreed to your job…" (October 26, 1947). It seems that all important decisions were made in consultation and not by the individual alone. The five members of the family were extremely close-knit – apparently closer to one another than to any "outsider," including spouses.

In the letters, Mordecai describes a very robust social life – roommates, parties, evenings out, and perilous situations faced with friends. His circle included many people who were or would become important, but after he left Israel, he gradually lost touch with everyone mentioned in the letters. I remember him talking about Carmi Charny, and they might have met a few times in the 1950s and 1960s, but they lost touch long before either died. In his early letters, Mordecai wrote that he preferred the "Palestinians," i.e., the Hebrew-speaking Jews of Palestine, to the American visitors or immigrants, and often expressed pride in his Hebrew – but it was clear that, in fact, his social life revolved around English speakers.

Growing up, I remember my father having a very small circle of friends. I think his closest friend was Rabbi David Greenberg, but they, too, lost touch long before either died. I am in touch with David's daughter, Susannah, and we recently reminisced about times spent in each other's homes and the closeness of our fathers. We struggled to understand how and why they lost touch. Despite the active social life he clearly enjoyed as a young man, he apparently was not good at preserving lasting friendships.

The letters discuss at least three women whom he considered as potential mates. At the outset of the correspondence he is waiting for an answer to a proposal of marriage made to Hadassah Frisch – but in none of his letters (that I have found) does he actually pine for her. He never speculates about what a life with her might be like, nor does he write of how bereft he would be if she were to reject him. I spoke with Hadassah when she was eighty-nine years old. Her version of their time together doesn't seem to add up to anything significant. In an email she explained that they went out on a few dates. She was "shocked" when he proposed to her. It seems that Mordecai misread the situation and proposed well before there was an appropriate basis for a marriage.

Mordecai cared deeply for Ann Strauss. They became true, close, supportive friends and he was genuinely anxious to help ease the pain of her tragic loss. As he tried, unsuccessfully, to convert that friendship into a romance, he admitted to his sister that he would have married Ann "at the drop of a syllable." The feelings he describes are raw, and real. When it becomes clear that she is not interested in a romantic relationship, his letters about Ann turn bitter and vindictive.

(Photo by Roy Shenkar)

Mordecai and Ann, 2006, four years after Ann's stroke

Kepi is the only woman featured in the correspondence with whom my father seems to have had a real romantic relationship. If I read the correspondence correctly, they were intimately involved with one other even while Mordecai's marriage proposal to Hadassah was outstanding. In his letters, he minimizes the importance of his relationship with Kepi, perhaps to keep his disapproving family at bay, but reading between the lines, I think she may have been more important to him than the letters suggest. She may even have been the prototype of the kind of women he sought; both she and my mother, Lilli, the woman Mordecai ultimately married, shared several important characteristics: both were beautiful and very smart; both were the youngest of four children; both were marginalized by parents to whom their brothers' education and professional success was far more important. This took a toll on both women.

As with all aspects of his life, Mordecai's family was actively involved in his love life. They expressed their firm opposition to one candidate and lauded the "qualifications" of others. Mordecai's mother, in particular, seemed far more interested in an advantageous match for her son than one based upon passion and love. Esther viewed the process in pragmatic terms. For example, she pushed Mordecai to date Mary Charchat, daughter of Isaac Charchat, the extremely wealthy president of the shipping firm United Cargo Corporation and the inventor of container shipping. Esther believed that other potential mates for her son "certainly cannot give you the things, standing, position, etc., that a moneyed *shidduch* can give you … and until Mary is married, or you are married, I shall always hope … unless there is somebody else in Israel who can meet the requirements of a wonderful wife, plus the possibility of putting you on your feet economically.…"[2] There is hardly a word in anyone's letters of love, romance, or intimacy. At times it seems that Mordecai, too, treated his search for a mate more like a position to be filled than a search for a soulmate. While there may have been lust, I see little evidence of romance or love.

Unfortunately, I have found no correspondence describing the evolution of my parents' courtship, only his tossed-off tease in a letter to his sister that he has been "going around with this English girl." Either he did not share any information with his family or those letters have been lost. It is easy to understand his attraction. In addition to being beautiful and smart, my mother was witty, adventurous, independent, and classy. On the other hand, she was not well educated and her family did not have useful social connections nor were they particularly well off financially. In this respect, choosing her might have reflected a certain rebelliousness on Mordecai's part. I have no idea how my grandparents felt about her initially, but later correspondence between my grandparents and parents reflects a warm and loving relationship.

---

2.   Letter of January 20, 1950.

* * *

Given how determined he seemed to remain in Israel, why did my father leave, returning only for the last years of his life? Even during the darkest moments of the war, Mordecai did not doubt for a second that the state he had dreamed of would come into existence and thrive, and that he would play his part in building it. He wrote passionate letters about his determination to stay and pleaded with his parents to stop pressuring him to return to America. Through the years I asked him several times why he left but never received a satisfying or serious response.

Perhaps, after the intensity and drama of the war and the birth of the state, the hard, day-to-day work of nation-building did not appeal to him. It is easy to imagine that after the romance and excitement of life during 1947–1949 had faded into the past, the daily reality of slowly building a modern country would seem dull. He also had some fundamental concerns: he was distressed by the Israeli tendency toward socialism and government control. At several points he expresses concern with the unrelenting censorship, the financial controls, and the "lack of democracy."

On a more personal level, Mordecai expected easy results. It is clear from several comments in his letters that he thought himself above having to start on the bottom rung and work his way up a career ladder, even though he did just that, successfully, at the *Post*. He was bored and unsatisfied with his work at PEC and wanted a path to a more financially comfortable existence. As difficult as it still is to make a comfortable living in Israel today, it was obviously even more difficult in the early years of the state, as Israel struggled to simultaneously build a successful and modern society, maintain its security, and absorb refugees.

For some reason, he thought the rabbinate offered an easier path, clearly misunderstanding his older brother's life and experience when he writes that he is jealous of Gershon's "easy life of contemplation and ideas."

Ultimately, while all these factors may have played a part, I believe the reason he left Israel was his sense of the inevitability of being a rabbi, like his father and brother before him. He used to jokingly refer to the rabbinate as "the family business." During a long-ago outing with my sons and me, my father explained that having finished three-plus years of rabbinical school, out of a total of four, he found that he "was not ready to be a rabbi." According to his perspective, he had asked for and received a year's leave, a year that stretched into almost four, after which he finally entered the rabbinate. Despite the very different impression from his letters, to Mordecai, it was apparently just a matter of how long he could delay the inevitable. In his memoirs, he specifically wrote that he "was simply stalling to avoid actually going into the rabbinate."

His hesitation may have been genetic. His father, although ordained as both an Orthodox and Conservative rabbi, had discovered early on that the life of a pulpit rabbi was not for him. Ultimately, he was a teacher and scholar. Shortly before he was offered the teaching post that would occupy him for most of his life, my grandfather wrote in his journal, with uncharacteristic bitterness:

> To the very same degree that a rabbinic position grows more possible, my reluctance to accept it increases. I fear the ugliness of the "congregation"; my soul refuses to embrace a framework created by the "members" – spiritual pygmies and dwarfs of the soul. (May 14, 1923)

Ironically, despite my father's apparent sense of the inevitable, it appears that my grandfather actually tried to free him from following the "family" path to the rabbinate. In his memoirs, my father wrote:

> Father approved of my getting a rabbinical education, but told me to "do something else: one rabbi in the family (my late brother, Gershon) is enough." Unfortunately, Ogden Nash was right when he said, "Children need someone to ignore; and that's what parents were invented for."

Mordecai's father had had a very different dream for his son – that he become a man of Hebrew letters. As is clear from a letter he wrote just before the declaration of the state (see chapter 19), his fantasy was that Mordecai would join the pantheon of Hebrew poets and authors, becoming an Israeli author who would sing the praises of the newly reconstituted homeland. There are hints in his letters of literary ambitions – the short story he sent to Maurice Samuel, for example. But they did not come to fruition. My father remained stubbornly tied to what became, ultimately, a doomed future in the rabbinate.

Given how fundamental Judaism was to Mordecai, there is surprisingly little in the correspondence (in my possession) about religion, either in general or in reference to the nature of religious observance in the nascent state.

Mordecai came from a home which practiced Conservative Judaism. In the US, Mordecai's father, Paul, gained Conservative ordination and an advanced degree in philosophy from a secular university on a decidedly non-religious subject, despite studying in prestigious Orthodox yeshivot in Russia and earning Orthodox rabbinical ordination at a very young age. Though Orthodox, Paul was clearly "enlightened." When I asked my father about, for example, his family's use of electricity on Shabbat, he told me that he and his brother would make sure that their father never went into a dark room on Shabbat, i.e., they would turn on the light for him.

In Palestine/Israel Mordecai faced religious challenges. Here was a young, religiously observant man who had nearly completed rabbinic ordination but then left home for life in a war zone, finding himself in a new society composed of Jews of wildly different backgrounds and levels of observance, but all fiercely Zionist, in their soon-to-be-established national homeland. It becomes clear from stray references in his letters that he gradually becomes less scrupulous in his observance of Jewish ritual law than he apparently had been in America. He also makes no effort to hide this from his father. In his early letters, Mordecai makes many references to how he is observing certain rituals – where he is going to pray on the holidays, and where he is taking his Shabbat meals. He describes his experience of various religious holidays, of going to the Western Wall, and of buying ritual objects. But then, later on, it becomes clear that he's not "keeping" Shabbat as he once did. Several times he describes having friends over to listen to records on Friday night. There are also times when he travels on Shabbat. He may also have needed to compromise on *kashrut* during the siege of Jerusalem. He is open about these lapses, but not so open (except with his sister) about his intimate relationship with Kepi.

Perhaps the lapses were due to the exigencies of living in a country at war, or part of the difficulty of being single and religious and trying to maintain ritual adherence when you're not part of a community doing the same thing. Perhaps they were due to the freedom of being in this new, Jewish Palestinian society. In the letters in my possession, Mordecai only makes oblique references to inconsistencies in his religious observance, and there are too few responses to be able to construct a clear picture of his attitude.

Despite his loosening of the bonds of Jewish law, I am struck by the fact that, like his father's letters, many of my father's letters are also sprinkled with liturgical and biblical references, especially those to his father and brother. He can express the deep emotions he felt after the vote for partition only via sacred literary allusions, tying a contemporary event to the great chain of Jewish history and tradition. These references were part of his basic vocabulary when it came to Israel. They reflect an intellectual, spiritual, and nationalistic orientation, if not necessarily a religiously observant one.

Many Jews who move to Israel and find themselves living as part of a cultural majority for the first time end up reassessing the Judaism they practiced in the Diaspora. Mordecai was no different. Despite this ambivalence, the level of religious knowledge and observance of the women in whom he was interested, along with their Zionist commitment, remained critical to him.

* * *

I read my father's letters to drink in his descriptions of Jerusalem, to learn about the war, and to meet some of the people he knew, but slowly came to realize that I had another goal: to understand my father's paradoxical nature; to reconcile his intelligence, academic and professional training with his lack of professional success; his active social life as a young man with his lack of friends as an older man; and perhaps most importantly, his deep literary sensitivity with his surprising apparent lack of empathy and interest in others. I have read my father's account of the vote for partition many times, but still cannot get through it without crying. I am moved by the story it tells, by the images he conjures, and perhaps most importantly, by the inner qualities he must have possessed that allowed him to write such a moving and heartfelt account. I realize now how much, throughout my life, I sought to elicit from him something of the sensibility revealed in these letters. I mourn the fact that he was not able to manifest that level of sensitivity more frequently to his family and friends.

My father's lack of empathy is especially hard to understand in light of his love of literature. Scholars of cognitive literary theory claim that reading literature helps us develop empathy. This is what supposedly happens when we immerse ourselves in another's world; stepping into their shoes, experiencing their joy and pain, we develop sensitivity and compassion. My father not only read literature voraciously, but wrote about it, often with a great deal of perception. But he did not seem to have developed empathy from his reading. The personal introspection present in his letters was illuminating but limited and not especially insightful, and his descriptions of others were often unfeeling, sometimes even callous. I can only suppose that his love of literature remained on the level of ideas, not feelings.

These are just some of the many qualities I saw in my father which I struggle to reconcile. I have an enormous personal stake in this process because how men feel about their fathers is fundamental to how they feel about themselves. We cannot accept or understand ourselves without first understanding and accepting our fathers. I, like most men, have always wondered how much like my father I am. I certainly look like him and sound like him! But what personality traits and skills did I inherit, and which qualities did I reject? What tendencies do I fail to overcome?

I have much to thank him for. Two of the most important aspects of my life come from him: my love of language and literature and the centrality of Israel and Zionism to my identity. Even though I worked in the investment industry, both in the US and in Israel, for many years, ultimately, my career was based upon the written word. One of the most satisfying tasks I undertook in my professional life was helping Israeli corporate chief executives identify and articulate their companies' strategies and present their financial results to investors, a job that cannot be done without the ability to listen carefully and write reasonably well. In addition to his ideological and intellectual gifts, my father also passed down to me a certain curiosity and manual dexterity; he taught me to fix things and to build bookcases, something I love doing with my own children.

As I focused on my attitude toward my father, I slowly began to understand that, however attached my father was to *his* father, like me, he too was probably struggling to understand *his* relationship with his father – wanting to please him, but also needing to become his own person. Their correspondence is filled with this kind of negotiation. But something unexpected happened while reading their correspondence – I fell in love with my grandfather, or at least with his written persona. It was incredible for me to discover how similar I am to him, particularly in temperament. My grandfather's letters are intimate and reflect a person totally engaged; he responds in depth to everything his son writes, with sensitivity, emotion and love. Paul was highly analytical, smart (with some curious lapses), and literate. He was also excessively empathetic and nervous, obsessed with his family, insecure, and something of a hypochondriac. I am just like him. Some of these attributes – like excessive empathy – exact a toll on me, but I wouldn't have it any other way. I think I would have adored him, and fantasize that he would have liked me. I suspect that we are kindred spirits. It is very painful to me that we didn't have the opportunity to know each other, especially in light of the deep and satisfying relationships I have with my own grandchildren. My cousin, Adam, who grew up not far from our grandparents, *did* have the relationship with our grandfather that I lacked. Adam told me that they used to walk together, hand in hand, and that my grandfather would both challenge and nurture him with great love and tenderness. I think the old adage is true – "grandparents and grandchildren are united against a common enemy." Relations between adjacent generations are complicated and fraught, but the relationship between alternate generations can be pure joy.

Reading the correspondence between my father and his father has given me some access to the nature of their relationship and, as a result, some thoughts as to what my father might have hoped for or expected from ours. Perhaps my father was frustrated that I did not venerate him the way he venerated his father. Mine demanded respect, but often did little to earn it, and was certainly not engaged with me (or with my sister) the way his father was with him.

I always felt guilty about my attitude toward him; that I was not a good son because I could not show him the kind of love and respect he craved. With the help of my wife, I took care of him during the last six years of his life but was always uncomfortable that I did not love him more. My wife would remind me that the commandment is to *honor* one's parents; it does not require us to *love* them. Honor is manifested by respect and behavior. I feared that I observed the letter of the law but not the spirit.

Perhaps the effort I have put into this project can be seen as a reflection of my openness to my father's most important experience, an experience that I deeply respect. This project has helped me understand aspects of my father's personality and life that were previously inaccessible to me. Maybe with this book, I have developed the understanding that he so desperately sought. I think he would have been thrilled with it, and I am sorry he was not here to participate in its evolution (and to answer some questions!). Perhaps by working on it together we would have developed the love and intimacy that I think we both wanted from each other. At one point, during my research, my daughter, Rachel, observed, "You seem to like him more now." That is certainly true. I am moved by the picture of my father as a twenty-five-year-old; by his descriptions of his life then, what he went through, what he thought, how he felt or thought he felt, by his struggle to understand, even if he didn't always get it right. I think he was extremely heroic and I am very proud of him. I have a much better idea of how he came to be who he was but will continue to ponder many questions for years to come.

Reading and rereading my father's letters has dramatically changed my relationship to Jerusalem. I always felt awed and privileged to live in this city, but the fact that my father lived here and fought here during the war makes this privilege all the more precious. As I walk around the city, I often find myself imagining the city as it was in 1948. I picture my father crossing the security zones with his press pass in order to sketch British military installations, and I am drawn to British-built buildings like the King David Hotel and the YMCA. I have eaten at the original Café Atara and visited many other places my father mentions. I scan the façades of buildings for the bullet holes left by the war, respectfully preserved, and am moved and strangely reassured. I feel my father's presence as I walk around Jerusalem.

This project has made me realize that I am a link in a "great chain," the third in a necklace of five generations. The correspondence has enabled me to look back toward my father, a member of the great generation that fought World War II and brought the State of Israel into being, and past him, to my grandfather, a member of the generation that fled persecution in Europe at the end of the nineteenth century. This book weaves together our three voices. I look ahead toward my children and to their children, who will grow up in an Israel radically different from the one their grandfather fought to establish. I am conscious of the nature of my relationship with my children and wonder how their children will see and judge them, and how they will remember me. I am awed that this chain extends across five generations and stretches from Czarist Russia, to America, to our own state over a century later. Our intergenerational relationships are braided together, bound up with our relationship to Israel.

* * *

I grew up in the United States with stories about how and when we would move (back) to Israel. I never believed them. And when, in the mid 1980s, my wife and I announced that we were making aliya, my mother was shocked. That I would make aliya, however, was never in question. Like others of my generation raised in Zionist households, I made the decision in the aftermath of the Six-Day War of 1967, when I was thirteen. My wife, Arlene, felt as strongly as I did. During our first date, in April of 1976, we probed each other about aliya. There would not have been a second date if either of us had not been aliya-oriented. We married in 1977, but remained in the US for eleven years in order to build the means we thought necessary to increase the likelihood of a successful aliya. Finally making the move in 1988, we raised our three children in Efrat, in Gush Etzion. We chose Efrat for many reasons, not least of which were the stories I had heard about the heroism of the Gush in 1948. All of my children served in the army (my younger son, David, is a career officer) and were educated here. Unfortunately, I was too old to serve, and like most Anglo immigrants (and my father and grandmother in their time), gravitated toward other English speakers.

I have often wondered how I could truly make Israel "mine." True, I taught many Israeli companies how to behave as public companies and contributed to the success of their public offerings in the US, but how could that compare with volunteering with the Haganah, and being a journalist embedded with a Palmach unit fighting for the birth of the State of Israel? I empathize with Art Spiegelman, whose graphic biography of his father's experience of the Holocaust and his exploration of their relationship, observes, "No matter what I accomplish it doesn't seem like much compared to surviving Auschwitz."[3] Exactly. It is interesting to me that, while awed by the historic times and full of admiration for the heroic behavior of his father, Spiegelman nevertheless expresses the same kind of impatience with his aging father as I felt toward mine.

Studying my father's life during this period has been invaluable. It may be part of the mourning process, my effort to separate and reconnect, grieve, make sense of, cherish, and release. The letters, memoirs, and documents my father left are a precious legacy, the greatest gift he could possibly have given me. I hope I have done them justice.

---

3. Art Spiegelman, *Maus II* (New York: Random House, 1991), p. 44.

Acknowledgments

What started as a project for my family, turned into a family project; each made invaluable contributions. I take pleasure in starting with my children, but in reverse birth order, beginning with my youngest, David.

David had a warm relationship with his grandfather and was instrumental in helping me to appreciate what a treasure these letters are. I may not have undertaken this project without his gentle, but firm, influence. His research was invaluable, especially with respect to military matters. His wife, Sara, also spurred on my research efforts.

I greatly benefitted from countless conversations with my son Ari about the fundamental nature of the book. From the earliest days, Ari raised, and helped me think through, such critical issues as the balance between the letters and the surrounding narrative and footnotes, which topics to highlight, and many other issues. These conversations were a source of joy and pleasure for me. His influence cannot be overstated.

My daughter, Rachel, lovingly translated my father's description of the night of the partition plan vote along with several other Hebrew texts.

My wife, Arlene, was my invaluable partner throughout. She read and corrected countless drafts and provided excellent judgment and advice. I doubt the book would have been possible without her efforts. I am incredibly grateful to her.

My sister, Jocelyn, was an enthusiastic and helpful supporter of this project.

My cousins, Michael and Adam, gave permission to quote from their parents' letters and offered their perspective on our grandparents. Adam shared many stories and provided important insights into our family.

Deborah Meghnagi Bailey edited early versions of the book and offered valuable research. She had a formative impact on shaping the book and provided crucial early support and encouragement and held me to a high research standard.

Shira Koppel translated the Hebrew language articles and letters (except those translated by my daughter, Rachel) and identified the numerous biblical and rabbinic references. I am in awe of the breadth of her knowledge and skills.

Yossi Klein Halevi had a critical role in shaping the book. I am very grateful to him both for his continuing guidance and his friendship.

I appreciate the encouragement and guidance of my early readers: Morton Landowne, Howie Nixon, Alan Edelstein, and Susannah Greenberg. Michael Tobin and Leona Toker read later versions and offered invaluable and detailed advice. Susannah also provided helpful guidance regarding the publishing world.

Warm thanks to Michael Grodin and to Daniel Gordis.

I am grateful to Shimri Salomon from the Haganah Museum for providing insight and context, for opening up the museum archives to me and my son, David, and for permission to reproduce images from the archives.

Heartfelt thanks to Elaine Moshe at the *Jerusalem Post* for permission to reprint my father's articles from the *Palestine Post*.

Thanks to Jeff Daube of the ZOA for obtaining permission for me to publish Mordecai's articles which appeared in the *New Palestine*.

One of the most enjoyable and moving aspects of this project was the opportunity to meet several of the people mentioned in my father's letters and/or their descendants. I am privileged to have spoken with Hadassah Frisch and to have gotten to know her brother, Larry, and daughter, Vivien. Kepi's daughter, Lydia, was very helpful and has become a dear friend. Ann Strauss's son, Roy and I have spent some wonderful time together and have shared information. I was also fortunate to spend time with Alexander Zvielli, the longest serving employee of the *Post*, before he died at age ninety-three. I was also glad to have had the opportunity to get to know Carmi Charny's brother, Israel.

Meeting David Nevo, the son of "Robbie" Rabinowitz, my father's favorite pressman and victim of the bombing of the *Palestine Post*, was especially moving – for both of us.

Developing relationships with many of the "second generation," sharing thoughts about our ancestors' experiences and filling in gaps in one another's knowledge, has been tremendously rewarding. I treasure these relationships.

It was wonderful spending time with Tzippy Porath (née Borowsky) who shared much of my father's experience in Jerusalem. I am grateful to her for allowing me to include parts of her "parallel" and interlocking experience of the history of Israel's birth. Her own, *Letters from Jerusalem: 1947–1948*, is fascinating.

Thanks to my old friend Michael Rosenfeld for permission to print the picture one of his parents took of my father the night of the UN vote.

Peter Ilani graciously allowed me to use a photograph his father, Ephraim, took. This is especially meaningful to me since his father introduced my parents to one another.

The staff at Toby Press has been a great pleasure to work with: Matthew Miller, Reuven Ziegler, Yehudit Singer, and editing wizards Ita and David Olesker. I am also grateful to David for his factual corrections and suggestions on both religious and historical matters. I am lucky to have had the benefit of his broad base of knowledge. I am delighted with Tani Bayer's cover design.

Thanks to Stuart Schnee, PR and media wiz, for his hard work and guidance.

Finally, it's probably rare to thank one's lawyers, but Sheila and Gerald Levine, husband and wife team of publishing lawyers, were enormously helpful and great to work with.

I am sure there are others who deserve my gratitude. I hope those I have inadvertently omitted will forgive me.

While many people have contributed information and made corrections, any mistakes that appear are mine alone.

Select Bibliography

Begin, Menachem. 1972. *The Revolt*. Tel Aviv: Steimatzky.

Bernadotte, Folke. 1950. *To Jerusalem*. London: Hodder and Stoughton.

Cesarani, David. 2009. *Major Farran's Hat: The Untold Story of the Struggle to Establish the Jewish State*. Cambridge MA: Da Capo Press.

Collins, Larry and Lapierre, Dominique. 1972. *O Jerusalem!* New York: Simon and Schuster.

Elston, D. R. 1960. *No Alternative*. London: Hutchinson.

Glubb, John Bagot. 1957. *A Soldier with the Arabs*. London: Hodder and Stoughton.

Golani, Matti. 2013. *Palestine between Politics and Terror, 1945–1947*. MA: Brandeis University Press.

Hoffman, Bruce. 2015. *Anonymous Soldiers: The Struggle for Israel, 1917–1947*. New York: Alfred A. Knopf.

Joseph, Dov, 1960. *The Faithful City: The Siege of Jerusalem, 1948*. New York: Simon and Schuster.

Koestler, Arthur. 1949. *Promise and Fulfillment Palestine 1917–1949*, New York: MacMillan.

Levin, Harry. 1950. *Jerusalem Embattled: A diary of the City under Siege, March 25, 1948 to July 18, 1948*. London: Victor Gollancz Ltd.

Miller, Nancy K. 2000. *Bequest and Betrayal: Memoirs of a Parent's Death*. Indiana: University of Indiana Press.

Millgram, Abraham, E. 1990. *Jerusalem Curiosities*. New York: The Jewish Publication Society.

Morris, Benny. 2009. *1948: The First Arab-Israeli War*. New Haven: Yale University Press.

Naor, Mordecai. 2010. *Atlit "Illegal Immigrant" Detention Camp: A Story of a Time and Place*. Mikveh Israel: Yehuda Dekel Library/Society for Preservation of Israel Heritage Sites.

———— (Ed.) 1988. *Jerusalem in 5708* (1948). (Hebrew) Jerusalem: Yad Ben-Zvi Institute Press.

———— 1987. *Haapala: Clandestine Immigration 1931–1948*. Ministry of Defence Publishing House.

Porath, Zipporah. 1998. *Letters from Jerusalem: The War of Independence and the Establishment of the State in the Eyes of an American Girl* (Scranton, PA).

Rabinovich, Itamar and Reinharz, Jehuda. 2007. *Israel in the Middle East: Documents and Readings on Society, Politics, and Foreign Relations, Pre-1948 to the Present*. MA: Brandeis University Press, 2nd edition.

Rogan, Eugene L and Shlaim, Avi, editors. 2010. *The War for Palestine: Rewriting the History of 1948*. Cambridge: Cambridge University Press.

Tal, David. 2014. *War in Palestine, 1948: Israeli and Arab Strategy and Diplomacy*. London: Routledge.

Tauber, Eliezer. 2017. *Deir Yassin: The End of the Myth. Israel:* Kinneret, Zmora-Bitan, Dvir.

Yarkoni, Hillel. *75 Years of Hebrew Shipping in Eretz Israel*. Israel Foreign Ministry.

OTHER SOURCES

On the Aliyah Bet:
http://paulsilverstone.com/immigration/Primary/index.html
Jewish Women's Archive Encyclopedia: https://jwa.org/encyclopedia
Palestine Post Online Archive1932–1950:
http://web.nli.org.il/sites/JPress/English/Pages/Palestine-Post.aspx
British Forces in Palestine: http://www.britishforcesinpalestine.org/index.html

About the Author

DANIEL CHERTOFF worked in the investment industry in both the United States and Israel as an analyst, as financial communications counsel, and as a venture capitalist. Before discovering the cache of letters, he was happily writing his doctoral dissertation in English literature at the Hebrew University. He is an associate editor of *Partial Answers*, an academic journal of literature and the history of ideas. Daniel and his wife, Arlene, live in Jerusalem.